LOVE
FOR
SALE

LOVE
FOR
SALE

A GLOBAL HISTORY OF PROSTITUTION

NILS RINGDAL

Translated from the Norwegian by

RICHARD DALY

Atlantic Books
London

First published in English in the United States of America in 2004 by Grove Press, an imprint of Grove/Atlantic, Inc.

First published in Great Britain in hardback in 2004 by Atlantic Books, an imprint of Grove Atlantic Ltd.

Originally published in Norwegian in 1997 by J. W. Cappelens Forlag a.s., Oslo, under the title *Verdens vanskeligste yrke: De prostituertes verdenshistone*. This English translation is published by arrangement with Tiderne Skifter, Copenhagen, and the financial support of NORLA Non-Fiction is gratefully acknowledged.

1 2 3 4 5 6 7 8 9

A CIP catalogue record for this book is available from the British Library.

ISBN 1 84354 314 1

Printed in Great Britain by MPG Books, Bodmin, Cornwall

Atlantic Books
An imprint of Grove Atlantic Ltd
Ormond House
26–27 Boswell Street
London WC1N 3JZ

CONTENTS

ILLUSTRATIONS

LOVE
FOR
SALE

INTRODUCTION

Butterfield 8, with its call-girl heroine working her way down the
alphabet of men from Amherst to Yale, appeared at a very
formative moment in my adolescence and impressed me forever
with the persona of the prostitute, whom I continue to revere.
The prostitute is not, as feminists claim, the victim of men, but
rather their conqueror, an outlaw, who controls the sexual
channels between nature and culture.
—Camille Paglia, *Vamps and Tramps*

The prostitute has traditionally stood as the symbol of sin, but precisely
in this capacity is regarded as a guarantor and stabilizer of morality and
matrimony in the rest of society. In the West, this view of prostitution held
sway until the latter part of the nineteenth century. Men of the upper classes
rarely married prostitutes. Thus, whores posed no threat. If a man paid a
visit to such a woman, it, like his subsequent venereal disease, was a secret
protected by the Hippocratic oath.

Much would change with the Victorian era, not least in Protestant
countries where the individual became much more preoccupied with
morality on a purely personal level. In Asia, this influence would not only
convert Christians but also create a new wave of morality among Hindus,
Confucians, and finally even Communists. In the West, Victorian morality influenced the awakening of both the women's and workers' movements.
Finally, even sexuality, family life, and prostitution tended to become
public issues. This tendency toward politicizing such questions became
even stronger in the latter half of the twentieth century. The new women's
movement, the gay-rights organizations, and the media have contributed
to this in their respective ways.

*　　*　　*

Prostitution, not the family is the theme of this book. But historians and social scientists have often seen the two institutions as polar opposites, both morally and culturally.

Relations between the two sexes have varied immensely in primitive cultures, ancient and modern civilizations, and through many and various historical periods. Nonetheless, families—nuclear units with a man, one or two women, and children—have been dominant. Yet family units have been organized in a number of different ways. Monogamy has alternated with polygamy, purchased brides and dowry have existed side by side or been cultural disparities; the free choice of partner or divorce has varied considerably. All these factors have a structuring impact on family and prostitution. The strength and status of the family define the status assigned to the prostitutes, as different family structures provide the men by various acceptance of extramarital sex. In some regions, and in small societies in particular phases of history, prostitution has almost put the institution of the family out of play. And every time the emphasis on family has diminished, this has had significant demographic effects. I have not weighed the various family or prostitution archetypes systematically against one another. But where I have discerned clear connections, I have pointed them out.

The conflict between family and prostitution as institutions can be viewed from a number of perspectives. As one of my favorite teachers once put it: Fixed and regulated relations between the two sexes have always provided the best conditions for stable child rearing and the continuation of the family line. Demographically, the impact of prostitution is easy to detect, since prostitutes have more sex but fewer children than women in stable families. Prostitutes have more abortions and venereal diseases and become more easily sterile, but still, many sex workers complete their terms of pregnancy and give birth to children. But the conditions are less propitious for rearing children, since there is a higher rate of infant and child mortality among the offspring of prostitutes.

One might also assess the opposition between family and prostitution in moral terms. The family obliges the man to feel responsibility for his children. For women, this may be something nature compels them to do, since very few women abandon their children, but men do so frequently.

In most societies, a man who takes responsibility for his children is considered more moral than one who does not. Understood in this way, the family is a positive servitude, while prostitution is a negative freedom. Moral assessments are challenging and often complicated to integrate into social-scientific or historical analyses. Maternity, love, and security are subjective entities, while sex can be more easily quantified. Like many others, I believe that a strict but loving parental couple, kind grandparents, pleasant aunts and uncles, siblings, and cousins represent optimal conditions for a child's growth and happiness. This may be a universal truth, as even the Victorians, whom so many of us love to hate, believed the same.

In today's high-tech society, it is easy to sublimate moral questions, because we are constantly confronted with "new" problems that pass themselves off as moral questions. Sex and reproduction, happiness and security, have, to an almost absurd degree, become themes of public debate in Europe and the U.S., though the discourse is political and not moral. Hypocrisy and ambiguous argument rule the day. Debaters pretend to argue a global perspective while they fight their own causes. To me it is a great moral paradox that we live in an overpopulated world where cross-border adoptions are difficult, but the world's wealthy women invest huge sums to fight infertility.

A right is negatively defined by the duty of others to respect it. Every time someone is offered a right, others must limit their own self-expression. The eighteenth-century definition of "human rights" to prevent discrimination—or punishment for beliefs, opinions, sexual preferences, or lifestyle—is consequently much easier to respect than the new set of positively defined rights that today is promoted by the selfish men and women of the West.

Informed members of the global society know that our world possesses neither the economy nor the technology to enable billions of people to enjoy the "right" to bear children or to have access to unlimited medical care. If this creates no ethical dilemma for those who champion such things as human rights, it is because they never intended the rights to apply to other than, let's say, Norwegians or Americans. With the whole world in mind, any right to sex or happiness for the handicapped, landmine victims, or the HIV-positive reveals itself as tragically naive.

The question of prostitution is equally complicated. Nobody has the right to sex, either unpaid or in exchange for payment: If nobody wants to sell sex, it is a crime to force anyone to do so. But when men or women do want to sell their bodies, they should have that full right without encountering punishment or discrimination. If the client behaves decently, the relationship between the sex buyer and the sex seller must be considered a purely private transaction.

Western single, lesbian, and infertile married women regularly maintain that it is their right to become mothers. The recognition of such a right requires economic support for biological intervention or adoption. Others argue that the woman's right in such cases should be weighed against the child's right to happiness and a normal life. I strongly reject this dilemma, because I do not accept the conceptual framework on which it is based.

But when a woman has already given birth to a child, we are dealing with a concrete moral problem. Woe to the person who, under the pretext of securing a child's happiness, takes it from the mother against her will on the grounds that she is a lesbian, prostitute, or both. In that case, the mother's right to an alternative sexual lifestyle is curtailed.

Much has happened since the Victorian era. But the parallels between old and new feminism, between media then and now, and between the syphilis and AIDS debates are nevertheless so striking that it is easy to doubt that the world has grown any wiser. A basic assumption underlying my text is that the Victorians are still among us—clad in postmodernism.

It is an adage that prostitution is the world's oldest profession. Since the Renaissance, fanciful speculators have maintained that prostitution is universal and comes into existence all by itself, due to women's natural responses to changes in the society.

This wild idea has even been developed into a model distinguishing "natural" from "hospitable" and "monetary" prostitution. Hospitable prostitution has been identified with primal foraging bands and sparsely populated societies without currencies, such as Eskimos/Inuits and Native Americans. But according to this model, natural prostitution must also be traced among lions and apes. The model implies that all women with many partners are seen as prostitutes. But a definition of prostitution that does not distinguish between the sale of sexual services and free sex with different partners is a contradiction and makes any concept of profession lose its meaning. Hunter, farmer, housewife, tribal chief and priest, and some crafts are, in any case, older.

Nineteenth-century evolutionist theory was inspired by biology's explanations of higher forms of animal life developing from earlier forms, with apes and humans as the highest species on top of the evolutionary pyramid. Johann Jacob Bachofen tried to apply this strange model to sex and gender through historical time. Bachofen argued that humankind had shifted away from the promiscuous freedom of the horde, through matriarchy, to patriarchy, a form of society that he considered to have developed in Mesopotamia, with Jewish, Egyptian, Roman, Indian, and Chinese variants. Lewis Morgan applied the construction to anthropology and Friedrich Engels through *The Origin of the Family, Private Property and the State* to Communist thought. Bachofen and Morgan saw primal promiscuity developing into prostitution with the advent of money and division of labor. Engels spoke of primal promiscuity and group marriage in original societies, which reached their next level of development with money, class divisions, and economic disequilibrium; he concluded that women in the brave new communist world would break free of all chains—and recapture their right to a virtuous life. Thus the old communist revealed the Victorian in himself.

The Bachofen-Engels tradition became quite influential, and even today Engels can be credited for his clarification that prostitution came into existence within the context of a state, religion, and private ownership and class division. Iwan Bloch wrote the first reflective history of prostitution under the same influence, and this may still enlighten some of the shadowy corners in the historical landscape of sex, prostitution, and religion. But in general, the Bachofen-Engels scheme has played out its role as a model of understanding, and today it can be traced only in the form of theoretical leftovers and sloppy conceptualizations in Marxist and feminist pamphlets.

In the meantime, both history and social anthropology have established a substantially wider base of empirical knowledge about early civilizations than the nineteenth-century evolutionists had at their disposal. We have valid proof that prostitution doesn't develop automatically in all societies. Twentieth-century anthropology has described a great number of different societies without prostitution (defined as sex exchanged for money or its equivalent).

Since prostitution is a complex profession, it requires learning, and it seems to spread through cultural diffusion. In both ancient Egypt and the Indus delta, prostitution developed at a later point of time than in Mesopotamia. Today it appears more logical to analyze prostitution as an almost unique cultural phenomenon that first developed in Mesopotamia and later spread to surrounding cultures in Egypt, Greece, and India. Prostitution in China may have developed independently, though it could also have traveled the Silk Road.

Although prostitution is neither universal nor found in all societies, the sex market has enjoyed formidable customer demand throughout history. There is every reason to wonder why this is so. Could Bertolt Brecht's designation of Man's *Sexuelle Sklavenstand* really be an accurate formula?

Humans are two-sexed creatures, and the physiological differences between the sexes have remained stable for tens of thousands of years, despite enormous social changes. Emphasis on sexual differences remained in disrepute for many years, but this has won greater acceptance, even in psychology and the humanities.

Just as men and women differ socially, so, too, do they differ in terms of sexuality. There is little to indicate that sexuality is weaker in the female than in the male, but they both develop and manifest themselves differently, physically and emotionally. Camille Paglia distinguishes between male Apollonian purposiveness and female Dionysian chaos; she has breathed new life into this classical distinction.

Simply by nature, men are promiscuous to a far greater degree than women. For thousands of years, women have tried to rein men in—often in alliance with sober-minded older men who themselves have experienced the destructiveness of unregulated promiscuity. Thus, in the civilizations of the East and the West, prostitution has been the predominant solution to the social dilemma created by male promiscuity. This has given rise to an ideological by-product, a bipolar concept of femininity—the madonna/ whore opposition, which instantly clouds and distorts both men's and women's understanding of the two genders.

Prostitution has by no means been equal at all times and in all places. It flourishes most extensively in evolutionary intermediary phases of history, during which a country or region is marked by a rapid upsurge in the population, urbanization, migration, and economic transformation. Prime examples have been the emerging Roman Empire, Western Europe in the 1800s, the Wild West era of the United States, Japan in the 1700s, and Southeast Asia today.

From ancient times, North America, the old East India, and Polynesia had a high degree of freedom for women but were unacquainted with prostitution. In the West, epochs of relative freedom for women have come and gone. Both the Roman Empire and the Age of Enlightenment were marked by high numbers of sexually liberated women who in no way were prostitutes but have almost disappeared from history. In the twentieth century, particularly after 1960, women's freedom has again increased.

Periods marked by many sexually free women have a special demographic profile. Usually, the increased freedom of women leads to a relative demographic falloff, combined with a relative decrease of and a higher specialization within the sex industry. Simultaneously, the freedom of women has another, independent demographic effect. Sexually liberated women resemble prostitutes insofar as they have more sex, but they conceive and give birth to fewer children. Some women simply do not want to become mothers. When this is the case, nobody should force them to do so. Many men become terrified by sexually liberated women and prefer same-sex relationships or a single or celibate life. Society ought to allow this as well. In purely sexual terms, we human beings are far from primitive animals. We might even be history's most complicated and sensitive species.

The bibliography demonstrates the enormous literature on prostitution: historical and medical studies, memoirs, biographies, and handbooks. I have gleaned more from some books than others, as I explain in greater detail in the postscript. My intention was to write a book with clear ideas and clear historical lines, which still left space for an individual approach.

Personal experiences and relationships have made it easy for me to share Camille Paglia's solidarity with, respect for, and understanding of people in the sex industry. My line of argument is nonetheless principled. With reason, respect, and reform, social relations can be created wherein women have great freedom without being dismissed, and different sexual choices can be accepted for both sexes. Presumably some in the future will also choose to sell sex, while others will purchase sexual services. If neither buyer nor seller suffers from want or acts under physical coercion, a sexual transaction cannot be considered more immoral than any other trade. Efficient sex with specialists may reveal itself to be beneficial for both individuals and society. In our times, price negotiations may be left to ICPR, the International Committee for Prostitutes' Rights. Much distress and deprivation would be alleviated, and social conditions in many countries changed, if their rates gained acceptance.

Foreword: The Whores and I

Like prostitutes, publishers are professional seducers. A brilliant and beautiful young editor planned to seduce me into writing a book about what she thought was the world's oldest profession, during a lunch in 1995. She was not prepared for my immediate and ecstatic response. Two weeks later, I scavenged London bookshops for recent and secondhand books related to a subject I had already been collecting books on for over ten years.

My lifelong partner, Dr. Georg Petersen, who was senior physician at the Oslo Municipal Board of Public Health when we met in the late 1970s, catalyzed my interest in this particular subject. After we had spent time in New York in 1981–1982, Georg initiated Oslo's measures to combat AIDS with an increasing number of coworkers, including an adviser who was the first female prostitute on the public payroll. Then he began many years of traveling in Africa, Asia, the U.S., and Geneva on behalf of the World Health Organization, focusing on AIDs. From 1989 on, I spent half the year wherever he was stationed, from Manila via Phnom Penh to Jakarta, where today he is the WHO representative and is responsible for all health in the country, not merely the sexual variety.

During the same period, I gradually shifted my attention from pure historical theory to writing history for a general audience. In my capacity as partner, I could travel and see most parts of the world, an experience that is conducive to thinking in global terms about many problems.

In 1991 we invited the leaders of the World Association of Prostitutes for drinks at home on Jorge Bocobo Street in Manila, with the formidable Priscilla Alexander heading the party. A memorable evening! I have never met such fearless, funny, and quick-witted union representatives. In New York, Berlin, Bangkok, Manila, Sydney, Jakarta, and Oslo, I regularly bump into people from the sex industry at night. I enjoy the girls' company, and I appreciate the respect they show me in their wisdom about all the variants of the male sex. With boys and men in the profession, too, I tend to flirt even more directly.

Three people who have all had a deep influence on my life and understanding have earned a living by selling sex. One is doing very well in a totally different profession; another is still working, virus-free, at the age of fifty. But a dear friend died of AIDS in 1987, a sweet and cunning black man and a star of the dance floor. His witty remarks and observations were so sharp that they never cease to boggle my mind.

A Note on Translation and This English Edition

A translation into a foreign language that the author has some command of easily forces him to some introspection. I have often been forced to ask: Was my writing unclear? Normally, the answer has been yes. No translation can clarify unclear text; maybe at its best it can hide the moments that lack clarity. I have tried to avoid that solution and have instead chosen to shorten, rewrite, and edit many parts of my original text in order to achieve more logic in the explanations and better chronology in the narrative. This has been done in several chapters but is most obvious in the two early and more complicated chapters about the origins of prostitution in ancient Mesopotamia and among the ancient Israelites. "Fallen Angels" was transformed into a separate chapter.

In the medieval and modern chapters, Scandinavian references have been taken out or limited. This edition also contains some new chapters and paragraphs written directly in English, like the chapter about Buddhism and two totally new chapters about Islam and the Ottoman Empire.

O N E

THE WHORE OF BABYLON

S he bears the name The Whore, the first prostitute we encounter in world literature. She appears in the four-thousand-year-old epic *Gilgamesh*. Like all superheroes, Gilgamesh is solitary, handsome, and brave, and in addition, a prince. His sexual appetite is enormous; he leaves no young maiden in peace, and hardly any young lad, either.

The people of his land must possess deep insight. They understand that Gilgamesh is so sex-mad simply because he is bored, and they pray to the gods to let him meet his equal. Thus, Enkidu comes to life, a man as big and strong as Gilgamesh, slightly shorter, although he looks more muscular and has a far hairier body. The nameless harlot enters the story next. She is called Harimtu, in ancient Babylonian, a term the lawgiver Hammurabi uses to refer to a low-class prostitute in one of Ishtar's temples.

Ishtar is an exciting and dangerous deity, simultaneously goddess of love and war. She is the daughter of the moon god, related to the superior gods and considered Queen of Heaven. Her main symbol is the planet Venus. She was venerated as both the morning and the evening star; she was born anew as a maiden every morning but became a whore every evening. As goddess of war, she is depicted with sword, bow, and quiver. She rides a lion, and is often depicted with several arms.

In Mesopotamia between the Tigris and Euphrates, different ethnic groups ruled in ancient times. The Sumerians built the first civilization, before the Babylonians took power, followed by the Assyrians, until the neo-Babylonians took over again. But religiously, the area remained stable, and although the Sumerians called the goddess Innana, she remained one and the same. She certainly lacked female rivals in the world of the gods. Some low-status goddesses were associated with birth and the role of mothering, but they were worshiped only locally, under simple names like Mama and Baba. The women in Ishtar's service helped the men who offered money to her temples, with the sacred powers of their bodies, yet the way in which the aristocratic women served her remained more of a holy secret. Ishtar calls herself protector of all prostitutes, including those who offered their bodies in doorways outside the temples or tempted the men in taverns. But when the goddess speaks about herself as a harlot, it has little to do with paid sex: She would make love to any man she happened to desire.

Enkidu lived out on the steppes as a savage until one day he encountered the harlot from Ishtar's temple in Uruk. He spent six days and seven nights with the *harimtu* woman, who lavished him with love of all kinds: maternal devotion, tenderness, mystical transcendence, and orgiastic sex. She also taught him to break bread and to drink wine, to clean and to take care of his body. This was far more than a quick screw; it amounted to an intensive course in civilization. Ishtar herself had authorized the harlot who educated the savage. After one intense week, all traces of savagery were gone: Enkidu had become civilized and prepared for life in urban society.

> *The Woman bared her Breasts,*
> *Untied her Loincloth and opened her Legs,*
> *And he took Possession of her Comeliness.*
> *She used not Restraint, but accepted his Ardor,*
> *She put aside her Robe and he lay upon her.*
> *She used on him, a Savage, a Woman's Wiles;*
> *His Passions responded to her.*
> *For six Days and seven Nights, Enkidu*
> *Approached and coupled with the Prostitute.*
> *After he was sated with her Charms,*
> *He set his Face towards his Game …*
> *Enkidu hastened after them, but found his Body bound.*
> *His Knees failed, when he tried to hunt his Game.*
> *Enkidu had become weak, his Speed not as before.*
> *But he had Intelligence. And wide was his Understanding.*

The harlot spoke to Enkidu of Gilgamesh: "He is a fabulous man, bursting with strength and ability to spread happiness." By now both heroes were eager to meet each other. Gilgamesh had a dream in which a star fell from the heavens, so big he could not lift it. But he was able to bend over it, as over a woman. He also dreamed of an ax. In the old Babylonian text, the reader encounters wordplay, since the words for *star/man* and *ax/male prostitute* sound almost identical. Gilgamesh's mother explained diplomatically that her son was about to meet his peer.

But two such heroes cannot become friends without a colossal brawl. It did not end before both found out that they were equal in strength and courage. The people were exultant, because Gilgamesh had finally met his match. The women prepared the bed, and the heroes kissed each other, became best friends, and planned to carry out great deeds—together. They continued to seduce young maidens and occasional lads, but at a less hectic pace than before. Their friendship had obviously tamed them both.

The Gilgamesh epic is drawn from versions dating from the Old Babylonian period, around 1800 B.C., and the following Assyrian times, but it was not known by the Greeks and the Romans, and it seems to have been forgotten for millennia. None of the texts we know today is complete, so different versions have been reconstructed based on Assyrian, Old and New Babylonian texts. The heroic poem might have a tiny base in real history, since the Sumerians were ruled by a king named Gilgamesh between 2750 and 2600 B.C., but it cannot be considered a historical text. Nevertheless, it is an extremely useful source for understanding social and sexual relations, love, respect, and violence between man and man, and between man and woman. Of utmost importance are what the poem explains about the goddess Ishtar and the sexual assistance offered by women in and around her temples.

Prostitution came into existence in its first and Western variety in and around Mesopotamian temples. There the temple was the city, the earthly residence of the god or goddess. There a deity received food and clothing, was washed, cared for, adored, and worshiped.

Most activities were concentrated around the temple. The building and maintenance of the irrigation system necessary for agriculture and other prerequisites for large-scale society were conducted from there. Markets grew up in front of the entrance. But economic activities also took place inside, where the grain silos and the tax offices were located. A god or goddess provided protection; money and precious metals were placed in locked chests and stored in the inner sanctum. Fees were paid, much as when one rents a safe-deposit box in a modern bank. The priests and priestess would loan money, too. Interest was given. The love goddess's temple in Lydia loaned King Croesus the initial money that enabled him to achieve legendary wealth.

Large temples were equipped with a stepped tower made of bricks, up to 150 feet high. At the top was a minuscule temple for *naditu*, highborn priestesses qualified for especially intense communication with the deity. An old Sumerian text quotes the goddess of love and fertility:

> *Who wants to plow my Womb?*
> *Who wants to plow the Grain that grows so high?*
> *Who wants to make my moistened Fields bear Fruit?*

The answer from the god who was her relative and lover reads:

> *Mighty Wife, the King wants to plow your Womb.*
> *God and the King will do it together.*

The *naditu* high priestesses took part in sacred weddings, *hieros gamos*, at which a king enacted the masculine part. The fertility of the earth would be secured through a symbolic sexual act between the earth's regent and the woman who represented the goddess. These rites were most common before and during the grain harvest; they were closely linked to the change of seasons and the grain that was sown and ripened: Like the grain, humans lived through fertilization, birth, and death.

Fearless theoreticians have proposed that sacred weddings in Mesopotamian temples have taken place since 6500 B.C. But the oldest text describing such rites dates "only" from 2800 B.C. and recounts how a high priestess waits outside the lapis lazuli—embellished door in front of the most holy of holies. A husband is expected—God and King in one person. The moment he arrives, the priestess leads him into the holy sanctum, where their symbolic wedding takes place. There are no witnesses, but even the lowliest of temple servants knows the sacred ceremony. These rites are normally interpreted as religious state ceremonies linked to a fertility cult. Some feminist scholars have seen them as a symbol of male dominance, since the king can bed any woman he so desires in his realm.

* * *

Infidels and visitors to Mesopotamia from neighboring societies may have already perceived the religious rites as more erotic and promiscuous than the participants did. But as the centuries passed, the male in the rites was replaced by a stone symbol representing the god, a fact that weakened the most sexual aspect of this most holy of rites.

We have still no absolute knowledge about how widespread the sacred weddings were under the Old Babylonian and later rulers of Mesopotamia. The great generalists of the nineteenth and early twentieth centuries knew much less than we do today, guessed at more, but were fearless in their theory and strong in their faith. What they believed represented a long tradition in itself, dating back to Herodotus, who wrote during the fourth century B.C. and founded the first Western comprehensive work of geography, anthropology, and history. Herodotus was learned and much traveled, interested and informed, and took great pleasure in recounting the strange behaviors of people to the east of Greece; in 440 B.C. he had even visited Babylon.

Biblical myths, psalms, and chronicles refer to Babylon with discernible religious pathos. The biblical texts have encountered critical readers since they were collected and canonized. Herodotus, "the father of history," met criticism in his own lifetime and was accused of inventing cock-and-bull stories to titillate his readers. But even as the centuries passed and the criticism was repeated, it never seemed to destroy the impression of Herodotus as a profound and reliable observer. Why, then, do we believe in Herodotus and not in the Bible? Because he seems to please and entertain his readers? Because he satisfies our prejudices? The most basic answer is simply that for a very long time, there was scarcely any reader who totally lost faith in this man.

In one of his most cited passages, Herodotus recounts how he personally observed Babylonian women copulating with unknown men in the temples of Ishtar. "And every woman did it," at least once in her lifetime. Most young maidens lost their virginity this way. But for the most ugly girls, this could take years, Herodotus concludes, most amusingly.

In Syria, Herodotus reported, women had to cut and sell their hair, or to offer their bodies for money and bring their earnings to the love goddess, whom they called Astarte. She had a son, Adonis, who also was her lover, and in the fall, there was a ritual ceremony mourning his death. Everybody wept for the god and attacked one another with fists and whips.

In the spring, a joyful feast symbolized Adonis being born anew. His statues were adorned with phalluses, while the women again sold either their hair or their bodies and subsequently donated their earnings to the temple.

Carthage, in North Africa, was founded by emigrants from Phoenicia and therefore counted among the lands "to the East" by both Greeks and Romans, who considered this culture akin to the Babylonian and the Syrian. All poor girls of Carthage had to serve some years in the temple of the love goddess to earn themselves a dowry, something rich girls received from their parents. The Phoenicians placed the temples to their love goddess on high cliffs along the coast—to help seafarers and their ships enter a port in the vicinity, reveals the Roman historian Valerius Maximus. He may be right. The problem is that most Greek and Roman narrators drew historical conclusions retrospectively, interpreting the past with fantasy and the stamp of their own historical period.

The ancient Babylonian empire that we glimpse through the Gilgamesh epic had run its course around 1200 B.C. On its heels came the Assyrians, followed by the New Babylonian empire. When Herodotus visited Babylon, it had fallen under Persia. But to what extent did this Babylon resemble the Mesopotamian culture of one or two millennia earlier?

Greek and Roman historians placed great store in the resemblance among the "barbarians" of Mesopotamia, Syria, Phoenicia, and Carthage. Today's researchers emphasize the differences between the various cultures and are skeptical of all statements where findings from one period or culture are validated over a greater region or over a longer time span. But for thousands of years, historians had little more knowledge about conditions and people of the past than the great narratives had given them. Gradually, archaeologists of the the nineteenth and twentieth centuries discovered papyrus manuscripts, clay tablets with religious inscriptions, tax records, lists of professions, laws from different periods, house equipment, and religious statues. This established new, much more exact knowledge about ancient Mesopotamia. Herodotus will still be read, just as the Bible will. Today we stand freer in relation to him than ever, but we may still trust him more than the Bible. However, while quite a few anecdotes have been whittled away, his better reports are accepted, reformulated, and clarified.

* * *

Bride-price and dowry are two customs that, each in its own way, have influenced the parties in a marriage. Bride-price reflects societies concerned with women primarily as labor power. When a father gives up a daughter, he is compensated in the form of payment for her labor, which, by virtue of her marriage, he and his family are losing. But a daughter sold off as a bride has brought nothing of her own into the marriage.

Dowry can be seen as recognition of a daughter as the inheritor to part of her parents' property. While sons often have to await their fathers' death before they inherit, the daughter receives her share in the form of the dowry, a direct or long-term payment from her family to her husband's family. This makes her more attractive as a partner, and a dowry can be seen as a guarantee for the woman. If she threatens to annul the marriage, her relatives can demand the return of their valuables.

But both dowry and bride-wealth have checks and balances. If a bride was expensive, it could take time to pay for her, which gave the expensive bride more freedom in the meantime. Phoenicians and Syrians gave their daughters dowries, while the Israelites paid for their brides. In Mesopotamia both bride-wealth and dowry seem to have been practiced side by side; Assyrian times have been so thoroughly studied that we know the customs in great detail and clearly see class difference reflected in the different customs. While the higher classes obtained brides with dowries, often including their own personal slaves, those who had less paid for their brides.

But Mesopotamian women did not enjoy particularly great freedom. A man who seduced another man's wife was not punished but fined. He then had to transfer a woman from his household to that of the man he had offended. There appears to have been no concern for the women involved. Men made the decisions and controlled the property within the family. Even women from the aristocracy had no jural protection for themselves or the wealth that stemmed from their dowry, but they could hand over the dowry to their children, if they so desired, before the husband's death. Divorce did occur from time to time, at the initiative of some few aristocratic women.

Both family and marriage did provide strong subordination, even of women of the aristocracy, and the fathers decided whether a daughter should get married or serve in a temple. We hardly know what the women wanted or preferred. But it is likely that some thought themselves better off with a life in a temple.

The poor seldom provided dowries for their daughters. They could sell the daughter as a bride or a slave but just as well send her to a temple. If the daughter was comely, the priests or priestesses would take an interest in her care and upbringing. In the temples of Ishtar, young girls learned to dance and sing to the honor of the deity and conduct themselves with modesty. The temples allowed for much more than fertility rites; they served as schools and residences, like the convents in Europe thousands of years later.

The temples of Ishtar were centers of knowledge about birth, birth control, and sexuality. Not only kings got to stay with the priestesses. Both aristocrats and men of lower rank hired women from the temples and made offerings to the goddess in return. Perhaps a man who spent time with a woman in service to the gods felt that sacred powers flowed over his body and his mind.

Religious inscriptions recount that many temple women possessed a power that could heal sexual problems and illnesses among men. Temple women were therefore nurses and sacred sex therapists. Magic texts that dealt with "satisfactions of the heart" were recited to make men healthy and strong. The magic oil used in massages was made according to an esoteric recipe known only to the women of the temples.

The young girls in the temples washed and anointed the divinity. As they grew older, they sang and danced and could be hired out to men whose eye they had caught. All the temple women, both the priestesses and their young assistants, did as they were asked in the honorable service of the goddess. Set against such a religious and myth-enshrouded background, a term like *prostitute* can give too many simple and modern connotations and summon ideas about quick tricks instead of sacred procedures.

The low-class prostitutes in taverns and inns lived beyond the temple walls in their own houses, called *gagû*, under the supervision of an older woman with a closer connection to the temple; some of the poor prostitutes seem to have worked in the temples earlier on as well. Sumerian clay tablets from 2400 B.C. show that the goddess of love considered herself linked both to whores at the inns and to male prostitutes, and publicly, she was associated with "high" ritual sexuality, roadhouse prostitution, and male prostitution.

Male prostitution seems to have just as old a link to temple rites and religious life as female, but to date, no one has managed to clarify this relationship fully. Some of the male prostitutes in Mesopotamia were eunuchs, priests who had ritually castrated themselves in submission to the goddess or another god. But since most priests dressed alike, some might have been called eunuchs without being such. A male prostitute could be a eunuch priest, a former priest, or only have a vague relation to the priests.

An aristocratic temple priestess had more freedom than her married cousins. She had the legal right to her own possessions, so she could buy and sell property and slaves. Also, the temple women of lower rank might be seen as having more freedom than married women. But were they any better off? A recently discovered Gilgamesh fragment recounts that Enkidu later reencountered the harlot who had tamed him. In the meantime, he had become confident and grown used to the urban way of life, but he was not convinced that civilization was better than life in the natural condition. Enkidu said that city life was worst for the harlots: many had to serve tramps and drunkards and could be beaten and tormented.

Old Babylonian laws distinguished clearly among the priestesses in temples, their assistants in service to the temple, and free prostitutes outside the temples. All three were in the service of the goddess of love; none of them lived the traditional roles of housewives or daughters. But some of the married women, in both the aristocracy and the lower classes, had spent some childhood and teenage years in the temples before their marriage. Their temple years did not disqualify them as wives, though several laws declared that men were forbidden to marry the poorest prostitutes who lived outside the temples. Assyrian laws did not allow poor prostitutes to wear veils or head coverings, while aristocrats, free women, and female slaves always had either a head covering, a veil, or both.

Poor girls who were brought up in the temples could earn themselves a little nest egg, a dowry, and thereby became more attractive than other low-class girls. But they might also pick up less attractive customs. It might be either good advice or a prejudiced warning behind this fatherly advice engraved on a clay tablet from four thousand years ago:

> *Do not a marry a Harlot,*
> *For she has with many lain,*

Nor a Priestess of the Temple
Who is consecrated to the Gods,
Nor a Temple Maiden,
Who has so many gratified,
She will leave you in a Pinch,
And her Words shall scorn your Name.

The mighty Mesopotamian goddess of love and war has continued to impress men and women thousands of years after her heyday. She is the oldest female deity of whom we have myths and records, and she has been considered the original goddess in whom all Indo-European peoples believed, during a lost era when women were said to dominate the world and God was of the female gender.

Archaeologists have found female goddesses with strongly developed breasts, thighs, and posteriors from the Middle Eastern, Western European, Russian, and Indian Neolithic periods. Primordial Venuses have been found over four times more often than male gods. The idea about one sole original goddess has had many adherents throughout different periods of history.

The Greeks and Romans venerated Aphrodite and Venus and, as the centuries passed, identified them increasingly with one another. As the Romans began to equate gods from regions even farther away with gods who already were well known, they declared that the Phoenicians had called Venus by the name Astarte. Already Herodotus had identified Ishtar with Astarte in Syria and Ashera in Canaan, Cybele in Phrygia, and Aphrodite in Asia Minor. The Romans turned this into dogma because they built their empire with the explicit ambition to unite and reconcile different cultures and religions. Over the years, all goddesses of the East were gathered up into one common deity—Magna Mater.

Even in far-off India, they worshiped goddesses resembling Ishtar and Venus. Hindu goddesses might be called Devi, Durga, or other names, but they were all seen as avatars of the same goddess. North and northwest of the Roman Empire, on Celtic, Nordic, and Germanic ground, fertility goddesses of other names were worshiped: Nerthus, Frøya, and Bamba. The planet Venus was known as the morning and evening star all the way from Scandinavia to India. So, although languages differ, the goddess of fertility remains the same.

In one way or another, all mother or love goddesses shared the habit of incestuous love relationships with a son or other close relative who also became a fertility symbol. In the myths, this male figure often died and was resurrected, in association with the seasonal drought and rain, with the sowing, growth, and harvesting of the grain. The half-subordinate son/lover/relative would be called Frøy, Osiris, Priapus, Eros, Adonis, Attis, Baal, Tammuz, or Shiva.

Studies on the relationship between feminine and masculine nature open for speculative explanations of this: Mother Earth is stable. The masculine principle has an inherent tendency toward erection, release, and collapse. These characteristics intrinsic to the male body and psyche can easily be understood in correspondence to the cycle of the seasons, and of life.

There is evidence that priestesses were central to the cult of the mother goddess right across the Indo-European cultural region, and it has been argued that this was appropriate because women most resembled the goddess. A woman's fertility and life-creating abilities gave her a natural priority of communication with the deity. This is why women became priestesses and oracles and performed entrancing dances with ritual sexual overtones.

It is exciting to let history start out with an original matriarchy and a mother cult that only much later was supplanted—or rather, defeated—by warlike men who countenanced male gods. Feminist researchers have found themselves especially attracted to the proposition that women were dominant in the oldest societies and the first religions. This position also seems to contain in itself a proof: What happened in the past can be repeated in the future. This proves that women's liberation is possible, and indeed a realistic political goal.

There is a strong feminist ambition and rich theological creativity behind the idea of one primordial female god. How much evidence, then, do we have to support the idea of one original mother goddess being worshiped all over the Indo-European linguistic area, from Ireland to India, in the earliest times? It is extremely difficult to say. More than ten thousand years passed between the earliest veneration of the goddesses and the times when various cultures developed the writing and languages that identified the goddesses under different names, then qualified them further through clothing, adornments, or the animals that bore them. Accordingly, to prove the existence of an original and more or less homogeneous goddess via empirical arguments is almost insurmountable.

Modern historians of religion consider all attempts to conflate old religions speculative and in strong contradiction to the empirical values and scientific methods that are the hallmarks of their discipline. They stress the individual character of the respective goddesses and place great weight on their differences, iconographically, culturally, and historically, and question even the least pretentious version—that the mother goddess in the Middle East was one and the same.

Everyone must have the freedom to believe in a god and to make her female—and, for example, call her the Great Mother. It still remains possible to concoct a primordial, feminist monotheism. But it is as impossible to prove that the mother goddess was at one point in history the one and only as it is to maintain today that there is only one God and that He is a male.

An empirical approach still allows us to state that the cults of the mother and the love goddess, however strong or extensive they originally were, declined in inverse proportion to the growth of cities and the prevalence of wars. In the days of yore, Ishtar was certainly a lady of great power, and was possibly worshiped with greater intensity and more rites than all goddesses elsewhere and at later points in history. But no one can claim unambiguously that she was the one and only primeval goddess. Questions about the gender of God and the origin of women's oppression thus have to be left behind as questions of faith.

Fortunately, prostitution is not a question of theology but a social phenomenon that can be limited, defined, weighed, and measured. Historians should approach it practically and trace it according to proof. An empirical approach in no way diminishes our curiosity about Ishtar, since we know that it was around her temples that history's earliest prostitution sprang up.

Ancient Egyptian papyrus and wall paintings, myths, and texts contain a variety of references to prostitution. But in Egypt, this phenomenon has never attracted the same attention as in Mesopotamia. This is because prostitution seems to be a younger, imported phenomenon, not a genuine or original element in Egyptian culture.

Ancient Egypt had very few fertility cults, and no goddess was as powerful as the male gods. Their leading female deity, Hathor, was a dangerous moon goddess linked to both life and the kingdom of death. But Egypt, too, had priestesses, and women predominantly worshiped Hathor. If distinctly sexual rituals existed around her or other gods, they can't have played the same role as in Mesopotamia. As prostitution gradually developed in Egypt, it did so independently of their own religion, and rather under influence from Mesopotamia and the cultures to the east.

Egypt was aristocratic and slave-based, but freeborn farmers played a greater role there than farther to the east. The lack of strong goddesses did not prohibit royal and aristocratic women from enjoying more freedom. Women had their own property and great freedom in the choice of husbands, including non-Egyptians. There was a ripple effect from elite women down to the class of farmers, who tended to be monogamous and faithful. Moreover, there are no traces of female infanticide, an absence that distinguishes Egyptian culture as far more woman-friendly.

Murals and burial-room paintings frequently portray women, and many in unusual roles: dining, and vomiting, at purely female banquets; fighting in the streets; trading in the markets. Their role in the household and as caretakers of children was highly emphasized. Male homosexuality is expressed through the well-known mythical story about Horus being seduced by his uncle Seth. But as with prostitution, Egyptian homosexuality seemed to be less widespread than in Greece and Mesopotamia. When sources from the New Kingdom give evidence of temple prostitution, this is seen as an influence from Mesopotamia.

Along with every new queen from the East came a new wave of cultural and religious influence. Isis was originally a local and unimportant goddess, but she would, as time passed, be linked by the priests to Osiris as wife and mother, due to foreign influence. In the New Kingdom, from 1600 B.C., Isis had become an independent mother goddess and started to be portrayed with her son Horus in her arms. Eventually, a love goddess also arrived. In the Middle East, this goddess would commonly be portrayed standing upright on a lion. Her wandering toward Egypt caused her to lose the lion as a mount; instead, she was given a lion's head, since they traditionally saw the gods with animal heads.

Later Egyptian papyrus depicts slave prostitutes painting their lips and couples in coital positions that suggest the male is engaged with a prostitute. A grave painting from Thebes shows a woman having intercourse while she plays a flute, a complex physical act requiring years of training. Late Egyptian narratives deal with the buying and selling of sex, and some parables mention prostitutes and clients by name. Moral stories reveal young men's experiences in a bordello; in proverbs, older men advise the younger to stay away from the public houses, ignore all the street prostitutes, marry, and settle down to family life. But all this moral literature dates from late periods of Egyptian history, after many generations of intermarriage between pharaohs and princesses from Mesopotamia.

Herodotus probably never visited Egypt, and Strabo stated that he wrote "more nonsense about Egypt than the East." In any case, his reports seem to be relevant only for the centuries before his own lifetime. Herodotus might be correct in his statement that the Greek prostitute Rhodopis was the most economically successful in the profession through all the ages of Egypt. It may even be true that she managed to build herself a pyramid from her earnings. But when Herodotus says that two so completely different pharaohs as Cheops in the Old Kingdom and Ramses twelve centuries later both built pyramids with money earned by their daughters' sale of sex, it is certainly nonsense. At its best, it might be used as an indicator for lack of stigma on prostitution in the Egypt of the last millennium B.C.; or that daughters of pharaohs made the most of their considerable freedom.

When Alexandria finally became the new capital of Egypt, in Hellenic and Roman times, prostitution reached great proportions, while women of all classes enjoyed lesser freedom. The goddess Isis would now be venerated around the Mediterranean, and religious paintings from these years portray her in flight with Horus in her arms. Quite often Isis is depicted seeking refuge in a bordello or healing the son of a bordello madam. But both Isis and the bordellos she visited bore few if any traces of the real ancient Egypt. They were mirroring a new Mediterranean culture where the Greeks had rescored an old song, from Mesopotamia.

Earlier generations of historians seldom stressed that the cultic duties in Mesopotamia's temples differed, and that the division of labor between women in the temples was considerable. When all women in the temples were depicted as temple prostitutes, this was a serious injustice to the existing hierarchy among the women.

Mesopotamia's temples were as class-divided as the society around them. Women from the aristocracy held title to the high priestess positions, and their sisters and cousins married the elite men of civil society. The high priestesses held property, were conspicuous in their clothing, wore noble headdresses and expensive jewelry. Ishtar was considered both virgin and whore, was venerated for both qualities, and needed priestesses of both kinds. *Ishtaritu,* a small group of highborn priestesses, lived in celibacy, while aristocratic women who took part in the holy rites were called *naditu.* The majority of the priestesses were *qadishtu,* a middle stratum who served as mystical therapists and helpers of men with sexual problems. To equate *qadishtu* with "courtesan," or luxurious whore, might be a secular misinterpretation, since the word clearly signifies "holy woman." This holiness has, on the other hand, led feminists to argue against the term *temple prostitute.* But why does a sexually explicit task for one make an aristocratic priestess less holy than her virgin cousin?

Low-class prostitutes—*harimtu*—frequented the saloons and taverns; they might have been purchased as slaves, and they might end their days as beggars. Perhaps fewer of the poorest prostitutes had a connection to the temples than was previously believed. Their temple connections weakened over a longer time span. Some modern feminist scholars question calling poor prostitutes temple women and openly admit their intention to tone down the sexual aspects of Mesopotamian deity worship. One might detect both upper-class arrogance and Victorian morality behind such intentions. It is also an insult to the goddess Ishtar!

Queen Semiramis is one of the few Old Babylonian women about whom there appears to be biographical data, above all because the Hellenic writer Ctesias penned her biography. He maintained that she was a prostitute who married King Ninos—the founder of Nineveh, who promoted the use of eunuchs, and devised the Hanging Gardens of Babylon. An Italian assyrologist has convincingly demonstrated that Semiramis probably is a mythical figure that Ctesias conflated with Samuramat, an Assyrian queen from around 800 B.C. In any case, if the Babylonian queen did exist, she probably would have participated in ritual sexual acts in her capacity as high priestess. To call any of them an ex-prostitute is a tendentious anachronism naively overtaken from the Greeks, who, in their enmity against the Persians to the east, painted all Easterners as barbarians and all their queens as whores. But modern feminists who want to rescue Mesopotamia's temple women from millennia of men's bad press commit a similar ideological mistake in portraying Mesopotamian priestesses on the level of today's modern women.

The goddess Ishtar even today speaks to us through old religious texts, in all her promiscuity as self-described whore. She showed up alone at the cheapest taverns and befriended the poorest prostitutes, saying that they mirrored something in her own divine nature. Ishtar was sexy and fertile but is not, strictly speaking, a mother goddess. She never gave her two sons so much as a thought, and thus became more of a bachelor's woman. But it is not always plain sailing to be a love goddess; for Ishtar was active and importunate and had strong, unrestrained individual lusts. As a result, she went through so many men that she could terrify even the most courageous. Ishtar once also lusted after Gilgamesh, according to the epic. But the superhero turned down the goddess of love, with the following devastating commentary:

> *You are like an Oven whose Fire is going out,*
> *A Door of Rushes that opens to the Storm,*
> *A Castle that tumbles down on the Hero's head,*
> *A Shoe that causes a Man to stumble.*
> *Which Lover can please you for all Time?*
> *Which Mate do you not find odious?*

When Ishtar was brushed off in such a manner, she replied in full fury, "Woe to you, Gilgamesh! Woe and disaster to you who insult me so!" Whereupon the two best friends Gilgamesh and Enkidu abandoned her, going off arm in arm. It is perhaps not difficult to guess what the goddess devised as the best way of getting even: Enkidu had to die!

Gilgamesh mourned over his friend's corpse for seven days: "Oh, Enkidu, you were the sword at my side, the bow in my hand, the dagger at my shoulder." For a long time Gilgamesh felt that life was no longer worth living: "He dresses his brother in bridal white … His howl is that of the lioness who has lost her young."

It has been a long time since the glory days of Mesopotamia, but the view of prostitution that we encounter in the Gilgamesh epic is surprisingly current. Enkidu had to die when the goddess so decreed, and he understood the fate that awaited him a few moments before he lay in the arms of death. In wrath, he slung out a curse on Ishtar and all her prostitutes. Who does not feel for a young, vigorous hero whose life ebbs away long before his time? But perhaps the most mind-boggling aspect is that young Enkidu's last, desperate utterances, four thousand years ago, were such an accurate prophecy:

> Oh, you sly Woman of the Night,
> Approach and hear your Fate.
> I curse you. Until the Eve of Times:
> The Streets shall be your Home.
> On tired Legs shall you stand in Shadow.
> The thirsty and the drunken smite you …
> Oh, Harlot, you Servant of Men,
> Kings and Princes shall love you.
> Young Men release their Belts.
> While the Old smile in their Beards.
> For Riches you shall both make and destroy.
> For you, the fertile Wife will be forsaken.
> While Priests shall wed you to the Gods.

T W O

PATRIARCHS AND PRIESTESSES

The oldest account of prostitution in the Bible is a learned story from Genesis. Its two main characters are the young woman Tamar and her father-in-law, Judah, one of the twelve sons of Jacob, who descended from the mythical forefather of the Israelites, Abraham.

Judah paid the full bride-price for Tamar, as was the custom, and gave her to his eldest son, who died as a result of unspecified evil deeds. Judah then handed the woman over to his second son, Onan. But Onan refused to have sex with Tamar and spilled his seed upon the ground, which caused him to die as well. Since neither of his sons had managed to impregnate Tamar, Judah sent her back to her relatives in widow's garb. To her, this was a shame. But in Judah's eyes, Tamar was a bad investment, a cow that had failed to produce any calves.

The story of Judah and Tamar belongs to a series of family histories created around 1000 B.C., retold for generations before they were finally written down in a narrative form so convincing that even today many believe them to be true. But even if Judah and Tamar may never have existed, their story does provide solid knowledge about life among the Israelites, the Western Semitic clans who consider Abraham their forefather and lived in Canaan between the River Jordan and the Mediterranean Sea from at least the second millennium before our era. Originally, they were semi-nomadic and moved around the territory with tents and livestock. This was a culture of male chauvinists. The father held power; kinship was reckoned through the male line. The father generally favored his eldest son but purchased brides and slave women for most sons. Abraham had married his half sister Sarah, who reached old age before finally producing a son. In the meantime, his slave Hagar had given birth to a son named Ishmael. As a widower, Abraham bought a new wife who bore him six sons.

Abraham gave away small parts of his herds to these young sons, but he sent them away while leaving most of his livestock to his favorite, Sarah's offspring, Isaac.

A woman's value was bargained, like that of cattle and goats. If a man could not get a good bride-price for a daughter and was too poor to wait, he might sell her more cheaply as a slave. Rape was considered a violation of another man's property, not of the woman's being or her virtue. When Judah, in his young days, caught the glance of a pretty girl alone in her tent, he did not ask anyone for permission to approach her. Then he followed the custom, paid the full virginal bride-price to her father, and married her. But when Dina, the sister of Judah, was raped, her brothers refused this solution and exacted a cruel revenge. This was the exception, however, not the rule.

Wives and daughters were put to work in and around the tents, while slave women tended the flocks, gathered fruits, and raised crops amid the seasonal movements of the herds between the highlands and the lowlands. It was not a luxurious life. The patriarch joined in the work; wives and slave women rose together at sunrise before starting their separate tasks.

Nomadic cattle keepers and shepherds preferred male gods and placed their greatest emphasis on the central role of the ox, while mother goddesses and male fertility gods tended to develop in agricultural societies in which religion was linked to annual crops and their yields. Most tribes in the Middle East worshiped gods of both sexes. But Abraham's descendants celebrated only one god, a masculine deity who seemed to have no name but revealed himself directly to Abraham and his descendants. Many generations later, it became clear that they had worshiped the same god, and then they were able to identify him by the name Yahweh, or Jehovah. Their neighbors called him a god of the hills, and he was worshiped in the greatest simplicity, on a hilltop near the houses or tents. His followers considered him omnipotent and omniscient, but unlike most other male gods, he was not promiscuous or conspicuously potent. Under exceptional circumstances, he could manifest himself as a snake. Normally, he appeared almost asexual: He was an extremely serious and solitary god but originally did not seem jealous or hostile toward rival gods.

When poor Tamar was returned to her kinsmen in disgrace, she was of the opinion that her childlessness was the fault of Judah's sons. This she intended to prove. One day she approached Judah's tents without her widow's cloak, heavily veiled, appearing to be a woman who offered sex in return for money. Her father-in-law did not recognize her when she asked: "What will you give me if I sleep with you?" "A goat," answered the old man and gave away his seal, his ring, and his staff as a deposit. Whereupon the young woman allowed her father-in-law to do with her as he wished.

The next day Judah sent a man to the village to look for the woman. He intended to keep his promise by paying for the sex and redeeming his belongings. But the villagers knew of no woman there who sold sexual favors. Slightly puzzled, Judah let the matter lie. Meanwhile, Tamar returned to her own kind, dressed as a widow. Three months later, it became obvious that she was pregnant. Since she was still under Judah's authority, he was furious: A widow who got pregnant was a whore who brought shame to him and his deceased sons. She ought to be burned alive! But when Tamar revealed the staff, the ring, and the seal to Judah, she proved the legitimacy of her actions: She had demonstrated that she was fertile and that Judah's sons, not she, had failed in the act of conception. This forced Judah to admit that he had done her an injustice.

Tamar gave birth to twins. Old Judah recognized the boys but refused to take Tamar as a spouse or give her to his third son, presumably because Tamar had shown herself to be more innovative and intelligent than was seemly for a woman. As the centuries passed, history would work equally well in Tamar's favor. The evangelist Matthew mentions her on his extremely short list of ancestral mothers to Jesus of Nazareth.

Tamar and Judah's story is the Old Testament's first reference to the sale of sex, but sources independent of Genesis corroborate that the sale of wives and daughters and of informal sex were widespread in Canaan in the days that we relate to Abraham's earliest descendants. The prostitutes were tolerated only if they were foreign girls, not descended from their own tribe. If a prostitute lived a sufficient distance from her male relatives, and her customers were unknown to her father or brothers, she brought no shame to them nor to the men she had sex with. Since prostitution had to occur far from the paternal house, the prostitutes were widows or orphans, freed slaves, young servant girls, or disobedient runaway daughters.

While there was nothing wrong with Judah's intercourse with a prostitute, it would have been disgraceful if he hadn't paid for the services, because prostitutes used to offer part of their earnings to a local shrine.

Abraham and his descendants respected other gods and goddesses of the region even when they did not worship them. Such tolerance would certainly diminish later.

Joseph, the younger brother of Judah, is the hero in the final chapters of Genesis. He was a golden boy, a paragon of male virtue, who was sold to foreigners by his brothers. He ended up in Egypt, where he bravely resisted seductions and false accusations of rape from Potiphar's sex-crazed wife. He was sent to jail and soon switched from being prisoner to prison administrator, then continued his career as Pharaoh's dream interpreter, with Asenath, the virtuous daughter of an Egyptian high priest, as his legal wife. He went on to became minister of agriculture and secured grain such that Egypt could survive with a surplus for seven years in a row, as famine hit the region.

In Canaan, Judah and his brothers were unprepared for the same famine and traveled all the way to Egypt to buy grain. Thus the brothers met again. Joseph was not angry. Quite the reverse—he cried for happiness when he heard that his old father was alive; and when he recognized his youngest brother, he served wine till everybody got drunk. According to the Scriptures, the twelve reunited brothers, their father, and all of their descendants remained in Egypt for generations.

Egyptian sources from the 1300s and the 1200s B.C. contain a number of references to Hebrew-speaking tribes from Canaan, so it is likely that a small group of Canaanites lived in Egypt, maybe partly as slaves. Genesis recounts how Moses finally took the lead in a rebellion and led his people home. He is the veritable central figure of the Old Testament and totally dominates Exodus and the following three books of the Pentateuch. These Scriptures are above all a collection of commandments, laws, and regulations. Through them the cult of Yahweh became established as an independent religion. Brilliant literary composition allows an exciting narrative to emerge out of all this heavy religious material, and Moses served simultaneously as the deity's direct mouthpiece and the interlocutor. Through the person of Moses, Yahweh appeared to be an impressive, active, businesslike god with a strong relationship to his chosen people. Now it became evident that it was he who previously governed and led their ancestors. Consequently, he could give the Israelites contractual promises for the future. Moses was the unifying figure in a narrative about a people's mystical wandering through their own history, symbolically represented as primitive nomadic life in the Sinai wilderness. Following this ritual cleansing, the narrative brings the public back almost to the present, morally empowered and spiritually impassioned.

The Book of Joshua links itself tightly to the Pentateuch and gives the wandering a grand finale in the form of a war between religions. The new hero is Joshua, a man with completely different attributes as strategist and warrior. According to the biblical accounts, foreigners with a deviant faith had overrun Canaan. Now Joshua besieged Jericho, razed it to the ground, and recaptured the country. In the middle of this turmoil appeared Rahab, the Bible's second named prostitute. She ran a house in Jericho, worshiped other gods, and offered her body for money as extra income. But nothing of this counterbalanced the help she gave Joshua in Jericho. Because she chose the right side, Rahab and her family were incorporated into the Israelites, and no reader has dared suspect that Rahab might have contemplated taking up her old profession again.

How much truth is there in the stories of Joshua, Rahab, and Jericho? It is very hard to find evidence of any battle of Jericho, and the recapture of Canaan seems very unlikely. Israelite tribes had lived in the Canaanite interior and mountains without interruption. If a small band wended its way back from Egypt or Sinai, it was hardly compelled to engage in much warfare along the way. There is another truth hidden behind these stories: From 1200 B.C., when the Israelites became sedentary and built their first towns, they entered a turbulent phase of their history, marked by dramatic population increase and social and religious change. Although the Battle of Jericho and the wandering in the wilderness may be regarded as myth, they do lend a brilliance of structure, goal, and meaning to the outlook of one religious party in these years of change.

The powerful Samson we meet in the Book of Judges was probably a real war hero from the years around 1000 B.C. His first love was a girl from the neighboring Philistine tribe, but his father denied them permission to marry. Samson was stubborn and strong, and in the end his father obtained the foreign girl his son desired. But for the powerful Samson, one woman was not enough. He could never resist the prostitutes in Gaza, where he was snared and deceived by one woman after another. The gorgeous Delilah seduced and captivated the champion and wormed his secrets out of him. Her powerful grip on him amounted to castration, the total loss of masculinity:

> *He goeth after her straightway,*
> *as an ox goeth to the slaughter*
> *or as a fool to the correction of the stocks.*
> *Till a dart strike through his liver;*
> *as a bird hasteth to the snare,*
> *and knoweth not that it is for his life.*

Similar episodes occurred in quite a few Israelite families, so Samson was a good representative for a time marked by intermarriages and a growing number of prostitutes. These women were, according to the Bible, always from the coastal countries of the Philistines and Phoenicians, and from the inlands, Edom or Moab. But the neighbors spoke the Canaanite language and lived almost like the Israelites. The only significant difference was in their religious practices. The increase in the cultivation of land at the expense of animal husbandry, the change of the seasons, sowing, and harvesting provided the Israelites with ideas about the soil and its fertility as ground for religious conceptions. Step by step, their god of the hills came under the influence of the god of the plains.

Israelite Scriptures pronounced it wrong to make images of deities. Archaeologists have nevertheless found innumerable figures of household gods in their houses, some of them dating as far back as 1200 B.C. The vast majority are female representatives of the goddess Ashera, who was known all over Canaan and resembles the Phoenician Astarte, venerated farther north. But the Philistines and Phoenicians represented the goddess Ashera/Astarte with hips, while the Israelites connected her large breasts to a cylinder-shaped lower body. This is usually seen as an indication that the Israelite Ashera was worshiped primarily as a life giver and mother and less as a sex goddess. Ashera's growing popularity among the Israelites was strengthened by intermarriage; for Ashera was venerated all over the region. It was only Yahweh who seemed to be exclusive to the Israelites.

We know less about Israelite women than their men, for several reasons. The biblical narratives could lead readers to believe that almost all men were bachelors. Far from it. It was not acceptable among the followers of Yahweh to live without a woman. The texts simply take for granted that good, unseen, and unheard women surrounded a man. Moses is named around three thousand times in the Pentateuch, his wife, Sippora, but three times, and we learn nothing of interest about her. None of Moses' many daughters are named. This means that they were all to a woman obedient, dutiful, and faithful. The few times we hear details about a female, it is usually a young maiden who casts her eyes to the ground and is particularly shy and passive. Biblical women are either good and faithful or bad and unfaithful. The ideal is the obedient housewife, the dutiful daughter, and the faithful slave. There are many, many of these, and they are not mentioned by name.

There is one amazingly nonconformist woman who appears in Judges: Deborah. Her husband is a real weakling, and the Israelites are in the process of losing their faith and their land. Then Deborah seizes the reins, defying all contemporary norms and commandments. She appears completely like a man: She judges in civil disputes, agitates for war, receives revelations from Yahweh, and even authors her own psalm of praise: "There was no leader to be found in Israel, nay, none before I stepped forward, I, Deborah, a mother of Israel."

Bad women inspire much more discussion. In the Old Testament, we read of queens putting on makeup, worshiping other gods, and dominating their men. As with the harlots, one bad quality almost automatically conjures up others. This is why the prophets thunder against queens and seem to detect a prostitute in every window, a harlot under every bush, unfaithful women filling the streets, and whores luring men at every corner of the road.

Despite a few bad apples, most Israelite women were nothing like that. They were diligent, hardworking, and busy; they bore responsibility for the growing of grain, vegetables, and wine grapes during daytime; and they prepared food before they started spinning or sewing. They had time for female-dominated religious ceremonies and puberty rites for their daughters. They danced the *meholot* using a tambourine or a drumlike *top*. The women's songs of lament and thanks could be addressed to both Ashera and Yahweh, but only Ashera received cakes when the women wanted to become fertile, and they burned incense solely to glorify Ashera.

The Israelites' first minor temples for Yahweh in Bethlehem, Sjilo, Hebron, and Dan were taken over from the Canaanites. The women worshiped Ashera in their homes, and most of them considered Ashera their deity, while Yahweh was the god of the men. As various religious currents met at historical crossroads, marriages were often arranged and alliances forged between priests and priestesses in service to different gods. In such situations, new myths develop that establish a "marriage" between the male and female deities, but the Israelites never felt the need to construct such a marriage. Everyone in Canaan knew that Ashera was married to Elohim, the lord of heaven, and that he and Yahweh were one entity, the one god whom the Israelites had always worshiped. Archaeology proves that from around 100 B.C., almost all Israelite families worshiped Yahweh and Ashera as man and wife, a clear demonstration of the religious compromise that had made the worship of Ashera benign and without risk.

Israelite menfolk loved to discuss moral and juridical questions and could dispute for hours on end. Most of all, they loved to slander the gods worshiped by their neighbors. The men dominated the cult of Yahweh as priests, singers, and musicians. As time passed, they grew zealous about distinguishing themselves from the foreigners, in dress, custom, and religion.

The Israelites spoke Hebrew, one of three Canaanite languages. Around 800 B.C., or perhaps a bit before, these languages developed a twenty-two-letter alphabet system that was a lot easier to learn than the Sumerian cuneiform or Egyptian hieroglyphics, with their thousands of icons and symbols. The Israelites quickly established a broad, democratic culture in which a considerable number of men and women could read. But when it came to writing down ancient myths, hymns, laments, parables, and laws, the men preserved this as their exclusive province.

It would take several hundred years to get all the texts we know as the Old Testament down on paper, and sections of the seemingly very old Pentateuch were assembled as late as 400 B.C. But already the first written texts reflected an era marked by religious blending and took clear stands against religious backsliding. One law forbade a man sexual rights over a female slave if she had already found herself a lover. Tattooing was forbidden, as was sex with animals or between men; there were also rules for when and under what conditions it was permitted to sell a daughter into slavery. But the Pentateuch made it crystal-clear that no man, under any circumstances, could allow his daughter to become a temple prostitute.

The Old Testament uses two different words that have traditionally been translated as *prostitute: Kadesh* is a very strong, pejorative term used on rare and significant occasions. Its literal meaning is "sacred evil," or witch or sorceress. But such words have never been used in biblical translations. Younger texts use *kadesh* most frequently and with a clearer connotation of religious worship. Theological tradition has often translated the word as "temple prostitute." Most likely, it referred to a woman involved in religious worship of the goddess Ashera—or worse, of a male idol like Baal. But given the strong patriarchal tenor of the culture, it is also quite possible that the idea of a woman leading a religious ceremony to honor the one and only Yahweh was so repulsive that the word was used in that context as well. If we assume that the word was used in all three situations, we are left with little knowledge about what such a woman actually did, but we may nevertheless conclude that the Pentateuch has no worse word to use about a female.

An old genealogical text in Samuel I, written down about 700 B.C., should attest to some of the social conditions of the day, although it places the events further back in time. The main characters are the high priest Eli and his two priestly sons. One day Eli discovered that his offspring had had sexual relations with some women who assisted them in their sacred devotions. This must reveal something much worse than pure sex. The common interpretation is that Eli's sons practiced religious worship that included sexual rites. Both Eli and his sons subsequently died, while the Ark of the Covenant was stolen, two horrors that demonstrated clear as day what such heathen activities would lead to.

This story is generally seen as the clearest example of Israelite temple prostitution, and it is the only case in which Yahweh's priests were clearly involved. Holy prostitution can hardly have been common among Yahweh's priests, since they had no official female helpers. The worship of Ashera was, however, led and dominated by women, who sang special songs for the goddess and wove garments for her. From around 100 B.C., she was worshiped more than ever, and a class of priestesses developed, two facts that made cultic sex and temple prostitution possible on a more permanent base. How regularly it occurred is hard to deduce.

The prophets had a vigorous pornographic repertoire of metaphors to use about infidels. Sometimes there was truth behind the accusations, sometimes not. This makes it difficult to decide how literally to interpret negative designations like *temple harlot* or *choirmaster*. A prophet might simply be referring to priests and priestesses serving other gods, while elsewhere they might accuse these servants of rival gods, and sometimes Yahweh's own priests, of promiscuity or homosexuality.

Liberal theology may have interpreted too many texts literally and given an impression of more prostitution and sexual aberration among the Israelites than would be expected in a small country with few and small towns. But it must be equally wrong to reduce all biblical temple prostitutes and whoremasters to a prophetic expletive- and sex-fixated fantasy.

"The Lord shall not be brought as sacrifices that which are the earnings of prostitution, or offerings from a eunuch," decrees the fourth book of the Pentateuch. The prohibition of homosexuality probably became emphasized, partly because many priests were alarmed by the Israelites' growing interest in another male deity, Baal. This old and formerly unimportant god of storms and fertility had been worshiped in gardens, beside springs, and in trees all over Canaan, and had even been seen as the son of Elohim. But now Baal's cult had become refined and elaborated, and if not the god himself then at least his priests and adherents gained in legitimacy. Such a change made Baal a far greater threat to Yahweh than Ashera. After all, Baal was male and had his own male priests. It also counted against Baal that he had a wife and sister, Anat, who called especially upon young maidens.

The Israelite priests responded with a propaganda campaign against Baal. His priests were called soft, effeminate, and homosexual. The terms did contain some truth: Baal's priests wore nice clothes, were well groomed, clean-shaven, and anointed their bodies with aromatic oils, while Yahweh's followers attached no particular importance to shaving and grooming. When the Israelitic texts repeatedly allude to both the barber's knife and eunuchs, this implies that some of the well-shaven priests practiced ritual castration as part of their worship; this was common in Syria and Babylon but has not been demonstrated among the followers of Baal in Israel.

The second and more common word for prostitute in the Bible is *zonah*, which is considerably weaker than *kadesh*. This term is most frequently translated as "harlot," but it appears in several hundred different contexts and seems to refer to everything from professional sex worker to tart or godless woman, sending every translator to the rack and thumbscrews. We hear in Judges that Jephtah was the son of a *zonah*, while two of his daughters took up their grandmother's profession. This might have been the case but could just as easily mean that the women in his family were socially and spiritually independent.

The Proverbs sometimes give fatherly advice to young men to keep away from a *zonah* in a manner we recognize from Mesopotamia and Egypt. From Proverbs 6:

> *My son, keep thy father's commandment,*
> *and forsake not the law of thy mother [...]*
> *For the commandment is a lamp; and the law is light;*
> *and reproofs of instruction are the way of life:*
> *To keep thee from the evil woman,*
> *from the flattery of the tongue of a strange woman.*
> *Lust not after her beauty in thine heart;*
> *neither let her take thee with her eyelids.*
> *For by means of a whorish woman*
> a man is brought *to a piece of bread:*
> *and the adulteress will hunt for the precious life.*
> *Can a man take fire in his bosom,*
> *and his clothes not be burned?*

But most warnings against *zonah* were sharpened by religious hostility: "Only the Wisdom of God can save a Man from the Charms of Harlots. For such Women have abandoned their Men and refuse to abide by the Laws of God," warns another proverb. Some try to define a *zonah* by her attitudes, as in Proverbs 7:

> *She is loud and stubborn;*
> *her feet abide not in her house.*
> *Now is she without, now in the streets*
> *and lieth in wait at every corner.*

It was always the harlot who lured a man into her snare, not the reverse. The Proverbs used a harlot as the explanation whenever a man lost control.

A man would in principle sin against Yahweh out of pride and rebellious-ness. But the common route to sin was to be lured from the straight and narrow path by a harlot.

Zonah was normally used without indication of money. It described a girl as free of her father and her brothers, and treacherous, especially toward the Israelites. A girl who did not want to move from her father's house to another man, as wife or slave, would have to sell her body to obtain freedom. But the Old Testament defined *zonah* more by sexual freedom and perfidiousness than her profession, and used the same word to designate neighboring women who brought a dowry into marriage. Unlike the daughters of Israel, she could gather her belongings and re-turn to her male relatives without embarrassment. As a woman with a dowry was free, she was called a harlot: "Listen to me, young Men, and obey. Don't go near her, stay away from where the Harlot walks, lest she tempt you and seduce you. She has been the Ruin of Multitudes. A vast Host of men have been her Victims. If you want to find the road to Hell, look for her House."

The sensuality, energy, and force of will that one might associate with the term *harlot* are a dangerous mix. Besides Tamar and Rahab, only one harlot is portrayed positively in the Old Testament, and that is Esther, who accepted being handed over as consort of the heathen king of Persia. But she kept her faith and was able to deceive all the foreign-ers and save her own people in the end. Esther was also obedient to her stepfather, and all her clever whoring was part of her service to God. At the end of her story, she won back the mantle of virtue, obedience, and fidelity.

King Solomon was Israel's prime state builder. Between 970 and 930 B.C., he managed to break down the old clan and tribe solidarity and estab-lish taxation, armed forces, bureaucracy, religious hierarchy, and cen-tral administration.

The Song of Solomon provided world literature with some of its sweet-est love poetry, but in fact it was not the king's own work; it was ascribed to him by later poets. Consequently, these texts cannot serve as proofs of Solomon's personal charisma or his seductive capacities. The queen of Sheba may have been a real princess passing through, but she may have been a mythic figure. Chronicles does state that one of Solomon's wives was an Egyptian princess and that aristocratic ladies from Moab, Ammon, Edom, and Sidon were co-wives. Contemporary sources from Egypt and Mesopotamia weaken any claim that Solomon's Jerusalem was a splendid capital led by a rich and powerful potentate. A few powerful Neo-Babylonian and Persian rulers of the first millennium surrounded themselves with up to three hundred wives and concubines. Solomon's wealth and power were nothing in comparison. The myth-creating propensities of the exiled Jewish authors in Babylon become especially obvious as they ascribed to Solomon seven hundred wives and three hundred concubines. They glorified their portrait of Solomon—consciously or not—to inspire their audience and establish that, like Babylon, Jerusalem had been rich and powerful once upon a time. Roman historians would reproduce this Jewish version of King Solomon uncritically, though other contemporary sources do not allow us to do the same.

But Solomon was, beyond doubt, the most effective ruler the Israelites ever had, and he certainly secured them a grand temple of their own. Obviously, this temple had a lot in common with major temples in the neighborhood, consecrated to other gods. The question is: How many gods were venerated in Solomon's temple?

Some Israelitic female servants at Solomon's court worshiped Yahweh, of course, but scarcely a single queen or mistress did, since they all came from non-Israelitic tribes, an unpleasant fact that no Old Testament text has managed to hide. Roman sources state that they worshiped Venus and Priapus, by which they meant Ashera and Baal. Indeed, Solomon's forty-year rule was distinguished by religious syncretism. His wish to reconcile different gods and religious rites was one of the secrets behind his successful state building. Yahweh was worshiped in the nave: The Ark of the Covenant was a sufficient symbol of his eternal presence. But the side temples were devoted to Ashera and Baal and contained images of them. Inside, the walls were decorated with erotic paintings of snakes, bulls, and other animals, while calves and goats were ritually sacrificed. In the rear apartments of the temple, it is likely that ritual sexual acts took place, as in Syria and Mesopotamia. That some Baal priests prostituted themselves is also probable, since this occurred in Phoenicia and Syria at the same time. Right outside, the temple women traded sex for cash. Trade and commerce flourished as never before, with prostitution as part of this commercial rise.

One of the king's wisest and best-known judgments occurred when two women were fighting over the same infant; each claimed he was her son. Solomon suggested cutting the child in two, thereby proving that the woman who chose to give up the child in order to spare his life was the true mother, because she loved him more. What tends to be omitted from Sunday school versions of this story is that tradition said the women were priestesses from Ashera's side temple and, especially in visual religious iconography, were depicted as prostitutes.

Chronicles describes Solomon with strange ambiguity, because the greatest among their kings pursued the worship of foreign gods. But to preserve his glory, the blame for this is shifted over to his son Rehoboam, who was influenced by his Ammonite mother, Na'amah. Indeed, when the authors wanted to disinfect Solomon, they found a woman to blame.

All texts that were written down in the Babylonian exile, four to five hundred years after the events they narrate, must be read critically. We must try to evaluate to what extent this foreign environment overshadowed the oral stories on which they were based. But although Chronicles is no contemporary source, it should be believed in its assertions about promotion of sacred prostitution and eunuch priests parallel with the worship of Ashera, independent of whether the blame is put on Solomon or Na'amah and Rehoboam. The writers in Babylon wanted to give a true narrative about Solomon and later kings and queens, but they were also trying to explain the fate of the Israelites as a result of moral backsliding. How much was anecdote or sensationalism and how much truth? Such questions do not have absolute answers.

Queen Jezebel was perhaps the most domineering personality in the Israel of 800 B.C. No human being is given a comparably dark portrait. It is virtually impossible to imagine anyone worse than her: the Whore of Babylon and the Queen of Sin in one seductive package.

Jezebel lived only a few centuries before her biography was written down, which suggests that many details in her story are true. The Israelite kingdom had been divided into two parts, Judah to the south and Israel to the north, where a new dynasty had ascended the throne. When King Ahab inherited the throne in 869 B.C., his marriage to Jezebel, the Phoenician princess from Tyros, became even more strategically important. The king allowed a blending of religions but may well have preferred Yahweh himself. The queen certainly did not, and it was she who made the decisions. Ahab is described as the archetypical henpecked husband, while Jezebel worshiped Baal and Ashera with burning intensity and intolerance. It is quite possible that it was she who fanned the embers of religious conflict until they burst with volcanic intensity.

But Jezebel was not alone in her warmongering. Some of Yahweh's prophets were also extremely intolerant and were thrown into blind rages by this queen who surrounded herself with eunuchs and promoted female priestesses. In the rites, she played the role of high priestess, and she might have participated in orgiastic rites dedicated to love and fertility. Moreover, said her detractors, she was greedy. Jezebel had cast her covetous eyes upon the lands of the well-to-do farmer Naboth and had him killed simply to satisfy her lust for good vineyards.

Jezebel would accept no religious compromise. She also fiercely resisted all ritual celebrations of the marriage between Ashera and Yahweh, which for over a century had been integrated into the daily worship of the majority of the population. Jezebel seems to have wanted to rescue "her" goddess from Yahweh and to bring his cult to a total end, initiating a regular massacre of his priests and prophets. Such a remorseless strategy would end with total victory or cruel defeat. There had been much religious uncertainty and liberalism for several centuries. Now the situation changed to hostile dogmatism and culminated in regular battles.

In this religious war, Jezebel led one of the armies; the rebel Jehu, with the skin-clad thundering prophet Elijah at his side, headed the side that finally won. At one time Elijah arranged a sacrificial competition between the priests of Yahweh and Baal at Mount Carmel, and won an astounding victory. Jezebel swore she would kill the prophet in revenge. Elijah found it prudent to leave, and withdrew all the way down to Sinai, where he lived in a cave and was fed by angels. When Yahweh told him to return, it was as the winning general.

Jezebel's fate was indeed cruel. She was the most implacable foe that Yahweh's adherents had ever encountered—and a woman, too. She realized that she was losing but was not reconciled to complete defeat. Instead, she decked herself out in full regalia, painted her eyelids green and her lips red, let down her hair, and took a seat in the window of the palace. This pose was both a royal and religious symbolic act. In such attire, she appeared as a sacred prostitute high priestess—simultaneously the earthly incarnation of the goddess Ashera and the queen of Israel.

Jezebel's idea must have been to project herself as so formidable in her queenly role, and so terrifying as high priestess, that no one would dare to unseat her. But the fanatical Jehu managed to intimidate three eunuchs so mortally that they chose to attack their high priestess and push her out the palace window. Her body hit the ground with a splash of blood spraying out in all directions. Frightened out of their wits, the royal horses trampled the queenly remains into oblivion. Then the dogs rushed forward, tore the flesh from her joints, and devoured it; the remains were slung on a dung heap. Jezebel's fate was painted with the most grotesque details that the authors of Chronicles could summon up, addressing the Israelites in exile who were confronted daily with related, wrongheaded religions.

The terrifying death of Jezebel was followed by massive killings of priests, priestesses, and all royal descendants venerating wrong gods, well planned and coordinated by the rebel Jehu. But these killings only kept the religious fire ardent. Later rulers in Israel, King Ahaziah and Queen Athaliah, remained true adherents of Ashera. The kings Amon and Manasse put the images of Ashera and Baal back on their spaces in the side temples of Jerusalem. The thundering prophets (Ezekiel 16: 26–28; Hoseas 4: 13; Amos 4: 1–7; Jeremiah 3: 3, 5, 6–7; Isaiah 23: 16–18) give us the clear message that Ashera and Baal continued to be venerated for the next 150 years, while harlots constantly wandered over the hills of Israel "and prostituted themselves under every tree" (Isaiah 2:3).

Maybe Yahweh's anger was the ultimate reason, but it is easy to find other explanations for why Israel was conquered by Assyria in 722 and its people abducted as prisoners. In 701, Judaea was invaded by the same enemy but was allowed some independence. But "the King was like a bird in a cage," and the inhabitants' fear of neighbors from the north grew to panic as the Assyrians were defeated by the even stronger Neo-Babylonians. In 621 B.C., the high priest Hilkia seems to have put in writing Moses' last sermons to his people. As the royal historian, Sjafan, read the texts to King Josiah, the latter, horrified, ripped his clothing asunder and set all his hopes on Yahweh's protection. This required worship in the good old down-home manner of Moses. At last the time was ripe for a religious reform movement. A contemporary text allowed Yahweh to complain straightforwardly to the prophet Jeremiah about the goddess wife his followers had imputed to him: "Don't you see what is happening in the streets of Jerusalem? No wonder my wrath is raging. Don't you see how children gather around Her, fathers ignite fires for Her, while the women knead dough and make cakes to this idol they call Goddess of Heaven? These offerings must stop!"

Josiah, Jeremiah, and a consenting female prophet, Hulda, took Yahweh at his word: It was time for his divorce from Ashera. Josiah destroyed Ashera's portrait in the temple, tore down the living quarters for her priestesses, and started a witch hunt against the prostitutes who had danced and made garments for the goddess. He concluded with a massive killing of the last priests of Baal. The revival of Yahweh spelled the end of the cult of Ashera and Baal. Yahweh's temple was cleansed, and the religious syncretism that had prevailed came to an end. For the authors of the Old Testament, this serves as the main explanation of a few decades' prolonged freedom for the kingdom of Judah.

Jewish folklore would later give a slightly different account. It tells that the wedding between Yahweh and Ashera had been prepared for centuries but never consummated. Yahweh had second thoughts and held them until the last minute, when he finally became man enough to send the goddess packing: She was altogether too demanding. In its worst versions, the myth says that Ashera married *Satan* instead—in revenge! Baal did receive new life as Beelzebub, another foul devil.

Although the cults of Ashera and Baal now came to a complete end among Hebrews, Ashera survived in folklore and continued to be worshiped among neighbors to the West and North. She even seems to emanate powers today. The many current archaeological findings that testify to the significance once accorded Ashera have made her a political problem for modern Israeli leaders. Archaeologists interested in Ashera figurines have, on several occasions, been prevented from publishing their findings. The Jewish right seems to fear Ashera and the religious syncretism she represents just as much as some of the prophets did.

Maybe they are justified? Ancient figurines of the goddess do impose doubt on Israel's present political ideology, closely linked as it is to dogmatic interpretations of ancient texts and Jewish history. If Ashera became famous again, she could undermine the dogmatics of modern Israel. What an inflammatory goddess!

* * *

Few present pornographers can match the strident thunder of the old prophets, who could coat any event with a sexual gloss. In 600 B.C., Ezekiel discerned ghastly whoremongers and shameless libidinous harlots wherever he went. The fall of Jerusalem was nigh!

And right he was! In 586 B.C. the Neo-Babylonian king Nebuchadnezzar besieged and occupied Jerusalem, razed Solomon's temple to the ground, and took the defeated Jews into captivity in the very center of world whoredom: Babylon. Both religious and secular prostitution blossomed to a level no Jew had imagined, and few fathers seemed to feel ashamed if their daughters became prostitutes; some of them started to grow up independent of the temples, in the commercial bordellos. The Israelite prisoners lived in their closed-off ghettos; one was within Babylon itself, and another was called Tel Aviv, located at the banks of a connected canal. During the Babylonian exile, the Hebrew prophets and authors did their utmost to consolidate their people's belief in the superiority of their religion; antagonism against foreign seed and customs marked everything they wrote and encapsulated their fear in one telling expression, the Whore of Babylon.

The Jews in Babylon prayed to Yahweh for a savior, and he finally heard them. He first pointed out with his finger on the wall to King Belzassar that he had been weighed, measured, and condemned. At the very same moment, the Persian king Cyrus seized Babylon. To the Jews, the liberal Cyrus represented the victory of good over evil, because he allowed religious freedom and let the Jews, if they chose, make their way home and to rebuild their temple in Jerusalem. But the majority remained, and later Persian kings continued to favor them as a fruitful connection for both parties.

Throughout the following centuries, one world power followed another as overlord over the former Canaan: Alexander the Great and his Ptolemaic followers in Alexandria; the Seleucids in Antioch. A century of freedom was followed by new subordination, this time to Rome. But memories of the Jewish-Persian connection remained, making the Jews suspect in the eyes of all later overlords.

In Ezekiel's rebuilt temple in Jerusalem, Yahweh ruled alone, his ex-wife and her priestesses gone for good. No Jewish moralists thundered against holy prostitution anymore, and the expression went out of fashion as a term of abuse. But there was sex for sale outside the temple, as before, and new prophets presided over the secular sale of sex, which had increased. Roman sources and apocryphal texts support the notion of widespread prostitution in the country that in Roman times would be called Palestine. In Jerusalem, Gaza, and Samaria, the harlots sang and played their harps, as the prophet Isaiah describes quite lyrically:

> *Take a harp, go about the city,*
> *thou harlot long forgotten;*
> *make sweet melody, sing many songs*
> *that you mayest be remembered.*

But many a whore simply shouted at passersby from her doorway. Some women used red paint to mark their houses as bordellos, after the Greek and Roman fashion. For Palestine was now under influence from the West as well, and even its prostitution began to imitate the sex industries of the leading cities of the day: Antioch, Alexandria, and Rome.

THREE

FALLEN ANGELS

Harlots, prostitutes, whores, or whatever we choose to call them are given a multilayered definition in the Old Testament, inclusive of everything bad that can be attributed to women. An explanation of what prostitution derives from may, however, be clarified through a close look at its prime narrative about creation and man's original sin.

What happened in the Garden of Eden? Did Eve straightforwardly destroy Adam and lead humanity out of Paradise into corruption and depravity? Leading Protestant female theologians agree that Eve is not a dominant figure in the Israelite canon. While one of the most problematic figures in the whole of the Scriptures, she is mentioned in only three short paragraphs, an odd mixture of creation myth and parable that explain the origin of sin. Then Eve is never mentioned again. And still: Genesis's narrative about man's fall has raised discussions in Christian and Jewish theology and folk belief for millennia.

The Jewish and Protestant traditions assign the greatest blame to the rebel archangel Satan and his party of fallen angels, and they emphasize how the eloquent phallic snake tempted Eve into the disaster of sin. The Roman Catholic Church blamed Eve and supported that view by canonizing a text from the second century B.C., sometimes called Ecclesiasticus, sometimes referred to by its author, Ben Zirah or Jesu Sirach. A related, somewhat younger text, the Book of Adam and Eve, even allows Eve to speak for herself and leaves no doubt about the source of sin and suffering. Eve says straight out that she is a deeply libidinous vessel, wicked and not to be trusted. This view of women differs from the dominating ideas of the Old Testament. There can be no emphasis on woman's weakness, since her sex seems innately obscene. During the last two centuries B.C., Greek Orphic mysticism had spread from Asia Minor to the Jews of the

Middle East, and the Greek Orphics stressed the weakness of the flesh, particularly in women. Orphic influence is clearly detectable in Ben Zirah's text but totally dominates the Book of Adam and Eve.

This text of Eve never became part of any canon; few read it today. But it was known and read in the ancient Christian Church, where the influence of Orphic mysticism continued to be strong, and its impact is easy to detect in the Epistles of Paul. The story of Eve and the apple from Genesis may appear to be an innocent tale, but thick-skulled and misogynist Greek influence upgraded it to a vision of horror.

Adam lived to the age of 930; Methuselah was 969 when he died. Christianity's and Judaism's most mythic texts account for the extraordinary longevity of the patriarchs' lives. Nobody bothered to find out Eve's life span. Her daughters are just as problematic. Between Eve and Sarah, Genesis reels off an almost endless list of men but only two women—Adah and Zillah, probably named only due to the renown of their sons, who changed human civilization. Adah's first son tamed the first cattle, and her second son created music; Zillah's son helped both as he created the first bronze and iron tools. Meanwhile, Adam and his descendants had been driven out of Paradise, clad in skins, bereft of apples and manna, and in most ways unprepared for the life that awaited them. Finally, God sent two handsome guardian angels, *grigori*, Azazel and Semjaza, to look after them. As early as in the seventh century B.C., Rabbi Elkiezer began a campaign against these two great mothers, presumably due to their assumed wicked sexual behavior: "When the angels fell from Heaven, the daughters of Cain examined them and showed them their genitalia. They had painted their eyes as harlots. After the angels had been seduced by the women, they took wives among them." Similar descriptions would be repeated in later and less venerable Jewish writings; obviously, the daughters of Eve barely needed to throw a glance at Azazel and Semjaza to discover that they were sexually useful. Then they applied paint to their faces and let themselves loose upon the angels. It had taken only a couple of generations on earth to make women as wild and aggressive as animals.

According to theology, God and Satan, angels and demons, exist outside time and history and beyond gender. They are ageless and sexless. But since human life, thought, and perception are sex- and gender-based, they all appear to us in human form, as male or female. How could civilizations ruled by men come to imagine God and Satan in a form other than their own sex? On the other hand, should images of God be avoided totally? To some extent, this applied to angels, too. The higher in the heavenly hierarchy, the more sexless they tend to be in human depictions. The archangels Uriel and Michael appear extremely manly and were indeed strong and powerful, while Gabriel and Raphael look almost like women. But such high-status angels always lack sexual organs when they are depicted. Angels of the lower orders appear more normal, to human eyes, at least. Guardian angels and others of lower rank are depicted with sexual organs, but smaller than those of humans. Angels are also said to be sexually passive, in no way seducers. But they may of course be seduced, as Adah and Zillah easily found out at the start of the time of man.

It is quite the opposite in the circles of hell, of course. The formerly fallen angels and their devil descendants appear to the human senses very well endowed, bisexual, or pansexual—and seductive. According to both Rabbi Elkiezer and later mythical sources, Adah and Zillah produced a number of descendants, with God's guardian angels as their fathers. The question of how angels and humans could beget children has engendered theological conflict. The practical conclusion, by the majority of those who have ventured opinions throughout history, is that mating angels with humans is like mating horses and donkeys: Children may come, but celestial bastards are not capable of populating the world in later generations. This point of view is the most humanistic position, especially when the same discussion arose over a millennium later, this time related to the offspring of humans and devils. Angels are never sexually offensive, though this should not count heavily against anyone, since angels are purely good by nature. But only women can get pregnant and be forced to justify their actions by pointing out how heavenly the father of their child really was.

While the Catholic Church gives the female sex the lion's share of the burden of male sin, both Jewish tradition and the later Protestants tend to explain sin with a concept of pure evil, something transcendent of the human realm. When women become harlots and men allow themselves to sin, it is due to demons' influence. And as both Jewish and Christian scholars would argue later, devils are not only purely evil but always out to seduce humans. For a man, such an experience can be tough enough. Women will suffer twice, both during the seduction and if they have to raise a child who may have inherited most personal qualities from its devil father. In such a mother's defense, she was seduced, if not raped. If the father really was a devil, the offspring would be left alive until it commits real, unforgivable evils as an adult. Tradition's wise "compromise" position in this complicated demonological dispute would allow many thousands of children to grow up. If the assumed bastard inherited sufficient human qualities, it might get a long life, but humanity would be protected, since it would never produce offspring. If the mother mistook a human seducer for a devil, this doubt also counted in the favor of the child.

History's first big debate about this issue broke out among Jewish literati in the second century B.C., precisely at the time of Ben Zirah. Its main theme was Eve and her descendants on the distaff side, sin and guilt in the Garden of Eden. Many posed Satan and his band of fallen angels against Eve and her descendants. Ben Zirah belonged to the minority who placed most of the blame on Eve. But the minority interpretations would prevail just as strongly into the future.

In some Jewish renderings, Eve's position as Adam's second wife counts in her defense. It reduces her status but explains her culpability. According to this competing myth of origin, the first woman in Adam's life was Lilith, a fallen female angel. But early in their relationship, Adam and Lilith encountered problems. Lilith was extraordinarily determined with her demands on poor Adam. She insisted, for instance, on being on top when they made love. Once when Adam tried to turn her toward the missionary position, she laughed right in his face, got up, and left. Promptly. Good Adam missed the bitch. He pined and regretted, but all in vain. Finally, he was provided with the much sweeter and more obedient Eve, while Lilith had sought out more compatible partners among other fallen angels.

We have more information about Lilith than the enigmatic Eve. Lilith was mentioned by the prophet Jesaiah, by Matthew, and in Revelations, and she has attracted a good many adherents through history. In the Middle East and along the Black Sea, she was known as the owl goddess, but also the goddess of love. In ancient reliefs, she was portrayed as a combination of snake, bird, and human. Some depictions showed her secretively holding the keys to life. Jewish and Christian folklore would eventually make Lilith the bride of Satan. Sometimes she was even portrayed as Virgin Mary's mirror opposite, in the triple role as Satan's mother, wife, and daughter.

Satan and Lilith reveal themselves particularly in Jewish mysticism and folklore. But Lilith has remained a lively challenge to male fantasy in general. Extraordinarily fertile, she was constantly giving birth to daughters, collectively called Liloth, a plural derivative of their mother's name. These she-devils had the frightful habit of seeking out men who slept alone, arriving in the dead of night and jumping on top of any poor soul sleeping the sleep of the just. Extremely virtuous and observant bachelors may wake up in time, scared by their unmistakably smutty laughter. These frightened young men fought their fear through jokes. For centuries, celibate Jewish and Christian men jokingly called themselves daughters of Lilith. The mother of all these devilish seductresses, the queen of hell herself, has for her part experienced a recent revival among esoteric feminists of the West. Women's bookstores, Jewish feminist periodicals, lesbian cafés, even a highly commercial music festival have been proudly named after her. Significantly, it was not the second, milder woman in Adam's life but his first and most difficult wife, the first female rebel of our civilization's most venerable myths, who has become the feminist symbol.

Although angels and devils in theory are beyond sex and gender, the individual angel or devil tends to appear with a majority of features of one sex. Some feminine angels have been associated with prostitution and the sale of sex, like Eiseth Zenuim and Agrat-Ba-Mahlat. Unfortunately, they are not guardian angels of prostitutes. They belong to the fallen party; accordingly, they promote evil and are normally described as Satan's brides and whores.

Asmodeus was the best known, most portrayed, and most attractive in this bad crowd. He has wandered from text to text, from the apocryphal Book of Tobit to Jewish folklore and Protestant fiction. Asmodeus was the personified whoremaster, the prince of hell, the greatest, most irresistible seducer. The only protection against him was intense prayer for the archangel Michael; only he would force Asmodeus to retreat. In all other situations, Asmodeus was victorious and bent both men and women to his sexual will. Although Lilith was the queen of hell, Satan's favorite was Na'amah, the Pleasant, who was also the mother of Asmodeus. Despite a rebellion against his father's reign, he was the most attractive to Satan and to every whore in his harem.

Hell shall thus be seen as populated by an army of seducers: Lilith and her daughters, Satan's whores and the angels of prostitution, with Asmodeus as spearhead. Everything they do is united into one idea—all have the same goal—to tempt and arouse humanity to greater sins. Satan might well be slightly sex-tired now and then, but he regains his power enlightened by his enormous, evil master plan, of which all whoredom and harlotry are parts. He certainly is obsessed—by his constant, evil plans against his one and only rival.

F O U R

G R E E K   L I B E R A L I S M

S ocrates was condemned to death in Athens in 399 B.C. because he allegedly "had faith in gods other than those the city believed in," and had "corrupted its youth." The seventy-one-year-old philosopher drained the poisoned vessel, but a good while before doing so, he sent away his wife, Xantippe. He didn't do this to spare her; he simply preferred to die surrounded by his young male admirers, such as the young Phaedon of Elis, who had just purchased his freedom from a brothel. The only woman Socrates might have accepted at his deathbed was the famous *hetæra* Aspasia. This reveals something about the old philosopher, and just as much about gender and prostitution in classical Greece.

While Athenian democracy and Greek culture were blossoming at their greatest exuberance in the fifth century B.C., Greek women were banished to a boring and virtuous domesticity. The men romped around in one another's company, intellectually, emotionally, and sexually. Slaves carried out the essential labor; foreigners conducted the trade and commerce. Demosthenes put it most appropriately when he said that Greek men of his day "had *hetæræ* for their pleasure, concubines to care for their bodies, and wives to secure the legitimacy of their descendants and keep their homes in order."

Around the year 550 B.C., Greek history experienced a turning point. Over the three or four hundred years of the Arcadian period, Greek culture had developed and spread from the mainland to Crete, Asia Minor, and Sicily. This was the period when the Greek city-states consolidated their culture and further developed a society that contrasted with their own older aristocracy and the barbarian civilizations, above all the Persian Empire, to their east.

In 499 B.C., Greek cities on the coast of Asia Minor tried to rise up against Persian hegemony. This caused two punitive expeditions, led by the Persian kings Darius and Xerxes. These assaults galvanized the Greeks into unity. All of a sudden, it looked as though their culture would either go under or triumph, for the Persian army was colossal, ten times greater than that of the Greeks. But it was only the Persians' aristocratic cavalry that was dangerous; the infantry consisted of slaves conscripted by force, of unwilling and unmotivated men who could in no way stand up to the Greeks' few but well-trained free citizens who were fighting for freedom, democracy, and Western values.

The Greek defensive war became a fertile ground for myth. A key concept from which much of Western political thought still derives is the fundamental opposition between the West and the East, between free men and barbaric hordes—an archetype created by the historians Herodotus, Thucydides, and Xenophon, as they described the struggles with the Persians.

Greek democracy, jurisprudence, literature, and military technology developed in opposition to these barbarians. But Greek sexuality also emerged in this opposition. The ideals of rational but warm male love and secularized, effective prostitution were created in contrast to the "un-healthy" love life among the "perverse barbarians" of the East. Their vase paintings illuminate this excellently. Young Greek males are frequently depicted as sexually passive but never as effeminate. Any Greek man, re-gardless of age, is athletic, muscular, and handsome. The sex organ of the Greek male is always portrayed as relatively small but infibulated. The foreskin is bound together ahead of the glans penis, something the Greeks found attractive, clean, and civilized. Prostitutes, the only women portrayed as naked, were also slim and shapely. By contrast, the barbarians were portrayed as slack and ugly; some resembled effeminate eunuchs, while others were fat and plain and equipped with large, ugly, slack genitals. Vase paintings indicate that the culture was xenophobic, promoting a belief that the Greeks were more intelligent and attractive and practiced much more aesthetic sex than the uncivilized barbarians of the East.

In the East, barbarian hordes were ruled by decadent kings and queens of intrigue, supported by local tyrant satraps, while Eastern temples were filled with hierodules, temple prostitutes, and eunuchs. In the West, the Greeks practiced political democracy, free philosophy, and learned science, athletic exercises, and manly love. Well-educated prostitutes were available for the elite, and publicly supervised bordellos catered to the commoners.

The best-paid Greek prostitutes were, in many ways, the world's first free women. Before this period, Egyptian, Mesopotamian, Lydian, and Persian princesses had mastered the refinement of their times and could dance, sing, and seduce lovers with poise and grace. But they were born and raised to this. The history of the Greek elite prostitutes is something else; they purchased their freedom, struggled for advancement, conquered literature, and conditioned and coaxed their bodies to ultimate beauty. Their labors allowed them to advance socially, through better and more handsome men, than the cleverest princesses of the East.

> *You, Solon, saw the city full of young men*
> *under the pressure of a natural need,*
> *and running wild and disreputable.*
> *So you bought up women and put them up for common use.*
> *There they all stand, all naked,*
> *so there's no pretending, what you see is what you get.*
> *Perhaps you don't feel so well, or feel aggrieved,*
> *the door is open, one coin, and in you jump.*
> *No prudery, no nonsense, no rejection.*
> *Instant sex is what you want, in any manner you wish.*
> *Once you've done, you can tell her to go to hell.*
> *She's a stranger to you now.*

This rather merciless tone is found in a fragment from a lost comedy by Philemon, *The Men from Delphi*, written in 290 B.C. Solon was the great statesman of Athens in the sixth century B.C. In one fell swoop, he managed to erase all the old outstanding debts, abolish the enslavement of debtors, codify civil law, and initiate the idea of an impersonal state, independent of any monarch or aristocracy. In other words, Solon founded Western democracy. An interval of tyrant leadership followed, before Athens turned back to the constitution Solon had established. All subsequent politics found their place within the forums of public debate and in accordance with the written laws from Solon's time.

But Solon is also the father of the sex industry, and his sexual reforms are closely linked to his other reforms. From the sixth century B.C., Athens and other Greek cities would show the rest of the Mediterranean world a well-organized and state-supervised prostitution trade disentangled from the religious and ritual boundaries that had largely marked the sale of sex in earlier periods. Solon's sexual reforms endured not least because he created the building complex that would later be called *porneia*, or "houses where people went naked," and purchased slave women and young slave girls to fill the houses. Last but not least, he trained the personnel, and he ensured a cheap enough admission that the political approval of a majority of his fellow citizens followed automatically.

From the sixth century B.C., one might encounter both female and male prostitutes in Athens and its port city of Piraeus. The sex industry quickly became a lucrative supplemental income for Athens and stole an important section of the market from the previously very popular Ephesus in Asia Minor, where a more old-fashioned, temple-related prostitution was still practiced. But prostitution flourished just as well in the neighboring city of Corinth, a port city opening to the West that had been a major center for maritime trade and transport since Arcadian times.

Fifty years after the Persian wars, Athens held the helmsman position among the Greek city-states. It was not yet the capital of any empire. On the Greek mainland, Corinth, Sparta, and Thebes were equally independent city-states in either alliance or opposition to Athens. Ephesus and Miletus in Asia Minor, Byzantium in the Straits of Bosphorus, and Syracuse in Sicily were also important, while Greek colonization had reached as far northwest as Massilia, or what today is Marseilles, in the south of France.

The classical period of Greek history consists of only the 150 years after the Persian wars. During this short period, Greek drama peaked, the popular assembly fostered one brilliant orator after another, and Greek philosophy, art, and architecture reached their zenith. All of these philosophers, dramatists, politicians, and artists sought the feminine company of the elite prostitutes—women more educated, elegant, and sexually liberated than the world had ever seen.

Men dominated Greek urban society. Both young and old worshiped others' bodies and masculine qualities. At the same time, brutal male wrestling and graceful dancing by both sexes were highly esteemed skills. It required no little beauty, intelligence, and wit from the women who were to make their mark with such competition. It was in this spirit that the *hetæra* Mania addressed two rivalrous athletes: "I went to bed with you, Leontinos, almost simultaneously with Antenor, for I was determined to find out once and for all what two Olympic victors could do for me on one and the same night!"

Strabo wrote antiquity's first comprehensive work on nature and culture. Later scholars have argued against the reliability of his figures, but no one has questioned his assertion that there were a thousand prostitutes in Corinth during the fifth century and almost as many in Athens. Both cities had between thirty and forty thousand inhabitants, which means that one in ten adult women were prostitutes. But conditions varied. Spartan women enjoyed greater freedom than other Greek females: They took part in sports and bore weapons. There were far fewer prostitutes in Sparta, but history has preserved the names of Spartan prostitutes. Cottina, who earned her wealth in Sparta, presented her home city, Corinth, with a bronze statue of a cow.

In most cities other than Athens, prostitution started out less secular, and for decades a majority of the prostitutes remained under the control of the temples of Aphrodite in Corinth, Cyprus, and elsewhere, or the Artemis temple in Ephesus. But soon all prostitution linked to Western temples would resemble the sex industry of Athens. Year by year, Greek, Egyptian, and Phoenician seamen looking for sex would notice fewer differences between one city and the next, since there were fewer rites, less religion, and more and more pure sex exchanged for money.

But religious sentiment did not disappear because sex became rational and secular. In Athens, the best-paid prostitutes could suddenly appear in public as priestesses of the love goddess Aphrodite, a role they continued to fulfill. These otherwise profane professional women would, when occasion called, dress up as divinities and invoke the protection of the gods.

The word *hora* is Greek, and only in the classical Greek period can this word be translated unproblematically as "female sex worker." The word's negative undertones developed quickly, however. But the Greeks employed a number of other designations, like *porne*, and suggestive metonyms like *bedroom upholstery* or *parish worker*. Even the word *dice* could be used to designate prostitutes. These women were objects that men would rub between their hands, then toss away.

The Greek female sex workers were divided into three clearly ranked classes. *Deichtrides* means girls on display; they were women of humble means who could be seen on display in the windows and doorways of *porneiæ*. Almost all were slaves who lived with a dirt floor and a few square feet of space. As if these miserable conditions weren't bad enough, both women and men regarded the *deichtrides* with great contempt. According to the laws, they were not allowed on the streets before nightfall, so that respectable women and minors could avoid encounters with them, although this rule was taken lightly in Piraeus and the harbor areas of Corinth. As children had the right to shout all kinds of filthy epithets at them, they had little desire to move around outdoors. The *deichtrides* were frequently afflicted with sexual diseases. Abortion was common among all Greek prostitutes, and gonorrhea and other infections contributed to low fertility. Many Greek men were under the mistaken impression that prostitutes were women who could not have children; they also believed that mixing the semen of many men during a short period of time neutralized fertility.

But prostitutes—even *deichtrides*—had children although fewer than did married women. A prostitute's daughter could be put to work in or near a bordello and, in time, take over from her mother. A son was another matter; many prostitutes staked everything they had to obtain entry for their sons into civil society. The war hero Themistocles is a vibrant symbol of the presence of prostitutes in Athens, and proof that a poor *deichtride* could attain a great deal through her son. Themistocles, despite a prostitute mother of such low status that she had to scrape together the proceeds from two-drachma customers to rear him, became Athens's leading politician during the Persian wars. As an adult, he became notorious for his wild orgies with *hetæræ*, yet every single time war or politics called, he put aside sex and sacrificed himself for his city.

Life was far better for the *auletrides,* the song-and-dance girls, who were free women with some skills and accomplishments. They appeared in public, played the flute and the zither or drums, and danced. Some of them could juggle, fence, and execute acrobatic moves similar to those one finds in the circus. One could book *auletrides* for entertainment at private parties, and these girls were subject to few restrictions. Their artistic talents

made them useful during festivals and ceremonies, when they could perform naked or in see-through drapery. *Auletrides* could earn good money
and make the transition to the highest class of prostitute smoothly. In contrast to the *deichtrides,* the *auletrides* were extremely popular among the
children and youth and were often celebrated under names such as the
Sparrow, Sunbeam, or Flower Girl.

    Hetæræ, or "companions," moved around most freely of all, even more
than the married wives of the citizens. In the afternoons the *hetæræ* prom-
enaded in the Ceramicus, a garden area that adjoined the Academy and
the Cemetery of Patriots. There were bushes, trees, and comfortable
benches here, and the gravestones were used as private mailboxes. A woman
could approach a headstone and note down with her eyeliner the name of
the man she was prepared to receive that evening. The client could reply
on the same headstone, the format being an introductory compliment followed by an offer in round figures. To succeed under such conditions, the
hetæræ had to be well known and limited in number. An Athenian census
around the year 400 B.C. put the population of *hetæræ* at 135; the number of
auletrides and *deichtrides* must have been many times higher.

    "Love me for all eternity, but do not be jealous if others do the same."
Asclepiades from Samos reveals in a poem to the *hetæra* Hermione that
she had these words, from his own verses, embroidered on a belt she always wore, with the text enwreathed in beautiful flowers. The *hetæræ* not
only constituted the elite of the prostitutes; many also considered them
the leaders among all women. It was said about the Athens of the fifth century B.C. that one saw no women other than *hetæræ* and *auletrides.* Wives and
girls from prosperous homes lived in obscure seclusion; the cheap prostitutes were stowed out of sight. *Hetæræ* and *auletrides* dominated the streets,
attended theatrical performances, and joined public processions. Indeed,
some of them even made their mark in politics.

    The top stratum of Greek prostitutes received their clients at elegant
dinners, paying *auletrides* to entertain their guests with song and dance
while they took care of philosophy, wit, flirtation, and sex. Sometimes they
engaged in regular bouts of drinking with their clients. Other occasions
were celebrated purely and simply through sex orgies. In most cases, the
activities took place in the *hetæræ*'s own well-appointed residences.

    From time to time, the *hetæræ* arranged parties where they did not
admit men, or in any case, not early in the evening. Evidence of this is in

a well-written letter from the frivolous Athenian Megara to her more philo-sophical girlfriend Bacchis, who had a literary bent that surpassed mere gossip writing. The lively Megara criticized Bacchis for not having ap-peared at the all-girl party simply because of an affair. Philomena, a third friend in their circle, had only just begun a more permanent relationship with a man, but that had not stopped her. She had sneaked out of the bedchamber to meet the other girls:

> We lived it up in the shadow of the trees, and although I had been tipsy before, I have never known what it is to be thoroughly drunk until now. The most hilarious moment of all was when Tryallis and Myrina began to compete over who could best wiggle her ass.... We had other competitions, too. As you know, when it comes to the belly, there is nobody who can beat Philomena. Yes, she is the only one who has never had to use hers for childbirth.... Afterward we went out into the streets and started up all kinds of pranks. Finally, we ended up in the house of Deximachos, in the Street of the Goldsmiths—I suppose you know the lad just inherited a fortune from his father....

Sappho of Mytilena, the famous poet, ran a school for women on the island of Lesbos. But she is best known for her lyrical poems, designed for recitation, many dealing with female love, between mothers and daugh-ters or between two closely involved women. The concept of lesbian love is her legacy to the world. It was later maintained that Sappho originally was a *hetæra*; modern scholars find this less probable. But it seems obvious that she had relationships with women of the *hetæra* class. Both the school she ran and the poetry she wrote would have been unthinkable without a broad stratum of well-educated, free, and independent women. Prostitu-tion is not mentioned in Sappho's lyrics, but the presence of the *hetæræ* is hard to miss. Moreover, in Sappho's time, the sale of sex was about the only possible choice of vocation for women who wanted to lead a free life.

As the business of prostitution spread in Athens and other cities, schools were founded that were purely sexual in nature. The speeches of Demosthenes make references to Nichareta, who purchased teenage girls in the slave market, trained them, and sold them for many times the origi-nal investment. But Nichareta seems to have taught her students to get rid of their slave bonds, too. Many did so, and some famous *hetæræ* of the day, like Nearea, would proudly admit that they were educated at the school of Nichareta.

*   *   *

The Greeks had several words for male prostitutes, but the most common was *hetairechos*. History always seems to preserve more details about men's lives, and that is also true, if a bit less so, of the female-dominated sex industry. When the Popular Assembly of Athens discussed prostitutes, it meant male prostitutes. A particularly famous debate was whether the politician and former wrestling champion Timarchos should be banned from politics in the mid-fourth century B.C. His enemies alleged that he had been a *hetairechos* in his youth and therefore could not be considered a free Athenian citizen. Over a week, the whole Athenian public discussed the youthful love affairs of the still-athletic-looking Timarchos.

Aeschines, who led the attacks, pointed out that as a young man, Timarchos had spent much time in a Piræus bathhouse, where wealthy men paid to admire his physique. The Greek attitude toward sex between men was somewhat ambiguous. The pejorative term *kinakosi* was used about effeminate homosexuals, in clear opposition to the *hoplite*, or warrior-citizen ideal, which can be construed as including clear homoerotic undertones in the context of manly faithful friendship. Aristophanes explained that sex for money hurt Greek feelings much more when it was the young men, rather than the women, who asked for money. It was by no means wrong of Timarchos to enjoy being admired as a male ideal, but it was wrong to make money on other men's admiration. The crucial question in this case seems to have been whether an earlier relationship between Timarchos and a man named Misgola, who no longer lived in Athens, had been of commercial or emotional nature. Aeschines was convinced that it was commercial; accordingly, Timarchos, who was well educated and knew the laws, should have signed himself into the public register of prostitutes. That, however, would have ruined his political career.

After the conclusion of the case, Athenians and subsequent history buffs were left with the impression that many youths at this time earned solid money by prostituting themselves. It was probably also true that most were slaves. Timarchos was lucky to have Athens's most eloquent statesman in his corner: Demosthenes himself spoke in his defense. Timarchos' supreme education and good family connections must also have counted in his favor. He was exonerated, but he had to live on with a somewhat frayed reputation.

This was not the only time the Public Assembly discussed male prostitution. A later dispute concerned the young *hetairechos* Theodotos. A man named Simon, who seemed to love him, accused another of the young man's customers of intentionally violating his body, and was the winner at the trial. These cases normally were brought against those who had prostituted themselves; after all, almost all of Athens was paying for sex. Most of these transactions were with women, but female matters were not normally public issues. Thus, the disputes about *hetairachoi* ought to be understood as public discussion on extramarital relations in general, regardless of whether women or young men were involved.

Most prostitutes were either slaves or women and on both grounds were excluded from the Popular Assembly. The literature reveals little about what proportions of the *auletrides* and *hetærae* were freeborn, but all cases where they were not free from birth, they had purchased their freedom to secure status and a good income. The most usual method was to establish a little fan club, which would guarantee the loan needed to buy oneself out of a *porneia*. When the debt was paid off, a free prostitute could concentrate on building up her or his income. One night with a *hetæra* cost hundreds of times more than a quickie in a brothel, so in purely economic terms, freedom was well worth the effort, and the sooner the better.

The *hetæræ* were much better paid than all other prostitutes, female or male, partly because their expenses were greater. The *hetæræ* offered lavish symbolic gifts to the gods and had to keep their bodies shapely and maintain beautiful homes. Their beds had to be soft, their garments elegant. The constant maintenance of pure physical beauty cost money and was one of their major daytime activities, besides reading.

The Corinthian Laïs had the most beautiful breasts of her time. She had philosophers from different schools of thought among her customers. The leading hedonist was the always luxuriously dressed, woman-loving Aristippus. He would take Laïs to the island of Ægina for two months each year, and he paid very well. The cynic Diogenes, on the other hand, was known to enjoy her favors for free. As Laïs ultimately became a theme in a philosophical dispute, Aristippus stated, "I am generous to Laïs in order to enjoy her myself, not to prevent others from the same pleasures."

When the famous Demosthenes signaled a planned visit, the price Laïs proposed was ten times higher than he had expected. The elderly statesman refused in the following dignified manner: "I am not prepared to pay such a high price for something of which I might very well come to be ashamed." Laïs reportedly replied, "I am not prepared to sell myself more cheaply, for in such an event, the shame would be mine."

> *I was a harlot in the city of Byzantium*
> *and granted to all the love that I sold.*
> *I am Kallihöe, experienced in all the voluptuous arts,*
> *lashed by the stings of love.*
> *Thomas has placed this epitaph on my grave,*
> *and thereby showed what passion dwelt in his soul.*
> *His heart melted and became as soft as wax.*

This tombstone epitaph from Byzantium is one of many found all over the Hellenistic world. Scenes from the sex workers' lives are found on innumerable vases and drinking vessels. Since the depiction of citizens' wives and daughters in a state of nakedness was taboo, nine out of ten women portrayed on Greek ceramics were *hetæræ* and *auletrides*, often depicted in titillating sexual positions that inspired discussion in the latter hours of a drinking binge.

Archaeology is only one of many sources of information about Greek prostitutes in classical and Hellenic times. The written sources are extensive and include census information, tax registers, and court records, in addition to a comprehensive epic and dramatic literature. One easily detects comments on prostitution in the works of Plato and Aristotle, and all the major and minor Greek historians. Aristophanes wrote a series of short *hetæræ* biographies, of which some fragments are extant, and he frequently portrayed prostitutes in his comedies, as did Menander and at least ten other writers of Greek comedies from whom we unfortunately have only fragments. Herondas wrote a textbook on prostitution in the fourth century B.C., which has since disappeared, while the learned Alciphron assembled letters from *hetæræ*, and Machaon of Sicyon collected a long series of anecdotal biographies about famous prostitutes.

In the second century A.D., the satirist Lucian from Samosata rounded out the Greek literature on prostitution. In addition to an otherwise rich and versatile body of historical writings, Lucian wrote twenty-four dialogues on prostitution that were so uncannily true to life that they cause even modern readers to burst into laughter. Lucian depicts the *hetæræ* Glycera and Thaïs discussing a handsome, wealthy officer with whom they both have had relations, but who, strangely enough, has fallen for an ugly nonprostitute. The women agree that there can be only one explanation— the ugly girl's mother must have bewitched the handsome warrior. Many of Lucian's dialogues are discussions between mothers and daughters in the sex industry on the subject of sex and its secrets. In one dialogue, a woman with twenty years' experience competes against a girl with only eight years. In Lucian's tenth dialogue, he has a young man visiting a whore for the sole purpose of pouring out his lamentations after his girlfriend has deserted him. In the witty thirteenth dialogue, two prostitutes' clients are ridiculed through a grandiose but pathetic sexual boasting competition.

But even several centuries before Lucian, there was a comprehensive Greek literature of learned and humorous writings about commercial sex. These and other writings show us that the history of prostitution, as a discipline of study, is over two thousand years old.

Most famous among all *hetæræ* in classical Greece were Aspasia and Phryne, two completely different women.

Aspasia was the daughter of Axiochus, from the Greek city of Miletus on the coast of Asia Minor. A free man of very little means, he sent his daughter to the local temple of Aphrodite, a completely acceptable way to get rid of an unwanted girl child. After various types of temple training, including sexual service, Aspasia made her way to Athens around 450 B.C., and started a career as a secular *hetæra*. Rather quickly, she became the major shareholder in one of the larger establishments and had several young women in her service. They were all elegant, highly articulate, and beautiful. That Aspasia herself was a beauty seems to be confirmed by a well-known statue of her. Moreover, she was said to be a master of rhetoric, witty and highly knowledgeable. All of Athens's leading citizens found themselves among the paying guests at her house from time to time, and they partook of her feasts and parties.

Pericles was the popularly elected leader of Athens, a great general in the concluding phase of the Persian wars, and the architect behind the Attic maritime alliance that secured Athens the leading position among Greek states in the years after these wars. Beyond doubt, he was the greatest statesman of the period. Pericles became Aspasia's first permanent lover, and he later left his wife for the *hetæra*. Aspasia had been tolerated, even admired, as his lover, but when she became his almost-wife, her status changed. Both poets and writers of comedies attacked her, while rumors blackened her name. Some alleged that she continued to work as a prostitute out of the home that she and Pericles shared.

When Pericles was publicly praised as the great Olympian, Aspasia was nicknamed Hera by the public wit. Comedians put Pericles onstage as Heracles the powerless, redressed as a housewife by the domineering Omphala, or growing feeble under the nagging sway of Deianeira. Plato, not usually known for gossip, maintained in the dialogue *Menexenos* that Aspasia tamed the great Pericles with a slipper, and purported that it was the *hetæra*, not the statesman, who wrote the speeches he gave before the Popular Assembly, a forum that forbade women both entry and the right to speak.

Aristophanes' comedy *The Acharnians* gives the impression that it was Aspasia, pure and simple, who caused the Peloponnesian wars, the feud between Sparta and Athens that for a time destroyed all internal solidarity among the Greeks. There was some truth behind the plot Aristophanes used. When some citizens of Megara abducted ten prostitutes from Athens, Aspasia worked tirelessly to get them back home. This was held against her popularly and ascribed as a major reason for the war that followed in 431 B.C.

The cool, almost queenly Aspasia was suddenly not only ridiculed in the theater but also mocked in the streets. As a final expression of popular revenge, she was hauled before the courts and indicted for corruption. At the same time, Pericles appeared just as weak as the comedians portrayed him. His power was in free fall, and his formerly brilliant speeches seemed heading in the same direction. He finally felt hopelessly isolated in the Popular Assembly. All he could think to do was throw his arms around his beloved Aspasia and burst noisily into tears. It was with his tears that he won the battle he could not win with words or swords. Aspasia was released and gained greater respectability thereafter.

When Pericles died in 429 B.C., Aspasia was a mature, wealthy woman, but her influence continued through her new lover, Lysicles, another prominent politician. She also ran a school for young women in which she taught philosophy and rhetoric. She did not teach sex, even though evil tongues continued to imply it. During these years, Aspasia moved in the social circles of Socrates, and Plato, who lived with the *hetæra* Arcanessa.

Socrates' preference for male love was common knowledge, but as his discussion partner, he accepted Aspasia and another philosophically well-schooled *hetæra* named Theodota. To her great delight, Aspasia lived to see the son she had with Pericles acknowledged as a legitimate member of the Popular Assembly.

The *hetæra* Phryne became almost as famous as Aspasia half a century later. Phryne—properly Mnesarete—came from the small town of Thesbia, in Boeotia, and spent her childhood picking capers, a painful and exhausting job that leaves no doubt she came from a very modest family. In her youth, she moved to Athens, where everybody agreed that she was extraordinarily beautiful. It did not take her long to understand that she could earn money from an appearance so striking that many were cowed by it. The comic poet Anaxilas compared her to Charybdis, who swallowed up both shipowners and their vessels.

Some young Athenian playboys once made a bet with Phryne. They were convinced that not even she could seduce the elderly Xenocrates, the most moralistic philosopher of Athens, and they meant to facilitate the task by getting him heavily drunk at a luxurious banquet. When Phryne finally appeared, the philosopher remained unmoved. The young men then demanded that she pay the price of the lost wager, but she refused. In her opinion, it had been a bet over a man of actual flesh and blood, not someone stone drunk and possessing the senses of a statue.

Phryne seldom revealed her total physical perfection at the public baths, and even her lovers usually got to see her only in dim light. But during religious festivals, Phryne felt it was right and appropriate to appear as the incarnation of a deity. On one occasion, during the Elysian mysteries that were performed annually a bit north of Athens, she removed her clothing garment by garment before an enormous spellbound crowd. When Poseidon or Aphrodite was celebrated in Piræus, Phryne would advance naked through the crowd, dive into the sea, and climb out again, in symbolic repetition of the goddess's mythic birth from the sea. With such an attitude and body, she could easily draw an admiring crowd. But her enemies grew proportionately.

In 340 B.C., she was charged with *asbeia*: impiety, an elastic concept, easy to apply to anyone losing popularity, and an accusation that left a lot to the feelings of the judges. As Phryne's case developed, the outcome hung on whether her beauty would be construed as witchcraft or of divine emanation. Two famous *hetæræ*, Bacchis and Myrina, convinced a client, the famous orator Hyperides, to undertake Phryne's defense. It would endanger the whole sex market if its most beautiful representative were convicted. The two women wrote several letters to each other in relation to the case. We still have them.

At one surprising moment in court, Hyperides went right up to Phryne and began to remove her clothing, garment by garment, just as she herself had done during the pervious year's Elysian mysteries. While people sat transfixed, he went ahead with his defense. "The judges were so seized by holy awe at the sight of the divinity that they did not venture to kill the prophetess and priestess of Aphrodite," wrote the historian Athenæus. Suddenly, the conclusion was clear: Phryne had not committed blasphemy but given expression to a religious feeling in the hearts and souls of most Greeks. While people no longer thought it likely that they would encounter the gods and demigods up in the hills, beside a spring, or along the bank of a river, they retained a powerful and aesthetically informed belief in the divine on earth.

Thus, Phryne survived the court case with undamaged charisma. She enjoyed a long life while keeping herself in top form, becoming very rich and, in old age, also generous. But when she offered to rebuild the Thebes city walls after their destruction by the Macedonians, the citizens turned her down. She had requested the following inscription on the walls: "Demolished by Philip of Macedonia, rebuilt by the *hetæra* Phryne." This was too much for the good citizens of Thebes, who preferred to live on without such fortifications.

The Macedonian king had successfully played the various Greek cities against one another before he achieved an alliance between Athens and Thebes in 338 B.C. and thereby put an end to Greek democracy. His son Alexander went on to defeat Darius, king of Persia, in battle after battle, and conquered Syria, Egypt, Mesopotamia, and the whole Persian heartland.

Alexander married Princess Roxana, from far-off Bachtria, but he seems to have held a special place in his heart for the bold, free-speaking Athenian-born Thaïs. According to Plutarch, she spent a wine-soaked night with Alexander right before the march on Persepolis, one of the Persian capital cities, and then she asked Alexander to be allowed, personally, to set fire to the palace of the long-dead king Xerxes—as revenge for the outrages the barbarian king had committed against Greek civilization 150 years before.

The new culture created by Alexander and his descendants would be known as the Hellenic Era. His court was a mix of effeminate Eastern eunuchs and beautiful Western *hetæræ,* a blend of Oriental despotism, Eastern religion, and Greek philosophy, literature, and science. Phoenicians, Jews, Babylonians, and Syrians began to live side by side, with Greek as their lingua franca. The trends of the times found their incarnation in the great new city that Alexander founded, naming it for himself, Alexandria, where the Nile meets the Mediterranean.

The great Macedonian fought his way to northern India but ended his life in Babylon. The ambitious Thaïs later married Alexander's Macedonian general, Ptolemaeus. Together, they founded a whole Hellenic dynasty in Egypt. Thaïs became a legend in her own lifetime, and there is an extensive literature about her. The witty Menander wrote one of his best comedies, *Phanion,* about Queen Thaïs, but he may have had personal reasons to be positive toward *hetæræ:* As a young writer, he had been supported by a *hetæra* named Glycera.

In Hellenic times, prostitution became a growth industry. Well-run bordellos shaped on the Athenian model were soon established in Antioch and Alexandria. Along with the modern bordellos, prostitution was still to be carried out in local temples, not least in small towns and remote areas where no other outlets existed.

Naturally, history knows the successful prostitutes best. There were many besides Thaïs who drew the long straw in life, as queens, consorts, and princesses. One *hetæra* married an aristocrat of Pergamon and became the mother to a later king; another son became the prince of Cyprus. Many of them married satraps, the vassals of Persian or Hellenic kings. The Greek *hetæræ* Gnathena and Glycera both ended up as queens in the Hellenic Seleucidian dynasty whose capital was Babylon. The *hetæra* Lamia became a royal concubine first in Alexandria and later in Macedonia. A majority of the Ptolemaic kings of Egypt did as their founder had and took *hetæræ* as wives. The wife of Ptolemeus IV, Agathoclea, may have been the most renowned among the many queens who started out as *hetæræ.* Whether it was true or not, the opinion of her time was that it was she who ruled Egypt.

The most famous among Egypt's queens, Cleopatra, was a politician of rank and a congenial seductress. Her charms blinded two of the most powerful men of the age—Julius Caesar and Mark Antony. This last feminine representative of the Ptolemaic dynasty often said with great pride that she had descended from generals and statesmen on her father's side, and from an unbroken line of *hetæræ* on her mother's side. Quite a noble mix.

FIVE

HINDU AMBIGUITY

Around 2500 B.C., a dark-skinned Dravidian people developed the first high culture in the lower Indus valley, present-day Baluchistan. Over the next eight hundred years, this culture expanded to the north, along the Indus, toward the Himalayas. Their religion seems to have been influenced by Mesopotamia; they worshiped fertility goddesses with deep devotion and probably also sexual rites. But since their main testament was in stone and their writings have never been deciphered, we have a very limited understanding of their culture.

Around 1700 B.C., an invasion by Aryans, warrior newcomers from the northwest, brought along male gods and a new, more usable language that would later be called Ancient Indian, Old Sanskrit, or Vedic. The older Dravidian culture was abruptly destroyed. The Aryans' Vedic texts were preserved for posterity when representatives of the culture that followed transcribed their texts a thousand years later. Vedic texts give no information about the pre-Vedic period; however, archaeology has demonstrated how goddess worship lost status as the Vedic culture took dominance.

The Vedic texts are among mankind's oldest writings, the oldest examples of an Indo-European language. Most texts are in prose, but the hymns display both erotic and religious meaning:

> *The womb of woman is an altar,*
> *Her nether hair is sacred grass,*
> *Her skin the cup of her body's sacred dram,*
> *The lips of her sex, the fire that consumeth all.*

Vedic texts give accounts of a mythic empire builder, Bharata, and prove that the people were acquainted with prostitution through references to "loose" women, female "vagabonds," and sexually active unmarried girls.

The Vedic word *sadharani* refers to a woman who offers sex for payment. The *Upanishads* describe sons of husbandless women and students who quarreled with such girls about payment, and they state that married women lacked the passion found among prostitutes. In Vedic times, most prostitutes seem to have dressed in red; even their gold jewelry was reddened, as this hue was assumed to scare away demons and give protection to those who chose to live in a moral gray zone.

A Vedic myth explains that Dirghatamas, a blind holy man, introduced the concept of sex for money to his people, but it leaves us without knowledge of his motives, friends, and enemies. If it is true that this blind man influenced or promoted prostitution, all we can say for sure is that such actions would have occurred during the centuries after 1700 B.C.

Chronological thinking is far from evident in ancient Indian texts. Explanations of historical institutions are rarely given other than in myths. Few actual princes are recorded as saying anything specific to servants, harlots, or sages known by name. Neither did the Vedic gods seem to interact with humans. Most phenomena were presented through old sayings, or were beheld by a holy seer in the immemorial past. By way of partial exploration, India's most ancient texts were passed down orally through more generations than those of any other culture before being recorded. But a more complete explanation must also include attitudes to time, the place of man in the universe, and our relation to transcendental forces.

More concrete historical information about cultural phenomena, including prostitution, was made available during the next historical period. Vedic civilization weakened from the turn of the millennium. Meanwhile, Hindu society, which shared some of the religious and linguistic characteristics of the Vedics but was more stratified, appeared on the Ganges plains. The kings of Maghada, to the north of present-day Bihar, were the most powerful.

Along with the spread of Hinduism, cultural and linguistic influences seem to have reached India from the northwest and spread from there to the south and southeast. The Persian Empire inspired the early kings of Maghada to preserve the orally transmitted Vedic texts in writing. Around 320. B.C., general Chandragupta Maurya—called Sandrakottos by the Greeks—made himself emperor of all the domains that came to be known as the Mauryan Empire. With all its subordinate vassal states, the Mauryan Empire would dominate the whole landmass later called India. Alexander the Great attacked its borders, but the departure of his occupying forces and his death prevented the incorporation of Indian territory into his empire. The principalities established by Alexander's generals did develop further lines of communication, most notably with the Mauryan rulers. Thus, Greek and Hellenic influences on the subcontinent persisted. Nevertheless, at that time Hindu culture was so firmly rooted that all later outside influences seemed superficial and unable to cause fundamental change in Indian society.

The early Hindu kingdoms were being established at the same time the West progressed from its mythical past and entered historical times, the character of which have been recorded in independent and contemporary written sources. As the exiled Jews in Babylon were documenting the final parts of their old texts, as the Romans started recording their lives in Latin, and as the Greeks thrilled themselves with all the arts of literacy, Sanskrit literature, too, was flourishing as never before. Naturally, it has often been compared to that of the Greeks and Romans in both quality and extent, but the comparison is not quite fair. While the Hindus produced a variety of literary and religious texts and laws in Sanskrit, they did not develop much in the way of a historical tradition.

Megasthenes, a Hellenic ambassador to the Mauryan Empire, provided the West with its first comprehensive report about India, including his complaint that nobody in India could think or speak in historical terms. Were the Greeks once again demonstrating their prejudice against Easterners? Later witnesses would state the same again and again. Maybe it is an expression of prejudice to point out the lack of historical sense within a foreign culture, but two independent expressions, prejudiced or not, should give sound reason to reflect upon the phenomenon they criticize. We can deduce extensive knowledge about ancient Hindu culture from its poetry, philosophy, and law, but we can rarely describe events in precise context, due to the weakness of Indian historical tradition, which would long continue to alienate travelers, invaders, and new rulers who continued to view Indian ways as fabulous or superstitious.

In the last centuries B.C., the number of Sanskrit/Hindu words for *prostitute* increased in both precision and quantity. There are more than three hundred different words for *prostitute* in late Sanskrit, something that signifies both a rich language and a comprehensive sex market. A learned luxury prostitute trained in the sixty-four arts alluded to in *The Kama Sutra* was a *ganika,* who was attended by *ganikadasi*; a temple prostitute was a *devadasi*; a cheap sex worker tempting men with her dress was a *vecya*; one who ran after men was a *pumscali*. There are words for holy prostitutes, for the hostesses of princes, lotus-scented creatures, soldiers' whores, procuresses, hip-wigglers, fish-stinking tarts, and completely base and vile women who offered cheap sex on the street.

Valmiki and Vatsyana are the most famous poets of late Sanskrit times. To Valmiki is ascribed the authorship of the epic *The Ramayana,* while the latter's most famous work is *The Kama Sutra,* an erotic handbook that also contains a subtle discussion on the political economy of prostitution: "If a *vecya* by her own reckoning is good to a man who is stingy, so friendly toward a man who considers himself irresistible and is so accustomed to winning hearts that he lowers her standard price, this must be considered a pure economic loss. . . . If a *ganika* can manage to obtain money from both a man with whom she has sexual relations and a man who is only in love with her, she must view this as a win-win situation. Men want pleasure, above all. Women want money."

Kautilya was the first political philosopher in Indian history, the closest adviser to Chandragupta, who successfully defended his empire against the West in the fourth century B.C. Kautilya has been called India's Machiavelli, due to his clearheaded script *The Arthasastra,* which describes social and economic conditions and, above all, taxation in the Mauryan Empire. A whole section is devoted to courtly prostitution and its supervision. In opposition to married women in India, the courtly *ganikas* were adept at reading and writing and of course could sing and dance. The *ganikas* could carry royal parasols and fans, wear gold jewelry and beautiful dresses, but they had to accept any man the king commanded them to join in bed. If they refused, they were whipped or fined. *Ganikas'* services were legally recognized; they could hold money and possess land and slaves.

In Kautilya's time, the Indian caste system consisted of Brahmin priests and nobility, *kshatryia,* while merchants, farmers, and artisans were put together with *ganikas* and other well-off prostitutes, musicians, and actors in the middle-class caste—the *vaishya.* Only people without houses, servants, or property were assigned to the low, purely working-class caste: the *shudra.* Kautilya stated that a middle- or lower-class woman did not lose status by being a prostitute, unless she took clients from castes lower than her own. However, a Brahmin woman who prostituted herself might be killed.

The *ganikas* had their own hierarchy as well. The top stratum was directly linked to the king. Others were admitted to the court of the queen and princesses, while the lowest ranks were available to servants and low-status guests. One of the royal *ganikas* would ceremonially be installed as the *arthasdastra*—stately courtesan—and could assign status to women of lower ranks and mediate disputes among the prostitutes. The privilege was often passed down to an *arthasdastra*'s chosen successor, since the position was also accompanied by a good income and less physical work. A good *arthasdastra* would take care of any sister, daughter, or cousin in the business, and her professional responsibility was to seek out the girls best qualified to carry the royal umbrella, prepare the food, or nurse the royal family. They all had to be obedient, beautiful, artistic, and able entertainers for the men of the royal household.

Naturally enough, India's men of the book and pen devoted most of their attention to describing the literate, artistic, and sometimes famous *ganikas*. Our knowledge about the poor prostitutes lacks similar detail. Those who worked outside the royal palace had to live in the south of the city, close to the soldiers' barracks. As in Egypt, Greece, and Mesopotamia, the poorest prostitutes were often slaves. They were as cheap as spittoons and addressed as *kumbas,* and also referred to by the equally lowly term *kumbadasi*. It is likely that the most important recruits to the ranks of poor prostitutes were daughters from very poor families and widows who did not want to join their dead husbands in the afterworld. In more recent Hindu literature, we read about married women who secretly became prostitutes, followed armies in times of war, stationed themselves in local bordellos and bathhouses, or conducted their affairs out in the marketplaces. But as early as the fourth century B.C., Kautilya had stated that poor prostitutes also had a claim to legal protection, something that afforded them much more protection against violence than their colleagues enjoyed in Europe. The precondition for this legal protection was that the prostitutes paid tax, calculated according to income. The tax register proved that a wealthy *ganika* and a poor *vecya* were equal in the eyes of the law: Both paid two days' earning per month in taxes.

Since the prostitutes were considered members of society, their clients could take legal action against those who did not fulfill their promises: If a woman had agreed to service a man and then changed her mind, she had to compensate him with double the sum they had settled upon.

Disputes between prostitutes and their clients were taken to the city or state *arthasdastra* to settle the issue.

A prostitute mother, or madam, was called *paricharicka* in Sanskrit. The word itself points to the existence of organized houses of prostitution in India's coastal cities, independent of princely harems and religious sanctuaries. In some passages of *The Ramayana* and *The Mahabharata,* the translators have traditionally chosen to describe these city houses as bordellos, even though the term frequently has negative connotations of military slave prostitution.

Any Hindu male or female who happened to meet a prostitute on the street considered it a good omen; conversely, a chance meeting with a widow heralded something negative. But a man was supposed to keep his visits to a prostitute secret from his wife. If she found out about it, she had full rights to howl and scream and even mistreat him. A Brahmin had to undergo a stipulated purification ritual after visiting a prostitute. The Hindu society indeed had its contradictions.

The mythical King Bhangasvana was allowed by the gods to father one hundred sons before he became a woman and gave birth to a hundred new sons. Because he was a very experienced human, the gods let him choose a further life as either of the two sexes. Bhangasvana chose to remain a woman: "Because in the union with the man, the woman has greater pleasure than the man has with the woman." Few cultures have extolled women's beauty as much, or treated women—at least outside of marriage—with such respect. Women could move freely outdoors and were never assaulted. The punishment for a man forcing himself on an unwilling woman was severe. Old wisdom stated that a woman enjoyed food twice as much as a man; she had four times as much insight, six times more courage, and eight times as much pleasure from sex. But despite this apparently enlightened attitude, at home a woman was a slave to her husband. An unfaithful wife received a terrible punishment. But an aristocratic man who moved around without learned courtesans was considered both unmanly and uncivilized.

Hindu culture was distinguished by great sexual freedom, combined with an ambiguous view of the female sex that visitors considered inconsistent or incomprehensible. A brief look at the Hindu gods might widen our understanding. The world of the gods was much more chaotic than that of the humans. In their wide pantheon, the Hindus consecrated two male gods above all others: The peaceful and worthy Vishnu lived harmoniously together with the mild Lakshmi, the paradigmatic Hindu housewife. Shiva, the destroyer, bore fires in his hands, wore skulls and snakes as jewelry, and was tied to his wife, Devi, in a stormy, warlike bondage relationship awash with extramarital activity on both sides. Devi, the Indian love goddess, was related to Ishtar and Venus; her *yoni,* or sacred vagina, was venerated both alone and together with a *lingam,* Shiva's sacred phallus. The chief Hindu goddess, here introduced as Devi, appeared in many different forms and carried different names while remaining the same deity. As Parvati or Gauri, she showed her maternal and wifely emanation; as Durga, she was unapproachable; as Kali, she was terrifying and castrating. The goddess rode on lions and tigers, carried the hacked-off heads of men in her hands, drank the blood of demons, and sat atop her lovers.

Rama and Krishna are the superheroes of Hinduism, young, attractive, and courageous—more than princes, almost gods, since they are viewed as avatars, earthly incarnations of the god Vishnu. This divine origin explains their power, and since, in the old sacred narratives, they appeared as dashing young men, they have all the qualities of fairy-tale princes.

Rama is the hero of *The Ramayana,* while Krishna appears in both *The Mahabharata* and *The Puranas.* The archer Rama is the archetypical faithful lover who goes through endless battles in search of his missing wife, Sita, without ever considering falling in love with anyone else. Krishna, the flutist, could not possibly behave as virtuously as Rama, because the hearts of all women, married or virgin, are set aflutter the very moment they set eyes upon Krishna; they undress and throw themselves in his arms on the spot. Prostitutes had good reason to view Krishna as their protector, since he seems almost to be one of them.

Both *The Ramayana* and *The Mahabharata* are full of prostitutes. Rama's father furnishes his son's army with "women who lived by their beauty, rich in the ability to find the right words . . . as entertainment for my son and his lost helpers." While Rama remains virtuous and faithful, his men get all the sexual attention they need. In the almost never-ending wars of *The Mahabharata,* one side seems to be victorious. Then the call is put out: "Send messengers into the city to tell about our victory, such that the young women might dress themselves in our honor, and play for us, with, in their lead, the sporting ladies of greatest beauty."

Megasthenes, in a text from the fourth century B.C., recounts how the wealthy and beautiful *ganika* Rupinika, of the holy city of Mathura—where Krishna carried out his early exploits and miracles—went to Krishna's temple to fan her god and dance and sing in his honor between visits from her customers. Rupinika was hardly the only one who served such different masters, then or later.

A Hindu hero would bring any woman luck, and sexual intimacy with such a man was honorable. Hinduism gave high rank to consensual sexual intercourse, while rape greatly dishonored the perpetrator as well as the victim. Sex for money lay somewhere in the middle. If a man could not convince a woman of the joy of making love with him, the introduction of money into the equation could assist in persuading her. Those who used the stick and the cane to pursue sex were denounced. The Hindu sex manuals warn against such behavior, while the laws promise stiff punishment in contrast to the West's traditionally weak condemnation of rape.

At the same time, Hindu myths associate women with death and the underworld, fire and snakes. *Ramayana* repeatedly expresses its contradictory views of women. In one passage, it states that once upon a time all creatures were of the same sex, spoke the same language, and were equally attractive. When the Creator decided to differentiate, he took out the best from all and created woman. In the next passage, we learn that woman is the root of all evil when the wise hermit Narada explains that the female sex lacks the male's moral strength. In *The Mahabharata*, young *ganikas* are praised for their beauty in one passage, while prostitutes are cursed in the next:

> *As bad as ten slaughterhouses is one roadside inn,*
> *As bad as ten roadside inns is one harlot,*
> *As bad as ten harlots is an evil king.*

Only Hindu princes had harems. A peasant would take a second wife only if he did not sire a son with his first spouse. With the exception of the *ganikas,* Hindu women received no education. Even aristocratic ladies were ignorant of reading, handicrafts, music, and dance.

Hinduism's favoritism of male children has great consequences. To be born as a woman was considered punishment for sins in an earlier life.

The bride-price was lower for a girl who had no brothers. The wife moved into the home of her husband's family. It was shameful to be unmarried, shameful to have adult unmarried daughters and sisters in the house. It was also shameful to sit back as a widow when the husband died. It was most honorable for a widow to throw herself on the funeral pyre with her husband.

A Hindu wife's task was to look after her man. No matter how he treated her, he ought to be treated as a god. A husband could therefore address his wife as *servant* or *slave.* Such relations between the sexes provided fertile conditions for a female role that was more emancipated, such as that of a *ganika,* a temple dancer, or a *vecya.* The problem for women who did choose these alternatives was that they still had to care for and satisfy males, either the gods of heaven or those who became their equivalent on earth, from kings to soldiers.

The overwhelming number of erotic paintings in Hindu secular culture, and the openly erotic sculptures adorning Hindu temples, have long impressed visitors as the most striking element in the culture. The Hindus imagined a heaven full of dancing ladies of the night, fairies or sex angels, the *apsaras,* who were more beautiful than any women on earth. Menaka was the foremost of them all. Learned Brahmins of the Middle Ages made lists of names, composed mythological censuses of *apsaras* and their companions and lovers—*gandharvas*—precisely as numbers and ranks of angels were discussed in Europe. The *apsaras* were inspirational to gods, heroes, and men. Against this background, it might seem less strange that the Hindu temples were decorated with images of *apsaras,* while the temples were filled with dancing *devadasi,* who in symbolic imitation should give men on earth care similar to what the gods received.

Young girls looked after India's temples and pagodas; adult women coddled the gods, much as daughters and wives did for their men at home, or as court ladies cared for the princes in their palaces. Every morning the temple girls sang and danced to honor the god; during the day they swept and cleaned, and fanned the images of the gods so that they would not grow hot in the heat of the day. In the evening they again sang and danced for the god; they were a joy and an inspiration for earthly men who visited the temples.

Old Hindu temples showed not only *apsaras* but also the mother goddess and female deities of the lower orders naked from the waist up. The temple dancers of the time were similarly scantily clad. Well into the twentieth century in South India, women could be seen outdoors with bare breasts, but over the last two centuries, even Hindu women steadily used longer clothing to cover themselves. This shows the later influence of Islam and Christianity.

Hindus painted and decorated their gods. Temple dancers might deck themselves out in similar ways with precious stones, perfume, and beautiful materials. Tattooing was common, and women painted themselves with saffron and blackened their eyelids. Necklaces, rings, and bracelets could be of copper, silver, or gold, depending upon income.

Temple prostitution, known to history from Babylon, Jerusalem, and Rome, would disappear in the West by the third or fourth century A.D. But in India it remained unchanged throughout the centuries, surviving not only Muslim rulers who tried to halt it but also British colonialists' criticism, and postindependence India's formal abolishment of temple prostitution in 1948. It is still in existence in a few temples in North India and is in full blossom in the southern portion of the subcontinent.

The heyday of temple prostitution seems to have been the first millennium A.D. When paid sex occurred in the temple environment, near the holy inner sanctum, the temples tended to derive a considerable income from it. Foreign travelers in India often described Brahmin priests on the hunt for beautiful young girls in the country villages. Priests and divinities had a common interest in recruiting the flower of youth of their region. There were various other ways a girl could become a temple prostitute. Many parents offered their firstborn to the temple, if she happened to be a girl; this was an alternative to infanticide, and it secured the help of the god in having a boy the next time around. Some girls were sold outright; others chose to serve there. A girl who had a *devadasi* as her mother had the deity as her father and thus was already part of the *devadasi* family. Self-castrated eunuchs could be found around the temples of the goddess as well. They could sing and dance at weddings and prostitute themselves. The Hindus developed an early taboo against homosexuality, but sex with a eunuch as a passive partner was quite acceptable.

There were dancers in many different temples and pagodas devoted to local gods. Shiva, the god of the cosmic dance, was the ally and protector of prostitutes, inside or outside the temples. No matter how old the girls were when they arrived, their formal consecration occurred with a ceremony when they were ten to twelve years old. They lost their maidenhood and became symbolically married to a tree, a knife, or a sword. In the Shiva temples, even the breaking of the hymen was ritualized, with Shiva worshiped in the form of a symbolic phallus, upon which the girls were ordered to take a seat. Before recorded history and in its earliest sources, most temple girls and Indian prostitutes generally were linked to the fertility cults of the maternal or love goddess, as in ancient Mesopotamia and later, around the eastern and southern Mediterranean region. But after about 500 B.C., there are few indications of sexual rites in the temples other than those of the girls' initiation and consecration, although prostitution continued.

The dancing girls were temple servants but were subordinate to male Brahmins who cared for sanctuary and led all the religious services. The girls were the adornment of the temples, and their presence attracted those who contributed substantially to the sacrificial gifts entering the holy sanctuary; they were admired locally, like present-day pop stars. The Brahmin who managed the coffers of the temple placed a high value on his girls, who would usually number ten or twelve in a lesser temple and many more in a major one. Hsuien Tsang, a Chinese traveler in the seventh century A.D., referred to hordes of temple dancers at Multan. When King Tajaraja built a pagoda in Tanjore, he furnished it with four hundred temple dancers. In the ancient Samanatha, there were usually five hundred *devadasi*. This would account for around-the-clock dancing and singing. The temples also engaged male musicians, as did the princely courts. Later, from the Hindu revival of the eighth century up until at least the British Empire, mainly trumpets and clarinetlike instruments were used. String instruments were hired and played by members of the barber caste. In the larger temples, an official would direct and compose religious songs and music in a way not too different from Western cathedrals. Since the girls' songs often dwelled on the erotic exploits of the gods, these songs gradually began to gain a reputation for obscenity. The dancing girls were not the only singers; the Brahmins also performed songs, theirs being of the highest spiritual content.

India's caste system was constantly changing, and with time, it became exceedingly complicated. Stringent restrictions were laid down concerning social intercourse, purity, and pollution with regard to the social uses of food and the conduct of marriage proposals and weddings. In the temples, strict divisions were upheld between the Brahmins and the ordinary castes. As time passed, hierarchic relations would be established between women and musicians as well. Prostitutes, musicians, and dancers would be assigned to lower castes. This might suggest that prostitution had lost status, but it can also be understood in another way—as democratization, since this made it easier for prostitutes to serve commoners.

Temple dancers needed money for clothes and jewelry, and some wished to support their families.. Supplementary income was to be gained from prostitution around the temples. Of course, not all dancers were prostitutes, since young girls in training might be allowed to dance before they were sexually initiated, while some elderly women would also be eminent dancers or choreographers but of less value to the temple as sex objects. This caused few religious problems, since Hindu gods were not jealous. Following a holy service, interested men could personally enter into an agreement about sex with a temple girl, but most preferred to do so through an older woman resident in the temple. Some wanted a room in the temple area, while well-to-do clients might take the girl home. Some *devadasi* found places to stay near the temple precinct. In such cases, the profits were divided: The temple got its share, the girl hers. Public officials, *dosandi paricha*, would make sure that the girls did not have sex with people of castes lower than their own. Pilgrims who had journeyed a great distance could have their bare feet kissed by the temple girls. This was done at no extra charge.

The temple girls and the eunuchs also derived some income from singing and dancing at weddings and other occasions. It was common practice to hire many of them all at once, in connection to an official function. Similarly, dancing girls could be asked to entertain at social gatherings, typically bidding each guest welcome, presenting him with a bowl of rose water, betel nuts, and fruit, or other gifts from the host. Later, they would dance and sing until the party came to an end. If a guest desired a private association with one of the girls, this was a matter between him and the matron who followed the girls like a shadow.

It is difficult to determine to what extent in ancient times women who danced at such events, and who were most frequently available for sexual services, were linked to a temple or operating independently. Conditions varied regionally and over time. But most men considered it more honorable to employ a dancer who was also in service to a deity rather than a purely secularized sex worker.

The Hindi, Bengali, Marathi, and Dravidian languages of today all distinguish between prostitutes with links to the temples and those without. This could certainly have been a less significant distinction in ancient times, although older texts hardly reveal particular antagonism between a temple servant and a luxury prostitute.

The full moon glowed, the earth quivered, and all the winds rested while the scent of lilies and other flowers wafted forth, full-blossomed and fragrant. At that very moment, all mankind became healthy and free of diseases, and all musical instruments played sweetly of their own accord, so joyful was that holy moment. Queen Maya, without pain, had given birth to her son Siddhartha in the Lumpini Garden in Kapitulavastu.

Myths have beautified the circumstances around the 563 B.C. birth of Prince Siddhartha, in the princely Sakya state of what is now southern Nepal. King Suddhodana's wife had been childless for so long, and the signs and prophecies made the king worry in the middle of all joy. When the wise sage Asita was called to the king, he explained that his son would become Buddha and leave his father's riches behind him. "What profit will it be if he becomes a Buddha?" said the realistic king, whereupon he put up guards around his castle to prevent any elderly, sick, dying, or Brahmins from entering.

During his upbringing, Prince Siddhartha saw or experienced nothing ugly, saw nobody poor or wretched. He was surrounded by only the most beautiful courtesans and courtiers and was entertained by the best musicians and dancers. Princes belonged to the Kshatryia, the warrior caste. When some Kshatryias mocked the king for Siddhartha's upbringing, the king arranged a tournament in which the prince engaged all the young men of the aristocracy in the warrior sports. He triumphed over them all. Thereupon, he married his beautiful cousin Yasodara, who gave him a son, without interrupting the sexual pleasures offered by all the most beautiful *ganikas* in the country. A secret flight out into the real world in the company of his stable boy and his white horse confronted him with age, sickness, and ugliness and left him in deep thought. At the age of twenty-nine, Prince Siddhartha left the palace to seek wisdom and understanding throughout the neighboring Maghada Empire and its subordinate states. He cut his hair and contemplated under a banyan tree, where he resisted Mara, the incarnation of evil, and Mara's three daughters, Tanhi, Rathi, and Raga—Property, Lust, and Passion—who were meant to lure him back to carnal thinking. These girls were always depicted as evil prostitutes in later Buddhist iconography. But Siddhartha Gautama resisted all evil and took the earth as his witness. At the age of thirty-five, he became Buddha, and held his first speech in a deer park near Benares. He preached and built up an everlasting sangha of followers before he died in 483 B.C. at the age of eighty.

Both the myths and the contemporary records of Siddhartha Gautama's life should contribute to a somewhat more chronological and systematic approach to questions of religion and history in India. Some of Gautama's closest followers were family, like his son, his half brother Ananda—who is credited with the collection and editing of the oldest sutras—and Ananda's mother, Gautama's aunt and foster mother, who became the first Buddhist nun. But the most prominent among Gautama's female follow- ers was Ambapali, a wealthy and rich *ganika,* possibly the richest and most schooled in the Maghada of her time. The learned *ganika* invited the young enlightenment-seeking Prince Siddhartha for lunch in the year 530 B.C. and was impressed. She offered large portions of her fortune to support the new Buddhist movement without changing her sources of income. Two other *ganikas* among his followers, Adahasi and the beau- tiful Vimala, did change their lifestyle, which contributed to their and Gautama Buddha's fame. Buddhist scholars put sexual abstinence ahead of carnal pleasure, but they did not consider the latter a sin. Buddhist temples were still decorated with *apsaras,* in the best tradition from Hindu architecture, and many *ganikas* believed in the Buddha's teaching but didn't change their lives.

Jataka contains stories from the life of the Buddha, written down long after his death in a younger, more popularly influenced version of San- skrit known as Pali. Buddhist texts take a dispassionate attitude toward prostitution, but *Jataka* and later Pali texts contain legends and parables about prostitutes. A *ganika* who had received advance payment from a young aristocrat almost died of starvation when he was called out to war; she felt she shouldn't serve a new client before the young man had reached the climax she had guaranteed him. Three thousand rupees was a vast sum for one night with a *ganika,* but it became a meager subsistence when stretched over three years.

Ashoka, who was probably the most congenial and effective ruler of the Mauryan Empire, was a tolerant king who allowed space for both Buddhism and Jainism. Even after Ashoka's empire fell apart, these new religions or sects continued to exist along with a new, clearly foreign religion: Christianity. But the Indian society retained its fundamental characteristics, even strengthening them when a Hindu revival took place in the fourth century A.D. The Gupta Dynasty would exhibit the purest veneration of Hindu culture that history has seen. The caste system had by then established its basic configuration. But in the university town of Nalanda, in Bihar, Buddhist and Hindu texts were studied with mathematics, medicine, and astronomy.

Sanskrit and more popularly influenced texts in Pali were now studied and written together. Both Hindus and Buddhists read parables to make young men keep their distance from prostitutes. A famous story described an unhappily married young man who fell desperately in love with a courtesan. With the help of her beautiful assistant, the courtesan led the young man to destroy all his father's riches.

Hindu farces written in medieval Indian (Prakrit) have made the *ganika* who turns ascetic into a well-known comedy figure. But tragic plays could just as well use a courtesan as the main character. A famous folk story centered on the faithful prostitute Vantasena. She cared so much for her favorite young client that, when he lost his fortune, she sacrificed all her own earnings and was willing to give her life for him.

Moral Hindu texts would continue to suggest that the Brahmins avoid the temples when the dancers performed, because of the association between the dancing girls and prostitution. The Brahmins were the girls' superiors, and prostitution was for princes, warriors, and merchants, not for Brahmins.

While Buddhist scholars rejected the Vedas as divine revelations and argued against the caste system and the belief in auspicious omens, the Hindus did not greet the Buddhists with equivalent skepticism. Prince Siddhartha or Lord Buddha was to be seen as the last avatar of Vishnu, while Buddhism, like Jainism, was considered another of the myriad Hindu sects. Thus Buddhism would expand to the southeast with Hinduism. While Buddhism gradually lost ground on the Indian subcontinent, it spread to China and later to Japan. Buddhist and Hindu regimes would replace each other in Southeast Asia without significant cultural change. India retained some Jainist enclaves but remained Hindu and caste-based just as strongly in the Tamil south. The Brahmins provided all new low-caste rulers with an acceptable genealogy, while the norms and customs of a stable society were preserved. Sects, religions, and secular groups have their own domains in a feudal structure that secured peaceful coexistence for many centuries. This ambiguous stability of Hindu society was not to change before Islam—a more aggressive religion—arrived on the scene much later.

SIX

ROME'S DAUGHTERS

A nyone who thinks young men ought to be forbidden affairs with prostitutes is certainly very ignorant of the freedom of our time, and indeed not in harmony with the customs of our ancestors. Name any epoch when this was not normal. When was such behavior ever censured or forbidden? These things have always been allowed. Prostitution is a legally sanctioned privilege." With such precision, Cicero, the orator and statesman, summarized his speech against his opponent Marcus Caelius Rufus at the Republican Senate of Rome in the year 60 B.C.

The Western world has obtained its fundamental view of prostitution from Rome. The views of Judaism and ancient Greece were put aside as Rome created its legacy. But this Rome was neither the mission center of Saint Peter and the popes nor the decadent Roman Empire, with its racial and religious mixing, sex orgies, and circuses. The basis for the Western view of prostitution and sexuality lies in an older culture—the patriarchal, moralistic Rome of the republic.

Cicero won the case, as usual, by demonstrating the conservative approach that Roman prostitution was an old trade, in existence from the mythic founding of the city and through the following centuries. According to legend, the twins Romulus and Remus were suckled by a she-wolf, but what has received less attention is that they were found by a goatherd whose wife, Larentia, raised them on income earned through the sale of sexual favors. Due to Larentia's many lovers, the other goatherds called her a she-wolf. According to the myth, she was able to buy one of the hills of Rome, the Palatine; Rome's first *lupanaria*, or bordello, would in that case be older than the city itself.

Western marriage also traces its roots back to the Roman republic. The society was surely patriarchal, but Roman matrons had more liberty than any other females of their time. Wives and daughters moved around freely,

were educated, and dressed elegantly. Some women participated in political life, particularly if their husbands were at war or administering subjugated
territories. Cornelia, the widowed mother of the famous Gracchus brothers, proved what political influence a Roman matron could have.

In temples consecrated to Venus, the Roman goddess of love, the normal rules were suspended: Matrons could be promiscuous and obtain counsel
from the priestesses on love techniques. One might meet male or female
prostitutes at the same place, since Venus and Adonis were in close alliance.
During celebrations to the goddess Flora, naked prostitutes dressed only in
garlands of flowers would dance and perform pantomimes. Divorce was not
uncommon. Like marriage, it had to be considered in light of economics and
family advancement.

Roman ethics, however, told the housewife to be faithful and the daughters to be virtuous. Accordingly, prostitutes could enter neither the temple
of Juno, where the cult of the wife and family was based, nor the temple of
Vesta, where maiden priestesses held sway. Family honor was the prime
virtue of Republican Rome, and the paradigm of the Roman matron was
the mythic Lucretia, who was forced into infidelity and responded by suicide, thus saving her own, her husband's, and the family's honor.

Above all, the Roman moral code separated sex and love. Love was
a pious devotion that ought to be reserved for parents and patria. In exceptional cases, similar feelings would develop between husband and wife,
but that required a lifelong marriage. Sex was something completely different. One could have sex with anyone who aroused lust, as long as no
man of rank, his wife, or his daughter was offended. While the Romans
had a relaxed view of sex, they greatly feared love. Slaves to love endangered family honor and self-respect. Worst of all were warm feelings toward subordinates, like servants, slaves, or prostitutes.

From 500 B.C. Rome had an official moral guardian, the censor.
Marcus Porcius Cato—the *senex,* or elder—would be remembered above
all others. Cato began to guard Rome's virtue in the year 184 B.C., when
the small city republic had started its expansion by means of warfare against
neighboring peoples. Their major foe, the Phoenician colony of Carthage,
resided to the south. One quote above all earned Cato eternal fame. Whatever he spoke about in the Senate, his conclusion was *Preaterea censeo
Carthaginem esse delendam:* "Moreover, I am of the opinion that Carthage
must be annihilated."

Cato is also the man behind one of the West's most famous quotes about prostitution. Observing a young patrician leaving a bordello, the old statesman raised his voice: "Blessed be thou for thy virtue . . . For when your veins are swelling with gross lust, you men should indeed drop in there, rather than grind some husband's private mill." But the old Roman was just as convinced that such visits should be done discreetly and not too often. Not many days later, when Cato saw the same young man on his way out of the same bordello, he retracted his praise.

A Roman patrician enjoyed unpaid sexual congress with his own household slaves, and the same rights as with a prostitute. In his own times and later, Cato Senex would be considered a guardian of Rome's borders and its morals. He felt it was completely within his rights to have sex with slave girls. When his own children criticized him for doing so, the guardian of morality had a ready answer: "Should I saddle my wife with sex at the wrong season?" Cato behaved rationally in all sexual matters, inside and outside his own household. If his male slaves wanted to have sex with the household's women servants, they could do so if they paid a small fee to Cato. As in all other matters, his ideal was that the authorities should exercise full control, plus earn the possible extra profit. The poet Horace would later summarize the old Roman virtuous times in this sarcastic poem:

> *When your passions are inflamed,*
> *and a common gratification is at hand,*
> *would you rather be consumed with desire*
> *than possess it? I would not.*
> *Don't we have servants and slaves,*
> *Ready and willing? So do as I,*
> *Be quick and frugal. Then forget it entirely.*

Public prostitution in Roman Republican times was supposed to stay mostly outside the city walls. Only on exceptional occasions were prostitutes allowed to participate in public life. Normally, prostitutes of the Roman republic would dance and juggle for the citizens of Rome on three annual occasions: during the high festival of Lupanaria, when the founding of the city was commemorated; in late April, when the goddess of love was celebrated as Venus Volgivava, a street girl; and in May the Floralia, devoted to Flora, the flower goddess, a prostitute who had bequeathed the earnings of her long career to the young Rome. Floralia was celebrated at the city's best party center, Circus Maximus, and tradition accorded the prostitutes pride of place.

While Marcus Porcius Cato was censor, he once attended Circus Maximus during the Floralia. As all the prostitutes stormed in naked, all eyes turned to the tough old man, and deathly silence fell over the gathering. Then the moral guardian got calmly to his feet, covered one eye with the corner of his toga, and walked out of Circus Maximus in full dignity. Ten minutes passed. Then the celebration carried on.

Roman tradition placed considerable weight on self-control. Not only politically but sexually. Those who could not control their emotions would succeed neither sexually nor be considered "real Romans." The many unhappy love relationships between poets and prostitutes that dominate Roman literature must be understood against such a background. The women whom the poets loved were not only beautiful and artistic; they also had literary accomplishments that made them suitable as muses. But the majority stood socially below the poets, who pursued them with pained, dishonorable masochism.

Ovid, or Publius Ovidius Naso, was among the most famous writers in the time of Emperor Augustus. He was in love with Corinna, who earned her daily bread by selling sex. This caused Ovid intense jealousy and pain. Ovid wrote about the technical details of love in a widely read poem, *Ars Amandi* (*The Art of Love*), which can also be viewed as a handbook on prostitution. Ovid enjoyed close relationships with many of the most gifted sex workers and knew the field very well. But Ovid's best and most personal love poems were devoted to his most beloved woman, Corinna, whose husband helped his wife obtain customers. To the poet, this husband became a natural enemy.

Ovid would, like many outspoken men of his time, end his days in political exile. Things did not turn out well for Corinna, either: A suitable existence for an old woman would have been to sell beauty preparations to younger prostitutes, or love potions to the girls' clients. But Corinna ended her days serving poor mariners along the banks of the Tiber.

The fates of Propertius and his beloved were still worse. This poet was in a love relationship that defied every Roman code of masculine honor. Self-effacing, indeed masochistic to the point of embarrassment, he became a walking dishonor to Roman manhood, but did so to the delight of succeeding generations of voyeuristic literary historians.

Who knows if the historian Hostilius is to blame? He armed his already mortally beautiful daughter with all the rules of art and furnished her with the best literary education of the day. According to tradition, she should have been called by the feminine form of her father's name—Hostilia. This name did not sound particularly sweet, so she changed it to the more elegant Cynthia. She was witty and refined; she could dance, sing, and play the lyre. She was not only unsurpassed as a literary critic; she could also set down rhymes and prosody. Additionally, she lived in great style, to a degree far beyond her means.

Cynthia was in no way a paradigm of virtue. She never considered it wrong to be paid for having sex with several men at the same time, even though she openly admitted that she preferred more generous contributions from a select few, preferably highly influential men. Her major patron for many years was a wealthy Roman public official, conveniently stationed across the Adriatic in Illyria. But it was the man who besieged her, and whom she most frequently rejected, who made her immortal.

Propertius would die young, in the year 15 B.C. He had considerable success in literature even during his lifetime, but little in love. Only on rare occasions was he allowed through Cynthia's door. Most of the time he had to sleep on her doorstep, or in some nearby place from which he could spy on her. "She loves neither power nor romance; she evaluates her lovers according to their pocketbooks," he lamented in a classical verse that summarized the feelings of many failed clients of elite prostitutes. Propertius wanted to have Cynthia all to himself.

There was no solution to the dilemma. In some elegies, Propertius complained about the rumors he heard about Cynthia; in others, he praised her beauty. Propertius' rejection, his heartbroken laments, and his praises gave resonance to all his poems. Propertius was demanding and unrealistic, but this does not make us empathize with Cynthia. One gets the impression that she was completely without compunction or conscience, and treated several other men with less respect than the aristocratic women of her day treated their slaves. But thanks to Propertius, Cynthia still appears in lines like these:

I relished fighting with you last night by the lamplight,
and hearing all your furious oaths.
Why overturn the table when mad with liquor,
and wildly hurl at me the wineglasses?
Come, come attack my hair with your savage temper
and scar my features with your pretty nails!
Dearest, threaten to burn my eyes to ashes,
split my robe wide open, and bare my breasts.

This magnetic female was to die under terrible circumstances, poisoned by an elderly prostitute she had known in her earlier days. The man who had employed the woman was, by all accounts, a freed slave with good contacts to Emperor Augustus and his house. Cynthia might have made an enemy of this ex-slave by rejecting him sexually, but it is more likely that she had only used her wit at his expense. Cynthia could express herself with such acid irony that she created mortal enemies in the course of a short chat; she was also extremely snobbish. Any former slave whom she encountered was likely to have been cut to the quick by one of her acid remarks.

The whole of Rome swarmed with rumors about the murder of this most elegant, eloquent, loved, and hated lady in the city. But nobody dared to take up her case. It can be fatal to be the most desirable woman of one's time.

By the beginning of the Christian era, Rome was no longer a peripheral republic in the western Mediterranean. The capital of Emperor Augustus and his descendants had grown to become the cosmopolitan center of the world.

Augustus, the nephew of Julius Caesar, became absolute ruler over an empire that stretched from Judaea and Egypt in the east to Hispania in the west and Gallia in the north; Britannia, far to the north, would be colonized a short time later. The empire took in some of the most important metropoles outside Rome, like Antioch, Alexandria, Byzantium, and Carthage. But the imperial capital predominated several times over. People flocked there in the hundreds of thousands: learned Greek tutors, rich Jews, speculative Egyptian mystics, illiterate Italian peasants, blond slaves taken as prisoners of war from Germania or Thrace, or the dark-haired slaves of Nubia.

At its greatest, Rome had a population of two and a half to three million. Those who did the work were slaves, freed slaves, or foreigners. Former slaves and slaves from the imperial or other patrician families engaged in trade and built fortunes rapidly. They did not bother to hide their gold or their precious stones, to the double annoyance of both the patricians and the poor city dwellers. In the later days of the empire, under 1 percent of the population was descended from the patricians of the republic. Italy's small farms had been transformed into huge slave-driven *latifundia,* while the former peasants had flocked to Rome and been renamed *proletarii,* with the status of free citizens. To its own inhabitants, Rome was a social state; any free citizen had the right to a minimal existence, bread from the state's purse, and circuses.

During the imperial times, any public official of the old school who pointed to the family as the basis of society, and of Rome's ancient gods and ideals, would receive sarcastic smiles and witty remarks. The middle class from the days of the republic—the knights, or nonaristocratic farmers who could afford to go to war on horseback—was by now almost wiped out, except within the imperial army and the lower levels of the provincial bureaucracy. The majority of Rome's population was the impoverished proletariat, together with a slave population of around a million. Very few undertook Roman marriages. Slaves had no right to them. At the same time, Jews, Egyptians, Phrygians, and Greeks had brought new religion and new philosophy to Rome, with a completely new concept of love and marriage.

Even in patrician families, marriage might be avoided. The patricians could have sex with other patricians, with slaves, or with prostitutes of either sex, then adopt the children they wanted, including their own offspring. Emperor Augustus tried to fine all who did not marry, and he rewarded women who had more than three children. But rebellious women from the upper classes entered themselves in the city's public registry of prostitutes. They may have lost a little status, but in return, they got to live as they pleased.

The moral philosopher Seneca was a teacher of the young emperor-to-be Nero. Seneca tried to imprint the old ideals on the youth and said in his defense: "He has not really done anything wrong. He just loves a male prostitute. Such things are normal. The boy is young. Give him time. Then he will improve and find himself a wife." But during the first century of the Christian era, the descendants of Augustus, like Nero and his second cousin Caligula, showed no interest in noble Roman matrons. The hard core of this Julian-Claudian dynasty permitted itself to fulfill its every desire, whether incestuous relations, several wives, or partners of both sexes and all races. Empress Messalina, the third wife of Claudius, hired Rome's most famed sex worker and brought her to the imperial palace to find out who could service the most men in one night, the empress or the whore. Messalina won.

The morals from the good old days of Cato and the Gracchus brothers had gone completely out of fashion. The discreet, almost virtuous harlots of Republican days were also gone. No sweet daughters of Flora and Venus were to be found. The sex workers of the empire were of a rather different brand, many times tougher and wilder.

Since half of the Roman population was uneducated, unemployed, and fed by the state, the sexual morals of the lower classes soon became just as lax. In effect, imperial Rome for the first time in history established sex as an available, usually inexpensive antidote to boredom (a luxury unknown to any but the aristocracy in earlier historical periods). But Rome's millions remained bored, in spite of the widespread availability of free or paid sex, in spite of the circuses and gladiatorial battles. The best-educated prostitutes received clients at home, by agreement, and followed the pattern of the Greek *hetæræ*'s gatherings. Some of them were Greek or Syrian; others only assumed Greek names because it was the fashion—Phlogis, Chloe, Chione, Lesbia, Saufeia, Thaïs. But many of the best-paid sex workers of the day had good solid Roman names, like Lydia, Celia, Marulla, and Delia.

Both paid and unpaid sex was found in the theaters, or in the *thermals,* the grand baths that distinguished the city. The bordellos were organized up against the city wall or right outside it, on the hills of Esquilin and Viminal, at Caelius and near Circus Maximus. Both free Romans and slaves, men and women, worked at the bordellos. Less organized sex establishments, called *fornices,* sprang up between the columns under the theaters. *Stabulas,* or stables, were open places where it was possible to organize orgies. One saw elegant, half-naked prostitutes along the Via Sacra, borne in litters without curtains. Their male competitors went around on foot. With explicit body language and blatant sexual noises, they made their availability clear.

A *meretrix,* "woman who earns money," was a free and locally born Roman woman sex worker who lived a tranquil everyday life until after the evening meal, or *merenda*. Thereupon she would station herself in a bordello and take up her night work. She was usually registered in the public index of prostitutes, paid her taxes, and did everything she could to stay on the right side of the authorities. A *meretrix* had to wear a man's toga; she was denied the use of the color purple, sandals, and flowered cloth, and could not put up her hair the way the Roman matrons did. Many prostitutes, both free and enslaved, wanted to distinguish themselves and began to color their hair red or blond, wear makeup, and dress in silks that enhanced their most important attributes. Women of good families could steal into the bordellos for the fun of it, or to earn extra money. They were called *famosas* and were disdained by all true whores.

The word *prostitute*, derived from Latin, literally refers to exposure of the genitalia, but the word was not in common use for the sale of sex until the late Middle Ages. The Romans had a more than sufficient vocabulary. A woman who attracted clients by means of shouted repartee was known as a *lupa* or she-wolf. A woman called *prostibula* in the days of the empire was just another *famosa*. Such people might also be called mosquitoes of the night, or street wanderers. A baker's girl sold small cakes in the form of female genitalia; a "cemetery worker" offered her services, both sex and professional mourning, in the graveyard. One encountered a *blitida* or a *copa* at an inn where cheap wine was sold; a "hen" was believed to steal money from her client, above the sum agreed upon; a *fellatrix* was specialized in the use of her mouth. Greek names always indicated sexual availability. *Doris* gave the perfect connotations—wild, poor, common, and Greek—and was used in plural about girls who stood naked in doorways.

Toward the end of the first century A.D., the satirist Martial authored the first guidebook to Rome's underworld, a catalog of the best and worst prostitutes. People of the day found his descriptions so apt that they thought he knew them all. He was certainly sober-minded in some of his descriptions, though strongly sarcastic in others:

> *Thaïs is the one who smells bad, worse than*
> *an old bucket, with hair the color of mold, alas,*
> *the stink of piss from a rutting tomcat, fish so rotten,*
> *yes indeed, this woman smells sicker than sick. . . .*
> *When naked, this witch goes to her toilet*
> *to blot out the stink with pomade*

and plaster herself with salve against all the garbage.
As if makeup, soap, and powder would help against the plague!
In any case, the result, it has to be said, is
that Thaïs still stinks—of Thaïs.

Martial's descriptions became public property and were sung on the street corners. Not all the prostitutes were happy about this. One reason for his crass, sarcastic descriptions was that he preferred young men. But Martial was not as scathing toward other women as he was to Thaïs.

The following text, left to posterity by a witty itinerant hobo from Aesernia, in Campania, gives a more everyday account of prostitution in Rome: "Erected in his lifetime by C. Calidus Eroticus, in honor of himself and Fannina Voluptas: Dear Innkeeper, my bill, please! You have put down wine, 1 penny; bread, 1 penny; food, 2 pennies. Agreed. Girl, 8 pennies. Agreed. Hay for my mule, 2 pennies. That damned animal will bankrupt me yet."

The *ediles* were Roman public servants who, from the days of the Republic, had supervised street life, public festivals, and the water supply. In imperial times, the power of the *ediles* crumbled. Caligula charged them with making sure that the brothels conformed to legal opening hours, from three in the afternoon until sunrise the following morning, and with registering all the sex workers of Rome. The *ediles* ended up as the vice squads of Rome. What a job!

When the *ediles* first tried to establish a full registry of Rome's brothels, they stated that there were sixty-four official bordellos in the city of two and a half million. The largest were enormous, like the famous Libidinium Consistrorium, the house of all kinds of lust. As the *ediles* began to register prostitutes by name, they stopped when they had collected the names of thirty-five thousand women and around two thousand men. "A prostitute is like a prosperous city," wrote Plautus, a poet comedian. "She cannot get on without a lot of men." His double metaphor tells a lot about both prostitution and Roman cities.

According to the laws, the *ediles'* duties included supervisory visits to unregistered promiscuous women. Some of them obviously enjoyed these surprise visits. Very often an irate father or a jealous suitor would pay the *ediles* to make them, so many women simply signed the registry to avoid problems with the *ediles*, relatives, or former lovers. Independent of class, a woman who regularly entertained different men would avoid all penalties, indictments, or unpleasant nocturnal visits. The registry served several different purposes and must be interpreted accordingly.

Male prostitution had never been so widespread as during the Roman Empire. Their activities were detailed in contemporary literature. It was a common belief that fellatio was better when performed by a man. Consequently, many men specialized in it, or in passive anal sex. Men who were looking for an active male partner might find him at a brothel or in a gladiator school, but they had to behave discreetly. Whenever it became common knowledge that a prominent man liked to play a passive sexual role, it was considered an attack on the honor of all patrician Roman males.

The Roman Empire distinguished itself from the rest of antiquity by treating male and female prostitution the same way. In the large bordellos, male and female prostitutes worked side by side; only smaller establishments were divided by sex. Unorganized male street prostitution flourished, perhaps even more prevalent than the female version, since the men could take more risks. The *ediles'* registries give long lists of names and biographical details about regular *procuri*, who served male clients, and *luperci*, gigolos who served mainly upper-class women.

Female sexual clients had hardly been seen before Roman imperial times. An especially well-trained athlete would have few problems attracting female customers. But women tended to demand more and pay less than men of the same class. Moreover, the possibilities for unpaid sexual relations were considerable. Rome was full of good-looking men with very little to do, so women paying for sex remained few and had to be wealthy.

The *ediles* had no prejudice against male prostitutes, but they vigorously tried to combat castration, whether the aim was sex work or religious observance. Rome had been familiar with *atti*, or *galli*, emasculated priests of Adonis, since Republican times, but had denied them entry to the capital until they obtained civil rights in 77 B.C. under the auspices of religious tolerance. There were three well-known means of castration: *Castrati* were cut cleanly and lacked both penis and testicles; *spadones* had lost their testicles through a process of dragging; the testicles of *thilibiae* had been bruised and crushed. Their seminal glands would be permanently disabled, but most were able to conduct partial intercourse. Martial stated in an ironic epigram why some women preferred sex with such men: "Do you ask, Pannychus, why your Celia only consorts with eunuchs? Celia wants the flowers of marriage, not the fruits." But most citizens, including the *ediles,* maintained the opinion that castration was a decadent custom from the East, in deep conflict with Roman traditions and morals. It wouldn't be of much help for a brothel owner to argue that there was a demand for eunuchs. The slave owners, the brothel managers, and the surgeons involved in castrations were punished. All societies have moral boundaries. Rome's fell between the knife and the male sexual organ.

Rome's best-known male prostitutes were its most adored actors and dancers, the superstars of the day. Mnester was an adored young prostitute actor with whom the emperor Caligula initiated a much publicized affair. Paris was an extremely handsome and virile actor with whom young Nero got involved. Nero, as emperor, would appear in public and private life with a beautiful but effeminate *castratus,* Sporus.

The third famous imperial male prostitute, Zoticus, was the escort of a much later emperor, Elagabaldus. The emperor became involved with him amid storms of scandal and proclaimed himself "the first imperial ally of all prostitutes of both sexes."

The Roman Empire provided prostitution with a new, partly foreign religious framework. Over the course of the centuries, Rome became marked more and more by deity worship and religious exercises of Eastern origin. One entered the Roman temples to pray to the Greek Demeter, the Phrygian Cybele, the Egyptian Isis, or Astarte from Carthage. They would all come to be worshiped under the collective identity of Magna Mater, who allowed her priestesses to prostitute themselves. New orgiastic rites developed wherein prostitution was integral to the cult. By way of comparison, the light and lusty Republican bacchanalias in honor of Venus and Flora look as innocent as Sunday schools.

In a society whose central institution was slavery, there are certain problems with the general use of the term *prostitution.* It would be wrong to identify as brothels all the various institutions of commercial sex. Many slaves worked without salary, all profit going to their owners. But these prostitutes were never called sex slaves, because that term already was reserved for free Romans who were obsessed with sex.

Emperor Domitian could be called a sex slave: He could not take a bath without a dozen slaves, and he certainly had sex with some of them. Such behavior indicates the surplus of labor power then. Yet there is no proof of more widespread prostitution in his time than during the reigns of earlier emperors. And Commodus' imperial residence, furnished with six hundred young women and men for sexual purposes, would not be called a brothel, because no guests had to pay at his orgies. It would be more accurate to say that the emperors of late imperial times established a new, wider, slave-based infrastructure for their sex and orgies.

Caligula's relationship with Mnester, young Nero's desire for the attractive Paris, and his "marriage" to Sporus ought to be seen primarily as signs of an absolute ruler's self-ordained right to sexual play and violence. But when members of the imperial family took a passive or masochistic role in a homosexual relationship, it was considered a loss of respect for the whole class to which these men belonged. What most shocked and provoked men of the time, and subsequent historians, about the emperor Augustus's daughter Julia, and the later empresses Messalina and Agrippina, was not their sexual excesses but the fact that they allowed slaves and proletarians to take dominant sexual roles.

All through the imperial times, there were slaves among the bordello prostitutes. Officially, the only slaves one could buy in Rome were prisoners of war. But throughout the reigns of the many different emperors, many of the most attractive young women and men were brought to the brothels from beyond the borders. Professional slave hunters always had an eye for healthy human beauty. Young, attractive, and well-built slaves were their best investment, as they were physically best equipped for transport and would always command a much better price.

Older, less healthy slaves were not likely to survive transport. They and the less attractive could be sold cheaply on the borders, because there was a great demand for sex workers there by Roman soldiers. Soldiers were not allowed to marry, though many spent half their lives in the army. The worst positioned among all the empire's slave prostitutes were those who had to work in the garrisons. They were locked into the tiniest cells, poorly clothed, and fed miserably. The army tried to use them effectively as long as they lasted; near the border, it was always cheaper to find new slaves than more food. There was a permanent and tacit protest among the soldiers; many found permanent lovers near the camps and boycotted the small, filthy sex cells.

The poet comedian Plautus described the tragic sides of prostitution in the most comprehensive manner. In one of his plays, a male slave says that he would prefer to spend his last days in a stone quarry with an iron weight locked over his shoulders than be a slave in the brothels. Lifting and carrying stones was, in most contemporaries' eyes, the worst form of slavery, so Plautus had an extremely dark view of the life of bordello slaves.

Who was worse off—a slave sex worker or a gladiator? A victorious gladiator was celebrated by all of Rome in the short seconds of his triumph, but only a minority of the gladiators were free men. The majority were slaves under a gladiator school or stable. Even the best fighter could lose his next match, and this often meant death. A slave sex worker with ambition and self-confidence normally had several ways to get free of bondage. They could attain a degree of freedom if clients purchased them for exclusive private use. It was more common, and wiser, to establish a fan club, with several fans as guarantors for a loan that bought the prostitute freedom. She or he later paid off the loan with interest.

The Roman Empire was a complex political system that continued to secure peace, law, and order in most parts of the realm, despite the decadence in the capital. At the periphery of the empire, life was more idyllic, except for the worst-positioned slaves. But if a slave owner took a posting in a quiet provincial capital, such as Aquileia or Cæsarea, the household slaves would enjoy the good life of the province as well. Such was the condition for hundreds of thousands. The life in the capital was widely heralded as everyone's desire, but there is little doubt that for many, the city of Rome was precisely the wrong place to be.

Three hundred years after Christ, the Roman Empire was not what it had been. German tribes were pressing against the boundaries of civilization to the north and east; the army increased its power as the authority of Rome lost ground. The social and economic conglomeration that comprised the empire was in a state of moral decomposition. The Roman state's prevailing religious cult was under competition from Eastern mystical sects, as well as Judaism and Gnostic, Arian, and Athanasic Christianity. Latin was spoken along with Greek, Celtic, and Aramaic.

Emperor Constantine was a man of his times, a successful army general, and the son of Helena, a disgraced imperial concubine. As he came into power in Gallia and Britannia, four fellow emperors rivaled his reign. But in 313 A.D., he was undisputed as emperor, and he allowed religious freedom across the empire. He had been backed by a faction of the Christian Church, led by Athanasius and Hieronymus, and he helped them condemn all rivals at the Church's Council of Nicea in the year 325. When his mother was declared a saint, this lent her son some divinity as well. Constantine concentrated the political power in his own hands, but he shifted its fulcrum to the east, where he established Byzantium as the new capital under the name Constantinople. But the following emperors were not able to retain one Christian empire. It became divided into an eastern part, around Constantinople, and a western part around Rome. The pressure grew, particularly from overpopulated Germanic tribes within and right across the boundaries. Eventually, it exploded when the Germanic tribes smashed the borders and conquered Rome. The Ostrogoths, Visigoths, Allemannians, and Franks established separate kingdoms in former Roman territory.

From the eastern capital of Constantinople, Christian emperors continued to hold power. In the sixth century, Emperor Justinian was the most impressive among them. He was born in Thrace, spoke Latin, and was an excellent army commander, but he would face his most serious problems at home. In the eyes of his contemporaries, the cause of his problems was his second wife, Theodora, in most people's eyes the actual ruler.

Theodora was a beautiful, magnetic woman whose appearance was grounds for myth. In her younger days, she was a prostitute and a talented actress, and she had first bewitched Justinian at the Circus, when she was in her mid-thirties and he was past fifty. She was the daughter of an innkeeper and a female acrobat and had, in her teens, advanced from a *fellatrix* to a *meretrix* who could satisfy ten athletes in one night. As an actress, she specialized "in mimicry and a virtuosity in the modern burlesque routine," wrote her biographer, Procopius, who obviously did not hold her in high esteem. Before this, she had been the mistress of a provincial governor in North Africa, but he gave her up, so she had to earn her way back to the Alexandrina bordellos on her own. "Never again," she swore. In Alexandria, she became a Christian, which may have facilitated Justinian's total intoxication.

Justinian convinced Emperor Justin, his uncle and adopted father, to change the law that forbade men of the senator class from marrying prostitutes. After Justinian's first wife died, he married Theodora in 525, at the new Hagia Sofia church, which filthy tongues said was dedicated to the Holy Whore. Two years later, Justinian became emperor and Theodora empress. Together, they would redefine marriage, in ways unseen since the Roman republic, many astonishingly modern. Theodora and Justinian penalized homosexual behavior in public places, though in their eyes, this did not preclude tolerance of such relationships. This tolerance was expressed in their protection of a close adviser, Strategius, who married his male lover, and Justinian furnished an Egyptian church with a side temple devoted to the male saints Serge and Bacchus, who had been beatified as a couple.

But the ruling imperial couple now battled all promiscuous behavior, with clear effects. Procuresses and brothel keepers were banished from the capital; sex in public bathhouses was forbidden; and the sexes were separated, so a mother had to bathe in a pool separate from her sons. "Mutual affection is the basis for marriage," stated Justinian. Justinian marriage law also laid out the legal basis for divorce, according to Christian principles of the time. Emperor Constantine had secured the legal rights of women who lived alone, be they prostitutes, divorcées, concubines, or virgins. A man was threatened with equal stringency for forcing himself upon any woman, no matter her social or marital standing.

The imperial couple had considerable success in establishing the doctrine whereby the emperor, not the pope, should be considered head of the Christian Church. Justinian and Theodora had a vision of a Christian constitution, a burning ambition that would entail either great reforms or their fall. Their rule was strong and strictly bureaucratic, in relation to society and the Church. They could not tolerate the philosophical school of Athens and closed it in 529. Justinian's generals conquered the Ostrogoths in Sicily, Rome, and Milan during the 530s, stopped further invasion by Slavic tribes to the north, and secured the borders to the east through peace with the Persians while pacifying the popes in Rome. This helped them keep the empire and the Church united awhile longer.

Empress Theodora was a fierce opponent of child labor, and she had her reasons for this. For millennia, poor people in the east had sold surplus daughters to temples. But as Christianity became state religion, it put an end to temple prostitution. But the sale of daughters continued, secularized as slavery. Theodora tried to make a law, but she wanted to punish only the traders, since the families were suffering enough already. Her aim was to put an end to the trade of young slaves through Constantinople, thereby setting an example for the rest of the realm. A new law promised freedom for any young slave who dared to accuse the men in the trade for pimping, or sale of slaves to bordellos. But this proved more difficult than she had foreseen. For many, fear of their owners was greater than faith in the imperial promises. Several of the cases against slave traders failed in court, and the man who had been charged took his slaves and left the capital.

Theodora tried to forbid minors entry to the remaining brothels and wanted to secure legal protection against rape for prostitutes and female slaves. It is no exaggeration to call Theodora the greatest woman of her time; she certainly was history's first prostitution reformer. Indeed, she knew all about the profession she wanted to reform. Theodora set up a former imperial palace as a permanent residence for the young prostitutes who had been forced into the trade, and called it Metanoia, or Repentance. The first nunnery for women was opened at Arles, in the southern Merovingian France of the time. The contrast between the two similar-looking institutions is striking. In the nunnery of Arles, entry was granted only to virtuous women of aristocratic background. While the first Western convent secured an inheritance for noble sons by providing fathers with a classy place to tuck away their daughters, the first Eastern nunnery was a social reformative institution for those who were poor and repentant.

Empress Theodora gave rise to a number of reforms that were social and woman-friendly, but few feminists have shown interest in this astonishing woman. Some blame might be attributed to her sarcastic biographer, Procopius, who was convinced that nearly all the former prostitutes in Theodora's foundation were unhappy and fled the place by jumping out the windows. This cannot possibly have happened to all, since the cloister existed for centuries.

The Byzantine capital was in a political turmoil, full of intrigue, slander, and rivalry. It certainly served the emperor to have a former actress as his wife. If the mob turned violent at the Circus, or a demonstration emerged, Theodora mastered the crowds. One slight gesture with her head made everybody in her presence stare, bewitched: The empress would get the attention of the whole populace the moment she seemed to lift a part of her dress. However, when the Hippodrome crowds turned against the imperial "blue" party in 532, she resorted to having North Germanic mercenaries slaughter parts of the crowd into submission.

In his *Secret History,* as Procopius called Theodora's biography, he put to work the whole rhetorical repertoire of the age into his description. There is little evidence that he lied about Theodora's childhood and youth, but he did describe her whole life as if all he wanted was to dishonor all her social reforms. The empress was in his eyes once and forever a whore, and the emperor was under her spell.

Theodora was probably the first former prostitute who became a Roman empress, but she was not history's first empress with a past. She had a vision of change, and she thought of others. The highborn Roman empresses of the preceding centuries, like Agrippina and Messalina, preferred gladiatorial fights and sex orgies to social reforms. When, on a whim, they became fascinated in prostitutes, their interest was exclusively competitive.

Of all the Roman empresses, I lift my glass to Theodora.

SEVEN

REPENTANT SINNERS

J esus of Nazareth died late Friday night during Easter, around the year 30 A.D. John the Baptist recorded that there were three women near the foot of the cross upon which Jesus had been crucified. The first two were Christ's mother, Mary, and Mary Salome, who was the mother of the Apostle brothers John and James. According to John, the third, Mary Magdalene, was the woman Jesus loved.

The evangelist Mark points out that both the Virgin Mary and Mary Magdalene stayed until the corpse was removed from the cross. All the male followers had lost courage and gone off fishing, though their master had predicted that he would rise from the dead. Only the women believed him, and of them all, Mary Magdalene was the most steadfast. According to John, she went alone to the grave on Sunday morning and found the stone rolled back from the crypt. Matthew maintains that Mary Magdalene and Mary Salome went together; the other evangelists describe a flock of women. But in all these accounts, Mary Magdalene was at the head of these female followers. She was the foremost of the female adherents, just as Peter was presented as the leader of the men.

It was truly unusual that an adult Jew should live alone in Palestine at that time. A man had to be married or live with a woman until he had fulfilled the society's minimum of one son and one daughter; only then might he choose to live alone. John the Baptist shunned women and lived as a hermit, but he was severely criticized for his lifestyle. Peter had a wife, but she seems to have stayed mostly at home. No Pharisee or scribe criticized Jesus for deviance in manners, other than that he could be too sensuous—he allowed his feet to be anointed with expensive balsam—and too liberal—he allowed female sinners to join his followers. The lack of stronger criticism would suggest that Jesus was considered perfectly normal and lived with a woman. But it seems very likely that something sinful adhered to this woman.

The apostle Paul, later so prominent, was a Roman citizen and had been strongly influenced by the Greek Orphics' negative view of women. The Orphics viewed the human body as the prison of the soul; Paul would introduce celibacy and campaign for an asexual lifestyle in the Old Church, so posterity believed that Jesus was celibate. If Jesus had children, the evangelists surely would have mentioned it. That he had a woman was so obvious it went without saying.

When Mary Magdalene saw the empty tomb, she went to fetch Peter, the leader of the men, so he could believe it for himself. When Peter had seen, Mary Magdalene wended her way back to the tomb. But she was not left alone. The first to come along were some angels. A moment later, Jesus himself stood there.

The conversation between Jesus and Mary Magdalene may be read as a farewell between two lovers. When Jesus set eyes on her, he said, merely, "Woman," the traditional greeting that a Jewish man of the time would use with the woman he loved. He consoled her as well as he could, but they could not embrace each other: "Do not touch me," he said carefully when she attempted to do so. This was because he was no longer a man of flesh and blood.

Who was this Mary Magdalene? And how great a sinner had she been before she met Jesus and became his beloved, as well as the leader of the women of his flock?

Christianity evolved within the physical and religious boundaries of the Roman Empire. In the first century, close to 10 percent of the empire's population were Christians and Jews, and the era was strongly marked by the loosening of family ties and promiscuity. The early Church would expend much time and energy on disputes about women and sex and female prostitutes. This had a lot to do with Mary Magdalene. But it also reflects the influence from goddess cults in Rome and, in the East, Orphism and Gnosticism. Only a small minority inside the Roman Empire distinguished clearly between Christians and Jews until the apostle Paul was imprisoned by Jews in Jerusalem in the 60s A.D., then released by the Romans. A few years later, the Romans destroyed the temple and sent the

Jews into their second exile. At the same time, they started the first persecutions of Christians.

After the year 70, the majority of the Christians were non-Jewish.
But for centuries, Mary Magdalene would cause struggles between the
different sects that in time would purge one another from the Church—
and later, between the popes of the West and the patriarchs of the Orthodox Church. Those who accorded Mary Magdalene a central place
in the doctrine defended the right of women to speak in gatherings and
maintained that human beings exist as both corporeal and sexual vessels. Behind the struggle over Mary Magdalene lay many generations of
battle between the sexes and demands for sexual freedom. In the long
run, the Mary Magdalene supporters would lose, and her defenders
would frequently be condemned as heretics. Today many consider them
martyrs.

But the search for the true, historical Mary Magdalene raises as many
problems as the search for the historical Jesus. In both cases the sources of
our knowledge about their lives must be scrutinized in all the variations
history has handed down. Let us start by taking a look at what the four
evangelists tell us about Mary Magdalene. The physician Luke introduces
a woman whom he calls Mary from Magdala, on the Sea of Galilee. Jesus
drove out of her seven demons, a high, almost mythic number. This was
advanced as evidence of sexual misconduct and prostitution. Even the word
Magdalene has been seen as a code for *prostitute*. Three evangelists recount
different versions of a sinning woman who washed the feet of Jesus with
her tears, kissed them repeatedly, and dried them with her hair before she
anointed him with precious ointments. Luke places this event at the home
of a Pharisee called Simon; John records Judas' complaints about Jesus
indulging in such luxury, instead of selling the ointment to feed the poor.
Jesus appears rather human in his reply: "She has covered my feet with
rare perfume. . . . Her sins are many, but are forgiven, for she loved me
much."

The female sinner whom Luke describes at Simon's house was said
to have had seven husbands. This expression is often viewed as a euphemism for the commercial sale of sex. John tells the story about his anoint-
ing analogously, but he reports that the event took place in Bethania,
where Jesus had three cousins on Joseph's side—Mary, Martha, and
Lazarus.

How many women actually put oil upon and cried at the feet of Jesus? Three? An unnamed prostitute, Mary from Bethania, and Mary from Magdala? It has been argued that these three women have been distilled into one, that they coalesced into the figure we customarily identify as the second most important woman in the New Testament, Mary Magdalene—the woman at the tomb, the woman whom "Jesus loved." But it is just as likely that there was a woman who was a relative of Jesus and a prostitute until she had her demons driven out, and thereafter began a love relationship with the son of God. The problem with this interpretation is that Mary Magdalene threatens to eclipse both Peter and Paul.

Much time was to pass before the veneration of the Virgin Mary in various parts of the Old Church. This worship developed partly under the influence of Egyptian religion, where Isis and the child Horus held dominant positions, though cults of the virgin in Rome and antisexuality currents in the Greek world also played their parts. But the sacred harlot was worshiped all over the Eastern and Roman world without interruption. Mary Magdalene was destined to get many adherents—and to cause stormy conflicts.

> *I am the first and the last,*
> *the honored and the scorned,*
> *the harlot and the holy one,*
> *the wife and the virgin,*
> *barren and fruitful.*

These words could easily have been taken as a revelation from Babylon's goddess Ishtar or the Syrian Astarte, but in fact this voice belongs to Mary Magdalene. It stems from an early Christian text that was well known, much read, and hotly discussed in the Old Church.

The Gospel according to Mary Magdalene is today known through a series of Greek fragments; they show a woman totally unfamiliar with Paul's idea that women in the congregation should remain silent. She made her own points on the parable about the mustard seed and commented on other subjects with authority. The Gospel depicted Peter becoming enraged and shouting: "Did He actually speak to a woman without us knowing about it? Should we all turn around and listen to her? Did He actually prefer her company to ours?" Mary Magdalene is just as central in another formerly widely read text, the Gospel according to Thomas, which also gives a somewhat different picture of both Jesus and Mary Magdalene than the four Gospels that eventually were canonized.

In an old psalm, Jesus himself urged Mary Magdalene to shake up the male disciples when, in despair, they had taken up their old trade of fishing on the Sea of Galilee. They should, he said, go out into the world and fish for the souls of men. It gave Mary Magdalene direction on what to say to them:

> *Stand up, let us go, 'tis your brothers calling ...*
> *Tell them: This is your Master ...*
> *Use all your cleverness and wisdom,*
> *Until you have brought the flocks back into the fold.*

A woman with such leadership qualities would certainly threaten all male followers who wanted to administer the legacy and the doctrine.

Several foreign ideas were influential as Christianity developed. Influence from Greek Orphism and neo-Platonism is especially clear in the Scriptures of Paul, while the Gospels of Mary Magdalene and Thomas bear marks of Gnostic influence. Gnosticism was a Jewish sect with strongholds in Alexandria and Damascus but also in Palestine during the century before Jesus. Large numbers of Christians and Jews were also influenced by Gnostic doctrines for the first two centuries after Jesus. But then the Greek bishop of Gaul, Irenaios, and the Latin author Tertullian, from Carthage, started a fierce campaign against Gnostic influence among Christians. Afterward, the Gnostic doctrines would be known mainly from their written texts. Tertullian was a hideous antifeminist, under Orphic and neo-Platonic influence, like the apostle Paul. In Tertullian's best-known text, *Apologeticus,* he fought against the participation of women in the Old Church: "Each and every one of you is an Eve. You destroyed man, God's image. And because of you, God's son had to die." But Tertullian's agitation can also be seen as a strong indication that women had much more power in the Old Church then.

At Egypt's Nag Hammadi in 1945, a fantastic rediscovery of old manuscripts reacquainted the world with literature that had been widely known in the Old Church, but was later lost and forgotten. The Gospel according to Philip, the First Apocalypse of James, and the Savior's Dialogue must all be considered Christian texts influenced by Gnosticism. In these texts, Mary Magdalene operates as a primary disciple of Jesus, and also as his partner, which increases her authority as a widow of the religious leader.

In the clerical hierarchy, among both the pure Gnostics and the Gnostic Christians, there was a high degree of gender equality. It was therefore natural to give pride of place to Mary Magdalene and maintain that the true Christian tradition flowed through her. According to Gnostic doctrine, female prophets and female archangels existed. The archangel Sophia had many sons, some of whom were her lovers; she had the power to arouse curiosity in tandem with sexual lust. For adherents of Mary Magdalene, however, it was problematic that non-Christian Gnostic texts like Pistis Sophia and the Gospel according to the Egyptians also made her a central character. Some of the later Gnostics developed a very ambitious project on behalf of Mary Magdalene, naming her Sophia Prunikos, "harlot of faith and wisdom." There was a dogma among some of the Gnostics that Jesus had given Mary Magdalene training in the arts of love before she became a prostitute. In one Gnostic text, Mary Magdalene was deeply involved in a discussion of principles with Peter. But instead of arguing further, she taunted him and told him off by referring to the extremely insignificant size of his penis. This single text might have caused more losses than gains for Mary Magdalene's followers.

In the third century A.D., the Persian Mani fused Gnostic, Christian, Persian, and Babylonian elements into a new religion known as Manicheanism. This made it even easier to accuse the Christian Gnostics of keeping bad company. In the following century, another faction inside the Christian Church caused a new split, as the charismatic Areios, from Alexandria, launched the doctrine that God was one, and so solitary in his male power that there was no place for any Mary Magdalene, Virgin Mary, or even Jesus of Nazareth, other than as small vehicles of prophecy.

At the Church Council of Nicea in 325, Athenaios manipulated the participants so well that only Areios and his two closest allies refused to sign the confession "that Jesus was of the same entity as God Himself." Bishop Hieronymus was the stage director as the synod determined which of the Jesus narratives and interpretive letters about his life and teachings would be considered true stories. If anyone continued to cherish writings other than the canon, it would be easy to hound them out of the Church and into the abyss of damnation. Through following synods in

Constantinople, Hippo, and Carthage, the main part of the Christian Church was united before the century was out, under a doctrine purged of Gnosticism and Arianism. Throughout the same period, the Jews decided which texts should be included in the Talmud.

One reason the Gnostics were considered heretics among a majority of Christians was their idea of a female cosmic principle predating the male's. Before the creator/demiurge was a timeless primal realm governed by a power they called Sophia, which meant "wisdom." This chaotic primal force could be seen as the mother of the creating or building god, but it was at the same time a wife for the creator. Sophia was a goddess variant of the old Eastern world. But although the Gnostics were defeated, elements of their belief were eventually incorporated into Christianity, somewhat halfheartedly, in the form of the Virgin Mary.

The Revelations of Saint John survived the purification processes. A number of scholars view this as a paradox. Strangely enough, this text allows Sophia to step forward and become Sophia Jesu, his bride, in a mystical, clearly erotically described reunion. No church authority has ever been able to explain convincingly whether this Sophia is the Gnostic archangel, Mary the Virgin Mother, or the holy whore Mary Magdalene.

Mary Magdalene has been regarded as the leading female disciple of Jesus for centuries. But when her supporters tried to place her at the center of the doctrine, they were shouted down by male-fixated Church fathers. In the fourth and fifth centuries, the common doctrine was that Mary Magdalene should no longer be counted as a leading disciple or priestess, since the text that said so had been banned. But few seemed to doubt she had been the mistress of Jesus. That was stated again and again in the more limited series of texts that were declared the canonic ground upon which Christian faith should rest.

The Old Church's skepticism toward the worship of saints was obdurate and strong. There were many reasons for this. The basilica form of the church buildings was an inheritance from heathen temples; a large number of them were built on old temple sites, and some were restored temple buildings. This allowed many features of the older religion to live on in the churches, often camouflaged as worship of saints.

Worship of a local saint indicated continuity in the veneration of an old local deity, perhaps incorporated into the new saint. In Gallia, many people venerated Saint Guignol, beyond doubt the best sexually endowed saint within the Church. In him the ancient phallic god of love, Priapus/Adonis, secured continued adoration.

The worship of the Virgin Mary, as the Mother of God, emerged in the eastern parts of the Roman Empire in churches built over former temples devoted to Aphrodite, Astarte, or Cybele. All these goddesses could be called both virgin and whore. But in many places, the tradition of assigning virginal qualities to the older goddesses was stronger, so earlier tradition became entrenched within Christianity. Pious Christian women from Syria and Asia Minor brought cakes and wine to Goddess Maria in the hope of becoming pregnant, as they had done in earlier times, long before Jesus of Nazareth was born.

Veneration of the Holy Mother Mary gradually spread west and north. For almost a millennium, the Maria Festivals bore clear marks of pre-Christian fertility cults. Now the flower-bedecked statue of Mary was paraded through the streets in the spring and fall, exactly as the old goddesses had been borne through the highways and byways of the city. Ennobled by Latin prayers and consecrated water, *aqua vitæ,* she who was both the mother of the one eternal God and the goddess of fertility was still worshiped.

The similarities were numerous. Mary had very close bonds to the God, as he was both her father and her son. In her capacity as virgin, she was a special protector of monks and men of celibacy, something that also tied in to another long tradition back through history, to the castrated priests of the East.

An alternative cult of the sacred harlot would absorb other religious sentiments related to goddess worship, and Mary Magdalene would not be the only holy prostitute venerated. Early Christian legend is speckled with converted prostitutes. These legends were always a good read. People easily took to heart the many narratives about women who had experienced the heat of love and afterward regretted it all the more deeply.

Thaïs, an Alexandrian ex-prostitute from the fourth century, would be remembered up to our own time, and she gained literary fame due to the learned German nun Hroswitha of Gandersheim, who in the 900s wrote a religious passion play about her. The passion play would encourage a number of later authors, a tradition completed by Anatole France's novel and Jules Massenet's opera in 1894.

Thaïs was raised Christian, but as she grew more and more beautiful, she developed a taste for fine clothes, costly jewels, and the good life, which were easy to acquire as long as she could sell her body for a high price. But Thaïs was not satisfied with "destroying herself for a mere bundle of real lovers"; no, indeed, she tried to be "the obsession of all men" and draw them all down into the dark pond of sin, as one version of the legend has it. Alexandria's most magnificent men squandered all their belongings and gold to spend time with the captivating Thaïs.

Her male counterpart in all these texts is Bishop Paphnutius, whose teacher, Antonius Pius, attended the Church Council of Nicea. Paphnutius could not fathom how a creature as beautiful as Thaïs could cause so much misfortune. In his curiosity, he saw no other possibility than to seek out Thaïs at home. Decked out as a client, the bishop entered the harlot's house. As a holy man, he immediately launched a deep discourse into the nature of sin, the road to salvation, and the passion of penitence—and morality won the day. Right away, in the flash of a sultry eye, Thaïs burned her clothes, gave away her jewels, and incarcerated herself in a cramped convent cell. She received food and water through a hole in the wall, but alas, there were no toilet facilities. Three years' worth of excrement filled her cell. When at last she was drowning in her own waste, Thaïs was immediately purified of all sin. A yeoman angel wafted her to heaven's door, where—freshly bathed, we hope—she entered paradise.

The Syrian Maria of Edessa, from the sixth century, shows many similar traits. Maria was the niece of Abraham, formerly the bishop of Bithynia near Byzantium, and she was left in his care when she was seven years old. Her ascetic uncle built a room outside his cell that was accessible only through a window. Thus Maria adapted to her uncle's way of life and spent all her time reading the Scriptures.

A young monk from the neighborhood also took part in the pious young woman's upbringing. One day he persuaded her to clamber out of the cell to pray with him. Who could deny a soul in need? In fact, his needs were quite intense. When Maria came to her senses, she realized that she was no longer a virgin and immediately understood that the only appropriate place for her was in the brothels. She traveled straight to Alexandria, the most sinful city of its day. At first Uncle Abraham did not notice that his niece had disappeared; he thought she had simplylost herself in deep meditation. But after two years, he found out about the liaison. He disguised himself as a soldier, cashed in a gold ring that a disciple had given him, and set off for Alexandria, where he found his niece, agreed on a price, and took her to his lodgings. The very moment she touched her uncle, the scent of his body triggered a cascade of tears, and she began to tell him about the pious life she once led with her hermit uncle in the wilderness. To comfort the crying girl, he ordered food. For the first time in fifty years, the hermit broke his self-imposed fast. Once they had eaten, he revealed himself. Maria immediately consented to return with him to the wilderness. Later, she became widely known for bringing about miracles and healing the sick. In the end, she qualified for beatification, just like her uncle.

Marianne, or Mary the Egyptian, chose to live alone in the desert after her conversion. For seventeen years, she survived on three slices of bread and a handful of wild herbs. Her fragrance was so overpowering that when she made the sign of the cross, she enabled people to walk on water. Her corpse was laid to rest in a lion's den, which caused the lion to abandon it, out of respect.

Pelagia, a dancer from Antioquia, was also called Margarito because of her beautiful trademark pearls. Pelagia repented all her sins the moment she met the holy bishop Nonnus. She borrowed his clothes and marched off into the desert, where she became known as the eunuch Pelagius and lived alone in a grotto near an olive grove. When her corpse was examined, it became obvious that this hermit was a woman and ought to be canonized as a female saint.

Some few but significant female saints of the Old Church did not start out as sinners but were honorable, unmarried adult women who lived independent lives. As the idea of convent life gained prominence in medieval times, the holy Catherine of Alexandria and the holy Caesarea of Cluny would be considered good models for the few leadership roles acceptable for women: prioress and mother superior.

The few married matrons who attained sainthood in the Old Church were rewarded for having produced a still more famous son. Elizabeth and Anna were the mothers of John the Baptist and the Virgin Mary, respectively. Saint Monica was the mother of Saint Augustine, and Saint Helena produced Constantine. But more female saints were young girls who would rather die than offer up their virtue, so they became martyrs: Lucia, Agnes, Barbara, Irene, Agape, Chionia, Marina, and many more. Everlasting virginity became the ecclesiastical ideal of womanhood many centuries before the convents came into being.

As far as the Virgin Mary was concerned, the Church began to preach that giving birth to Jesus had left her virginity untouched. It would later be pointed out that her intense prayer during the birth spared her pain and ensured that the blood of birth never befouled her. A marriage of the flesh was a concession to the lust of fallen humanity. But Mary's marriage to Joseph was completely devoid of sex and therefore comparable to life in celibacy.

It is astonishing that, against all this female virtue, so many former prostitutes of late antiquity were canonized: Pelagia, Thaïs, and the many Mary Magdalene facsimiles were only the most famous of a bevy of saintly prostitutes around the eastern Mediterranean. After some centuries, the West got its share: Saint Aphra ran an Augsburg brothel in the fourth century but died a martyr after some ecclesiastical clients of prostitution converted her. Upon her death, three of her prostitute colleagues took care of her corpse, and for this they became Saints Digna, Eunomia, and Eutropia. Saint Vreka of Liège and Saint Verena of Zurzach were prostitutes who also attained sainthood after many years of penitence.

Indeed, the concept of the female penitent sinner never lost its appeal, and stories about beautiful women with a lewd past would continue to grip both men and women. But of course these stories required a happy end— in penitence and celibacy.

In the legends of the Old Church, a male figure—distinct from the old sage who rescues a young sinner—shows up just as frequently: the healthy, handsome, but virtuous youth who stays away from all women. Such a young man would never dream of bringing about the salvation of a female prostitute; he would spurn all harlots as if they carried the plague.

John the Baptist was a role model for these young men. He bravely spurned all of womankind, including the seductive princess Salome. But among the apostles, Paul was the most sex- and woman-hostile. It was he who, under the influence of Orphic skepticism for women, worked up the rejection of females into a theology. According to Paul, even the most minimal physical contact with a woman damaged a man, and intercourse with a prostitute befouled the holy body of Christ.

The legends that promoted this message became many and scary. The holy Johannes Chrysostomos pushed a harlot off a cliff in Syria around the year 380 to demonstrate his opposition to lascivious temptation. Tertullian of Carthage embraced eunuchs in his disgust for women, declaring, "The kingdom of heaven is thrown open to eunuchs." At the end of the fourth century, the Church father Hieronymus led the efforts to bring out the first complete edition of the Bible in Latin, the Vulgata. Hieronymus was also a hermit and polymath, and he told the story of a young man who was confined to a wonderful garden with an equally beautiful prostitute. He defended his honor by biting off his tongue and spitting it in the face of the woman. The almost omniscient Hieronymus would be considered one of the fathers of the Church, but when it came to prostitution, he showed little analytical talent. He seemed to label any promiscuous woman a whore, much in the way of the Old Testament's prophets. Whether the woman was paid for her services didn't factor in to his judgments.

The most prominent among the Church fathers, Augustine, showed a more refined understanding. Born in Carthage, he ended his days as bishop of Hipporegius. But he had a past, both philosophically and sexually, before his conversion to Christianity. Augustine's life can be divided into three distinct periods: his Manichean youth, his neo-Platonist early manhood, and his Christian maturity. In his wild youth, Augustine visited lots of prostitutes and engaged in a number of love affairs. In his early manhood, the neo-Platonists taught him to blame the women for that earlier wildness. When his pious Christian mother, Monica, and Bishop Ambrosius of Milan were finally able to influence him, and the latter pointed out that neo-Platonism and Christian beliefs did not contradict each other, Augustine converted to Christianity and celibacy.

In old age, Augustine would preach morality with a power proportional to the wildness of his youth. His autobiography, *Confessions,* consolidated his fame as a great sinner, which in turn gave weight to his preaching. Augustine never stopped reflecting on his own life path. This man who, as a youth, had adored sacred prostitutes and purchased sex from profane whores would formulate the famous metaphor about man's "two heads," with the more unruly one dangling between his legs. Augustine pointed out the male sexual organ's strong urge to live its own life, and noted the resulting conflict between body and soul.

With such a complex view of the male body, Augustine developed a Christian doctrine of sexuality connecting back to republican Roman views. Prostitution was necessary in human society as a safety valve, to dam the overflow of unbridled lust: *Aufer meretrices de rebus humanis, tubaveris omnia libidinibus*—or, "Banish prostitutes from humankind, and capricious lusts will overflow society," said Augustine in 386. This doctrine would later be established almost as a theological dogma; it was to become the most widely cited statement on prostitution of all time.

Augustine would, as a Church father, defend prostitution as a bulwark against general immorality. His view would influence the future of the Church much more than the imprecise thundering moralism of the Old Testament, and it weakened the apostle Paul's indiscriminate rejection of all female flesh as dirty. In the post-Augustine era, the Church expended much energy on promoting celibacy, but it still defended marriage, both to secure the continuation of human life on earth, and to preserve the choice of celibacy or marriage. Within the Church, celibacy would be ranked above marriage, widowhood above remarriage, and virginity as the noblest way of life for a woman. Within a marriage, friendship between man and wife was a virtue, but a sexual relationship was not regarded as a sin so long as it provided offspring.

With Augustine established as the foremost Church father, the defenders of women's sensuality had lost their last battle. Prostitution was tolerated. But prostitutes would be excommunicated from their local congregations. Christian men were urged to stay away from prostitutes, but they would be forgiven if they could not resist. The Church would no longer try to eliminate prostitution from society. Neither would Mary Magdalene be totally removed from the Scriptures. In the long run, the Church was served by the legends about her and the other women sinners who, like Augustine himself, became penitent, celibate, and ultimately were rewarded with the status of saints.

Gregory, who would be known as the Great, was from old and noble Roman political stock, a dynamic and ambitious man who started his career studying law and taking up political commissions in a collapsing Rome.

Gregory had to be offered the papacy repeatedly before he grudgingly took
it up in the year 590. Thereafter, he began to reorganize the convents and
monasteries, the liturgy, theology, and the Church's economy at a more
rapid tempo than any of his predecessors. All of a sudden everything was
in order. Rome may not have been built in a day, but the pope's Church
almost was.

Members of the victorious party from the 300s—Hieronymus,
Ambrosius, and their learned contemporary Cassian—all encountered
massive logistical problems as they looked into the Mary Magdalene question. Augustine managed to solve parts of the problem toward the end of
that century, but Gregory would be the only one strong enough to chop
through the Gordian knot that Mary Magdalene had become for the
Church. Gregory did not give a damn about what the apostles had written. He came straight out and issued a decree that this woman had not been
the lover of Jesus. The evangelists had meant only to explain that Jesus
liked this woman, nothing more.

Gregory understood how impractical it would be for the Church to
leave the issue unclarified in the long run. Had Jesus engaged in sexual
relations with Mary Magdalene? It was not only prostitution that created
problems but also their family relationship. The official theology then was
that no one could marry or have sexual relations with a relative. In part,
this was the Church's way of dealing with overpopulation. The Church
permitted relations only between people who were more than seven collateral generations apart. Parents and siblings were relations of the first
generation; uncles, aunts, and cousins were the second; second cousins
made up the third.

With a papal decree, the High Middle Ages simplified it from seven
to four collateral generations. Even so, the relationship between Jesus and
Mary Magdalene would have been very much illegal and improper. The
Church could have clarified and defended the relationship, and stressed
that the common genealogy was through Joseph, who could not be considered Jesus' flesh-and-blood father. But there were certain unpleasant
associations adhering to the relationship.

Gregory was a born problem solver. In this matter, the question was
to dispense with all sexual ambiguity via a papal interpretation that was
pure and simple. Mary Magdalene hailed from a village around Bethania,
where the family owned a handsome estate called Magdala. The apostles

described this woman as dearly beloved, because she was young and related to Jesus. Like John, she was a cousin, and the only other person to whom the apostles applied this strong term. John was dearly beloved by Jesus in his capacity as the youngest cousin on his mother's side, and he was the darling of the whole family, not simply of Jesus. Mary Magdalene could then be someone with whom it was possible to coexist, so long as one regarded her in the same light as John. She was as sweet and sensitive a girl as he was the golden boy. Accordingly, both had to become the Master's favorite relatives.

Suddenly, the girl was a typical little sister, coddled and spoiled. On the other hand, she had two extremely noble older siblings, her sister Martha, who was strong enough to kill a dragon but still used all her force to cook and comfort her more fragile younger sister, and her pious brother Lazarus. There was no doubt that it was due to her beauty and sensuality that the little sister was lured out onto the wild streets. But then she met her good cousin, who guided her back onto the path of righteousness. She'd had sex with others, yes, but never had she been Jesus' lover. Gregory the Great laid this down with the utmost finality, and nobody dared venture the slightest doubt. So Gregory got things the way he wanted them—almost.

In both Byzantium and the previous Eastern branches of the Church, Mary Magdalene had been seen as a former prostitute and sinner. In certain circles of the West, many continued to view this woman as Jesus' lover. Of course, Gregory's decree was of great use to the Church, but such a hot rumor cannot be squelched with the wave of a hand.

The Old Church allowed for two different traditions about Mary Magdalene's later life. The Greek Christians were convinced that she had gone along with Mary, mother of Jesus, to Ephesus, and faithfully looked after Mary until her death. The problem with this legend was its support of the notion that Mary Magdalene was the daughter-in-law. A different Latin legend would be propagated by the pope in Rome and, in the end, given the authorized force of Abbé Odo de Cluny's 920s manuscript *In Veneratione Mariae Madalenae*. Odo de Cluny systematically organized the biblical stories into one logical narrative, which explains to us that Jesus' young cousin had first been in love with the young John. Their marriage was prepared in the village of Cana, in Galilee. But when Jesus showed up for the wedding, he urged John to devote his life to preaching. This propelled Mary Magdalene into prostitution. But in the house of Simon the Pharisee, Jesus met his young kinswoman again. She sank to his feet, kissed them, and wept. He drove the demons out of her, and she joined his flock of disciples. Some years following the death of Jesus, she was exiled from Palestine. Together with Martha and Lazarus, disciples and faithful retainers, she boarded a ship without rudder, sails, or oars. But God steered them safely to the Roman city of Massilia, in Gaul.

Mary Magdalene was the first to disembark the vessel. She was so extraordinarily beautiful and spoke so eloquently about Christ and against the worship of idols that people immediately listened and believed. When Mary Magdalene roused a Gallic princess from death, an increasing number of people converted to the Christian faith.

Lazarus became the first bishop of Massilia. Meanwhile, Mary Magdalene lived alone and penitent in the woods of Saint Baume, praying and confiding with the angels. Every day they took her up to heaven, where she became acquainted with the celestial nourishment that would be her ultimate reward. Unlike Lazarus, Mary Magdalene did not suffer a martyr's death. She expired calmly, surrounded by angels and disciples, in the care of the ever faithful Martha, who grieved for eight days, then gave up her own life. Mary Magdalene's relics are the holiest items in southern and eastern France, now lodged in the Romanesque cloister of Vézelay, in the valley of the Yonne, where pilgrims continue to flock. Her feast day is July 22.

EIGHT

TANG CHINA'S
PLEASURE WOMEN

Yü Hsüan-chi was the name of a girl from Chang'an—the capital of Tang Dynasty China, present-day Xi'an—located a goodly way into northern China, along the Yellow or Huangho River. Yü was born in the year 844, at a phase of China's history that coincided with the time of Charlemagne in Europe. She came from a poor craftsman family, but had joie de vivre, beauty, and intelligence, as well as a natural talent for song and dance. At twelve or thirteen, Yü had already begun her liaisons with the young students who flocked to Chang'an, most of them from the civil-servant nobility, who would in time become mandarins.

This young girl was under nobody's supervision and seems to have taken the initiative to meet the students herself. They quickly discovered her many talents, not least her poetic genius, something that made her extremely popular. It is above all her poetry that has given Yü her place in Chinese history. The Chang'an students soon began to shower her with gifts, which inspired her into sexual relations with some of them. Early on, she developed into a luxury prostitute of the day.

According to older Chinese historians, this vocation was already well established; tradition says that there was "always" prostitution, which means as early as the ninth or the eighth century B.C., when China still consisted of smaller feudal states.

The philosopher and statesman Kuang Chung, adviser to the first Huan of Ch'i—the strongest state of that time, centered in the middle of the Huangho River valley—had set up the first bordellos in China, according to tradition. Kuang's rationale was to increase the flow of money into the state coffers, and in this he succeeded.

China is the only civilization for which one has solid reason to believe that prostitution developed independent of influence from the West.

In this light, it is particularly interesting to contemplate how far back in history it was possible to buy and sell sexual services. However, histories recorded by later writers cannot serve as evidence of actual prostitution. China's historians have had a tendency to interpret the events of older periods in light of their own time and age, and to use present-day concepts to describe old social conventions.

Here, the historical tradition may contain a kernel of truth: Petty princes and men of the weakening imperial family seem to have sought out the prince of Ch'i to buy beautiful women who would grace their homes or harems. But the prince's adviser seems to be described more correctly as a slave trader than as a brothel keeper.

When, centuries later, the Han Dynasty united and consolidated China, urban living, trade, and commerce had influenced all social relations. From the time of Emperor Wu Ti, around 100 B.C., archaeological finds and imperial accounting records give a clear impression of great numbers of prostitutes serving as appendages to the imperial army. These women could, against cash payment, be used by officers and common soldiers. In the larger cities, privately owned brothels were available to craftsmen and merchants as well. These brothels were called *ch'ang-chia*, or "the houses with the singing girls," and some were furnished with the greatest luxuries of the time.

But it was the Tang Dynasty, in the 700s and 800s, that produced an exceedingly rich and comprehensive body of historical and literary material on prostitution. Ever since, Chinese literature has included stories about the most famous prostitutes, and recited poetry written by them and in their honor. Yü Hsüan-chi's poems might be the best known among these. They are still read and analyzed in the schools and universities of China.

As Yü neared the end of her teenage years, a student from a good mandarin family talked her into moving to his province, maybe without revealing that his parents had already sought a wife of equivalent social standing for their son. In social terms, Yü represented nobody but herself and would become the subsequent, or number two wife. In ninth-century China, for a craftsman's daughter without powerful alliances, this would have been about the best fortune she could have dreamed of. If Yü had behaved herself properly, neither the first wife nor the first wife's family would have had any reason to postpone the arrangement.

But in most people's eyes, Yü Hsüan-chi did not behave herself. She appeared emotional and demanding and expected a life and a love that hardly any man could give her, especially not a young mandarin out in the Chinese provinces. Some of the love poems Yü wrote in this period have survived, and those who appreciate the nuances of Tang poetry agree that her work makes for a stormy read. In most cultures, the idea of romantic love deals with basic emotions directed toward someone unattainable. Raw and direct love poetry may become totally overwhelming when a woman depicts her beloved man as out of reach, or as someone she thought she had obtained, but in practice their love remains forever unrequited.

Yü's poetry deals with conflicting feelings in a genuinely Chinese manner and is therefore almost impossible to translate. But obviously, it refers to the three various moral outlooks, with separate views of men, women, and sexuality that glaringly opposed one another, though they were allowed to exist. The doctrines all stem from texts dating back to around 500 B.C., but they achieved their respective glory and honor at slightly different times. Confucianism was a kind of official moral doctrine, while Taoism and Buddhism resembled religions. All three influenced Chinese behavior and outlook before, during, and after the Tang period. The pragmatically minded Chinese understood that it paid to live calmly with them all, and to pluck a bit from each doctrine. Most Chinese throughout history married in the Taoist manner but chose to be buried in a Confucian way.

In outlook on humanity, these three doctrines find themselves in deep conflict, and this may be debilitating for those who think deeply, especially if they happen to be female. Confucianism taught that women were creatures of lower standing, and suggested that the two sexes live relatively separate lives in family and society. Women were not seen as possessing anything that might sustain a man, culturally or spiritually. Confucian morality was designed to advance the family and secure fatherhood with virtuous daughters and faithful wives. Accordingly, marriages were arranged to strengthen families and alliances. Taoism and Tantric Buddhism had different views on women and sexuality: Sexual activity was stressed, as was the way a man should be stimulated by a woman, since she represented sex, which incorporated the essence and the life force of men. Taoism stimulated men toward sexual life within and outside matrimony, and not least, it strongly defended sex for money. This doctrine found adherents among well-read prostitutes.

The temples and monasteries—where women could gain entrance and become members—disseminated Taoist and Buddhist mystical teachings. But Confucianism dominated civil service and the imperial court and was strong in the universities. The young men who studied in Chang'an were expected to take up careers and often came from influential families, so they were stamped by the Confucian way of thinking. We have no reason to expect Yü Hsüan-chi to have been sympathetic to the Confucian view of women. We do not know, however, whether she came to her senses about this before she was installed out in the provinces.

We have to read Yü's love poems as biographical evidence to guess what happened between Yü and her husband. We have good reason to expect that their sex life had been important when he first showed an interest in her, although it is also conceivable that it had become secondary to him sometime before he asked her to join his family. In any case, she soon began to experience their love in a totally different way.

Any son of a mandarin family would know how important it was to have children with the woman his family had chosen for him; two families with common descendants represented a formidable alliance. According to Confucian thinking, kinship was superior to the single individual, and Yü's partner hardly would have thought otherwise. Biographical interpretation of her poetry indicates that she was soon dissatisfied by their sex life.

Taoism advanced all sexual activities positively. But no matter how much time a man devoted to it, he could allow himself to expend his seed only when he wanted to produce children. According to Confucian doctrine, Yü could never serve him in this purpose. As Number Two Wife she could never dare contemplate being the mother of her husband's children. She had no family of importance, no ancestors to boast about. She realized that she could not keep her lover company when he traveled; nor could she contemplate being a mother. She was fated to remain childless, a locked-up secondary wife of a man who had become intellectually bored by his first wife. Yü would meet no one outside the families of her husband and his number one wife. They were all virtuous and well turned out, but they were stuffy and, like the upper class in general, devoid of any literary appreciation whatsoever.

A year and a half into the young prospective mandarin's second marriage, Yü was seen as demanding, impertinent, temperamental, and acerbic. When she eventually extricated herself from this Confucian family prison, she sought moral support and strength in a Taoist convent near the capital, where former prostitutes lived alongside widows, women separated from their husbands, young girls with no marital experience and little hope of achieving it. In Taoist nunneries of the period, quite a lot of wine was consumed; the Taoist priests had a lucrative sideline supplying the cloistered communities. Additionally, the more broad-minded female members of the cloister entertained guests almost as in the city's brothels.

Wine was a scarce resource during the Tang Dynasty. To drink a great deal was a sign of status, and the prostitutes competed with the men. Women who were able to tolerate a lot of wine were highly esteemed. It was not until the Ming Dynasty, half a millennium later, that Chinese wine production became so cheap that a drunken prostitute, nun or mandarin, lost any status in society.

Yü Hsüan-chi spent one and a half wine-soaked years in the Taoist nunnery. Then she fell in love again, this time with the most famous male poet of the day, Wen T'ing-yün. For a while, they traveled around the empire; sometimes she took him along, or he took her. Meanwhile, she became seriously established as the literary and cultural hostess of the ninth-century Chinese literary intellectual set.

Ancient Chinese cities were proud of their foremost ladies of the night, who moved around freely with entourages, were organized in guilds, and paid taxes. During the Sung Dynasty of the 1200s and 1300s, they played a ceremonial role in the weddings of the upper classes, and took part in the singing and dancing.

Chinese chronicles from all early dynasties report homosexual relations between men of the same age and social status, between older aristocrats and young men of lower rank, and with eunuchs, particularly from the imperial circles. Male prostitution, however, came late to China and spread during the Sung Dynasty, when one could find male prostitutes, usually dressed in female finery, in the streets and in the bordellos of varying degrees of luxury.

Chou Mi, who wrote in the fourteenth century, distinguished among three classes of female prostitutes, with the well-schooled and cultivated courtesans at the top, and the prostitutes of the wine bars and bordellos—the so-called *ch'ing-lou,* or *ch'ang-lou,* the houses of singing girls or houses with green rooms—as the middle stratum. The poor prostitutes of the streets and cheap brothels never enjoyed any status. During the Sung Dynasty, when prostitution was more widespread, cheap prostitution was forbidden in certain provinces.

The cheap prostitutes gathered together in large establishments. Brothels were normally built for special customer groups, like sailors in the harbor districts of the port cities. The authorities also normally saw it as their duty to supply *ying-chi,* or girls, to any army in the field. In peacetime, these girls were often sent back to the privately organized sex industry.

The brothel clients were young city males from middle and lower classes. Many larger brothels were state-owned. The least expensive brothel prostitutes often had criminal backgrounds or were relatives of criminals; the police and civil servants recruited some of them for law and order in red-light districts and other shady parts of the cities. It was not uncommon for daughters from families with many children to be sold directly to the brothels, while others regularly were stolen away, or shanghaied, from their villages by specialized traders. This was especially easy when wars were raging along the periphery of the expanding Han Chinese imperial civilization. Here, the linguistic and ethnic minorities were unable to put up much resistance to the Chinese human traders, with their weapons and horses.

Whether the bordellos were small and private, or large and public, they were, like so much else in China, regulated, supervised, and taxed. The bureaucracy had centuries of experience and followed age-old principles.

The middle-stratum prostitutes were organized into guilds, as were the richest. All these guilds paid taxes. Brothel owners paid tax on behalf of the business they conducted with slave and impoverished prostitutes. On the other hand, all prostitution enjoyed a certain degree of public protection. Large bordellos had their own permanent security forces, and this was not only to secure the well-being of the establishment, the prostitutes, and the clients; they were also used as enforcers against competition from unregistered, non-tax-paying youths of both sexes who tried to work the streets as free agents.

Unfortunately, the women of the brothels did not appeal to the writers of the Tang and Sung Dynasties the way the literary prostitutes did, so it is difficult to determine how great the differences would have been from brothel to brothel, or how much pressure was used to bridle the large numbers of impoverished prostitutes, how hungry they were and how much they suffered, or how early they died.

But some facts do emerge: Those brothel women who experienced the love of a seaman, or a craftsman from a city in the interior, could have their freedom purchased by their paramour, then be taken to the man's home province—but for this to occur, the woman had to have all of China's benevolent gods on her side. There were not many poor girls who won such a premier prize in that particular Chinese lottery.

The Tang Dynasty men's competitive lust was not particularly strong in the sexual arena. But China's mandarins, officers, and merchants had just as much competitive drive as men in other cultures, although they pestered one another less with sexual braggadocio; and families of upper-class males worked to furnish their homes with women. Chinese women of good families were neither artistic nor literary. They were expected to behave in a manner that was courteous and modest, and they were expected to be pretty. These qualities were enjoyed by the husband alone. No man of power and influence showed himself in public with women from his own household.

But even if China's men hardly competed over sex, they did compete over women, particularly those renowned for their style. By the time of the Tang Dynasty, prostitutes were key figures in the life of elegance and fashion. The man who could possess a well-known woman poet or singer of the day was deemed a man of culture and refinement, and as such, he gained social status. Public servants or writers with intellectual aspirations would frequently take along well-schooled prostitutes when they went on important journeys or official visits; these women had presence and were capable of intelligent conversation. Consequently, it was not primarily sex appeal and beauty that drove the rich mandarin to support his respective literary or musical urban prostitute; rather, it was her status, which might secure him a reputation for good taste and style.

The fact that China's men were preoccupied with such desires came to affect Yü's life more and more as she, now in her twenties, became more and more famous. When prominent prostitutes were described in literary or biographical works, it was their abilities in song, dance, and literature that were mentioned first, and their appearance only subsequently. The abilities to engage in disarming repartee and to overcome a sudden dismissal or an emotional defeat were highly valued. They made it possible for the men to be confidential, relaxed, and emotional in the company of these women, without feeling that they suffered any loss to their manhood.

In the final analysis, a prosperous prostitute spent just as much energy on her career as did the men who reached the top of military, political, or commercial life. The more famous she became, the less sexual she had to appear. A high-ranking pleasure woman demanded a protracted wooing before bestowing her attentions upon a man. A distinctive literature of romantic love developed in the circles around an almost unattainable woman. Some felt that this was to the good.

Yü obviously approved to a far lesser degree. She was not only witty and elegant but also extremely sensual, emotional, and quick. She was not always pleased to be coveted for snobbish and cultural reasons. Why would she, who knew the nuances of language, be pleased by heated love poetry written for one reason? Once again, she began to feel imprisoned, this time not by Confucian and provincial family life, but by the fashionable, avant-garde capital-city life. What was horrible about her success was that it caused her pain; she was stifled by her own myth.

By now Yü had become the foremost sex symbol of her day. What did that imply? In this case, not a very good sex life. This still seems to be something she constantly dreamed about. Her rich, influential, middle-aged mandarin patrons either had wives and lovers from before, were afraid of her sexually, or were plainly interested in her only as a trophy. Few of the powerful male trendsetters in the capital city felt grounds for jealousy if a woman prostitute whom they supported had sexual relations with another, perhaps younger man who played no particular role in society. The condition was simply that those who possessed power and status should be treated with full respect.

There is much to indicate that Yü had enjoyed stripping away the hypocrisy of the snobbish game in which she was enveloped and constricted. But whether she consciously set in motion a campaign of provocation, or whether everything happened out of desperation and confusion, Yü's erotic escapades became more and more numerous. Scandal followed scandal, and everyone looked for the logic behind what she did, but nobody found it. People in Chang'an spoke all the more about the latest thing she had said to one or another minister, or about which young student or poet she had been to bed with most recently.

Yü Hsüan-chi's life was the least typical of any that one might focus upon from among the hundreds of thousands of Chinese prostitutes during the 800s. There is a good deal of information about a handful of other high-class pleasure women, and we know their good poetry, beautiful paintings, and sought-after drawings; they all reached a ripe old prosperous age. On the other hand, thousands of prostitutes died very young, departing from life in such a state of misery that society did not consider them worth remembering. Yü's life was totally different—she died young, rich, and beautiful, tremendously famous, and famously loathed and despised.

Yü Hsüan-chi's last poems were sublime. She wrote them at the moment when the thread of her destiny was about to snap. In the inner social circle of the most influential mandarins, she ruthlessly and recklessly played men of influence against one another, then revealed in the very next breath that a young man of whom they probably had never heard was head and shoulders above them all, in both wit and refinement. For one possessed of such a stiletto tongue, she should have made sure she played at least one card correctly, so she could have kept one friend and ally.

But Yü lived as though she had the most powerful family relations in China, when in reality she had more enemies than the emperor. She probably realized she would never get the chance to grow old. The thought of fading away, slowly but surely, is particularly hard to face for some. Perhaps she wanted to scintillate eternally and knew that the magic formula involved dying young. Finally, everything in Yü's life coalesced into a catastrophe. A group of political public servants of her acquaintance indicted her with having whipped and beaten her serving girl to death, and they mobilized a series of bizarre false witnesses. Yü had the temperament, as half the capital city knew—not a few had seen her in action under the influence of a surfeit of wine—but this! This smacked of an actual plot.

Alas, if only she had not been playing for such high stakes, and with such negligence, the signature of one powerful mandarin would have been enough to save her. But not one man of power came forward to help. She was convicted, condemned to death, and executed in 871, at age twenty-seven. One of her very last poems lamented the absence of her lover before death:

> *Separated from you,*
> *What can I offer?*
> *Only this single poem,*
> *Stained with my bright tears.*

Yü Hsüan-chi was no saint; nor was she a martyr. Nevertheless, she came to stand as China's goddess of love during her short historical moment on earth. She came, she saw, and she conquered, but she did not find happiness.

N I N E

MUHAMMAD'S WOMEN

The prophet Muhammad considered Eve the first woman of humankind. But she was far from the top of the list of perfect women. In his opinion, the first among the world's four most perfect women was Aysiah, the pharaonic queen who set aside her unbelieving husband in favor of the belief propagated by Prophet Musa/Moses. The second perfect woman was Maryam/Mary, who gave birth to Isa/Jesus "out of nothing."

Muhammad's first wife, Khadijah, must have been the most perfect of all perfect women. She is ranked as the second most holy person in Islam after the prophet himself, and she gave birth to the fourth perfect woman, Muhammad's favorite daughter, Fatimah.

The prophet and the wealthy widow and successful businesswoman Khadijah entered into a monogamous marriage when he was twenty-five and she was forty. She was wise and devout but open-minded, and bore him sons who died in infancy plus four daughters. When Khadijah died, Muhammad was forty, and he missed her terribly. While he was still mourning her loss, the angel Gabriel came to him, sleeping in solitude on Mount Hira, and said, "Recite!" Muhammad hesitated, but the angel urged him until he said, "What shall I recite?" Then he repeated after the angel, "In the name of the Lord, who created all things, who created man from clots of blood," the verses that would begin the scripture which later became known as the Qu'ran.

After his revelations, Muhammad became a religious leader. He remarried in Mecca twice, with a short interval between, then took four new wives in Medina. Three of his new wives were also widows, and one was divorced. All belonged to his inner circle; two were also daughters of his most trusted friends. His second most favored wife, Aysiah, was the daughter of Abu Bhakr, who would take over the religious leadership from

Muhammad and become *caliph* after his death, followed by Umar, who was Muhammad's father-in-law.

Muhammad took another six wives. In Islamic tradition, these measures are considered tactical, politically necessary. One wife was the daughter of his archenemy; another was a Coptic Christian slave whom he received as a gift from the ruler of Egypt; while two beautiful Jewesses, Maryiah and Safiah, converted and served as proof that the prophet had received his revelations from the same god as theirs, and that his teachings were the most contemporary and appropriate.

Muhammad differed strongly from those he named as prophets before him, Ibrahim/Abraham, Musa/Moses, and especially Isa/Jesus. He also differed from former prophets, insofar as he became a ruler himself in Medina, and came to wield political, juridical, and religious authority. After an eight-year struggle, he conquered Mecca and established his *umma,* or inner circle. He promulgated laws, collected taxes, sent out diplomats, and made war and peace. The *umma* was soon to become an empire. After Muhammad died, the following rulers became *caliphs,* or deputies of God. The Muslim empire would extend far eastward, sometimes beyond the borders of India and China; westward along the Mediterranean until it eventually reached the Atlantic; southward to black Africa; and northward to the lands of white Europeans. Right in the middle of the empire, Jews and Christians continued to live under Muslim domination. They were tolerated but treated as nonbelievers, since they never accepted the idea that the god who had revealed himself to Muhammad was the same as theirs, and thus represented the latest and in fact most updated version of God's wishes for humankind.

Muhammad's empire would soon be split in two. The first two *caliphs* had been elected to their position, but they also held strong positions as the prophet's fathers-in law. Two sons-in-law of the prophet became the next *caliphs,* first Othman, then Ali, who had married Muhammad's beloved daughter Fatimah, and additionally was adopted by the prophet. But both in turn were murdered. When Ali's son Hussain was murdered, the Muslims split. One faction would accept only the descendants of Ali as leader and became known as the Shi'ites. This was

Ali's party, and its capital was Damascus, in Syria. The other faction continued to elect their *caliphs* and considered this approach more democratic, in accord with tradition, or Sunni. Their rule from Medina would be known as the Umayyads.

Be they Shi'a or Sunni, marriage remained a problem. It was not only the prophet who had many wives. Ali, too, had married a perfect woman, Fatimah, who gave birth to the prophet's only male descendants. But who could replace a perfect woman? Ali needed nine new wives after Fatimah's death. Although monogamy had proved possible, it would have been hard to promote if the early Muslim scholars had wanted to do so. Polygamy was quite widespread among followers of different faiths in the world where Islam developed; they tried to restrict the number of wives to four. But Islamic scholars clearly accorded marriage higher respect than most other religions did, while still holding celibacy and single life in very low esteem. Chastity was promoted only among the very young and unmarried, especially girls. Close friendship among men was also highly esteemed, and it led to acceptance of intimate experiments before marriage. When the Qu'ran says, "Tell the believing men to lower their gaze from looking at forbidden things and protect their private parts from illegal sexual acts," it is usually taken as a warning to adult Muslim men.

But in general, there is a sex-friendly tone in Muslim texts, from the Qu'ran to profane literature. Ascetics and eunuchs are deviant creatures; Allah finds nothing wrong with sexual desires, as long as they do not threaten society, and seems to promote a happy sex life for both man and woman— except during the woman's *haid*, or menstruation, when she is considered polluted and can neither pray, read the Qu'ran, nor have sex.

Another rule: "Say to the believing women that they should lower their gaze and guard their modesty. They shall not display their beauty and ornaments, except what most ordinarily appears thereof." A proper woman should cover her beauty, both her body and her jewelry, in the presence of unrelated men. Inside her home, she was allowed to expose all her beauty and sensuality, to sing, dance, and entertain her husband, her father, her brothers and nephews on both sides. Nor did she feel shy toward very young and old servants, who were immune to sexual temptation, or male servants free of physical needs, those who lacked vigor. In pure female company, female sensuality might be even more exposed. Beatuty did not make any woman or young man bad—on the contrary.

The Qu'ran is above all a collection of rules and regulations and devotes innumerable paragraphs to proper behavior between husband and wife. It urges a father to make sure his sons and daughters marry properly, and to marry male and female slaves and servants to each other, especially if they are virtuous, fit for marriage, and belong to the right faith.

The polygamy that the prophet's early followers practiced gave the wives a more secure position than their neighbors'. The Qu'ran clearly states that a man has social and economic responsibility for all his wives, including those he divorces and those who divorce him with legitimate reason, as long as the divorced woman does not marry again.

When polygamy was extended into harems during the later Umayyad period, it broke the rule for the number of permissible wives and allowed concubines. Although the man who could afford a harem would father numerous offspring, the average wife or concubine would have fewer children. Thus, the harem prohibited overpopulation and provided safe conditions for children and women.

Polygamy was not only to man's advantage. The Qu'ran states that the man who sexually avoids one of his wives over six months and the man who commits adultery both give their wives grounds for divorce. Adultery must also be severely punished.

A polygamous, antiadulterous society should give good reason for severely limiting prostitution. And it did so, as Islam spread to Morocco and Spain, Turkey and farther east, and throughout India to the East Indies and Africa. "Force not your maids into prostitution in order that you make a gain, if they desire chastity. But if anyone compels them to prostitution, Allah is most forgiving to those women, because they have been forced to do this evil act unwillingly." The Qu'ran deals explicitly with prostitution, speaking especially against those who trade slave girls to brothels. This would lead us to assume that very few prostitutes in those parts of the world where it flourished independent of the spread of Islam were born Muslims.

Zina is a strong, pejorative word in the Qu'ran, clearly stronger than the Jewish and Christian *sin*, but it has similar sexual connotations. *Zina* is among the best reasons for divorce, and it applies to both sexes; it refers to abnormal sexual behavior among men and shameless appearance among women. Adultery is not only *zina*; it requires additional heavy punishment, since the property of another male believer has been violated.

But not all extramarital sex is considered adultery. The Qu'ran does not condemn men who pay for sex with women who offer it willingly. Sex with nonbelievers far from the household would hardly be called adulterous. The Islamic world had an open structure, with many enclaves of nonbelievers in separate areas of the cities. Like polygamy, prostitution was a very old and widespread social phenomenon that continued to be practiced by the nonbelievers within the empire. Prostitutes of Muslim origins would be found occasionally, and over the centuries they would even comprise a majority in the brothels of cities like Cairo and Aleppo, where prostitutes had to pay taxes and certify their birth and religion to the officials. Low-class Muslim women in these big cities would take up other professions forbidden them by the Qu'ran, such as nursing in hospitals with male patients, or attending baths. But in general, Islam discouraged prostitution, among Muslim-born girls in particular, and presumably even more among Shi'ites than among Sunni Muslims. Some prostitutes were always accessible in the cities, but the rule was that a prostitute and her brothel owner were foreign and belonged to one of the oppressed minorities. The girl would be either a Christian slave from the periphery of the Byzantine Empire or Jewish.

In the early 700s A.D., the Umayyads began to experience serious defeats, in 732 by the Catholic Charlemagne at Poitiers, in south-central France, and twice by the Byzantines. While their power was weakened in North Africa, rival Islamic sects formed an alliance at home and gained Persian support. The result was a murder of the last Umayyad governor of Central Asia, followed by a number of Arab-Persian tribal wars. The Abbaside family ultimately toppled the governorship, and its own dynasty was established, a line descending from Muhammad's uncle and accepted by the Shi'ites, since their line of succession from Ali had died out. In the Abbaside dynasty, the caliphate became hereditary. The Abbasides shifted their attention from North Africa and Europe to Central Asia and Persia. But rather than being rewarded, the Shi'ites, who had contributed to the rise of the Abbasides, were driven back.

Harun al-Rashid, whom we meet in the *Arabian Nights,* was the most splendid of the Abbaside *caliphs.* He kept a court of barbaric and sybaritic splendor, a wonderful imitation of the wonders of Byzantium, at Baghdad, which had been founded on the edges of the glorious, now ruined old capitals of Mesopotamia and Persia, Babylon and Ctesiphon. Baghdad grew rapidly and would soon reach half a million inhabitants, eclipsing Basra and Damascus in size and importance. This new Abbaside capital was polyglot, multiracial, and multireligious. It copied lifestyles from Byzantium and the Persian Sassanian Empire. If the austere nomadic Muslims had not learned sophistication before, they certainly did now. The traditional wellborn Muslim woman had been able to negotiate the terms of her marriage. Harun al-Rashid copied the practice of Persian Sassanian nobility by purchasing numerous well-trained slave women as concubines, along with eunuchs to guard them. Other members of the ruling elite and some wealthy merchants followed his example.

Eunuchs, who in ancient times were castrated for purely religious purposes, had under Persian rule been transformed into guards or household employ, due to the emotionless neutrality ascribed to them. While the Qu'ran explicitly forbade castration, the custom continued. The prerequisites were only that the castrates be nonbelievers and that the demasculinization take place far from any holy ground. But Muslim men would adopt another Persian custom: taking young male *ghulam,* or uncastrated, slaves into their households, for sexual purposes. This custom was not forbidden by the Qu'ran, as Muhammad probably never imagined the possibility.

Harun al-Rashid's first wife, Zubayda, would become more influential than any other Muslim woman for several centuries. She left an eternal mark on fashion and Muslim women's taste, but even she could not prevent the growth of harems, which weakened the position of all Muslim wives, although they never lost their right to inheritance and independent economic enterprise. One must understand that Muslims outside the old Arab territories were converts from other religions, in particular Christianity, Judaism, Manichaeism, and Zoroastrianism. The converts understood Islam in terms of assumptions from those heritages. Though the trade in slaves for private sexual use diminished women's authority, Islam nevertheless continued to limit institutionalized prostitution wherever it gained influence.

Harun al-Rashid's times gave rise to a much greater variety of literature that supplements the Qu'ran, for anyone eager to find out how Islamic men actually lived their sexual lives. The Qu'ran itself started the revolution of Arab literature, creating new forms that were better fit for the new sophisticated, elegant, and urban Muslims. The traditional *quassida*, a panegyric poem to a successful warrior, began to die out. Among the poetic forms of a more settled and sedentary life was the *ghazal*. Although abstinence is considered abnormal for a man, it put its mark on some elegiac love poems addressed to Muslim women, who become almost divine, since they were inaccessible for the poet. But with instruments and music as metaphors, the male organs were nevertheless able to create an ecstatic love fantasy.

The *khamnyia* gave more direct reference to the actual love life of the Abbaside Muslims. These down-to-earth Bacchanalian verses praised the joys of wine and the lovemaking that could be realized almost on the spot, as with slaves in the neighborhood. In the poems, the women might be camouflaged as grazing gazelles that the poet knew exactly how to hunt for. Slave girls belonged to the female section of the household and were not easily accessible. A wife might choose to regard such a small side step in a serious light, consider it *zina*, and demand divorce. Access to a slave girl in another man's household required several go-betweens who all had to be so well paid that the hunt became an expensive endeavor. But beautiful slave boys walked around freely, easily available for a small sum of money, right on the spot. In spite of their slave status, these young men could use their bodies to make money for themselves. In this slightly exceptional form, prostitution flourished in the corners of many a Muslim household, as described by the most famous poet of the time, Abu-Nuwas:

> *A clever young lewdster made his rivals amaze.*
> *He swam in abundance, having been poor all his days.*
> *"Why," I asked, "do you stare with that skeptical squint,*
> *Since he holds a veritable royal mint*
> *Hidden in his baggy britches,*
> *The source of his well-earned riches?"*

Although some believers hoped that Islam would conquer the world, the Muslims had to interact with nonbelievers in many different ways. On long journeys, almost all Muslim merchants had sex, and there again they preferred women to boys. Sex far from home with nonbelievers was certainly not adultery, since it couldn't be seen as offending another male Muslim. Muslim merchants in Africa or Southeast Asia would accept a female companion for the night as a token of hospitality from their trading partner.

In the Mediterranean, and along the trading routes through India to China, prostitution flourished. A good believer should, however, not stay away from home too long. If his journey lasted over six months, he had done injustice to his wife or wives by not giving them the sexual pleasure they were legally entitled to.

The Islamic armies provide other proof that prostitution was in serious retreat where Islam flourished. Allah's soldiers were powerful and victorious. Those who died would get their heavenly rewards; the survivors needed worldly satisfaction. But although a Muslim male witness was required for punishment of a male rapist, it was considered an evil act, even toward the enemy's women. Thus rape was not common, nor did prostitute quarters grow up around Islamic garrisons; nor was an advancing army followed by a female "army" of prostitutes, as was the case with armies to the west and the east. Islamic soldiers were supposed to get their pleasure from consenting women and would normally take a second local wife, independent of her belief. Even if the marriage was considered short-term or the woman was a concubine, both Muslim army leaders and soldiers still felt responsible for the women and their offspring, not least in questions of faith.

Thus it was that Islam's surprisingly quick and successful expansion was due to success in both war—and love.

TEN

GUILDS AND CLOISTERS,
ROGUES AND RAPISTS

On altar cloths in medieval Europe, the Holy Family was dressed as local townsfolk or peasantry, bowing in penitence. Cities and villages were crammed with symbolic representations of the family as the founding pillar of society. But to a growing degree, these values would end up in conflict. Beginning in the 1300s and for the next 150 years, popular literature poked fun at the Church's values. Love stories from the 1400s never end with marriage and wedding bells but with successful sexual penetration. The literature gives the impression that all wives were unfaithful, that most men were cuckolded, and that young monks thought of nothing but sex. "Marriage is a trap" was a common expression. The late Middle Ages have been called a time without morals.

This characterization is apt, for prostitution now enjoyed better conditions and was of greater extent than both before and after. *Prostibula publica,* or public whorehouses, existed from Naples to London, Nuremberg, and Leipzig. The French words *borde, bordieau,* and *bordelet* corresponded to the Italian *bordello* and were derived from the Saxon *borda,* meaning "little house"; the English *brothel,* however, is derived from the word for *wrecked* or *wasted.* Everyday male language was full of euphemisms like *the cloister, the woman's house, Auntie's residence, the rose garden, the pighouse,* or *the prison.* The parallel between cloister and brothel, nuns and prostitutes, soon developed into an archetype. The reasons were obvious: The cloistered communities were the only living arrangement known outside the family.

The Germanic terms *hore/hure/whore* and *whoredom* are well known from ecclesiastical legislation and theology, but they had no clear direct reference to paid sex. On the contrary, they referred to all kinds of extramarital sex, independent of whether one earned money from it. A whore normally would be not a prostitute but a loose woman. The Scandinavian *frille* was almost devoid of negative connotations, somewhat like a live-in partner of today. Many city women lived in permanent unmarried relationships because they could not afford to marry; because the Church, due to the partners' genealogical proximity, did not sanction their relationship; or because the woman's breadwinner was a priest, monk, or out-of-town merchant.

Everybody in the medieval world knew the difference between a married woman, a mistress, a whore, and an actual prostitute. A professional female sex worker was described in Latin as *meretrix;* in Italy as *puta* or *puttana; garce, ribaud, fille joyeuse,* or *fillette* in France; *strumpet* or *harlot* in England; while most Germans would call her *dirne.* Farther north, *puta, portkone, and skjøge* were in use, but many preferred prettier designations, like *nuns* and *novices.*

Before the 1200s, the sale of sex had been rare as far north as Scandinavia because serfdom was widespread, and peasants and heathen chiefs could avail themselves of female serfs when they desired sexual variation. They regularly accepted their offspring as heirs. Trade and Christianity, however, turned the wild Vikings into civilized Europeans, and during the late 1200s, the few Nordic cities had grown enough to support women who sold sex. Large well-run establishments never came into existence in Scandinavia, and prostitution remained more informally organized, but the growing sex industry might be taken as proof that Scandinavia had become a part of Western civilization.

Dijon, in Burgundy's northern Rhône Valley, and Bergen, on Norway's western coast, are among the medieval cities where prostitution has been studied in great detail. In 1485, Dijon housed eighteen small whorehouses, each with two or three girls, all run by widows or the wives of craftsmen. In addition, there were two large bordellos, plus a public bath with professional management. Altogether, there were a hundred professional prostitutes. Bergen was half as populous, with only eight thousand inhabitants, but it had just as many prostitutes. Both the large contingent of unmarried men in the Hanseatic League's trading enclave, on the waterfront, and the concentration of churches and monasteries provided a solid group of clients. A tax register from 1521 shows that 150 unmarried women lived in Bergen independent of their families. A third of them were mistresses or lovers of the clerics or merchants, while about a hundred probably were regular prostitutes. That Dijon did not have more sex workers than Bergen was due not to different morals but to demography and geography. Central Europe was full of towns and cities. There were girls for sale both in the towns and along the main highways. In the sparsely populated north, there was hardly any sex for sale outside of the five major cities. Consequently, those women who set themselves up in business had the whole region as their market.

Two thirds of the prostitutes in Dijon were born within the district, daughters or widows of poor craftsmen. Many came into the trade at sixteen or seventeen, quite often after a form of abduction or rape. Bergen was smaller but more international, and it provided visitors with girls from every outpost of the north. In the cosmopolitan Florence, two thirds of the prostitutes were born in Germany or the Netherlands. The biggest city of the time, Paris, had a larger and more international sex industry than any other place in the Western world.

> *Agh, once was I so young and brisk*
> *and fair as a day in spring.*
> *I lured both cleric and the priest . . .*
> *till their purses didn't hold a thing.*

Such were the mutterings of an aging woman of pleasure from the circles of the notorious poet and provocateur François Villon in Paris of the mid-1400s.

Bologna and Venice had distinctly designated whoring districts as early as the 1260s. In England, official supervision of prostitution was under way just as early, but the development toward more public supervision and interference in the sex trade moved in fits and starts; the prince or the city council governing during a period might want increased supervision, then their successors might pay considerably less attention to the issue. But when the Great Council of Venice ratified a decree in 1358 that declared prostitution "absolutely indispensable to the world," this was a definite sign of the times. Most of central Europe had by then undertaken official registration and supervisory inspections. In France, official prostitution was most developed in the south and along the Rhône Valley, but by the 1300s, it had spread north toward Flanders and east to the cities of southern Germany. By the 1400s, organized bordello prostitution was predominant over half of Europe. Even in the smaller towns of Europe's southern and western regions, one could usually find a tiny whorehouse with five to ten women, and in the cities, all the larger prostitution establishments were located in separate red-light districts.

The majority of medieval cities had public baths, too, which were beneficial in terms of hygiene. In addition, the baths offered small rooms without bathtubs, because visits to the baths were not made only for of washing. The largest baths contained rooms for social gatherings and a kitchen serving pâtés and wines. By paying a little extra, a man could obtain a single room and the company of a young woman, an employee of the bath, or he could bring along a woman who had caught his eye. A seemingly virtuous wife from the neighborhood would officially go to the baths to do her ablutions, but she might as easily embark on a little bout of lovemaking in an intimate cubicle with her lover.

One first paid the bath owner a fee for entry, then to the bath wife a sum that depended upon how much help one had been given to wash, groom, and shave, and how much beer one had consumed. One paid the bath wife for any sexual services rendered as well. In Bergen, the first bathhouse was built on royal ground in the 1230s. In England, Germany, and farther north, there were more baths than brothels. In London, they were called *stews* and had names like the Stag, the Clique, and the Swan.

Down through the ages, the sale of sex had been primarily a women's business. In the bordellos, the baths, and the whorehouses, older women were usually responsible for the supervision of day-to-day affairs and would be called the *madam,* or *maquerelle* in French, but in most languages, the euphemism *the abbess* would be understood immediately. Like all convents, they were ultimately under papal jurisdiction, since prostitution now fell under the aegis of an official civil servant, called in French *le roi de ribaudes,* or *rex ribaudorum,* the king of knaves and rascals. In addition to overseeing prostitution, this official arrested and whipped rapists, thieves, and madmen and was frequently the chief executioner. Between 1214 and 1449, the royal palace in Paris also had such an official on its staff. But his line of work was so noble a public posting that it deserved a different job description. He had exclusive control over the royal court's prostitutes, the fine selection of beauties who were at the disposal of the king and his courtiers, their guests and retainers.

Late medieval religious literature indicates only two roads out of prostitution. The unlucky sinner could either be saved by entering a monastic order or, in the ideal case, be rescued directly to heaven—quite often by the Virgin Mary herself. Christian canon laws implied that it was impossible for a prostitute to marry and settle down with a family, but they never explicitly forbade it; English civil laws prohibited prostitutes from marrying, but no other country had corresponding statutes. In the real world, however, many prostitutes had husbands or lived out of wedlock with the father of their children. In Paris, Dijon, and Lyon, a third of the prostitutes were legally married, and among the unmarried, a good many had live-in partners who might earn their daily bread by pimping, or recruiting clients for the houses where their girlfriends worked, to which they themselves were attached.

François Villon, writer, brawler, and whoremonger of the 1400s, was the permanent partner of a prostitute and at times a procurer. In 1455, Villon gave his girlfriend and her other men a poetical tribute, "La Ballade de la Grande-Margot." The subject of this lyric is a vivacious prostitute with such joie de vivre that later historians have been able to identify her from a series of court cases of that time. We can catch a glimpse of both his tenderness toward Margot and his dispassionately healthy good sense:

> *Because I'm sheltered by a whoring bitch*
> *Am I surely not a scoundrel or a swine?*
> *She has a mass of clients from the rich.*
> *At doing what men like, she is just fine.*
> *When guests approach, I fly to fetch the wine*
> *and on the table put the cheese and fruit da nova,*
> *And the bed, too, of course gets handed over.*
> *If he be beneficent and his purse is strong,*
> *then I say, Stay the night, Ol' Rover,*
> *in this brothel where we all belong.*

Villon spent his life in a Paris with one hundred thousand inhabitants. Contemporary observers estimated that between five and six thousand women lived off the fruits of prostitution. The Federation of Parisian Harlots, the city's guild for whores, reported four thousand members when in 1474 it received an official gift from Louis IX. When we add those who were not guild members, we have grounds to believe that every fourth woman in her twenties prostituted herself in the Paris of the 1400s. The cause of this was the enormous disproportion between the sexes in that great city. Paris was packed with students and soldiers, priests and monks, courtiers and clerks in service to the state, most of them young men not yet in a position to marry. Many moved to the provinces when they reached the age of thirty and were able to marry, but as long as they were young and single, they constituted the customer base for Paris's prostitution.

In 1400 the French sex workers' guild mounted an action against a girl who was behaving in a way that they felt damaged their professional ethics. She "kept" a young man who, in the opinion of the guild, did not reciprocate sufficiently. It was quite all right if a woman prostitute confined herself to a permanent client and became his mistress, but the reverse did not wash. A man living with a prostitute needed either his own job or one at the bordello. But this particular, very handsome, and extremely lazy youngster refused either solution and subsequently had to desert his love, the guild of prostitutes, and Paris.

Villon's lady love, Fat Margot, competed for customers in Paris with M the Idol, Floria-from-the-Bush, Isabelle who was always saying "Yes, by Christ," Aliz-from-Berne, Big Jeanne from Brittany, and Marion la Peautarde. In Bergen, too, they had good pungent nicknames for the older women in the trade. Maggie-Five-Finger-Ass lodged in the Rector's Cellar, while Anne-the-Fresh-Offering lived nearby. Katrin-the-Snake, Kristina-Noisy-Fart, and Snow White Marina seem to have shared both a house and clients; just down the road lived Big Ragnhild, Danish Karin, and Citzele Thunder. Some of the other Bergen women of stamina were called Magga Ass, Karina Flourstick, and Christina Pig-Rye.

In southern Europe, loose women could travel far and wide and sell their bodies along the highways, indeed, high up in the valleys and deep within the thinly populated forest regions. Such traffic was difficult without the benefit of male company. But a woman who could not support a man full-time could arrange for protection from a beggar or a vagabond. Itinerant prostitutes could, if they were tired, sick, or undernourished, seek out temporary accommodation at a nunnery. It was a Christian duty to open the gates to lone female travelers. The thinking was that needy souls should be taken care of in the cloistered community, and there given strength of faith and morality. But most of them went back out to work when they had satisfied their hunger or regained their health.

In the 1480s, Pope Sixtus IV undertook a census of the Roman population and came up with seven thousand prostitutes out of a population of seventy thousand. There were fewer women in Rome than in Paris, but more prostitutes. It is possible that the Roman count did not distinguish between permanent lovers of the clergy and women who required many men to earn an income. There is, however, no room for doubt that prostitution was booming in Rome. Following a visit to the papal city, Bishop Robert Grosseteste, one of the most talented statesmen of King Henry III of England, reported: "But just as the wealth of the entire world would be insufficient to satisfy the greed of Rome, so too would all the world's prostitutes be unable to satisfy the lusts of Rome."

Antonius Panormita, who wrote under the pen name Becadelli, composed the poem "Hermaphroditus" in the 1490s in tribute to Cosimo de Medici; in it, he described what in his time were considered the obscenities of the Florentine bordellos: nudity, dancing, and masturbation. More advanced sexual arts or acrobatic numbers were never notable in Europe's brothels until the sixteenth and seventeenth centuries, and even then only among the best-paid prostitutes of Venice and Paris.

Measured against modern times, medieval brothel sex was extremely traditional. For its own time, it was also unusually clean. "Before intercourse, a woman should clean her inner organs with a finger wrapped in wool, and dry herself inside and out with a completely clean piece of cloth, and then spread her legs as widely as possible so that all the moisture runs away. Thereupon she should dry herself once more, and dab her sex organ with powder and rose water. She is now ready to approach the client." Those who knew the rules drawn up by Trotuta of Salerno were aware of how to prepare themselves for a client. Most of the brothel madams across

Europe in the late Middle Ages transmitted the knowledge to the girls in their service.

A local abbess or madam had many things to do. She had to recruit—but not young runaway nuns or girls under the age of thirteen or fourteen—she had to give a certain amount of instruction on hygiene, and she had to make the clients aware of several dominant rules, for instance small brothels welcomed many clients, but never two who were related. The madam also had to report to the local authorities anything she learned from her girls about the out-of-town clients.

In theory, no girl should enter into relations with men from her home area, or with boys under the age of sixteen. Jews and Muslims, of course, could not be allowed to sleep with Christian prostitutes; the girls had clear instructions to withdraw if they discovered a circumcised client. The madam also made sure that the girls did not allow anal sex or intense kissing though it was very unusual for anyone to offer her body in any way but the most orthodox. Oral sex was considered unclean, and anal sex was a great sin. The preferred position in all brothels was vaginal penetration, with the woman lying on her back and the man on top. The doctrine of the Church Fathers decreed that this was the only position acceptable to God, whether in the whorehouse or the marriage bed. The local abbess made sure that the rules were followed. Due to regular complaints from the neighbors, we have a rich body of litigation material that testifies to what went on. It was extremely seldom that they told about anything worse than naked bodies and sex standing up.

Right from the 1300s, it was commonly forbidden either to visit a house of prostitution or to take a bath during Lent or on the religious high holidays. During that century, there were regular negotiations between bordello owners and the authorities concerning opening and closing hours, and rental adjustments on the establishments during the ascetic season of Lent, but this was only a remnant of times that had a greater respect for the Church calendar. By the 1400s, it was only at Christmas and during Easter week that people refrained from visiting the bordellos and the girls got a holiday.

In his "Ballad of Good Doctrine," the witty François Villon gives a brilliant account of how easy it was for a man to waste everything he had on a strumpet:

Now whether you peddle indulgences,
or learn to use loaded dice,
or counterfeit coins and get burned
like those traitors without any faith
who are boiled in hot oil, or if
you're a crook who's always out filching,
where goes the money you make?
All to the girls and the taverns.

If you rhyme, jest, play cymbals or lute
like a foolish and shameless impostor,
or if you're a mummer, magician, or flutist,
or if in the towns and the cities
you do farces, plays, or moralities, or if
you're a winner at dice, at cards, or at ninepins,
it soon is all gone (do you hear?)
all to the girls and the taverns.

Neither the Church nor the civil authorities of the late Middle Ages saw any great injury to morality when young lads had sex with prostitutes. All over Europe, the majority of clients were local lads, merchants, students, or soldiers. But approximately every fifth client was a cleric. Whoring was of course considered a worse sin for a priest or a monk than for a soldier. Only one out of ten clients seems to have been from out of town. Many clients were married, even though in the eyes of the Church, their sin was greater than for either the young and unmarried or the celibate clerics.

Attention to such moral breaches and the Church's ability to levy fines on unlawful clients varied considerably. In 1403, in Florence, men over the age of thirty were forbidden to visit any brothel, and each had to undertake a moral pledge. The idea was that by refusing men over thirty admission to paid sex, sexual need would force more of them into holy matrimony.

Medieval homosexuality was conducted much more discreetly but was combated much more intensively. During the 1400s, it seemed to spread in both sacred and secular circles, so some prominent Church authorities intensified their struggle against it. Bernhard of Siena and

Girolamo Savonarola conducted separate campaigns against homosexual practices. In 1460, in Venice, a council was established precisely to fight this evil: the Collegium Sodomitorum. The literature of the day alludes to the occasional young man who sold sex in or near the brothels. Normally, these few were younger brothers or sons of madams or second-generation prostitutes. But no official documents or registries refer to male prostitution during the late Middle Ages. The fact that male prostitution was never regulated or taxed points to more than moral taboo. It clearly also indicates that the enterprise never reached very great proportions, at least not from the economic perspective.

Female prostitutes, on the other hand, never needed to hide in the late Middle Ages. Everyone could see who they were, and everyone knew where they lived, just as one knew the goldsmith, the cooper, and the shoemaker. Indeed, harlots were organized in guilds, exactly as craftsmen were; they also wore characteristic clothing and lived on specific streets, which can be seen in street names. Many cities had a Women's Street, a Rose Alley, or a Maria Hill. Berlin's Rosenstrasse led down to the River Spree; the bridge there was called Jungfraubrücke, or Maiden Bridge. Many prostitution streets went under the name Well Street, for it was here that a man came to drink from the well of love. One might not speak of Whore Street or Vagabond Path, but there were places like Lift-the-Skirt Alley and Flesh Parade.

Literary masterpieces from the late Middle Ages, such as *The Decameron* and *Canterbury Tales,* and popular narratives and fables reveal a world in which husbands were cheated and deceived by lusty young wives with lovesick students and monks, and where prostitutes were standard figures, well-integrated participants in the ceremonial and everyday city life, while their offspring were cared for by godfathers and godmothers. The real world was not too different. The guild-organized, cake-baking, generally well-received harlots were the characteristic norm, but many prostitutes' lives of the period were painful and dangerous, a fact rarely alluded to in fiction.

An Avignon city ordinance of 1441 stressed that an officially registered prostitute was duty-bound to buy any goods that she had fingered in the market. This might indicate that some of the girls were threatened, almost like lepers. But such laws are easy to misunderstand. Normally, they were holdovers from stronger ordinances from the early Middle Ages, and they were, as the centuries passed, more and more rarely enforced. Sauvignon's proper and well-run guild of harlots participated with banners and drums during all processions or festivals and would have protested if this law were put into practice.

In Paris, the court's prostitute elite presented flowers to the king on Saint Valentine's Day. Mary Magdalene's saint's day in July was another natural day of celebration. It is more tricky to explain why Ascension Day was the holy day when prostitutes participated most visibly. All over France, the prostitutes prepared batter for cakes that the city council distributed to the poor. In Nîmes and Nantes, the bathhouse owners—encircled by near - naked female attendants from the baths—received a large sum of money from the mayor. At least half of France celebrated Ascension Day as a festival marked by trumpet salutes, cities decorated with floral garlands, and lightly clad whores reveling in the streets.

By the late Middle Ages, dress codes were being enforced, seemingly with full consent from the prostitutes' guilds. "The commonest Women and Harlots should bear upon their Heads a Cap half red, half black, no Garments better than for an Adventuress, and no Linen better than the Drapery on a Shilling," was the regulation laid down by King Hans of Denmark-Norway in 1496. In Vienna the prostitutes were told to wear yellow scarves, in Leipzig, yellow capes with blue lining. In Milan they commonly wore black capes, in Berne and Zurich red toques, and in Florence bells on their caps and gloves. The widespread scarlet cord symbolized the rope that the Bible's Rahab had used to help Joshua and his men. But in Toulouse the cord was white, and in Dijon and Avignon all women prostitutes wore a circular white mark. Other cities demanded prostitutes walk around bareheaded, however cold and rainy the day.

But wherever statutes of a city forbade prostitutes to wear precious textiles, exotic leather belts, or fine silver belt buckles, there would be a great many prostitutes who dressed however they pleased. In big cities like Paris and Venice, the rich prostitutes became more and more noticeable every decade, sometimes wearing more gorgeous gowns and more expensive jewelry than their sisters from the aristocracy. The official civil servants certainly confiscated some clothing, furs, or jewels and made a tidy profit reselling them. The wise prostitute spent her time more profitably by getting a new client and a new dress than by protesting.

Contemporary female athletes probably don't know what tradition their Western predecessors belonged to: Whores were the first sportswomen of medieval Europe. They took part in various sporting competitions during city festivals, like running and ball games , and performed kicks, leaps, and cartwheels that no woman of virtue could allow herself so much as to contemplate. On special occasions they might perform clad as the original Eve in the Garden of Eden, which would be good publicity for many girls to show off their bodies in this way. The public did not complain. When the events were over, the prostitutes dealt out prizes, frequently in symbolic colors associated with the prostitution guild of their hometown.

A strange mixture of guild and cloister mentality marked the image of the sex workers of the late Middle Ages. The girls underwent ceremonies and rituals of initiation in their "nunneries"; they ate together daily and shared expenses democratically, particularly the weekly sum they had to pay the night watch of the district, who did his best to offer them protection.

But if the commoners were normally tolerant toward prostitution and prostitutes, the mood could change rapidly in times of crisis. A collective pressure to clean up might set in after a poor harvest, or if the death rate suddenly rose, or if a high-ranking Church official announced an official visit. In one second, people could retreat from a good set of measures toward prostitutes and start a riot. The harlots might be seen with entirely different eyes, going from whores with hearts of gold to scapegoats for all misfortune.

Gang rape was a common phenomenon in the late Middle Ages. Any woman traveling the streets alone at unorthodox times or in unusual places was in danger of being raped. The attackers signaled their approach by shouting "whore," which legalized the deed.

Historians studing Dijon and Venice of the 1400s and 1500s have found hundreds of such rapes every year. Everything indicates that these cities were representative of general conditions. Only on very rare occasions were the gangs of young men punished. Many rapes were never reported, so the phenomenon was probably much more extensive than the figures indicate.

Such attacks on women prostitutes were simultaniously a way of securing unpaid sex and a common form of initiation. Young lads developed sporting instincts and a sense of team spirit, and they could congratulate themselves for defending public morality. The gangs usually consisted of five or six male youths—in exceptional circumstances as many as fifteen—from around eighteen to twenty, under a leader who was seldom over twenty-five. It is an indication of the weakening morality of the Church that these gangs called themselves monastic brotherhoods, even referring to their leader as the prince, king, or abbot. The gangs acted openly; the city councils knew exactly what was going on, and the younger council members were frequently members of a gang. If a member of such a group were to get married, his circle of friends carried out rites of a more innocent type, that is, without rape; on such occasions they might let loose on a donkey. Normally, a young man would leave the gang the day he married. But exceptions did occur, particularly if a newly married man had had a central position in his group; then he could allow himself to continue with the game until he was thirty.

The gang rapes of the 1400s and 1500s have been analyzed as an expression of turbulent times, but also as liberation from the authority of the Church. Some have indicated influence from the Franciscan order, which was known to be particularly liberal on all questions of male sexuality.

Medieval prostitutes were popular and generally well protected, but they were devoid of any judicial/legal rights; they could neither inherit property nor stand as witnesses in court, so it was complicated to accuse men of violence. Having sex with a prostitute against her will was considered almost legal, according to the statutes of civil and Church authorities, and it was not really a criminal act to rape or gang-rape a prostitute. To rape an innocent girl might be regrettable, unless one had reason to believe she had behaved like a whore. It was the duty of fathers to protect their daughters, and husbands their wives. Maidens had to defend their virtue; they could go about only in daylight with any degree of security, and then only with a chaperone. A pretty woman who dressed in a forward manner and went about sans escort was deemed guilty if she happened to be raped. This scared girls into virtuous attire and home-based domestic activity. Rape functioned as a disincentive to unruly women and a general form of oppression of actual prostitutes; in the corridors of power, it was tolerated, indeed encouraged.

The horny young men, according to the thinking of the time, found biblical legitimation in Genesis. When Jacob's daughter Dina was raped, it brought shame to her father and brothers, so they took gruesome revenge on the culprit and his family.

In the canonical registry of sins, rape was only a subsidiary form of whoredom, admittedly more violent in form, but viewed as no worse a sin. And there was much in Church doctrine that legitimized the activity;

Thomas Aquinas gave this opinion: "A victim of violent seduction will, if she does not marry her seducer, find it difficult to marry. Thus it is that she can easily be led into those debaucheries against which, until then, only her virtue has defended her."

In very exceptional circumstances, young girls were on hand at ritual rapes during the early 1500s. Such a girl was not touched so long as she was part of the moral fellowship in her capacity as future wife to an older member of the gang, or even the abbot. Some few women dared to protest the gang rapes. Marguerite Chasserat from Lyon used harsh words about the practice, which now seem strikingly ahead of her times:

> We innocent women are always being hunted by men who believe they have a right to everything in the world, and that they themselves stand above the law, while at the same time not owing us anything. Without ado they allow themselves to destroy with the baseness of the vagabond. We can ... be indicted for infidelity if we are so much as out of the man's line of vision for a minute. We are certainly not wives and comrades, but rather prisoners captured from an enemy. On the street corner and at the tavern and immoral places that I could never give name to, men throw themselves at us women, tear us to pieces, curse us and accuse us of everything possible, and demand things of us that they themselves would never dream of offering.

The "finest" sex sport was the gang rape of the lover of an unpopular priest. By taking her, they punished a whore and revenged themselves on the priest. Not even the lovers of bishops could avoid meeting such treatment. And if ecclesiastical circles wanted to punish the gang of rapists openly, it was such an intricate process that the clerical plaintiffs were almost always the greater losers.

Any woman with a cleric as a lover would know that she led a risky life, so most of them avoided the dangers of the dark. Young, inexperienced girls did not have such good instincts. When they became victims of the boys' gangs, the damage was usually irremediable, and the road to the brothels swift. Support within the girl's family and neighborhood was rare. Any girl who was raped had behaved as a temptress. Obviously, she was a bad girl, and her rape brought shame to her family. As most such misdeeds were accepted, the vicious circle sprang into being like a self-fulfilling prophecy. This had to be God's will. The rape was proof that she was a whore. Ergo, she had no choice other than to became one by profession.

Above left, a kadesh or biblical harlot, intended to look historically correct, in a late-nineteenth-century German Bible illustration (Archiv für Kunst und Geschichte, Berlin). Right, Egyptian prostitute and client. Papyrus, ca. 1500 B.C. (British Museum, London).

A sex demon pays a nocturnal visit to a terror-stricken Christian. During the medieval times a sex demon in female form would be called a liloth (after the fallen angel Lilith) or a succubus, while a male demon was an incubus. Demons that misled men—the moral sex—were considered the most dangerous (Mary Evans Picture Library).

Above, a Greek ceramic drinking vessel decorated with a mature athletic man who is about to beat a prostitute. A younger man is rushing to help the woman (Staatliches Museum, Berlin). The cane in the picture might be considered a weapon, but could also indicate that the young man is a little lame. At right, an Indian drawing from the 1700s. The god Krishna was the special protector of prostitutes. Here Krishna (in tree) observes a group of gopi, or shepherdesses, who were said to always disrobe at the very sound of his flute (Werner Forman Archive). In spite of the significant influence the great Mughal emperor in Delhi, who was a Muslim, had on Indian culture at this time, the style of the drawing is noticeably Hindu.

Above, a bordello sign from Pompeii reading TO THE SISTERS. The madam is looking after her girls. Three Roman goddesses were associated with prostitution:
Venus, Flora, and Pheronia (Staatliches Museum, Berlin). Below, a man purchased
tokens like these at Rome's major brothels and gave them away to the one or many
who awakened his taste (Bibliothèque Nationale, Paris).

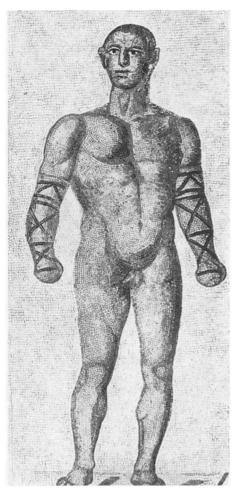

Sex work and athletics were linked in imperial Rome. Those who wanted a beefier specimen than the men in Rome's bordellos hired their pleasure at a gladiator school instead. Martial wrote that male and a few female customers competed for the best gladiators. Female prostitutes were the only Roman women who regularly practiced sports. The gladiator at left can still be admired in Caracalla's thermal baths in Rome (Scala/Terme de Caracalla, Rome), while the female sex worker in the Sicily mosaic at right works out with barbells (Scala/Piazza Armerina, Sicily).

✦ Le Chastel d'Amours ✦

faulx semblant ·· Malebouche ··

Above, "Storming the Fortress of Love," an illustration from the manuscript "Champion de Dames," a contribution to the women's debate of the 1400s (Mary Evans Picture Library). Right, a brothel scene from "The Shepherd's Calendar," 1503. A prostitute is in the bath with a client as a second plays the lute. Venus, the goddess of love, has a symbolic pedagogical function in the picture (Archiv für Kunst und Geschichte, Berlin).

Above, a Chinese drawing from the 1600s. The young girl points her bound feet toward the man's genitals. He is easily identified as either a student or one who has recently achieved mandarin status. Intramarital sex was never depicted or poeticized in China, so this girl is likely either a luxury prostitute or a mistress or second wife (Werner Forman Archive). Below, a love encounter between a young samurai and a Tayu whore in the prostitution district of Yoshiwara, 1600s (Bridgeman Art Library).

Agostino Caracchi made a number of erotic drawings; a series from 1602 titled "Heavenly Love" were a particular high point in his work and erotic art in general (Galleria dell'Accademia, Venice).

Above, notorious royal mistress Nell Gwynn. In the 1600s women of high social rank often posed for famous painters, as long as they were exhibited as mythical archetypes. It was Nell Gwynn who broke this tradition by appearing as herself, for example, in Sir Peter Lely's painting from 1680 (Dennys Eyre/Bouwer Bequest, Chiddingstone Castle). Below, a selection from "The Harlot's Progress," a series of etchings from the 1740s by William Hogarth. In the first scene a healthy country lass meets a painted and cynical madam and takes the first step on the road to ruin (British Museum, London).

E L E V E N

C E L E S T I A L   W H O R E S

No conceivable diplomatic seating arrangement could make for a more byzantine intrigue than the ranking of Christianity's elite in heaven. But the Florentine poet Dante Alighieri dared to take up such a task in his *Divina Commedia* early in the fourteenth century.

Here we are given the final judgment on popes and kings, poets and fictive figures from the Bible, the classical writers, philosophers, heathens, sinners, and libertines of antiquity, even friends and enemies of Dante. The writer played God and determined who was to end up where, from the depths of the inferno to the cooler spheres of purgatory and right up into the lofty heights of paradise. What courage!

For human beings, the Rose of Paradise is the highest sphere in the celestial world. Only God and the angels have it better, but they have been there for all eternity and do not need to seek entrance. Still, it must have been quite a struggle to enter the Rose of Paradise, where there is space for only the most noble of souls. Here the Virgin Mary is the hostess; as Queen of Heaven, she enjoys the highest ranking of all.

At Virgin Mary's table we find a considerable number of women. We also encounter Moses, the foremost prophets, and the elite among the Church Fathers, like Saint Augustine, Saint Benedict, and Saint Francis of Assisi. Anna, the Queen Mother, virginal like her daughter, the Virgin Mary, has an exalted seat on par with Saint Peter. Dante seated his heart's desire, the young Beatrice, with Saint Lucia of Syracuse and the most pious women from the Old Testament: Sarah, Rebecca, and Ruth.

As at any celebrated dinner party, there were many who did not receive invitations: Peter's wife; Anna's husband, Joachim, stepfather to the Virgin Mary, the carpenter Joseph. Among Mary's relatives, only John the Baptist and her nephews James and John were present, but they were, after all, numbers two and three in the flock of disciples. Though Mary's sister, their mother, was another central disciple, she and the other relatives of Jesus are deemed too insignificant. The patriarch Jacob is enthroned with his youngest wife, Rachel, but without Leah, his daughter Dina, or his slave wives Bilha and Silpa.

On the other hand, Eve has made her way back to paradise. Cleansed of original sin, she sits sharing intimacies with Mary. What is most noticeable is the absence of Mary Magdalene. This can have only one explanation: She was a woman with a past.

But there is more to paradise than just the Rose of Paradise. There seems to be room up there even for a Norwegian saint—Olav. But a Viking warrior must be given a less exalted ranking, in one of several simpler but perhaps more pleasant heavens, like the Venus Heaven. It is located in a deeper and darker cloud cover and represents, according to Dante, the eternal existence that people envisioned in the old heathen times.

Some might judge the Venus Heaven the most attractive place to spend eternity. There is a lot to indicate that Dante himself had a weakness for precisely this corner of the firmament. He placed a couple of the sensuous but deeply reflective contemporary moralists whom he admired—two male poets like himself, and, lo and behold, a noble Lombardian courtesan by the name of Cunizza. In the Venus Heaven, one also encounters the foremost harlot of the Old Testament, Rahab, who assisted Joshua in the Battle of Jericho with her long scarlet rope.

Mary Magdalene is not to be found in the Venus Heaven, either. Dante could not possibly send her to purgatory, since she was a saint. In Dante's *Divina Commedia,* the Bible's third most important woman has simply not been seated. Here lies the core of the problem.

Dante cannot have forgotten her. In his day, Mary Magdalene was worshiped as never before; she was the patron saint of guild-organized whores, raped women, hairdressers, perfume makers, glove makers, gardeners, wine dealers, and schoolchildren. A newly founded order of nuns had been dedicated to Mary Magdalene and other women sinners who wanted to do penance. The legend of her life had been canonized and was extremely popular. The painter Giotto, a contemporary of Dante in his hometown of Florence, gave pride of place to Mary Magdalene in his altarpieces and other paintings, as did painters throughout Europe. She frequently figured in passion plays that were performed in the street markets during religious holy days. In a small church in Paris that the prostitutes had built with their own means one could see the Egyptian Mary on the altarpiece, not in the role of the penitent hermit but with her skirts up. The words written in gold leaf under the painting read: "How the Holy Woman had to turn up her skirts to pay for her Journey."

Dante's exclusion of Mary Magdalene and all the other canonized prostitutes from heaven reveals the puritanism in this Florentine writer, who had scarcely any sexual experience and never even spoke to the young Beatrice whom he loved with infinite intensity. But this points to the core of the ambivalence that, during the Middle Ages, the Church held toward prostitution.

Mary Magdalene and her carnal sisters were useful to the Church's earthly goals. But in God's actual heaven, the matter was regarded more sternly; such women were not allowed to slip in, no matter how holy they had been declared.

"Prostitution in the cities is like the toilets of the palaces. Take them away and the palaces will be destroyed by the stench and putrefaction." Thomas Aquinas, the leading theologian of the thirteenth century—perhaps of the whole of the Middle Ages—felt that prostitution was associated with sewage. It was a necessary evil, but it gave off a stink. This double-tongued theological argument was firmly in the tradition of the Church Fathers, from Saint Augustine via Gratian and Ruffin and right into the late Middle Ages.

With the reform movement of popes Gregory VI and Gregory VII in the late eleventh century, the Church agitated for marriage as the only acceptable framework for sex, and undertook sexual abstinence in the priesthood. Celibacy, the ecclesiastical pet theme from Paul to Augustine, became more of a practiced policy than ever. The campaign certainly had a theological dimension but also sought to keep Church property in Church hands.

The result was as planned. The number of lovers and mistresses among the ordained was reduced, and fewer children of priests and monks entered the world. Above all, the Church increased its economic power and scared the priests out of giving away Church property. But celibacy had one effect that had not been anticipated. Priests and monks increasingly had sex with one another. Celibacy actually led to more sin against nature.

No matter how strongly one battled against carnal lust, some monks and priests—abbots and cardinals, too—could not resist sexual temptations. In such a context, prostitution was the least of the evils. Openly consorting with women had to be fought; a practicing prostitute could be excommunicated from the Church, and a whoremonger could be punished—mildly. Homosexual acts were worse than a visit to a prostitute, particularly for priests and monks, perhaps because such encounters between men of the cloth—or where such men tempted younger ones—might challenge the clerical hierarchy.

At the same time, theologians of the medieval period also conducted discussions about taxing the prostitution trade, reforming prostitutes, and producing theologically marketable defenses of men who contacted prostitutes. This had to do with making sure the clients of whores would not be considered great venal sinners; they worried a lot less about the prostitutes.

There were many reasons why Pope Innocent III issued a decree in 1198 declaring the high moral value of marrying a reformed prostitute. The decree represented an attempt at social rehabilitation of prostitutes, since the Church now gave its blessing to such marriages. At the same time, it legitimized personal association with loose women; men could now say that their interactions were for the purpose of bringing sinners back to the path of the righteous. The clerics could not admit to having a formal marriage, but they could insist that moral improvement was their goal.

The Church's double standard toward prostitution created the foundation for a new source of ecclesiastical income. In 1309, Bishop Johann of Strasbourg himself built a brothel. It yielded double profits: first from the sale of sex, and thereafter in fines levied upon the guilty. All the clergy in Strasbourg enjoyed the new and modern bordello—some openly, as clients, others in the course of their moral inspections—while the profits were shared.

Since olden times, Southwark has been a prostitution area on the south side of the Thames, across from the city of London. As a bishop, Saint Swithin of Winchester built a nunnery in Southwark, and later a whole district for whores. The supervision of prostitutes would be delegated to the secular authorities, but as before, the profits went to the diocese, and the whores from that district were known all over London as Winchester Geese. In 1161, Henry II decreed the revenue from the Southwark brothels to be a royal privilege awarded to the bishopric. This privilege stood for approximately five hundred years. As a consequence, London could have more churches built from the proceeds of prostitution than any other large European city, with the exception of Rome.

Thomas Aquinas spent many long hours reflecting upon when, and under what conditions, the Church could accept taxes or income from prostitution without becoming morally defiled. In his day, there were few men of the cloth who thought so deeply about these questions. The syphilitic Pope Sixtus IV reformed the taxation of Rome's whoring districts in 1471 and managed to increase Church revenues considerably. Thus it was that the whores of Rome contributed to the building of Saint Peter's Cathedral. There is always a bright and lucrative future for effective sin.

In the legends of late antiquity and the Middle Ages, and in passion plays where the main female character is a prostitute, the hero is always a man, and he always saves her for the faith and a good life on the path toward virtue. The archetype is the story of Jesus and Mary Magdalene.

Didactic literature of the Middle Ages was rich in respectable whoremongers with upright aims. The still-extant theology of the late Middle Ages said that one could, strictly speaking, undertake marriage to a prostitute only if she had left all sin behind.

Most of the men who wanted to marry a repentant prostitute had probably met her during her active working life. But a man who had relations with a woman still involved in the sex industry was, theologically speaking, considered a whoremaster or destroyer of marriages, even if he intended to marry her. Thus, fines had to be levied on him, even when he was contributing to her rehabilitation. Such theology had its positive side for the Church's coffers. Anyone who married a reformed prostitute had to be vigilant, lest she backslide into her old habits. The Church taught that women had a greater natural tendency to sin than men did; this was their genetic inheritance from Eve.

From the early Middle Ages onward, Western Europe's convents had a tradition of recruiting aristocratic women interested in learning and scholarship. Many convents had links to the Benedictines, but general knowledge was more central to the lives of the nuns than theology. The abbey of Gandersheim, in southern Germany, became an important center of women's learning in the tenth century. Beginning in the twelfth century, some nunneries began to recruit from the peasantry and common people. These women normally received a subordinate status as lay sisters and were assigned to practical and social functions. In the thirteenth century, the Catholic Church began to encourage the convents to recruit repentant prostitutes. In 1227 Gregory IX founded the Order of Saint Mary Magdalene, a practically oriented subsection of the otherwise very learned Dominicans. The newly converted ex-prostitutes were called White Sisters and always wore white to show that they could never wash themselves sufficiently clean of sin.

The White Sisters put their mark on the fourteenth century. They had the support of the pope, both politically and in the form of lavish gifts. At the same time, other orders of nuns started to accept reformed prostitutes, depending somewhat upon social status, theological orientation, and the local abbess's social priorities.

The character of Mary Magdalene appealed to the medieval world like never before, among both artists and the common people. At this point in history, it had nothing to do with a particular semantic interpretation of theology but rather with aesthetic conventions and social relations. The artists used motifs from the Bible and from antiquity when they thematized the problems of the day. Mary Magdalene was one of the best-known biblical characters, an archetypical figure with whom it was easy to identify. She was young and sensuous, fragile in the temptations of the flesh, but her soul was pious and good.

In paintings that portray Jesus being taken down from the cross, Giotto, his students, and many others portray Mary Magdalene as having stolen the spotlight away from the Virgin Mary, who more or less swoons at the side of the picture, where she is attended by her sister and the rest of the women. Mary Magdalene is right in the middle of the picture, embracing the deceased or kissing his tears. The whole biblical narrative around *noli me tangere,* in which the disembodied Savior and the flesh-and-blood Woman meet on Easter morning, became an extremely common motif of the Middle Ages.

Odo of Cluny's official version of the legend was much read, but other accounts and religious dramas about her also made their mark on four-teenth-century Europe. The Dominicans wrote many texts that steadily won greater numbers of readers; in addition, they had supervision over the White Sisters.

All of Christian Europe was familiar with Mary Magdalene's stay among the sick and the leprous, with her disputes with the Pharisees, her longing for Jesus, and her life of penitence out in the wilderness. The fact that her role always had something of the rebel to it can in part be attrib-uted to the popularity of the passion plays. In many of them, Mary Magdalene defended the common people, as indeed some outspoken har-lots have done at various points in history. Mary Magdalene was thus a spokeswoman for the people, such as she possibly had been within the ranks of the disciples.

As the Middle Ages slowly slipped into the Renaissance, Mary Magdalene became more and more sensual. In the Gothic period, she had always been clad in red and often wore a cowl, but as the years passed, more and more of her hair was revealed: It was always long and blond, and always the same hue that contemporary prostitutes used when coloring their hair. During the Renaissance, Mary Magdalene began to bare her bosom as well. This woman was repentant, but she looked sensuous and carnal, with her full white breasts and tear-glistening eyes, with her hair down and a jar of salve for all weary men.

During the Renaissance, Mary Magdalene was often painted with a book in her hands, partly because legend said she was a skillful pros-elytizer, but partly to underline the fact that many prostitutes were quick-witted and learned women. Among Mary Magdalene's other common symbolic attributes were the crown of thorns and the crucifix, which likened her distinctly to Jesus. Other Renaissance paintings show a ghostly head or a mirror indicating her vanity, while ball games, musical instruments, and many young suitors all attested to a frivolous life.

All major painters of the Renaissance and the Baroque periods bus-ied themselves with Mary Magdalene, although Rembrandt showed her only in a group picture. Botticelli, Vermeer, El Greco, and Hieronymus Bosch all painted her. She is found in woodcuts by both Lucas Cranach and Albrecht Dürer. Godefredus Batavus, who painted on commission for

François I of France in the 1500s, inspired a wave of Mary Magdalene paintings.

Pintoreccio, Titian, and Tintoretto portrayed Mary Magdalene, using the most beautiful courtesans of the day as their models. Vanozza dei Cattani and Giulia Farnese would, ironically enough, run directly from their artists' sittings to private meetings—both sexual and philosophical —with popes and cardinals. Antonio Correggio was the Italian painter who most often portrayed Mary Magdalene, but the Dutch painter Peter Paul Rubens, who studied under both Titian and Correggio, set the Magdalene record—he painted her alone and in sorrow, thoughtful in front of a mirror, in discussion with her big sister Martha, at the feet of Jesus, and with Martha in the background, in front of the grave of their brother Lazarus, or as a naked, penitent hermit far far out in the wilderness.

In a religious play of 1437 by Eustache Mercadé, Mary Magdalene introduced herself in a monologue:

> *I am available to everyone,*
> *to each and all, don't be afraid.*
> *Here is my body, I yield it*
> *to all who'd take their lust in or with it.*

This description of Mary Magdalene was quite traditional, if one ignores the fact that the speaker is not a prostitute, though she does go from man to man, full of hope that she will encounter that one great true love. In the course of her search, Mary Magdalene describes herself as a public woman.

Many theologians of the Middle Ages saw little value in distinguishing between women who took payment and women who merely went to bed with many. Promiscuity, sensuality, bad morals, and a need for money were all factors when one defined who was a public woman. From Gratian and on into the late Middle Ages, there was one theological line of argument that maintained, "The woman who is accessible to the lust of many men is a whore." Bartholomeus Brixiensis maintained that a harlot was "one who copulates indiscriminately—like the dogs." Individual theologians stated that any woman who did not blush at the very thought of sex was, in her heart, a harlot.

The more pragmatically oriented theologians quantified the line between the normally sinful nature of woman and a real harlot. The objective numerical standard that most ecclesiastics ended up with was forty: Any woman who had intercourse with more than forty men was a true harlot, no matter how she earned her daily bread.

In Eustache Mercadé's passion play and many contemporary paintings, Mary Magdalene was depicted as a liberated, spoiled upper-class woman. French painters in the sixteenth century would picture her out on a stag hunt with young cavaliers and a hunting falcon in hand, or in the middle of a dance, encircled by flutists and drummers. In one painting, Peter Paul Rubens furnished her with African slaves, and in his play, Mercadé gave her two ladies-in-waiting named Perusine and Pasifae, and portrayed her playing with her jewels while she admired herself in the mirror. Her sister Martha then rebuked her. The incident provides a psychological explanation for Mary Magdalene's whims and caprices. Mercadé thus let Martha explain to us that the siblings lost their father when her little sister was but a child. And without a father in the house, who can guide and bring up a carefree and lighthearted girl?

Eustache Mercadé's play is presented in aristocratic trappings, but his story line has a strong moral and a happy ending. This woman finds what she has been looking for, namely, she meets the most handsome of the world's gallant cavaliers, indeed, the best of all men. Who else but Jesus Christ?

"You will never come to hear other than reproaches. Any weak man will denounce you. Keep your distance from my lusty behavior. Do not take any risks on my behalf. My dear sister, look after yourself." Mary Magdalene spoke these words to Martha in another, slightly more recent passion play by Jehan Michel. She explained how she could feel in her body the whole world's condemnation of prostitutes. It was for this reason that the sisters had to break all contact, since a bad woman can pervert the most virtuous. In an older play by Arnould Grebán, Martha severed ties with her sister. As the variations in the portrayals of Mary Magdalene expanded, the degree of poetic license also had greater latitude. And many were just as influenced by the plays they saw on the streets and in the squares as by the homilies of the priests. Within the Catholic Church, they began to see a need for a major retouching of this woman's biography.

Olivier Maillard, a militantly moral bishop who castigated sinners not only in Nantes and Anjou but also in Brittany during the late fifteenth century, tried, through a long series of sermons, to create a new precedent in the portrayal of Mary Magdalene. Maillard was fond of recounting the story of a young woman who committed a mass of sins in her heart. He heavily underlined that Mary Magdalene was but a woman afflicted with sinful fantasies. From this angle, it became easier to create a space between her and the guild-organized prostitutes of Maillard's day. Maillard was actually striving to prevent the spread of practices that had arisen, namely that the guild-organized whores were actively taking part in public celebrations, year by year, in greater numbers.

Like Olivier Maillard, the moralizing sixteenth-century ecclesiastic Michel Menot would categorically state that "far too many sinful rumors circulated around the figure of Mary Magdalene." These rumors were obviously based on the fact that she was a mature woman who had moved around more freely in Palestine than other women dared to do in the time of Jesus.

Paralleling these revisionist pronouncements was a new and critical tradition to the Mary Magdalene literature. The Renaissance's great French humanist professor at the Sorbonne, Jacques Lefèvre d'Etaples—who called himself Father Stapulensis—published his text *De Maria Magdalena et triduo Christi desceptatio* in 1517. Lefèvre was a shrewd biblical interpreter and textual critic, something he had in common with both Luther and Erasmus. He became the first to demonstrate the ways the official portrait of Mary Magdalene had changed to serve the needs of the Church.

In Protestant countries, it was never common to identify Mary of Magdala with Mary of Bethania. But the two are reminiscent of one another. They were both prayer-house groupies with long wild hair and teary eyes: "A calm moment at the feet of Jesus. And exalted words from his own mouth. When Jesus and I are alone, ah, then it is indeed pleasant to be here."

There are not many who have given much thought to which Mary sang out in exultation on Easter morning, "Just think, even I who am the most insignificant of the nobodies, I too can sing out with joy." What was the basis for this "insignificance"? Perhaps it was the fate of all young women, both great and small, to be sinners. Hebbel's bourgeois drama of 1844, *Maria Magdalena,* set in contemporary times, was influenced by Gretchen from Goethe's *Faust,* so Hebbel's Mary became a naive, seduced, small-town girl who atoned for her sins by committing suicide.

Fifteen hundred years of papal theology, effectively promoted by painters and writers, had changed the picture of the Old Testament's second most important woman from love goddess and ex-prostitute to a girl with a teenager's longings for love who did no more than toy obsessively with the idea of sin. The promiscuous Mary Magdalene was almost rooted out of history until she rose again as a hippie. The Andrew Lloyd Webber musical *Jesus Christ Superstar* and Martin Scorsese's film *The Last Temptation of Christ* breathed new life into this mythic woman.

Back in the fourteenth century, Dante Alighieri dared introduce us to Mary Magdalene. He didn't make room for many women at all, apart from the few noble creatures clustered at the feet of the Virgin Mary.

Apart from the fact that the oddest guilds and professions have sneaked into hell and purgatory, Dante's mentions of prostitutes and ex-prostitutes are few and far between. Emperor Justinian had a whole song devoted to him in *Paradiso;* Empress Theodora, the social reformer with a past, did not get a single line. Dante frequently used the world *harlot* in *Purgatorio,* but only as a metaphor for the Catholic Church. By the midpoint of his vast work, he had not mentioned a single prostitute, though he devoted considerable space to male libertines, not least homosexual poets of the Middle Ages. Perhaps sensual men fascinated the puritanical Dante; he had scarcely any experience of sensual, reflective women. The Renaissance, which gave rise to this type of woman, still had not arrived.

In the upper echelons of hell, we understand that there must be some prostitutes wandering around. On the eighth level of Hades, we find the money-grubbers, including men who earn their daily bread in the sex trade, whoremasters and ruffians, and men who seduce women toward prostitution. The neighboring level belonged to the sycophants, with many prostitutes among them, even though Dante mentioned only one, Thaïs. But most Dante commentators admit that he was thinking of a fictive character from a comedy by Terance. It is equally likely that he had in mind the totality of women in her profession.

Dante anchored his whole view of prostitutes in the notion that they offer love on false premises. Their major sins are a lack of real feeling and untrustworthiness in love, not the sale of sex. For Dante, as for so many others, it was not the economic element of prostitution that weighed most heavily.

Joannes Andrea, a French theologian from the early fourteenth century, developed his concept of prostitution along the same lines as Dante. Andrea maintained that there was deception lurking in the behavior of all prostitutes: They swindled all men, because no one alone got to have their bodies and hearts. So there was no place for such women in heaven. And though Mary Magdalene was said to be the woman Jesus thought most highly of, it should be remembered that the eternal social gathering constructed by Dante is the dinner party of the mother of Jesus. And no mother in the Western world has ever considered a repentant sinner suitable company for her beloved son.

Dante's own sweetheart, Beatrice, died a virgin at nineteen. He had seen the girl just twice: once at nine, in a red dress, and once at eighteen, in white. Mary Queen of Heaven, born from a virgin, became a virgin again herself after giving birth, and ended up a virgin in heaven, too. Such a mother might admit only someone like Beatrice as a suitable companion for her son. Think of what a revolution it would have been to introduce into heaven an ideal of womanhood who was fleshly and carnal.

Dante was not the man to do such a thing. It was Oscar Wilde, six hundred years later, who did so. In his philosophical memorandum *De profundis,* Wilde wrote, "Mary Magdalene, when she sees Christ, breaks the rich vase of alabaster that one of her seven lovers had given her, and spills the odorous spices over His tired dusty feet, and for that moment's sake, sits forever with Ruth and Beatrice in the tresses of the snow-white Rose of Paradise."

TWELVE

THE WAR OF THE ROSES

If she knows what's good for her, a wise wife will persuade her husband that when the jackdaw has chattered about her infidelity, the bird was crazy. She will back this up with the testimony of her own dear maid: "Deceite, weeping, spinning God hath yive / To wommen kindely (naturually) whil they may live." In his *Canterbury Tales,* written in the fourteenth century, Geoffrey Chaucer lets the Wife of Bath comment on her five marriages. She has managed to lie and calculate and suffer through her husbands. As she sees it, a married woman has to tolerate just as much as any prostitute. With a fresh turn of phrase, she airs her views about her husbands:

> For wynnying wolde I al his lust endure,
> And make me a feyned appetit.

It was not until her fifth marriage that she was able to choose her mate on the basis of her own desires. But Chaucer still puts into her mouth words flush with feminine joie de vivre:

> Lo, heere the wise kyng, daun Salomon,
> I trowe he hadde wyves many oon.
> As wolde God it leveful were to me
> To be refresshed half so ofte as he! . . .
> Blessed be God that I have wedded five! . . .
> Welcome the sixte, whan that evere he shal.

Earlier literature of the Middle Ages had been marked by rather different and higher ideals; "romantic" love poetry rose among the princely courts of southern France, northern Italy, and southern Germany in the transition period between the twelfth and thirteenth centuries, and it led to a flourishing literature that would later reach other parts of Europe. Chretien de Troyes and Walter von der Vogelweide were but two from a century in which the density of poetic creativity in central Europe was enormous.

Medieval Europe was in the process of becoming overpopulated, something that affected the nobles as much as it did the serfs and peasantry. A majority of the young sons of the nobility knew that they would go through life without being able to start a family. Superfluous noble daughters found refuge in abbeys and convents. Superfluous aristocratic sons created more discord, for they preferred the wild life of young bachelors at their region's royal court. They practiced jousting and the other arts of chivalry, went on crusades, and wrote romantic poetry to women they knew to be unattainable.

In the poems of courtly love, and in contemporary troubadour lyrics, love is defined as a sacred mystique and a noble longing. In the great narrative poems, the literary heroes and heroines are historical figures from the nobility or fictional figures. The love poems deal with unattainable women, queens, or even the Virgin Mary.

A great many poems were adoring homages to the aristocratic wife who presided at court. Queen Eleanor of Aquitaine, Countess Ermengarde of Narbonne, and other countesses of the thirteenth century regularly stepped forward symbolically as the queen of all hearts when they acted as judges in literary games and competitions. In addition to her moral and literary rulings, the royal or leading aristocratic wife set the tone at court, defending "pure" love as more noble than "compromised," or carnal, love; or declaring female infidelity more unkind than the masculine variety.

The source of inspiration for such poetry should have a lot more of the exalted goddess in her than the practical palace hostess. But the women of the poems are studied only from the position of noble adoration, with precious little physical desire in evidence.

Many have wondered if there was something else at the base of these grandiloquent expressions. Did the young troubadours have relations with one another that they were transmitting, camouflaged in code? Or were there a lot more of these high-and-mighty virgins at court than one would normally expect? At the same time, these super-romantic knights and troubadours had many experiences in the realm of love that the literature does not communicate particularly well. The courteous nobleman was not restrained by sentimentality in his everyday live. His carnal needs were expressed in rapes of servants and peasants and visits to prostitutes. But no troubadour would dream of writing so much as a single stanza to a woman who belonged to any of these social classes.

The fourteenth century arose with new ideas about love, yet they were associated with poems and verse romances from earlier in the Middle Ages. "Women ought to color their hair, use makeup, and wear brassieres." This was not Jane Fonda speaking, but the woman who kept and guarded the rose in a French allegory from the same time, *The Romance of the Rose*. This female figure can be interpreted as a sort of brothel hostess and madam. Nature has created women for free love, and marriage is nothing but a straitjacket, says this woman guardian. The real art is to love as many as possible. If a person loves but one, things end in tragedy, maybe even as badly as with Dido and Medea. *The Romance of the Rose* promoted promiscuous love and visits to prostitutes.

A woman took the lead in a formidable battle against all this. Christine de Pizan has been identified by most scholars as the first feminist in world history. She was also the first woman in history to argue against all prostitution. Back in the fifteenth century, she earned many enemies, and she is still capable of causing provocation today. Nickie Roberts, an ex-prostitute and historian, writes, "Christine is often cited as a pioneer of women's liberation. In reality she was one of the Middle Ages' highly conservative snobs."

Christine de Pizan was born in Tuscany but lived almost her whole life in France. England and France were fighting their way through a series of wars that were later called the Hundred Years' War. Plague epidemics ravaged the land, and both peasants and city dwellers mounted rebellions. But neither war nor want diminished the upper classes' demand for luxury. Young noblemen treated sexual life as though it were a sport.

For many years, Christine de Pizan lived like a poet laureate, writing poetry commissioned by the rich and aristocratic; she has also been decribed as the first professional woman writer in history. She took center stage in a discussion that has been called France's first literary controversy, Europe's first secular moral debate, and the world's first public discussion on the role of women. It is perhaps most illuminating to say that this was the fifteenth century's debate on pornography and its destructive properties.

The core of the controversy seems to have been the apparently innocuous allegorical verse romance called *Le Roman de la Rose*. However, allegorical formulations can be provocative when one interprets all the symbols as obscene. In 1400 this text was used as an erotically stimulating evening's read, and a practical collection of arguments for sexual abandonment, especially at court.

> *The whole hill was here a-burst with roses,*
> *the fairest of the land . . .*
> *I long to be there among the richest blossoms.*

The rose is the symbol of woman, and of love. *The Romance of the Rose* was understood to be an encouragement and guide to young men who wanted to pluck as many such flowers as possible.

Those who defended the book were referred to as rosephiles. They were not sex-mad noblemen but classically educated humanists, like the abbot of Honoré Bonet and Jean de Montreuil, the gifted secretary to the king of Burgundy. Christine de Pizan led the faction called rosephobes, together with Jean Gerson, the royal chancellor, the highest public official at the University of Paris. Theologically, he was closer to a mystic than a committed textual critic. This literary feud is still referred to as *La Querelle des Femmes*. That a woman could give rise to a battle is nothing new, but this fight was totally new to European intellectual history and its main theme groundbreaking for its time—women and women's points of view.

Charles the Wise of France was the fourteenth century's least knightly and chivalrous monarch, slight of frame and no athlete. He was both devout and bookish. Perhaps it was because he played his cards so wisely that he regained control over his chaotic and fractured country.

Tomasso de Pizzano, a doctor and astrologer in Pisa, was called to Paris to assist this clever king. Tomasso arrived in 1368 with his bright four-year-old daughter. Both Tomasso and Charles the Wise passed away, but Christine and her relatives remained at court in the Louvre, since at the age of fifteen, she had been married off to the secretary of the king.

The new king, the young Charles VI, ordered that portraits be painted of all the daughters of dukes from the Holy Roman Empire, to make it easier for him to choose the most beautiful to be his wife. In 1388, Isabeau of Bavaria arrived in Paris with a blast of pomp and ceremony the likes of which no one had ever seen. The style-conscious historian Jean Froissart used obscene wordplay and ambiguous formulations when he described the episode in his chronicles. This caused the royal wedding to be viewed as a warning that once again the country was in for a period of decline.

Within the Louvre, the tone was set by two beautiful daughters of dukes, since the equally stunning Valentine of Lombardy had been married to the king's younger and more libidinously agile brother, Louis d'Orleans, a love- and pleasure-mad dandy and dancer.

Christine de Pizan disliked the happy chatter and the wild and licentious parties at court. Still in her twenties, she felt much older than the ducal daughters setting the tone. Though her husband was considerably older, she was constantly pregnant. She had barely reached the age of thirty when she became a widow and had to leave the court with her three children, relatives, and servants. How could an aristocratic woman of the Middle Ages with no income from landed property feed so many mouths?

The situation might have led even the less virtuous to despair. She probably lay awake for some nights wondering about the future, and had certainly sent out one or two ingratiating letters to the court; but in the end Christine suddenly decided that she would live by her pen. She secured a ten-year literary engagement, saving herself and her children and dependent relatives from an extremely brutal transition from the easy life at court to which they had become so accustomed. The poems that saved Christine de Pizan were grandiose, formal, decorous tributes that the king and highest nobles ordered for great occasions. The pay was generous; perhaps some courtiers felt pity for this learned and strong widow whom they had seen at court for so many years. Her more independent, scholarly writings brought in less income, but they were the works that secured her a place in history.

The Romance of the Rose is characterized by allegorical thought and has a detailed, rigid structure. On the surface, the romance portrays the dream and scruples of a nineteen-year-old man on the hunt for love. In this work, love is represented by a rose or a sea of roses. The woman who is the guardian of the rose of love is one of many counselors; Amor is the most important assistant. But it is the goddess Venus who helps the youngster to victory over both Shame and Fear. In the end, this young man is able to pluck the flower that he so desires, and make use of both his natural tools and his pilgrim's staff.

Today this versified allegory is known in two different versions. The original version, by Guillaume de Lorris, dates back to the 1230s and relates to *De Amore,* a surprising and half-ironic erotic textbook written by Andreas Capellanus, who in turn built upon Ovid. What most clearly distinguishes the original version from contemporary courtly love poetry is that the nineteen-year-old actually plucks his rose; in a word, he is victorious in love.

But *The Romance of the Rose* read in Paris around 1400 was five times longer, more didactic, more rational—and more pornographic. It was rewritten by Jean de Meun. His version fades into an explicit, even blasphemous redemption for the libidinous hero. It holds no shock value for people of today, but in the late Middle Ages, the very assertion of cutting down or mastering a rose, plucking its petals one by one, and drinking its nectar shocked some to the depths of their being, while for others it was an erotic stimulant.

In *The Romance of the Rose,* the woman guarding the rose of love explains to the young man that paying visits to prostitutes is a natural solution for those on a quest for love. For her part, the prostitute gains both a good purse and a surfeit of love. The text was considered a direct defense of prostitution, which, during the transition from the fourteenth to the fifteenth centuries, had become a burgeoning profession.

In 1398, Honoré Bonet published *Rejoinder to Master Jean de Meun and the Rose,* proposing that a nobleman should live as "freely and naturally" as the peasantry. This could be interpreted as an endorsement of marriage between noblemen and commoner women, but it could legitimate male sexual behavior with servant girls, and even noblewomen. Right before Bonet published his text, the king's courtiers had decked themselves out as savages and rampaged through the Louvre, assaulting the ladies of the court, raping servant girls here and there, shrieking and howling. Shortly thereafter, a group of young prostitutes arrived "from an abbey in Toulouse" to bring joy to the king's brother and other gentlemen of the court, and lessen the sexual pressure on the ladies of the court. Court prostitutes continued to be a permanent feature of life in the Louvre.

King Charles VI did not participate in this fun. Following a riding accident in 1392, he suffered from long bouts of madness, and for the most part sat alone, weighed down by strange and heavy thoughts. He was later referred to as Charles the Mad. But this was not the reason why the court changed its style; rather, the direction of the country was weakened by the rivalry between the king's uncles, led by Philip of Burgundy, and the handsome Louis, Comte d'Orleans, who had all the young women at court on his side.

France was politically split. New wars were threatening, and the people were suffering. But in the Louvre, the aristocracy decked themselves out and pursued the practices of love as a form of play—sometimes violently. *Le Roman de la Rose* told people to behave naturally, to pay attention to how cows and bulls frolicked in the meadows, and try to behave the same way. After Queen Isabeau got herself a sheep farm in 1398, she regularly dressed herself and her ladies-in-waiting as shepherdesses, with her favorites decked out as shepherds. Right in the middle of Paris, they were singing the songs of goatherds and copying the peasants' simple dance steps. Jean de Brie and other poets who mastered bucolic poetry, praising the simple life on the land, were all the rage.

But one member of the royal family was seen less frequently in the Louvre: Philip of Burgundy. He ruled over Burgundy, Flanders, Brabant, and Luxembourg almost as a separate state. His court in Dijon was dominated by order and better morals, something that Christine de Pizan and other rosephobes pointed out as frequently as they could.

Chaucer translated the original version of *Le Roman de la Rose* into English. His *Canterbury Tales,* as well as his lyric tales about Amor and his female saints, *Legende of Good Women,* disturbed Christine de Pizan, as did Boccaccio's *Amorosa Visione* and *Il Decamerone.* In her eyes, all these works give the same false depiction of women as did *Le Roman de la Rose.* She believed all leading writers of her time painted women as evil, untrustworthy, or superficial and showed them with no other desires than for clothing and finery, while they deceived their husbands and brought marriage into disrepute. Her main goal was to provide an alternative view of womanhood: showing women as virtuous and generally learned but devoid of sexual desire. None of Christine's ideal women would ever dream of deceiving their husbands.

Christine's first written critique of *The Romance of the Rose* and other contemporary writings, and her principled defense of the female sex, came out in 1401 under the title *Epître au Dieu d'Amour,* or "Epistle to the God of Love." Christine felt it wasn't she who had started the literary feud but Honoré Bonet, with his statement in defense of Master Jean de Meun. But Christine now took the lead, and the following year, she put out a lesser statement by way of continuation: *Dit la Rose,* or "Regarding the Rose."

Christine de Pizan was now thirty-six and had in all likelihood given up any hope of remarrying. Christine's later biographers have interpreted her criticism of promiscuous men and her defense of virtuous women as a loss of lust for life. Early on in her writing career, she wrote some pastoral and mythological poetry, such as "l'Epître d'Otha et Hector," and in these poems, love was given such free rein that they could be described as moderately rosephile.

In 1402, Christine de Pizan wrote a letter to Queen Isabeau in Paris, urging her to intervene in the literary battle between rosephiles and rosephobes. Christine was six years older than Isabeau and knew her well from her years at court. It is possible that Christine imagined the queen would take up the moral cudgels, as queens of the late Middle Ages were wont to do. But the times had changed considerably. Christine's request could also be interpreted as a demand for literary censorship, or as a suggestion for initiatives against immorality at court, in Paris, and in other cities across France. Her bold letter turned a literary debate among a number of learned men into an issue of public concern. "I have many enemies," wrote Christine de Pizan to Queen Isabeau, with justification. In the late Middle Ages, it could be dangerous, even deadly, to raise political or literary opposition to immorality. It is fair to say that Christine de Pizan may have been one of her time's most courageous women.

Beautifully coordinated with Christine's letter, Jean Gerson was giving a series of fire-and-brimstone sermons in Paris. His audience was composed of aristocrats, city merchants, and students, men as well as women. Superficially, his speeches brought to mind the warnings being dished out around the countryside at this time by itinerant and only lightly schooled preachers about the downfall of the world. It was easy to declare itinerant preachers heretics, and to toss them in prison, but

Jean Gerson ranked higher than any other ecclesiastic in service to the king of France. When he spoke on the corruption of morality, with direct citations from the most immoral book of the day, *Le Roman de la Rose,* half of France quaked.

Using a chaste tone, Christine commented on the upper classes of her day. Side by side with the chaste lives of women were the erotic escapades, wars, and wild partying that characterized male immorality. In *La Cité des Dames* of 1405, she traced out an alternative, women-dominated ideal society governed by the goddesses Reason, Integrity, and Justice. A series of historically renowned women appear in the text, following the pattern of a book Boccaccio had written fifty years earlier on famous women.

The basis for calling Christine de Pizan a feminist becomes still clearer here than in her earlier writings. She was the first to launch the principled idea that women's ideas can oppose men's. She did not simply criticize immoral men; she also struck out at the scholars of the Church for their contention that Eve was mainly responsible for the fall from grace and the expulsion from the Garden of Eden; she also noted other negative concepts of women in the Bible.

Christine de Pizan earnestly entreated the prostitutes of Paris to abandon their profession. The worst thing about prostitution was that it gave a bad name to womanhood. If women stopped practicing prostitution and began to live decent lives, the women of the aristocracy would be met with greater respect by the men of their own class, and women commoners would be better treated by the men of theirs. Though the reasoning is frankly feminist, it gave no indication of a democratic temperament.

Christine de Pizan knew almost nothing about everyday life among students and prostitutes in the Paris of her day, so she was uncompromising in her opposition to prostitution. She argued that it would feel good for a woman prostitute to repent and begin a new, simple, and virtuous life in one of the prettiest corners of Paris.

Christine de Pizan sent her own daughter to a Dominican convent and frequently pointed out what a good safe life a woman could have as a nun. If a woman did not choose the cloistered life to avoid prostitution, she ought to surround herself with good neighbors and work as a servant for a noble family, in the home of a merchant, or even, in times of great need, a tradesman. Christine had given scarcely a thought to how five thousand Parisian prostitutes were going to obtain such secure employment.

Prostitution caused the parting of the ways among rosephobes, and in particular between Christine de Pizan and Jean Gerson, who was a mystic by nature but knew life's realities well. Year in and year out, by the bright light of day and in the middle of the night, he had observed the ten thousand students of Paris for whom he was to some extent responsible. To Gerson, prostitution minimized the numbers of what were called blind rapes (rapes by strangers), so it had to be tolerated as the lesser evil. In his sermons, Gerson emphasized a celibate life, but if a young unmarried man felt that carnal lust was about to overwhelm him, he was given permission to visit a prostitute to regain his peace of mind.

Christine de Pizan had never considered rape and prostitution in a joint perspective. She scarcely touched rape in her criticism of *The Romance of the Rose*. The theme was more thoroughly dealt with in *The City of Ladies*. For her, rape was evidence that women and men often had opposing views. It was extremely common among men of the late Middle Ages to maintain that women liked to be raped, even though they protested. This fundamental view is referred to in *The City of Ladies,* but the goddess Integrity rejects this contention sharply, and concludes by saying that the man who commits rape deserves the stiffest punishment.

In subsequent periods, the question of who "won" *La Querelle des Femmes* would frequently come up for discussion. It is natural to describe the result as a compromise. The courts in the two Burgundies, Burgund and Bourgogne, instituted some arrangements that would change European concepts of love and the relations between the sexes. These arrangements have been called *the courts of love,* but they could just as well have been called courtrooms of gender equality, dance schools, or courses for the nobles in modern customs. Jean de Montreuil was the key person in Burgundy; the rosephiles thus became master of ceremonies, though the aim was to improve all customs and practices, particularly to teach young men respect for the opposite sex. The practical exercises involved sitting calmly at a table with women, conversing with these strange and distant creatures, who, for their part, improved their collection of scientific data on the male sex. In addition, there was some resumption of the thirteenth century's competitions in proposals of marriage, poetry composition, and the performance of love ballads.

The women had the pleasure of playing judges over the men's proposals of marriage and could distribute the prizes and award the grades. As long as the festivities continued, any man had to respect the virtue of all participating women. Later historians have described the courts of love as nothing more than sex orgies, which is both paradoxical and wrong. The arrangements tried to create a mutual understanding between the sexes and refinement of behavior among the noblemen of the late Middle Ages. And with the passage of time, this bore fruit—very gradually, men learned that they had to look up to not only the queen but many in the ranks of womanhood.

What Christine de Pizan thought of the courts of love in Burgund and Bourgogne we do not know. She lived for over sixty years but spent her last twenty in a convent, probably with her daughter. Shortly before she died in 1430, she stepped once again into the literary arena with a poem that was an inspired eulogy to Jeanne d'Arc, the saintly virgin who, dressed as a man, had inspired all the French troops near the close of the Hundred Years' War. The great achievements of Jeanne d'Arc had set an eternal example and brought honor and glory to womanhood, Christine declared in her eulogy. Christine de Pizan could give her blessings to war, in the literary arena, and on the battlefield, as long as virtuous women were in the lead.

T H I R T E E N

P O X ,   P U N I S H M E N T ,
A N D   P E N I T E N C E

S yphilis was first identified among French soldiers in Naples in 1495. From there it spread to the rest of Europe. The Danish historian Hans Vaning reported that it reached Copenhagen the same year. Certainly it had done so by 1496, when the malady reached northern Germany. This one-year lag did not give the Germans much of an advantage, since the disease spread like wildfire.

Christopher Columbus called it the disease of the Indies, the French called it *le mal de Naples,* while in Italy and England, they talked about the French pox. The Turks said it was a disease of Christendom, and the Chinese said it was a Portuguese epidemic.

The term *syphilis* derives from a poem. A shepherd in disease-ridden Haiti bore the name Syphilus in a 1530 poem written by a well-informed Veronese doctor and writer named Giolamo Fracastoro. The author had a pedagogical objective and succeeded in winning general acceptance of the theory that the disease had been imported from the New World. But even today the origin of the disease is disputed. Some believe it started out in Africa. Definite evidence that it came to Europe from across the Atlantic has never been produced.

Syphilis manifests itself from two to ten weeks after infection, in the form of boils on the genitals or other body parts. The boils disappear after three to eight weeks, leaving only a slight scarring. For two years after infection, one is dangerously infectious without realizing it. In its second stage, syphilis manifests itself through fevers, headaches, and sore throats, but the danger of infection gradually lessens. At the end, some become completely healthy; for others, if they have not died yet of other causes, a third stage sets in. Third-stage syphilis is anything but a beautiful death.

Syphilis is significant to any understanding of social and cultural history in the years following 1500. It influenced the thoughts and behavior of scholars and laymen, physicians, theologians, and politicians. Syphilis also influenced the public debate on prostitution.

The term *venereal disease* is derived from Venus, the Roman goddess of love. As early as 1495, Emperor Maximilian of Habsburg issued a decree that explained the illness as a result of common immorality. Both the emperor and the populace considered prostitutes particularly responsible for syphilis and other venereal diseases. By no means does this indicate that people understood how syphilis worked. Both doctors and patients assumed it was passed through food, breast milk, clothing, and the air. But whenever an epidemic was on its way, people looked for scapegoats. Women who were suspected of being syphilitic were hunted down and expelled from a number of cities at the beginning of the sixteenth century, with Paris and Strasbourg most noted for their witch-hunters. Many brothels were also closed down, and hospitals often refused to accept syphilitic patients. King Hans of Denmark-Norway closed all public baths.

In one of his paintings, Sandro Botticelli gave expression to how anxiety over syphilis became a hunt for scapegoats. *Mystical Crucifixion* shows Mary Magdalene tearfully embracing the cross of Jesus Christ, with the whole panorama of syphilis-infected Florence in the background. It is as though the harlot in the foreground, not the man on the cross, must assume all guilt on behalf of humanity.

"A woman who is convicted of prostitution is brought into the council room, the executioner binds her hands, and attaches a large poster to her back. Everyone can read the details of her sins. . . . Then the woman is taken to a rock in the middle of the river where she is placed in an iron cage and submerged three times, but not so much as to drown her. All the inhabitants of the city are present to attend the circus. Then the poor girl is brought to prison." This is the way a woman prostitute was punished in Toulouse in the 1560s, for that city belongs to the part of France where the Huguenots— the French Protestants—were most strongly on the offensive. Similar episodes could be observed from Sweden to Scotland, Switzerland to Silesia.

Luther, Zwingli, and Calvin had ignited independent religious uprising in central and northern Europe between 1520 and 1550. Protestantism spread particularly quickly thanks to the invention of the printing press. Most of the sixteenth century would be marked by the Reformation and the Counter-Reformation, which in turn caused many moral and political changes.

Of course, the new religious currents had their own considerable weight. But the anguish over syphilis that marked the first part of the century gave the religious and moral purification that grasped Europe so forcefully in the latter half a second character—as an epilogue to the syphilis scare.

All major Protestant doctrines place marriage more centrally than does Roman Catholic theology, while the Protestants look more mildly on sex before marriage. The Virgin Mary's position was decentralized concurrent with the decreased stress on virginity; Catholic celibacy, for its part, was considered a camouflage, hiding the fornication of churchmen.

The Protestants stepped up the struggle against prostitution, for in their eyes, prostitution, celibacy, and the pope's Church were closely bound together. Ordinary priests and monks, common city dwellers and peasants, had long questioned the financial emphasis of the Catholic Church and the hedonistic lifestyle of so many higher clergy.

The struggle against the papacy and the Church gave opposition to prostitution a religious legitimacy. The sale of sex was as good as acknowledged by the papists, who themselves made use of prostitutes. Conversely, any true Christian had to struggle without compromise against all such activities: "With the help of our true enemies, the Devil has sent whores here to the earth in order to destroy our young men," wrote Luther. "Any who engage in such a trade must first give up the name of Christ, and admit that they are heathens." Luther felt that control and supervision of immorality was a civil and not an ecclesiastical affair, and thought the secular authorities should punish infidelity, rape, and whoring when they took place in the light of day. Sins that were committed out of sight, however, received their just deserts from the Lord above. In practice, the Protestants began to treat the prostitutes as though they were heathens or Jews. Such women did not belong to Christian society; they were regarded as enemies of Christendom.

Calvin was even more of a fulminator than Luther, and still more unconditional in his struggle against sin. Any fornication, Calvin stated, was against the will of God. The prostitutes had to give up their trade—and fast in penance—or be banished from Geneva. In 1556 he proposed the death penalty for prostitution. This law was not ratified, but two Genevan prostitutes were executed in 1560.

In a very short time, and over much of Europe, by force or free will, people began to shift religion, moral outlook, and political leadership. These types of fundamental changes generally unleash other strong forces, including a sense of instability. People find release from their anxieties by behaving aggressively toward minorities—Jews, prostitutes, and other deviants from the social majority.

Huguenot Toulouse and Languedoc were in no way exceptional. All over Europe, the pillory, houses of castigation, and the shaving of heads were becoming solutions to every problem, including prostitution. It was as though people suddenly preferred to wound and destroy those they had earlier sought consolation from.

In Germany, shaving the heads of women considered to be shameless had been common in the early Middle Ages. Now there was a resurgence of taking the law into one's own hands, not only in Germany but also in southern France and Scandinavia. In Huguenot-controlled Languedoc, prostitutes who had sought clients outdoors at night were sent naked through the streets of the larger cities by day, before being ceremonially shoved out through the city gates. In smaller towns, the newly converted could go on the attack against the perhaps five or six local prostitutes, whipping and beating them and cutting off their ears.

Scandinavia, in Europe's northern and less urbanized periphery, switched to Lutheran Protestantism with relative ease, but Luther would soon be taken with mortal seriousness in all questions of central religious dogma—and more peripheral questions within the overall doctrine, like prostitution. In 1546, King Christian III declared to the bishops in Denmark and Norway that prostitutes had to be expelled from the hospitals: "Women ... who formerly in their Youth and Vigour have lived in open Fornication, and led an improper Life and beyond that became corrupted by the Pox, the French Pox ... Each and everyone must therefore be on guard and reject such an evil and loose Way of Life." In the 1560s, prostitutes were to be "punished and driven from Place to Place for as long as it takes, until they become ashamed, and further, correct and better themselves."

The first and greatest Protestant bishop in the north was Peder Palladius, who came directly from Luther's Wittenberg to reform Denmark and Norway. During the 1550s, Palladius spoke out against prostitution in the austere spirit of Luther, but added a touch of Viking rage:

> Now indeed there sit many of the Harlots of Filth, both in the Marketplace and yonder Village, where you may well watch and be warned. She keeps bad Beer in her Jug. If you do drink of this with her, all you get for your Pains are both Shame and Injury, and the Dregs lead to the Pox and other Evils, which I shall not name for the Sake of Decency, such that this young Jude of the fields, runs to her like a Dog across the Commons—that by its own Volition runs after a Bitch. Such a one in the end gets all besmeared and soiled and sinks into Corruption.

The majority of Europe's public sex institutions were closed by the middle of the sixteenth century. In Geneva all open prostitution was forbidden from 1524; in Ulm they closed the brothels in 1537. This process spread from city to city through the 1540s and 1550s. London's brothels were closed in 1546. In Strasbourg the prostitutes sent a petition to the city council in which they asked for an alternative form of work—or husbands—before the brothels were closed down. It did not help much. In 1561, Charles IX of France closed down the very last brothels in Paris and a number of other French cities.

The Catholic Church had to show that its morality was just as high as that of the Protestants. In 1563 the Papal Nuncio of Trentino in southern Tyrol forbade both all forms of prostitution and the annulment of marriages; the same year all the remaining bordellos in Italy were closed, as well as in the small German Catholic principalities. Only in Zurich and some other unrestricted Swiss and German cities was it still possible to organize prostitution despite Calvin, Luther, and the pope.

The Catholic Counter-Reformation was marked by just as strong a sense of morality as the Protestant storm in the north. Emperor Ferdinand established a chastity committee to oversee morality. A great many city dwellers were punished; still greater numbers lost their income. Pope Pius V tried to clean up the immorality in his own backyard. In 1566, on the saint's day of Mary Magdalene herself, July 22, he was audacious enough to abolish all prostitution in the city of Rome. The reactions were much more vehement than he had anticipated. The urban merchant class stood up right away with resolutions that predicted an economic crisis. Ambassadors from Spain, Portugal, and Florence submitted identical protests. Within two weeks, Rome was seized by hysteria. Twenty-five thousand people became refugees—there were roughly five or six thousand working prostitutes, but when one also took into account their dependent relatives, lovers, and servants, the numbers increased exponentially. In August, Pope Pius modified his orders, and the prostitutes were given the right to remain in Rome. Nonetheless, this papal action drastically reduced the numbers of prostitutes, and the Church's income from prostitution sank as women continued to flee the trade.

To the north, things took their most brutal turn in the small Danish city of Helsingør. In July 1574, Fredrik II required the city council to arrest all of the city's prostitutes, flog them publicly, and drive them out of the city. If a woman dared to return, her ears were to be sliced from her head. Were she so intrepid as to come back a third time, she was to be "tressed up in a Sack and sunk." But things were not as fanatical farther south, perhaps because prostitution had not been as extensive. In 1584 Bergen still had seven "tolerated houses." In Copenhagen, Peder Palladius confirmed—without his customary fire and brimstone—that there were women's houses both in Rosengaarden, at the city limits to Copenhagen, and within the Royal City.

Head shaving, flogging, and the removal of ears would spread to Scandinavia in the late sixteenth and early seventeenth centuries. But no one was drowned, even though this method was now sanctioned by law. Even the prostitutes of Helsingør survived, although some were maimed.

In Rome, Pope Pius had been forced to beat something of a retreat. But in 1586, Pope Sixtus V declared that the death penalty would be imposed on prostitution and "sins against nature." Sixtus V intended his command to be followed all over the Catholic world. There were some death sentences, but not many. For their part, the Lutherans continued to shave off both hair and ears; the Calvinists branded, and burdened with large stones carried around the city, and employed the stocks in public places. Given the stringent new laws in both Catholic and Protestant regions, one might have expected far worse conditions, indeed, mass persecutions. But fortunately, this did not happen.

Prostitution had fallen into a state of ill repute during the sixteenth century. The sex business was an occupation many sought to leave behind them. Many a poverty-stricken girl would pin her hopes on another solution, and spend some of her youthful years in a life that resembled the brothel and the cloister.

In the late Middle Ages, the prostitute who wanted to enter the trade had an alternative in what were called the Magdalene homes. In the course of the Renaissance, these institutions took over the work of administering to prostitutes from the abbeys and convents that had previously done so in both Catholic and Protestant Europe. A woman who sought a place in a Magdalene home did not need to make any sacred pledge of future chastity; she was allowed to concentrate on slow self-improvement toward a traditional way of life, preferably as a married wife and mother. Women were dissuaded from attempting this way of life alone—that is, outside the institution.

If they managed to get so far, the women of the Magdalene homes carried out pious and healthy work for the man who owned the home: sewing, weaving, spinning, washing. The pay at a Magdalene home was particularly low, so a smart entrepreneur could make great profits from offering work to penitent women sinners.

It is perhaps paradoxical that a number of young women sought out the homes without having experienced prostitution. Many of them lied, confessing to a life of sin in order to get on the dole and find a home where they got food and clothing and learned to sew and spin. Some reported that their parents had told them to say they'd been in a relationship with a rich man who had left them in the lurch; others found it expedient to prostitute themselves for a short while to qualify for admission.

But the eye of the needle was narrow; professional matrons inspected every candidate for the Magdalene homes, looked for physical signs of a life in prostitution, and posed crafty and intricate questions. They wanted well-qualified sinners, women with a "real" past. Many did not pass the last and most conclusive test: They had to swear on the heart of the Virgin Mary that they had not become prostitutes for the purpose of getting into the home.

The woman who took the name of the Virgin Mary in vain, and lied about a past as a prostitute, was qualified as a penitent woman sinner and received a good new life at public expense. This was a sign that the Church's control over people's minds had weakened.

Obviously, prostitution was less extensive during the 1600s than it had been earlier or would become later. But in a Europe that continued to be marked by religious conflict and the Counter-Reformation, it was possible to have a future in prostitution—for a few, at least. Through the whole century, prostitutes continued to live by themselves and in small whorehouses in Protestant and Catholic Europe. Some few lived very elegantly, most in discreet destitution. But no more public regulation of the trade was undertaken. And all open debate about prostitution subsided.

F O U R T E E N

S P L E N D O R   A N D   M I S E R Y
O F   T H E   C O U R T E S A N S

Veronica Franco was the mistress of two Renaissance painters, Jacobo Tintoretto and Paolo Veronese, who both regularly used her as a model. She spoke seven languages fluently, wrote sensual poetry, exchanged letters with Michel de Montaigne, and played the flute. Veronica Franco was a mixture of the beautiful and the trendsetting when it came to fashion; she was the sole woman of her day who succeeded in seducing Henri III of France, who otherwise desired only men.

Imperia Cognata modeled for Raphael when he created *Parnassus, The Transfiguration,* and several other paintings, and was immortalized by the Renaissance writer Matteo Bandello. Imperia took hundreds of ducats for a single night with a foreign client; it was she who invented bedsheets of black silk, which made such an effective contrast to her own pale skin as she relaxed between marble columns in the light of gigantic bronze candelabras. Imperia Cognata knew many men but preferred stable relations with bankers. Angelo del Bufalo paid for her extravagant apartment with its marble, brocade, and lapis lazuli. A Spanish grandee searched in vain for something into which he could spit and in the end was forced to use the face of a male servant. Imperia insisted that her clients arrive full of wit and good humor, and depart after discreetly leaving behind a costly gift.

In the sixteenth and seventeenth centuries, a new character appeared on the European stage: the courtesan, named from the Italian, *la cortegiana.* The masculine form, *il cortegiano,* or in French, *le courtesan,* denotes a man of the royal court. The rules that governed the behavior of such a man were described in detail in Baldassare Castiglione's dialogue *Il Cortegiano.* The women who accompanied such men in public had to move in similar circles. Contemporary artists immortalized a great many of them. The beauty of the women in Italian Renaissance paintings cannot be ascribed just to the painters; their models were more beautiful and erotically self-assured than any women Europe had seen before.

Many courtesans named themselves after their city of origin, such as Camilla de Pisa, Beatrice da Ferrara, and Alessandra Fiorentina; others created names with connotations of power, like Imperia Cognata and Isabella da Luna. But a courtesan was not a public woman; she was far from available to all, and commanded the highest prices. A kiss from Veronica Franco would cost a Venetian worker six months' wages. Poets, painters, and rich men fought for Veronica's favors, and most of them were rejected.

Renaissance writers made sharp distinctions between prostitutes and courtesans. A courtesan was richly attired, lived respectably, and would scarcely be seen at a public bath or in a brothel. She preferred to receive at home but could pay visits with a chaperone; she was never exposed to the taunts and jeers of young lads about town.

Italy's courtesans developed a unique *civilità puttanesca,* a high etiquette of whoring. The women had to be neat and clean, delicate, well dressed, cunning at the card table and board games, and proficient in arithmetic. Their business acumen was adapted to the rising class of merchant capitalists—they were modern and economically rational people.

"I swear, by the same great Fortune you are destined to make, dear Pippa, that lust will be the least of all desires in your life. Just because you are simply too concerned with alluring others of their inner Secrets." Antonia, an elderly courtesan "who bears on her body the boils and scars left by syphilis, contracted to her in her profession as a prostitute," states this in a dialogue by the learned Pietro Aretino; Antonia is teaching the teenager Pippa some secrets of the trade. "You should understand," wrote Veronica Franco in her younger days to an even younger admirer, "that anyone thirsting for my love must show the strictest discipline in his studies. If only my fortune had been great enough, I would have spent my whole life in the Libraries, and shared my free time with only the most learned of men."

A courtesan had to be able to speak several languages, recite poetry, and play at least two musical instruments, and preferably be a proficient singer. The most learned of them wrote and spoke Latin, and some also Greek.

Courtesans were soon to appear in Paris as well. The foremost representative of the art in the late seventeenth century, Ninon de Lenclos, had such spirit and elegance that young men would swarm after her until she was eighty. Molière and Boileau were Ninon's close friends; even Voltaire admired her. Cardinal Richelieu offered her 150,000 gold coins to become his mistress. She declined, saying that such a large sum was improper to receive from a lover, and at the same time it was too little to compensate for the unpleasantness of a life with a man she did not love. What times those were—when a harlot dared to say such a thing to France's most powerful man.

In a pasquinade, a Neapolitan jingle of the sixteenth century, we find the following rueful message:

> *Seek not the courtesan*
> *Hold back the best ye can,*
> *For like her whoring sister,*
> *She beguiles both lord and mister:*
> *She purloins the virtue, prick and purse,*
> *Know this, lad, or get thee to a nurse.*

French moralists like Guillaume Coquillard, Olivier Maillard, and Michel Menot often pointed out that a courtesan could be more dangerous than an ordinary prostitute because she was expensive enough to ruin one young nobleman after another.

 With the dawning of the Renaissance in northern Italy and France, one found the flower of Europe's aristocracy, rich merchants, and public servants all on their knees in thrall to the leading prostitutes of the day; some of these women were even born in the whorehouse. What had happened? Earlier, and for centuries, the nobles had been able to take their sexual pleasure from almost any woman at will. But now they were all too willing to pay a stern piper for female company. The Renaissance would change Europe in complex ways. Evidence that many men now looked on women with greater respect is to be found in the fact that active instruction was conducted in decent social conduct and how to respect and venerate women. This was something that had been in progress in the principalities of Burgund and

Bourgogne since the fifteenth century, in the form of courtly love. Centuries of higher education and generations of domestication of the noblemen of the late Middle Ages were finally showing results. During the Renaissance, impeccable manners and high respect for women were in fashion. At the same time, a steadily growing number of women were schooled in the literary and musical arts. Courtesans of the sixteenth century were the first to take advantage of the greater emotional refinement and sexual self-discipline that had developed among the upper echelons of Europe's male sex.

Without the fifteenth century's basic training in comporting oneself in the proper gallant, chivalrous manner, this romantic relationship between noblemen and luxury prostitutes would not have been possible. Romantic love had, up till now, been a privilege of the aristocracy. Now romance was becoming increasingly democratic and human. Thus it was both possible and socially acceptable to fall in love with a prostitute and give in to her charms. Besides, the courtesans had one thing in common with the Virgin Mary and all those queens the troubadours had sung about: they were also slightly out of reach. For those who dreamed about only one woman, it was devastating to think that she was constantly meeting new men.

"Majestically the carriages roll through the narrow streets of Rome; the Via Sacra is not free, nor is the Via Lata. They pass directly down the avenues, clothed in splendor; and they are carried over the Ponte Sisto in insolent glory," wrote one sixteenth-century Venetian following a visit to Rome.

La Strada del Populo was the street in Rome best known for its streetwalkers, but it did not have such a bad reputation that decent people could not take their promenades there. The courtesan Giuliana Ferrarese had cardinals and men of wealth as her clients; she was well clad and well mannered and anything but a woman of the street, though it is conceivable that she, too, could have captured one or another of her rich suitors out on the street.

One day, with deliberate intent, Giuliana Ferrarese offended a woman of virtue and position right in the middle of La Strada del Populo. The honorable lady shrieked and raged and used volleys of language so foul that it would have desecrated the souls of ten bishops. The cultivated

Giuliana Ferrarese smiled amiably and replied in her refined Italian, "I do most humbly beg your pardon, dear lady. I now understand that indeed you have a greater right to promenade down this street than I do." With the arrival of the courtesans, prostitution came out of the shade and stepped into the sun-drenched piazzas of the Italian cities.

The cultural influence of prostitutes streamed into the rich and vibrant northern Italian cities. A beautiful woman was not to smile or laugh in such a manner that she revealed more than six teeth, a courtesan's affectation probably originated to conceal teeth that may have been missing. Giovanni Boccaccio reflected the tone of the day when he declared that a woman of ideal beauty had blond hair. Things became even more difficult for Italian womanhood when the abbot of the Monastery of San Salvatore wrote a dialogue about female beauty, *Dialogo delle belezze Donne,* in which he placed great weight on "the blue eyes of a goddess" and only as a last resort accepted "the shining brown" ones. Like antiquity's Roman prostitutes, the courtesans of the Renaissance colored their hair blond; they used a mixture of chamomile and marigold flowers, henna, and lemon, but were forced to keep the eye color with which nature had blessed them.

"There are two types of women," wrote Thomas Heywood, a commentator on the sex industry of his day. "The better type are not only wiser and better schooled, but at the same time more discreet than men—and much more persevering in the sport of love." For Heywood, it was the courtesans alone who occupied this category, and he preferred those he met in Rome and northern Italy, although they could also be encountered in France and England. The women of the second category were far worse—"humorless, bad-tempered, weak-minded purveyors of gossip, so foolish that the only suitable place for them was the Devil's own dungheap." Not only the brave housewives of the Renaissance, but considerable numbers of lower-class prostitutes were included in that second category.

The madonna figure went out of fashion during the 1400s and 1500s, while the courtesans sailed right in. King François I of France had several mistresses, and his liberal and literary sister Margareta da Navarra immortalized the courtesans of the Renaissance in her book *Heptameron.* But the courtesans contributed to the mythologizing, since considerable numbers of them were also writers and poets. The courtesans were simply the leading women of these centuries, both sexually and intellectually.

The mistress of Charles VII of France, Agnes Sorel, was a woman of slight pedigree and debatable virtue, but she was inducted into the aristocracy as Madame de Beauté. Agnes would captivate the imagination of all France. In some of the poems that praise her, she is, strangely enough, presented as a virgin, as if the king had never touched her:

> *Noble are you, Agnes,*
> *only because*
> *your deeds are more honorable*
> *across the whole of France,*
> *rather than within some cloister*
> *with the most pious nuns, or solitary devotees.*

Tradition has it that Charles VII himself wrote these lines, though they are obviously a snippet of popular poetry. The French continued to regard women through conventional eyes, so Agnes was transformed into a holy virgin of almost the same dimensions as her slightly older contemporary Jeanne d'Arc.

But who knows? Perhaps indeed it was his love for Agnes that drove Charles to unite France once again, and to bring peace and order to the country? And if this were so, how much greater would Agnes Sorel's virtue be!

Pietro Aretino had supporters and detractors from the moment his dialogues came out. For some, he still stands as a brave campaigner for sexual freedom; for others, he is an ironic critic of his society. A third group would consider him a victim of the tyranny imposed on frail mortals by the sex drive. Certain biographers have felt that Aretino was entrusted with the secrets of the courtesans because his own mother belonged to the trade, but there is no real evidence about this. Aretino never talked about his mother in such terms; nor can she be identified in Venice's registry of prostitutes. What we do know is that this satirical writer grew up with a beautiful and cultivated mother who sat as a model for a whole series of painters of the day. Perhaps she had features in common with Veronica Franco and Imperia Cognata. But beautiful women have existed in history who were not courtesans, even in Venice.

While the courtesans were both learned and beautiful, it did not necessarily follow that their ethical standards were as impressive. Lucrezia, one of Aretino's fictive courtesans, helped a client take the life of a mortal enemy without getting a single drop of blood on her fingers; she simply told one client at precisely what time another would be finished. How was she to know that her client, still somewhat dazed by their love tryst, would receive an iron rod through his skull as soon as he left her house?

The self-same Lucrezia also knew the importance of good word of mouth. She told her clients that on nights when the star-studded heavens were clear, or the moon shone down upon the earth, she was generally unable to sleep and had to get out of bed and walk around a little, completely nude, often in front of the window. She was not at all shy about allowing the men in the street to glimpse her perfect figure. This proved very good for business.

One of the last of Aretino's saucy dialogues pitted three women of the trade against one another; the middle-aged syphilitic Antonia; her professional sister, Nanna; and the latter's daughter, Pippa, still an apprentice to the profession. Nanna explained to her daughter how she could be compared to a soldier: She was paid to do what it was wrong to do, and for her pains, she met with ambivalence in society. In addition she, like the soldier, was always on call.

Nanna seemed never to have any peace and quiet, neither out in the world nor at home. As she explained to Pippa:

> For when she is sleepy, she cannot sleep; she must stay awake to caress some scurvy man, a huge, ugly buffalo.... If she is at table, every fly looks like a silkworm to him; and if she gives the tiniest morsel to someone else, he grumbles and fumes with rage, gnawing at his bread.... We are prodded and pushed and manhandled from all avenues, and in all ways, day and night, and any whore who does not consent to all the filth they can think of, would die of hunger. One man wants boiled meat, the other wants roast; and they have discovered the "aperture behind," "the legs on the shoulders," "the Gianetta style," "the crane," "the tortoise," "crouch on the belfry," "the stirrup," "the grazing sheep," and other postures more far-fetched and extravagant than a stage actor's prancing, so finally I would cry, "Oh, world, may God be with you!," though I am ashamed to say it. In short, nowadays they make an anatomy of any lady whatsoever; so learn how to live, Pippa, and learn how to manage, or else I'll see you in hell.

Henry IV of France, the king who seemed to give no more thought to Paris than he did to high mass, changed mistresses more often than religions.

During his reign, the court prostitutes from the lower rungs of the social ladder, as in days of yore, were housed in small secluded dwellings some distance from the royal palaces.

But with the king's favorite mistress, it was another story. Henry IV thought his mistress should take part in the affairs of court, as did the queen, Maria de Medici, and the rest of the aristocracy. Henry IV's first mistress, Henriette d'Entrague, was first made a marquise, then a duchess; Gabrielle d'Estrée was the next in line. Maria de Medici raged for a while—this was going a bit far, perhaps—but the tone had been set for similar arrangements in courts throughout Europe.

Royal mistresses received substantially greater prestige and status, and prostitution began to flourish at the periphery of the court. In the sixteenth and seventeenth centuries, sexual frivolity with the royal courtiers was a career move for beautiful women and their families. Those women—and a few handsome men—who put themselves at the sexual disposition of a king seldom received ready money; rather, they got diamond jewelry, houses, horses and carriages, and with time they also received high aristocratic titles for themselves and their families.

> *Peace is his aim, his gentleness is such,*
> *And love he loves, for he loves fucking much . . .*
> *Restless he rolls about from whore to whore,*
> *A merry monarch, scandalous and poor.*

So wrote the witty poet John Wilmot, earl of Rochester, about Charles II of England in the 1670s. Even though he was the king's whoremonger, and was by nature manic-depressive, Rochester was as wholeheartedly a libertine as his monarch. He would help the king, well disguised, gain entrance to even the most basic whorehouse in Newmarket. There were rumors that on one of these escapades, the earl of Rochester abandoned the king of England in a brothel without money. A contemporary writer, Theophilus Cibber, recounts that Charles II, unrecognized, had been refused credit by the local madam and was made the general butt of laughter. The earl of Rochester's liberal attitude did not mean he was always polite and gracious toward his lord and monarch, as witnessed by a poem he wrote, speaking in a voice he claims to be that of His Majesty:

I rise at eleven, I dine at two,
I get drunk before seven, and the next thing I do,
Is send for my whore. . . .
At once she bereaves me of money and cunt,
I storm and I roar, and I fall in a rage,
And missing my whore, I bugger my page.

One of Charles II's more permanent mistresses was the merchant's daughter Barbara Palmer. When she was introduced at court, she was married, but after a few nights with His Majesty, she saw to it that her husband was elevated to an earl. Later, she, too, received an aristocratic title with ironic undertones—Baroness Nonesuch. After putting in many years in the monarch's bed, she became duchess of Cleveland, and under this name, she went down in history as one of the most promiscuous women of the English court. A list that her enemies made up of all her lovers included circus performers, actors, and pageboys, but there was at least one exception: the founding father of the aristocratic Churchill family. As an aging duchess, she neither paid for nor accepted money for sex, for she had invested all her sexual capital and could age without worry and at the same time be gratified by half the city.

How did one become a courtesan in Rome or Venice, or a royal mistress in London or Paris? There were no courtesan schools, but these women all required schooling. It was not enough to possess white teeth and a well-endowed bosom. The life of the Roman courtesan Tullia d'Aragonza is perhaps representative. Her mother had been a prostitute and her father a man of the cloth. Her mother was the not unknown Giuliana Ferrarese, who had had many rich clients; however, she bore her daughter in an unattractive ramshackle brick building in Campo Marzio de San Trifone. Both the mother and the infant were lucky that the birth father was a cardinal and admitted his paternity. Lodovico d'Aragonza paid for his daughter's education as long as he held on to power in a Rome that seethed with intrigue. When he fell from grace and was forced to leave the papal city, Giuliana's new lover stepped in to contribute to the education of Tullia, who was now in Siena, learning to speak the country's most beautiful Italian.

Not many years later, Rome would lay itself out at the feet of the well-educated, beautiful, and quick-witted Tullia. Her mother also benefited from her daughter's triumphs. Many excellent schools had helped to make Tullia d'Aragonza a formidable poet and storyteller, and she wrote perfectly in French and Latin, played the harp, and knew all the fashionable dances. She became a trendsetter in haute couture and was more elegant than anyone else in Rome.

The Englishwoman Nell Gwynn was also the daughter of a prostitute, born in a London whorehouse in 1650. Her extremely fat mother was the madam, and her sister Rose became a prostitute. Nell started out as an actress at exactly the moment when it became acceptable for women to go on stage. She was amusing and quick-witted; the theatrical world taught her how to behave like a lady, and generated a crowd of paying admirers. George Villiers, duke of Buckingham, was among the many who took notice of the clever, high-spirited, and sweet-tempered thespian, and it was he who managed to introduce the city's most talented prostitute to the nobility of England. The first time Nell Gwynn was introduced to King Charles II, however, she was tactless enough to ask him directly for money. One could expect diamonds, privileges, and titles, but not cash. And Nell Gwynn learned. The next time His Majesty invited her, she was discretion itself. With the passage of time, she had two sons with a royal father; both were ennobled and granted landed estates.

The French Jeanne du Barry grew up with a single mother who ran a tavern and from time to time worked as a prostitute. In time, the mother married and enjoyed a calmer, more orderly life. Jeanne was, like most comfortably-off daughters of whores, sent to a convent. She went to Paris when she was eighteen and was swiftly recruited by an obscure count who specialized in giving the finishing touches to first-class prostitutes. Equipped with new manners, real diamonds, false identity papers, and a fictive marriage contract to a nonexistent count, Jeanne was ready for Versailles.

A few courtesans were born into the nobility's own inner circles. Louis de Mally was the marquis de Nestlé, but he was deeply in debt. On the other side of the ledger, he had five extraordinarily beautiful daughters; three of them went from man to man within the aristocracy, then became ladies-in-waiting to Queen Maria and simultaneous mistresses to Louis XV, not always an auspicious combination. The marquis, however, cooperated with the king's counselors, who did not want Louis involved with women who had political ambitions, which the Nestlé family did not have. In return, the marquis had his debts paid and received a generous lifetime annuity. Even in the very best circles, there can be a living wage in prostitution.

Jeanne-Antoinette Poisson was dazzlingly beautiful but from a bourgeois family background. When she was twenty-five, she by accident met Louis XV at a masked ball, dressed as Cinderella. Despite opposition within the aristocracy, she became the monarch's mistress and, in accord with convention, had to be upgraded to a marquise. Thereafter, she was known as Madame de Pompadour and acquired great political power and influence. She was also a trendsetter for coiffures and clothing and much else that came to be named after Madame.

Madame de Pompadour was wise enough to see that all this good fortune would not continue forever. She secured for herself the administration of the royal mistresses, something that well qualified her to be called "madam." In the game park at Versailles, she built a house where King Louis got to choose his partners, one every night. The girls lived in seclusion, but by day they received instruction in dance, singing, and painting. The whole court knew about them but did not know that the king was their sponsor; they had been told that the faithful nightly guest was a Polish count in exile. When one of the girls suspected the truth, she was removed to a madhouse before she could spread the story further.

Among the "great" courtesans and mistresses, there was but one who ended up a moralist and prostitution reformer. This was Françoise d'Aubigné, best known as Madame de Maintenon. Among her lovers were the writer Paul Scarron and Louis XIV. In her old age, she became a defender of French classicism's ethical dramatist Jean Racine. In Racine's biblical dramas, *Esther* and *Athalie,* we meet the queens and heathen priestesses of Israel and Babylon, and all of Racine's contemporaries thought they found discreet allusions to Madame de Maintenon and her past.

During the 1530s, Tullia d'Aragonza became famous throwing the most elegant parties that Rome had ever seen. The Medici popes were permanent fixtures on the guest list. When, at one point, the hostess's honor suffered a derogatory remark, the whole of Rome's aristocracy rushed to her assistance, with a young count in the lead.

It was the misstep of her life when Tullia openly showed that she preferred the company of a portly German client to that of Rome's young and supple aristocrats. Money, which had lain so heavily on the scales, left when the German Croesus departed from Rome. The young men about town set in motion a whisper campaign, and suddenly, Tullia was out of fashion. She also lost all the support she had enjoyed from the authorities and was forced to abandon Rome abruptly.

She hoped to reestablish herself in Ferrara, where a liberal atmosphere prevailed. She wrote beautiful poetry and was admitted to the salon of Victoria Colonna, the leading woman writer of Italy in the sixteenth century. A French diplomat who had no idea who the newcomer was wrote a glowing report to Paris about "a goddess of a woman" who sang her arias like a lark and conducted intelligent conversation on any theme from theology to geopolitics: "And at the same time there are none who dare approach her, not even the brilliant Marquis de Pescara."

Ferrara was too small a place for a woman of Tullia's reputation. Nor was Venice exactly what Tullia had expected. The learned humanist Bernardo Tasso, father to the poet Torquato Tasso, was completely smitten by her, but he was in no position to subsidize her lifestyle. At the same time, the courtesans of Venice were meeting with success in their campaign against intruders. Tullia's next stop was Siena, where she tried to live a neutral life for some years as a duly wedded wife. But there, too, she was sought out at home and harassed by the police, who wanted to drive her out of her home and place her in the red-light district. For they believed that it was there and nowhere else that she belonged. Neither princely lovers nor literary fame hindered the Italian policemen from harassing whores whenever they felt like it.

Tullia penned a letter of supplication—in the form of a sonnet— to the duke of Tuscany, who offered her protection in Florence. At long last, she was back in intellectual society, and in her later days, she would keep contact with one of the leading Renaissance humanists, Benedetto Varchi. Titian had immortalized Varchi in a portrait of the day but used other, and Venetian, courtesans—not Tullia—as models for his many Venus and Mary Magdalene paintings. Tullia d'Aragonza made her wise friend the main character in one of her best-known works, the dialogue *Dell'infinità d'amore,* which deals with the great diversity of physical love and its limits.

When Tullia d'Aragonza returned to Rome some years later, she lived a less stylish life. The new pope, Paul III, sent people to humiliate her: They made her wear a veil, which was obligatory garb for common prostitutes.

Consequently, Tullia d'Aragonza spent her last years wandering the streets of Rome dressed in the simple habit of a whore—several decades after last selling her body. Pietro Aretino had left Rome at the same time. The pope had wanted to send out a warning. It was perhaps not surprising, then, that his first victims were Italy's most immoral writer and the most famous luxury prostitute, she with the best turn of phrase.

How, then, did they die, these courtesans? Imperia Cognata died at the beginning of the sixteenth century, barely thirty years of age. A messenger was sent from Pope Julius II with oil for the extreme unction. Rome's best doctors sat at her bedside. As soon as her death bulletin came out, it spread through the streets to the sorrowing population. Imperia Cognata left behind a fortune that she bequeathed for the paving of Strada del Populo, where so many harlots who had enjoyed less success than she had had to earn their daily bread on their feet.

Veronica Franco died in Venice at the end of the sixteenth century. She also left behind a large fortune but bequeathed it to a Magdalene home. This was perhaps a sign that she had changed her views on certain features of the life she had led in her youth.

Nell Gwynn lived out her life in England without acquiring an aristocratic title. She used her own name and introduced herself, publicly and with great relish, as "the king's Protestant whore." It was this direct, unaffected manner that endeared her to the people. Verses and stanzas portrayed her as the symbol of healthy Protestant womanhood. England's first feminist, Aphra Behn, dedicated her drama, *The Feign'd Courtesan*, to Nell Gwynn out of respect and admiration. When "Little" Nell died in 1687, there was an outpouring of national sorrow.

Tullia d'Aragonza wrote her own testament in faultless Latin before she died in 1556 at just over fifty. Had it not been for the thirty-five books and eleven volumes of personal memoirs she left behind, one would have thought she was some poor streetwalker and not one of her century's most admired women. At the time of her death, Tullia did not own so much as a single jewel—only three gowns, five good unwashed bedsheets, two pillows, one carpet, and four chairs.

FIFTEEN

LOVE IN THE SOUTH SEAS

Imagine what it must have been like when H.M.S. *Bounty* dropped anchor on Tahiti in the historic year of 1788. Everybody on board was enchanted with the island and overwhelmed by the affectionate welcome they received from both men and women. With the exception of the strict Captain Bligh, they all soon fell in love, several times each. But the dreamland had its dark side. After some months, venereal disease spread, along with jealous dramas. Far from all the Tahitian girls were pleased with the first white men they chose and simply took a new one.

The story of the *Bounty* has been committed to film many times, and in every version, Fletcher Christian, the first mate and second in command after the captain, is the most handsome of all the white men. Both English historical records and actual events in Tahiti give the clear impression that this cinematic convention was true to popular opinion back in 1788. After having passed from embrace to embrace for a time, he ended up with the island's princess, Mauatuas, whom he christened Isabella. Christian's male orderly, or *tyo,* was the only person Isabella allowed him to sleep with, if she was tired. In this sexual dreamland, the princess made the decisions.

Down through the ages, European and Chinese travelers in Southeast Asia and the Pacific have described the region's women as scantily clad, loving, and sexually inviting. Visitors of today have a strikingly similar impression, most of them focusing on peripheral islands. There, social relations seem less affected by centuries of political and technological changes, and many white men still dream of experiencing the same delights as the *Bounty* sailors. But the soft "hello" and the delicate flirtation with which one is greeted are not invitations to a one-night stand. The woman, not the man, brings a mutually binding relationship to fruition, if that is what she wants.

Along the beaches of the South China Sea and the Pacific, prostitution is, even at the beginning of the twenty-first century, considered a culturally foreign phenomenon. Any careful observer who listens to a girl's voice and watches her gait will be able to determine whether she is one of the island's own or an abandoned short-term adventurer from Manila or mainland Southeast Asia. Cash-oriented sex behavior in this setting is conspicuously brutal, as though these endless sandy beaches and the coconut palms call upon softer and milder female initiatives.

For many centuries, Puritan Europeans felt that all men and women of the South Seas should be called whores and adulterers, with precisely the same meaning as back home. Westerners with more open minds learned that if they were not to the taste of a local woman, no amount of money could make her change their mind. The women had little need for cash but showed their value through the work they carried out, and they were accustomed to taking ample care of their desires.

Antonio Pigafetta, the observant Italian mariner who kept a diary during Magellan's great circumnavigation in the 1520s, was such a lively raconteur that even today his book remains a source of great enjoyment. One reason for this might be that Pigafetta was extremely curious. Without bashfulness, he questioned people on all the islands that the expedition visited—about both sex and genitalia—and got answers. His diligence resulted in a text rich in detail; for example, he was able to explain how and why the men of the Philippines and Borneo installed an iron or gold pin in their glans penis: "The men say they do so because the women want to have it like that; those who leave it alone, don't get to have any contact with women."

On other islands in the region, people practiced quasi-surgical alterations of the sexual organs that today we would consider a cross between piercing and circumcision. In contrast to those common in Africa, all interventions were designed to bring women greater sexual pleasure.

Jacob Cornelius van Neck, a Dutch merchant, visited various harbors in Southeast Asia around the year 1600, including the Muslim state Pattani, on the northern part of the Melaccan Peninsula, where the rajah was a vassal to the king of Siam. Van Neck described the women of Pattani: "The young women were equally straightforward about which European or Chinese merchant they liked, and proposed to become their short-term wives. Thus would she become his cook and servant by day, and his wife by night. But he should not sleep with other women—and she should not speak to other men. When his ship was about to leave the city, they parted from one another as good friends, and she received the fee agreed upon— before marriage."

During the 1600s, more European traders came into contact with the East Indies and Indochina, today's Southeast Asia. The region would remind them politically of Europe a couple of centuries earlier. In the Southeast, there existed royal power, mercantile trade, craft workers, and city dwellers. Only one European feature was not to be found—prostitutes.

Monuments like Angkor Wat in Cambodia and Borubudur in central Java prove the existence of old civilizations resembling those of India and China. In Burma, Siam, Cambodia, Vietnam, and Java, kings resided in their capitals, conducted wars with one another, and tried to levy taxes on the burgeoning trade, almost as in Europe. Because the interior was inhospitable, the rivers and coastline bound these kingdoms together. The feudal kingdoms on the mainland had their vassal states in the mountainous regions, while on the islands to the south, there was a series of more independent small Muslim sultans. Although the political and bureaucratic systems were simpler and the written culture poorer than in India or China, all visitors from the West, China, and the Arab and Indian worlds agreed that this part of the globe was civilized.

When the Westerners left civilization and traveled farther southeast, they discovered New Guinea, Australia, and the lesser Melanesian islands. Here they were met with warfare from populations living at a lower level of development. To European eyes, these darker peoples were indeed primitive and wild.

During the 1700s, the European explorers would sail even farther east and discover more islands, much farther out in the Pacific Ocean—the islands of Polynesia. The explorers of these islands, like Louis de Bougainville and James Cook, concluded that they were back in civilization. These island societies resembled Southeast Asia more than the primitive Melanesia, with small kingdoms on Tonga, Tahiti, and Hawaii. The Polynesians were lighter in skin, amiable in manners, and sexually attractive to the Europeans. In terms of language and culture, the Polynesians had so much in common with Southeast Asia that Westerners found adjustment very easy.

* * *

Far into the 1800s, Westerners remained guests in Southeast Asia and the Pacific and conducted their mercantile trade in niches of the foreign cultures. Very few had the desire to re-create the region in their own image.

The more the Europeans observed, the more surprised they were. Most impressive were the friendly and accommodating body language and the light, body-clinging attire of the women. These women gave birth, looked after their homes, and took part in agricultural work, more involved in political life and trade than women in India, China, or Europe. They sometimes bore weapons. The powerful sultans of Aceh, in Northern Sumatra, preferred to surround themselves with a bodyguard of unmarried women. Women were considered less trigger-happy, shot only when it was absolutely necessary, and felt a stronger solidarity with their ruler.

Southeast Asian and Polynesian men mostly moved to their wives' houses or villages upon marriage, which gave the woman as many allies as the man if conflicts arose in the marriage. One can therefore speak of a matriarchal society, a cultural feature that defines both regions, in sharp contrast to the patriarchal societies of India, China, and Japan and the primitive male-chauvinist societies of Melanesia.

Politically, sexually, and economically, the relationship between the sexes in Southeast Asia and Polynesia was rather equal. Women commonly chose to have abortions on their own terms, sexual intercourse before marriage was widespread, and those dissatisfied with their husbands easily got divorced.

Christianity and Islam have different concepts of women's position in society and their sexual pleasure. The arrival of those two religions in Polynesia and Southeast Asia explains to some extent why women's freedom has weakened over the past 150 years. But much has continued as before: The piercing that fascinated Pigafetta is still practiced in peripheral Philippines and Borneo, although less frequently than before.

Islam reached Melacca, Java, Sumatra, Borneo, and the southern parts of Mindanao and Sulawesi just a century or two before the Europeans introduced Christianity to the region. All over this area, indigenous religion was pushed aside by Islam, and Hinduism today remains dominant only in Bali. The low marriage age that the Europeans explicitly registered among the aristocrats in the many small sultanates was proof of the power of Islam. But in the highlands of mainland Southeast Asia, Sumatra, Borneo, and the northern Philippines, the Moluccas, Flores, Timor, and the

Polynesian islands, Christianity gradually eroded most traces of ancestor worship and animism. Only the Theravada Buddhism of Burma, Siam, and Cambodia resisted the pressure, but even here, influence from Christianity revised the equality between the sexes. In Vietnam, Christianity, Confucianism, and Buddhism would live side by side and even give birth to new religious blendings.

During the same period, increased wealth transformed women of the aristocracy into more dependent and decorative assets. The Ramayana, Southeast Asia's most widespread secular text, which inspired many ballet and theater performances, also contributed to a new view of women as more passive creatures, first within the aristocracy and gradually down through the middle classes. Aristocratic women from Theravada Buddhist states were still allowed sexual freedom with men of equal or superior social standing.

Southeast Asian and Polynesian women of the lower classes also enjoyed more freedom than women in other parts of the world, in spite of the Muslim, Western, and Chinese influence. Parallel with the religious and economic changes, the region became urbanized, which affected the sex roles in villages and cities. An increasing number of European, Muslim, and Chinese businessmen came into the region, and as the number of single foreign males rose, a sexual culture developed in accord with the expectations of the itinerant Chinese, Indian, Arab, and European merchants.

Prostitution had been unknown in Southeast Asia before the year 1500, but it expanded through the centuries in direct proportion to the numbers of Western, Arab, and Chinese businessmen and their growing prejudice against free sex with native women.

The Dutchman van Neck—who with particular intimacy had described the old temporary-marriage institution with Malayan women— also in the early 1600s observed something that resembled European and Chinese prostitution, in Pattani and other ports: women who made themselves available for sexual services on a one-time basis, in return for a cash payment. When van Neck investigated it turned out that these women were slaves of the local sultan or prince, and it was he who had initiated the move to obtain extra income. When the governor of the Philippines, Gomez Dasmariñas, visited the sultan of Brunei in his floating capital a couple of decades later, he observed the same phenomenon. The sultan's female slaves rowed out to meet the Spanish galleons to offer their services for cash—for the sultan. Since slavery has a spontaneous tendency to lead to sexual abuse, it is easy to confuse this phenomenon with poverty-stricken prostitution. While slavery in Southeast Asia had older roots, prostitution was a new cultural trait sprung from foreign merchants' preference to pay for sex.

In Ayuttayah, the original capital of Siam, one of the king's civil servants was given the task of supervising the six hundred slave women the king used to satisfy the demand for sex among the growing numbers of European and Chinese merchants. When the capital was moved closer to the coast and renamed Bangkok, visiting Europeans reported on booming prostitution both there and in Rangoon, where the king of Burma hired out great barracks of slave women prostitutes to foreign merchants on short-term contracts. Up until World War II, the royal families monopolized the income from the sex trade in Thailand, while the Cambodian queen Kossamak kept full control right up to the American coup d'état of 1970.

In the small Muslim sultanates, there was a growing skepticism against the infidel Europeans and Chinese. This endangered the traditional temporary marriages with itinerant foreigners, and during the 1800s, the sultans began to promote prostitution, following the example of the Buddhist kings but also on the assumption that such intercourse would diminish the foreigners' influence over their own women.

In the late 1800s, Southeast Asia and the Pacific underwent enormous economic and political changes. The Dutch, British, French, for a few years the Germans, and finally the Americans and Australians divided the region and secured political and economic control over their own spheres of influence. Partly through warfare, and partly through pressure and threats, the local rulers were defeated or pacified.

Mines and plantations were established over the whole region, which increased the presence of white businessmen and their assistants. Thousands upon thousands of Chinese coolies were imported from the southern provinces of China to the Philippines, Java, the Malay Peninsula, and Sumatra. Indians were sent to Fiji and the Chinese to Hawaii; the aboriginal populations of Australia and Melanesia were freighted back and forth between the islands. Forced-labor recruits submitted only when they were too far away from home to escape.

As the production of raw materials increased, so did world trade. The population soared, mostly in the coastal cities and the economic trading zones. A marked shortage of womenfolk occurred among mariners, the urban population, miners, and plantation workers, but they could obtain female company in different ways. Some chose the companionship of Vietnamese, Malayan, or Polynesian women lovers on the rubber plantation or the mine site. They occasionally availed themselves of the diversions provided by a Japanese prostitute in the nearest coastal city. Chinese law forbade married men from leaving China, and a coolie's wage could hardly feed a family. For the coolies, a visit to a prostitute was almost the only alternative to celibacy or homosexuality.

Southeast Asian women learned from the immigrant East Asian and European prostitutes, and an increasing number began to charge for pleasuring merchants, sailors, and Chinese coolies. Finally, Southeast Asian men were pulled into the newly developed circulation of prostitution. During the 1900s, Thais and Vietnamese, and Malays from Manila to Jakarta, began to appreciate periodic visits to prostitutes. It was more practical and a lot cheaper than to permanently maintain the traditional second wife.

Polynesia is more sparsely populated, and is located outside the world. It still is considered an idyll for both men and women, and prostitution is little developed. This might be explained by other factors. Protestantism rules strongly, and for strategic geopolitical reasons, the region receives such great economic support from the U.S.A. and France that few women feel the need to prostitute themselves.

The urbanized and overpopulated Southeast Asia, on the other hand, today has the greatest number of prostitutes relative to its total population. Obviously, there are many rational considerations behind this development. It nevertheless remains a great historical paradox that the Chinese and European men who went to Southeast Asia were offered the pleasures of love for free. But instead of free South Seas love under the gentle swish of the palm trees, they preferred quantifiable sex illuminated by the ubiquitous red lanterns.

SIXTEEN

FANNY HILL

J ohn Cleland's praised and detested libertine novel of 1748, *Fanny Hill: The Memoirs of a Woman of Pleasure,* was banned by the English censors of its day. Even in our time it has been branded as pornographic and depraved.

Despite all this, the book was translated into many languages, while in England it was published illegally. In the end, it came out in a cleaned-up and morally upgraded version that history has since, rightly, forgotten. Unfortunately, the virtuous branch of literary criticism has concealed the book's literary value by discussing only the commotion it created and its underground character, not its content. But in its unexpurgated form, *Fanny Hill* is rich reading and clearly literary even today. Additionally, it is a source of manifold insights into prostitution, sexual life, and sex-role patterns of the eighteenth century.

John Cleland was an educated and well-traveled gentleman with important posts in the colonies of the Middle East, India, and the East Indies. He obviously had personal experience with prostitutes in England and India, male as well as female. His book is central in an important debate on sexual morality, individual freedom, ambition, and prostitution in England and France of the eighteenth century. Other writers were publishing books on related themes then, too.

William Hogarth's oil paintings and etchings from English street life, with one series entitled *The Harlot's Progress,* came out about the same time. While Cleland's novel portrayed prostitution as a key road toward social advancement, Hogarth's paintings gave the opposite message, depicting the advance of women into alcoholism and misery. Nonetheless, Hogarth believed that a prostitute could have a heart of gold even if her fate was far from kind, and he urged his countryfolk to sympathize and "save" her and her sisters.

The question of which of these artists was right cannot be answered. Cleland's heroine, Fanny, was in no way representative of the majority. Of this Cleland was conscious, and all his life he continued to write about the brothels. In his later books, which would probably now be forgotten if not for *Fanny Hill,* many prostitutes had a grim fate. Fanny, however, became the best-known "happy hooker" in world literature.

Fanny Hill is truly a sunshine story. Not only do we get the explicit details of exciting sexual exploits—which the heroine always enjoys—but we also encounter great romantic love. Charles, the lover, is at the outset a student with a better social background than peasant girl Fanny's.

Fanny's story is told through a series of letters to a girlfriend in the same trade. We learn everything about how Fanny felt, from the moment she caught a glimpse of her dream hero, fully debauched but sleeping the sleep of the just in the lounge at the brothel where Fanny served as an apprentice: "Oh, Lord, what a sight! Neither the passage of years nor the vicissitudes of fate can ever obliterate the impression his appearance made on me. . . . Even the faintness and pallor in this face, where the momentary triumph of the lily over the rose, due to the debaucheries of the night, drew from me the most beautiful thoughts united with an indescribable bliss." Obviously, this was love at first sight. And, surprise of surprises, Charles felt exactly the same—as he woke with a hangover—and cast an eye over the angel Fanny.

Because Fanny was still a novice in the sex trade, she had not yet, praise the Lord, had her sexual debut. A second, equally significant stroke of luck was the fact that her heart's desire had inherited permanent economic support from his grandmother. This made it easy for the two youngsters to escape from the brothel together.

The following day, Charles returned to the brothel with his solicitor to retrieve Fanny's belongings. He then quit boozing and carousing and used Granny's money on Fanny and a cozy little flat. The two youngsters lived in a free relationship, but Charles had the best of intentions. Without a blush, the writer gives us every detail about how Charles transformed Fanny from a virgin to a woman.

Later, fate would drive the lovers apart. Fanny turned to prostitution, not always of the prettiest kind. But she was always decently installed, in her own well-furnished apartment, with a servant girl.

Toward the end, the lovers reunited. Fanny had by then had an abortion. In all other ways, she was still young and healthy in body and soul, had steered clear of venereal diseases and alcoholism, common problems among her sisters in the trade during the 1700s. Charles, for his part, became an even more attractive human being: "His travels had made him more manly and a charming beard contributed to making him more mature, something that went unremarked in league with a mixture of dignity, security and kindness. But he had lost none of his powerful, muscular physique, which continued to glow with vigor and was a true joy to my eyes and hands," Fanny confided. She explained that deep in her heart, she loved only Charles, but her love was not of the type that precluded unfettered abandoned sex with other men. Such had happened in the meantime, often at Fanny's own initiative. Charles had had important experiences and exciting adventures in the English colonies, but he had made no fortune. Fanny, who had prostituted herself all over London, had saved money that grew into a small fortune when she inherited the estate of an old suitor. Charles, after deep thought and fond entreaties, was persuaded to take Fanny's money to start his own business. Later, his beloved Fanny, now a married woman, devoted herself to the upbringing of "the loveliest children anyone has ever seen."

Fanny Hill's story is almost too fantastic to believe. But Cleland does contrast Fanny with her friend Emily, a more believable example of the successful eighteenth-century prostitute. Emily was naive but good-hearted. She met a man of her own class but told him she was the widow of a drowned sailor. He believed her, and her happiness was thus secured. Emily "took great delight in domestic life in a completely natural way, with such stability and skill that it appeared she had never taken a single step from the correct path of virtue."

A contemporary English social reformer estimated the number of prostitutes in London at the time of *Fanny Hill* to be three thousand, while the city's total population was verging on a million. Male prostitutes were also to be found, but only a few hundred at most. Prostitution was still not a dominant feature of London life. However, contemporary sources make it clear that most prostitutes suffered much grimmer fates than both Fanny and Emily in Cleland's book. Like most London girls, Fanny and Emily married in their early twenties. Few real prostitutes were over the age of twenty-five, but this does not mean that most of them ended up happily married. London's Magdalene Hospital has kept good statistics about the girls they took care of in the decades after the 1750s, the period that Cleland pretends to describe. Six percent of the young prostitutes treated at Magdalene eventually married and raised families. Around 50 percent accepted the hospital's effort to contact family members from the suburbs or the countryside, and returned home, although some of them were in such miserable condition that they had no reason to expect a warm welcome. Some girls died, others ran away, while every fourth girl left the hospital to reenter the sex trade and make more money or marry, even though they were past the ideal age for both.

John Cleland has been accused of depicting the prostitution of the 1700s "with all the pain removed." But he does give a vivid description of Fanny, her sisters in the trade, their customers, and the young men they seduce and pay for; and periodically, a homosexual pops up in the text. All in all, this gives an interesting introduction to London around 1750, when the force of urban growth, proto-industrial conditions, and cultural exchanges with the world had in a few decades created a new and much more open urban society.

Cleland's book is marked by a modern outlook on women, men, and sex roles, and has an astonishingly modern view of prostitution analyzed as a product of poverty and need combined with free choice. Prostitution is posited as a possible road to social advancement, which was true, for a lucky few. Social climbing from village simplicity to bourgeois stability, "from rags to riches," might be seen as a basic theme in the relatively new, important literary genre of the 1700s—the novel.

The new wave of French and British novels was speckled with servant girls and orphans, all struggling to make a better life. Thoughts of the future forced characters in the novels of the 1700s to analyze whether it was expedient to maintain one's virtue or cast it to the wind. Most heroes and heroines did climb socially, but they employed exceedingly different methods, simply because the authors thought differently about the issue. Some felt it best to be super-virtuous; others let their heroes stake their future on vice. Daniel Defoe, the author of *Robinson Crusoe,* also wrote novels whose main characters were women. Two of them early on decided to become prostitutes: *Roxana, or The Fortunate Mistress* might be more exactly described as a novel about a courtesan than a common whore. But Moll Flanders set herself up differently. Her life story has the august and imposing title *The Fortunes and the Misfortunes of the Famous Moll Flanders, Who was born in Newgate, and during a Life of Threescore Years, besides her Childhood, was Twelve Years a Whore, five Times a Wife, Twelve Years a Thief, Eight Years a Transported Felon in Virginia, at Last grew rich and dy'd a Penitent. Written from her own Memorandums.*

"I want to become a *gentlewoman,*" declared the foundling Moll at only six years of age. From the time of her milk teeth, our heroine was completely determined to avoid a life of diligent domestic servitude, or endless weaving and spinning. She wanted to learn to sing and dance, to study languages, and to see the world, a sensationally modern message in 1722. Fifty years earlier such a thought in a woman, no matter what age, would have been mutinous. But Defoe could allow his readers to meet a foundling with such a hope, because all of England had been seized by changes and optimistic visions of the future.

Both Moll Flanders and Roxana decided to sell their bodies of their own accord, and each experienced both triumph and defeat. Moll would learn a lot more than to sing, dance, and sell her body. She was in no way too good to steal, but she still ended up as owner of her own plantation in America.

The first French novelist to write about prostitution was Abbé Prévost, who did so ten years after Defoe. In Prévost's novel *Manon Lescaut,* prostitution is not linked to any hope of social advancement; rather, it is focused mainly on a great romantic love. Prostitution appears only as a means of maintaining the lifestyle the hero and heroine feel their love demands. The heroine Manon and her lover, the Chevalier de Grieux, both descended from the well-heeled classes but were shielded from their own sensuality by their respective families. When the couple first met, she was about to enter a convent and he the Order of Malta. The meeting was disastrous—love at first sight. Both of them instantly understood that it would last for all eternity.

But this beautiful sensuous couple craved everything life can give, and let their love depend upon silk and champagne, theater visits and domestic servants, in order to satisfy the great love's need for luxurious scenic props. Manon's solution in the service of love was to sell herself to men she did not love, first secretly, then gradually, with her lover's blessing. Manon had a rather coarse brother who thought the young Chevalier to be as pretty as any girl and proposed that he sell his body as well. Chevalier preferred more dangerous but more "manly" methods of obtaining money—card sharking and grand larceny.

Manon and the Chevalier became more and more familiar with silks, champagne, chambermaids, and valets before they started the slide into ruin and damnation. For Prévost, pleasurable self-indulgence was the explanation of prostitution. Thus he took his seat among the conservative moralists who warned the aristocracy against giving their servants cast-off clothing and ornaments, because luxury instilled dependency, particularly among the poor. Any servant who got to feel real silk against her skin would fall prey to the ungovernable lust for more luxury. However well intended, such gifts could drive even innocent souls down into prostitution. The moral was clear—subordinates should be kept firmly in place, in their itchy homespun!

Abbé Prévost's social message was moderation and self-control among all classes, a conservative theme that flew in the face of the progress-oriented, optimistic challenges posed to the privileged of the old feudal society by the likes of Defoe and Cleland. Prévost's conservative moral outlook forced him to end his novel with tragedy—in French Louisiana in North America. The Chevalier de Grieux had committed murder, and Manon was expelled from France and died in tragic exile.

Thus the novel had developed three immortal heroines before Cleland: Roxana, Moll, and Manon. Cleland had learned from both Defoe and Prévost, thematically and stylistically, but was innovative in letting Fanny be the first real professional prostitute in the history of the novel. In his book, the brothel for the first time becomes the main stage.

Cleland's book has to be understood in another literary context. It relates to Samuel Richardson's enormously successful epistolary novel *Pamela, or Virtue Rewarded*. After its publication in 1740, a Pamela fever seized the reading public from France to the U.S., and in England particularly, the novel was followed by copies, parodies, and travesties.

Richardson's heroine, Pamela, was a servant on a large landed estate and bore the extremely common surname of Andrews, an idealized member of the small shopkeeper class who would never dream of prostituting herself, either for love or for possessions and gold. Nonetheless, she was firmly determined to scramble up into good society, and to capture a husband from the highest possible social level. Pamela was inexplicably patient, rational, and beautiful—a diligent woman as Christian in outlook as a parson's wife. Richardson's novel took the epistolary form, a collection of exhortative letters in which Pamela explained in detail to her siblings how she was constantly besieged by young and old, handsome and ugly, noble and common—men who all had the same goal, to get Pamela to bed. But she prized her maidenhead over everything else as the road to the accumulation of capital, the card on which she staked everything. Indeed, virtue was rewarded. Pamela married a landed gentleman. Her calculation struck a note and proved that a woman's virtue was worth more than short-term happiness and transient romance. This was Pamela's message to her siblings, Richardson's message to the world.

Henry Fielding was the most dynamic among the British novelists of the 1700s. He had an extensive knowledge of prostitution from his brother Tom, an active social reformer and cofounder of London's first police force. The Fielding brothers regarded poverty as the main explanation for both prostitution and crime, and were inclined to offer their assistance "to reform those prostitutes who are willing to return to virtue and obtain an honest livelihood by severe industry."

Fielding started out as a writer of comedies, then followed with a series of travesties and was soon considered Richardson's main opponent in the literary and moral debate of the day. In his sarcastic pamphlet about Shamela, Fielding played fiercely on the words *sham* and *shame*. Shamela lacked all of Pamela's virtues. But this was precisely why she was successful in social climbing. In *Joseph Andrews*, Fielding's irony was milder and sweeter. Here Pamela's life story was tested, or rather retold with irony, with a switch in gender roles. The handsome Joseph Andrews was explicitly presented as the brother of the famous Pamela. He was just as virtuous as his sister and wrote alarming letters to her about all the cruel women of nobility who were hunting him down, intent upon robbing him of his virtue.

Henry Fielding's longest, best, and most famous novel, about the orphaned Tom Jones, may be seen as an extended version of *Joseph Andrews*. Tom, who seemed early on to be another of Pamela's brothers, felt no concern for his virtue; he was a man of action and adventure socially and sexually.

While Fielding constantly tried out new approaches and ideas, the steadfast Richardson did nothing to expand his sense of reality or compensate for his lack of knowledge about prostitution. He made it a central theme in his next book, *Clarissa, or The History of a Young Lady,* published in 1748.

Clarissa, too, tried to keep her faith in virtue. But she was not sly and suspicious, like Pamela. The man she thought loved her shut her up in a brothel and forced himself upon her, although they were still far from being legally married. The shock was immense, and the wretched Clarissa died almost at once. The description of professional prostitutes ought to scare any young woman from ever leaving home after sundown, or from trusting any young man she met independent of her family.

Fielding and Cleland shared an ironic opposition to Richardson's flat moralism. And Cleland made a number of the same references to the Pamela fever as Fielding. Fanny's letters borrowed form and style from Pamela's, and Fanny inherited her name from the girl Joseph Andrews loved and married, whom Fielding made Pamela's sister-in-law. The eighteenth-century English novel was stuffed to bursting with literary incest.

The witty Fielding was better able than any of his contemporaries to clarify the stark changes occurring in the traditional male and female roles during England's dynamic eighteenth century. His novel from 1747, *The Female Husband, or The Surprising History of Mrs. Mary, Alias Mr. George Hamilton,* had lesbian love as its theme. The very same year, Nathanael Lancester published a novel with an unmistakably gay hero, *The Pretty Gentleman, or The Softness of Manners Vindicated.* But England was far ahead of the rest of Europe in economic, social, and cultural development. The publishers of Paris, Leipzig, or Bologna hesitated to translate these two books. Female husbands and pretty gentlemen existed all over Europe, but they in no way embodied their times in the same way as the virtuous, beautiful, and ambitious young servants like Pamela and Joseph Andrews, Fanny Hill and Tom Jones, with their less radical gender roles.

Prostitutes and prostitution remained the main theme in the novels Cleland wrote after his world success with *Fanny Hill.* It suddenly became fashionable to describe brothels and prostitution in England and France, with the juiciest examples of the genre being the anonymous 1749

Satan's Harvest Home, or The Present State of Whorecraft, Adultery, Fornication, Procuring, Pimping and Sodomy, and Charles de Granval's hard porn *Le Bourdel, le Jean-Foutre puni*, published anonymously in English under the title *The Brothel, or Johnny Fuckalot Meets His Reward.* Among the profusion of contemporary writings on the theme, one might also mention *The Prostitutes of Quality, or Adultery à la Mode*, and *An Account of the Triumphant Death of F.S.A., Converted Prostitute Who Died April 1763, Aged 26*, written by Martin Madan, an exceedingly moralistic Protestant cleric.

The literary bordello reigning in England and France led all the foremost writers of the day—Montesquieu, Rousseau, Diderot, and Choderlos de Laclos—to touch on prostitution. But a couple of decades would pass before a French novel had as great a success as the English translations. When the Marquis de Sade and Restif de la Bretonne established themselves as counterparts to Cleland and Richardson, France began to hum just as hectically as England twenty years earlier.

French novels found new angles to throw light on virtue punished and vice rewarded. One could read about Justine, Juliette, Félicia, Aline, and Fanchette—one young girl after another who struggled against temptation in brothels, castles, and inhospitable cellars. In the end, they fell or triumphed, ending up with riches and husbands, in prison, or in the grave.

Samuel Johnson's dictionary of 1755 demonstrated the new awareness of the 1700s for women and prostitution. He pedagogically stated that one commonly defines the word *whore* in two ways, one traditional and one modern. According to Johnson, a whore is a woman who in an unlawful manner has sexual intercourse before or beyond marriage. The word now normally describes a woman who takes money from men as payment for sexual favors.

Fanny Hill was a whore in this modern sense of the word, for she was a working prostitute who had abandoned the work and wended her way back to civil society's more traditional role as a married woman and mother. Fanny, who allegedly authored her letters at an adult age, also revealed a Christian temperament and knew that it was right and proper to feel remorse. Fanny, alias John Cleland, as though in a state of remorse and repentance, wrote, "If I have portrayed Vice in all its happiest colors . . . and decorated it with flowers, this has been such that as an offering to the altar of Virtue it will be higher, more august and valuable." The irony becomes still more clear when at the end the heroine said that it was to alert a healthy contempt for vice that good fathers, acting as masters of ceremonies, took their sons through the dens of London: "For must one not know the touchstones of Vice before one can condemn them?"

It was not only the prostitutes painted in glorious colors. The same can be said of their employers. Male ruffians and pimps were banished from Fanny's world, while the madams, Fanny's employers—Mrs. Brown early in the book, Mrs. Cole later on—were described as pious, devout abbesses, loving stepmothers, or amiable governesses. Mrs. Cole was most likely modeled on a living person. In any case, she has to be a madam of the best class. She raised her girls in an exemplary manner and "was implacably opposed to those who seduced the innocent, and restricted her acquisition to the unfortunate young women who had lost their virtue . . . and saved them from the gutter."

This book fascinates a modern reader not only as cultural history but also because the pornographic passages still make for exciting reading. They demonstrate so strikingly the eighteenth century's understanding of anatomical functions, blood and tissue, and other technical-mechanistic features of the human body. From a history of ideas point of view, it is perhaps not surprising that a male writer allows this knowledge to influence his depiction of the male sexual organ.

That a woman—be she from the 1700s or from the present day—described male sexuality as mechanistically as Fanny has been referred to as a feature of the novel that is not very realistic, yet the exclusion of these passages would have radically reduced the novel's piquant entertainment value and enduring praise.

In *Manon Lescaut*, the Chevalier de Grieux decided to take up gambling rather than selling his body, which he left to his wife. In the most obviously underground brothel novels of the eighteenth century, there was explicit treatment of male prostitution. This theme was also touched upon in Fanny's letters. On several occasions, she recounted that young men got paid for performing sexual services.

Fanny understood this even as a novice in the prostitution trade, spying upon an older colleague—an old wreck of a woman, "a procuress . . . with breasts . . . never have I seen such an enormous pair . . . that reached all the way down to her navel." Early on, this fearsome matron allowed herself the satisfaction of a destitute but attractive young man, "a tall and muscular young cavalier grenadier, built like a Hercules." After making his contribution, he received payment, "a present that, as far as I could see, consisted of three or four gold coins."

Later, Fanny established a relationship with a handsome and well-endowed young man, and she paid him every time they had sex, even though the boy was nineteen and she seventeen. At that time, Fanny was being maintained by an older gentleman and was in good economic straits. Accordingly, she paid exactly one guinea for each encounter with this nineteen-year-old's divine physique. She confided to her epistolary girlfriend that she did not want the boy to develop a conspicuous expenditure of money. It appears that the women of the time were in agreement that young men who earned money from sex did not have the same ability to save money that young women did.

That women paid men money for sexual services was a fact in eighteenth-century London, but hardly a frequent occurrence. It was much more common for young men to prostitute themselves with male clients. Documents from eighteenth-century law courts show that young men operated as agents for the vice squad in relation to actions against homosexual men. London in the 1700s had many clubs, or Molly Houses, where men who desired sex with other men went.

In Paris, one could find organized male brothels in the 1770s. During that decade the authorities began investigating and registering young men working in brothels just as they did women. Nobody has exhaustively studied how widespread male prostitution was in the London of John Cleland's day, or in the years that followed. Even without clear empirical numbers, many sex- and sex-role-interested literary historians feel that there is a homoerotic subtext to Cleland's book, based on the fact that male bodies and male sex organs are described in such detail. The book has always had a broader appeal to homosexual readers than any other pornographic literature of the time.

Many have been of the opinion that Cleland had connections to the unique London subculture of sodomites, or Molly men. Intercourse between persons of the same sex was recounted in several passages. It was through a happy lesbian session with the slightly older Mrs. Phoebe Ayers that Fanny, with her maidenhead intact, had her sexual apprenticeship.

Later, her dear friend Emily went to a masquerade ball dressed as a shepherd boy. The gentleman who subsequently invited her out to a more attractive inn got quite a surprise when, unwrapping his new confection, he discovered her sex. He solved the problem by letting loose on her posterior, which until that very moment she had never dreamed of defending.

The two young women greatly enjoyed discussing this episode. Later, Fanny described homosexual men in extremely prejudiced terms after spying upon two young men performing anal intercourse. She had to balance on a chair to watch through a hole in the wall. She then lost her balance, fell, and scared the young men away, so she was unable to report them to the police. Her more experienced girlfriend agreed that in her place, she would have reported this incident to the morality squad, since such men were "devoid of all manly virtue and filled only with the worst vices and follies of womankind . . . equally detestable as they are absurd in their enormous inconsequence with regard to avoiding and condemning women while at the same time aping all their manners, expressions, language and gait."

Compared to some of the sadomasochistic episodes in which Fanny herself participated, this short and innocent anal penetration appears almost a boyish prank. It is therefore of interest that the storyteller philosophized over the incident: "Apart from whatever effect this outrageous vice has had in other times and other lands, in our own latitudes this seems to be a sinful sign of pestilence."

It is significant that it is the voice of a well-traveled English gentleman we hear, whether or not one chooses to believe him honorable. An uneducated young English woman cannot possibly be considered to have set such a formulation down on paper.

In *Fanny Hill* and later on, John Cleland married off many of his prostitute heroines to men who were above them socially. Like the Marquis de Sade, he felt that vice rather than virtue had a greater possibility of leading to happiness.

The painter William Hogarth and the writer Samuel Richardson portrayed prostitutes as dying of drink and venereal disease. It is likely that all these various fates occurred in their day. It must have been a bit more difficult to return to a respectable and virtuous civil life than what

Fanny expressed in her letters, but it is obvious that thousands of women did precisely that in reality.

The Magdalene Hospital in London, the source of some of the most reliable material on eighteenth-century prostitution, did not admit girls with venereal diseases. Neither the hospital nor the police had any dealings with women who camouflaged their activities so well that they never had anything to do with the public authorities or charitable organizations. Without appropriate empirical figures, we have to content ourselves with the consideration that the lower strata of London's prostitutes could have ended up on the sorry road portrayed by Hogarth and Richardson, while girls with better resources could have lived more in league with the descriptions of Cleland and Defoe. Life, like literature, is full of both happy endings and tragedies.

The novel is a true child of the 1700s. In its deep structure, the novel deals with growth and maturity, the search for and establishment of identity. Outwardly, this happens via the hunt for happiness and the work of building a career; experiments with unusual sex and work roles were typical phenomena in the second half of the eighteenth century and intimately bound up with identity.

Eighteenth-century novels allow us to meet women and men, heterosexual and homosexual, who took responsibility for their own lives. Along with the novel came virtue and vice, prostitution, marriage, and other sexual lifestyles chosen by women and men to maintain their independence.

Fanny Hill provided contemporary literature with a new theme—the responsibility of the individual over her or his own life. Cleland showed how a young woman would try out a historically new free life in a more free society. And whether or not one chooses to read this book as a homosexual writer's boy fantasies in female garb, as a more traditional male fantasy, or as an almost-true story about a happy hooker from the beginning of the Industrial Revolution, no present-day reader can help being surprised by the hearty pulse and myriad reckless antics it described.

SEVENTEEN

HARA-KIRI

The 1904 opera *Madama Butterfly* ends with a suicide right in the middle of the stage. Giacomo Puccini wrote the music; the libretto was based on a text by J. L. Long, an American who knew Japan at least superficially. The opera's heroine is the high-class prostitute Cio-Cio-San from Nagasaki, who believed she had found true love with the upstanding American lieutenant Pinkerton. He had to go home; she dreamed of and longed for him. Three years later, he returned with a straitlaced American wife, their only mission being to pick up his son. Cio-Cio-San thrust a knife into her own abdomen, committing ritual Japanese suicide—hara-kiri or seppuku—a convincing proof of true love. Interpreting this act requires understanding of the unique elements of Japanese prostitution and the feelings of love and honor in this culture.

Japanese myths point to indigenous fertility rites and to Korean female shamans as the origin of prostitution, but it might be due to Chinese influence during the Nara Period in the eighth century A.D. Written sources described itinerant beggarlike women who sold their bodies in exchange for very low payment. Slavery entered Japan from China at the same time, but neither farmers nor feudal lords seem to have needed slaves or poor women for sexual purposes, since sex was practiced quite freely and was easily available from women of their own classes.

In the Heian Period, between 800 and 1200, the influence of China was still making itself felt on all forms of culture. Kyoto became the new, more urban capital, while the power of the emperor grew along with the population. As Japan developed an increased social stratification and division of labor, prostitution followed the same pattern. Some prostitutes entered new roles as entertainers, becoming better paid and much more in demand.

The 1200s horrified Japan as Kublai Khan and his Mongol hordes entered the islands. The Mongol foot soldiers outnumbered the horseback-riding military gentry—the samurai or bushi—ten to one. The samurai offered resistance but seemed to be on the road to defeat. By pure luck, a typhoon wrecked the Mongols' ships.

Japan was not invaded again. But the shock and shame of what was felt to be a loss resulted in over two centuries of political crisis and civil war. By the early 1600s, the feudal lords—daimyo—were pacified and the emperor was reduced to a ceremonial godlike figure virtually imprisoned in Kyoto, while all real power was concentrated in the hands of the gen-eralissimo, or shogun. The shoguns of the Tokugawa Dynasty would rule Japan as military dictators for over three centuries.

The Tokugawa rulers brought peace and order. For a time Japan experienced cultural and religious exchange with the West, but the results were not uniformly welcomed. At the beginning of the 1600s, the shogun carried out massacres of Christians and missionaries and reduced all con-tact with China and the Europeans to minimal commercialism through Nagasaki and a few other coastal towns. In the meantime, the shogun had built his own fort in Edo—or Tokyo, a former fishing village that now ex-ploded with a population reaching 150,000 by 1600 and passing one mil-lion in the 1700s.

During the Tokugawa Period, Japan counted 250 families as daimyo or high nobility. Some were descendants of pacified lines of former feudal lords; other lines were of imperial or shogun descent. The daimyo lords moved between their holdings and Edo, where they held high-level heredi-tary bureaucratic positions. Their families remained in Edo as symbolic hostages for the sake of peace whenever the lords left to administer their own lands and local capitals. Thus the daimyos' wives and daughters and the shogun's wives and concubines were the leading ladies of the time.

The samurai were the military gentry, and originally lived on per-manent incomes from their former landed fiefs, but during the shogunate, their income diminished in disproportion with the urbanization of the country. They resided in the daimyos' urban forts or in Edo, where they held lower bureaucratic posts. A growing majority were bachelors. For pro-fessional warriors with no more wars to fight, life became slightly artifi-cial, and the samurai suffered a steady erosion of their purchasing powers. They seemed less inclined toward philosophy than in earlier times. Their sense of honor was based more on a sense of face than on devotion to real principles, and they behaved according to a roughly recognized Bushido, manly way of honor.

The strut and haughty glare of a samurai were meant to scare any civilian from his path and to prohibit civilians from the thought of rising above their allotted place. The samurai arrogance was backed by razor-sharp swords; however, these were used much less than modern films would have us believe. In Edo, the samurai mostly encountered their own kind and could not challenge one another continally; they were forced by law to restrain from competitive and aggressive behavior. Of course, there were differences among them. Samurai from central districts had wealthy parents who sent their sons to the best schools, where they were taught martial arts and a strong sense of superiority to commoners, absolute loyalty to their lords, the tricky ways of mealtime etiquette, body posture, calligraphy, and the oral translation of Confucian texts from Chinese pictographs into Japanese. A wealthy samurai's suits of armor would be decorated with lacquer, ivory, and precious metals, his hairstyle refined. Samurai from distant provinces had less money, wore old-fashioned armor, and were often poor readers and poets. But they could be ruthless tacticians and tough fighters, especially if they came from the north, where the rough environment contributed to their austerity.

The samurai class rarely produced ladies. The disparity between the sexes was much greater among samurai than in all other classes. If a samurai married, it would normally be late in life. He chose his wife for political and economic reasons and demanded the strictest fidelity from her, just as he had to show absolute loyalty to his daimyo lord. These women had no schools in which to learn proper behavior; this made it easier to be dismissed by their husbands as the samurais developed more civilized standards of womanhood.

Few samurai could afford to take families along on their semiannual sojourns to the capital, and many preferred to save all expenses connected to a family for as long as possible. A single samurai required all his income to cover his own expenses in Edo; and while inflation benefited the merchant class, many samurai ended up almost as poor as farmers.

Foreigners could not market their wares in Edo, but local merchants flocked to the capital. Most of them left their families in their home provinces. Edo became virtually a men's city, overpopulated by single men, most of them samurai. No other capital in history seems to have developed a male urban culture to the same extreme degree. Japanese society closed itself off in mythical isolation and entered an era that set the standard for all subsequent politics and culture, for Kabuki theater and haiku poetry, *tayu* prostitution and geisha entertainment.

For a time, homosexuality flourished wildly among the samurai. The custom spread from Buddhist monks via the shogun's court. While the monks seemed to prefer early-puberty *chico*, the samurai more often had sex with *wakashu*— young samurai between fifteen and twenty. The new love ideal of the times—*shudo*, love between men—was linked by opposition and similarity to the Bushido. While *shudo* would have a fertile ground in the male-fixated samurai society, with so few women available, it became a challenge to samurai ethics. In cases where two lovers were samurai of the same rank, there had to be a clear age difference between lover, *nenja*, and beloved, *wakashu*. Besides, according to samurai ethics, a *wakashu* could have only one lover in life. In any other case, he would become a prostitute, *kagema*.

Then one of the shoguns, thinking he could kill two birds with one stone, tried to ennoble heterosexual prostitution in Edo. Homosexual relationships between monks or samurai would continue, but more discreetly, while it continued to be acceptable to love actors (*yaro*) or professional male prostitutes when the new walled-in citadel of love, called Yoshiwara, was founded in 1618, near the shogun's fortress. After a great fire at the end of the century, this city within the city was moved a few kilometers up the Sumida River by the Asakusa temples. For two hundred years, a fantastic, complex prostitution and love cult would flourish there, leaving its mark on all subsequent Japanese culture.

The highest-paid prostitutes—*tayu*—were praised in song and described in haiku and novels. They resembled courtiers, priests, actors, and intellectuals as they lived and were recruited outside the rigid class system. They were all social outcasts but enjoyed more freedom than the rest of society, as long as they caused no unrest. The walled-in Yoshiwara was in no way the only prostitution district. Cheap brothels with *hashi* girls and bathing houses with *yuna* women were spread around Edo and other cities, side by side with elegant prostitution enclaves like Kyoto's Shimabara, Nagasaki's elegant Mayama, and Osaka's flowering Shinmachi district. Male prostitution flourished, especially in Kyoto and Osaka, due to the many monks in these cities, but also in downtown Edo. Yoshiwara was the largest and most important prostitution district. Aside from the shogun's and the emperor's court, there was no other place where etiquette was so dense and complicated. Edo was the city; Yoshiwara epitomized the very concept of Japanese love. Everything in Yoshiwara was noble, ritualized, and enjoyed the blessing of the state.

Yoshiwara was not viewed as a necessary evil. To the contrary, it was celebrated, worshiped, and sung about. Sources are overwhelming: detailed maps, sex guides, novels, drawings and paintings, legal material, tax records, and historical accounts. They give the convincing impression that in no other place or period of human history have so many men been so fixated on, so singularly obsessed by, female prostitutes.

The client reached Yoshiwara in one of four ways. Those who intended to indulge in the cheapest prostitutes could trudge the one and a half miles along the country road. But this might be fraught with danger, especially if one wanted to return to Edo before the city gates closed. Even a samurai could be set upon if he had partaken of a surfeit of sake and sexual excitement and now longed only for his tatami mattress in the south of Edo. Taxis could be worth their price for the return—sedan chairs were not too expensive to hire. A slim riverboat called a *yoki* was so intimately linked in men's imaginations with Yoshiwara that the very word had an arousing effect. A particularly impatient young customer would hire many oarsmen and enjoy the delight of passing most of his rivals on his way up the Sumida River.

The ultimate in stylish arrivals was by horseback, preferably on a proud white steed. A young mounted samurai wearing white leather trousers, a white silk kimono, his shining black hair set up, and both his short and his long sword in matching white sheaths must have been an impressive sight. Very few owned horses. Normally, they were hired for the occasional visit, and along with the horse came a singing stable boy who followed behind.

Most guests stopped under a tall willow tree just outside the great gateway into Yoshiwara, or at one of the roadside teahouses. There they would brush off the dust, fix their hair, and check their appearance. Now they were ready. The upcoming love encounter would, in the most

romantic cases, last until sunrise, as contemplated in an anonymous poem
of the time:

> *What time is it? Late! must go.*
> *Your smile tells me to hurry up.*
> *How unkind time is!*

A poor samurai went straight to a cheap brothel near the gate, where he
could take a direct look at the most reasonable girls. To meet a prostitute
of high rank and price, one first had to visit an *agoya,* an elegant hotel with
a courtyard garden. Entrance was permitted only to those who were known
or carried a recommendation as a guarantee of background and economic
standing. If the client requested a visit with a specific girl, he composed a
letter that was delivered directly to the girl, normally quartered some
streets away.

The visitor would order sake and food for himself and his entourage,
and usually hired actors and musicians to perform sketches and sing merry
songs while he chatted with the great watermelon, or the hotel owner and
his wife. Then the renowned *tayu* would arrive with her entourage. Leading the procession came the adult woman chaperone, followed by one or
two young girls serving their apprenticeship, then a couple of prostitutes
of lower rank. From the late 1700s, it became customary to take along a
couple of geisha, male or female entertainers who were versed in traditional song, music, and storytelling and knew all the rituals of the tea ceremonies. A young male servant, a *shinzo,* carried the *tayu*'s bedclothes and
extra equipment in a chest, if she did not happen to be a resident in that
house. The girl was very beautiful, elegantly made up, with her hair swept
into one of a variety of fashions. The cut of her hair and robe by law distinguished her from the women of the aristocracy. But this would make
her look no less fashionable, in her costume of expensive silk with precious prints or embroideries, as carefully made up as any aristocratic lady.
Artistic creativity and fashion flourish best in freedom. So, paradoxically,
Yoshiwara set the fashion trend that the ladies in Edo later copied, with
the necessary adjustments of color and symbols. Toward the mid-1800s
the train of the *tayu*'s costume would increase to the almost absurd length
of five meters—a true bridal gown indeed. Occasionally, the girl would
wear a kimono on top, especially if it was extremely cold. But she never

wore shoes. Even on the coldest winter days, she arrived barefoot, carried by her *shinzo*. Her naked feet were powdered to appear as white as possible. Feet and calves sexually aroused the customers. It was crucial that they be tiny, elegant, and white, no matter the cost.

The *tayu* would now seat herself diagonally opposite her suitor. She would not look at him, speak, or smile, even if he was a regular customer or her absolute favorite. The hosts would bring sake and two small porcelain cups. Thereafter the customer and his chosen lady underwent a short version of a ceremony used in weddings of the same period.

A girl could desist from participation in this ceremony and signal her unwillingness to have intercourse with the man. But this would bring so much disgrace that few wished to expose a man to such loss of face. The usual way for a girl to reject her suitor was, when they finally were alone, to symbolically turn up the lamp or lie down with her back to him.

A luxury Yoshiwara prostitute did not have to go to bed with just anyone who called upon her. "Busy five months ahead," might be said when inquiries were made. It was possible for a client to appeal to the gentleman's instinct of a rival caller, making it clear that a girl was his favorite, asking the rival to yield his place in line for the evening. There was etiquette among honorable samurai; perhaps the first client realized that the girl would not take an equally great pleasure in him, knowing that her favorite was in Yoshiwara but had been unable to jump the line.

Formally, all were equal in Yoshiwara. Only money and love counted. Swords, which otherwise divided daimyo, samurai, and merchants in society, were put aside on arrival. However, if a high daimyo lord came to Yoshiwara, it was necessary for reasons of security to make a simple written mark on the house he was visiting. In theory, his hasty return to Edo might be demanded at any time. Thus a daimyo was never anonymous. On the other hand, the shogun, who himself had up to fifteen concubines, regularly issued decrees to prevent that class from visiting the Yoshiwara women, but in vain.

Most girls immediately distinguished merchant from samurai, since the latter's body language would be easy to recognize even without swords and in spite of the hat many put on to appear neutral. All daimyo and samurai were in theory sufficiently literate to master the art of haiku poetry. But the *shinzo* were well versed, too—and developed their own parody of haiku to make fun of samurai of the baser sort.

Excuse me, noble maiden,
but Edo's rough-rade samurai
have stumbled in again!

Even a daimyo could be rejected in the bedchamber. There were suitors aplenty. It was more prestigious but politically more dangerous to reject a daimyo.

All walls in Yoshiwara were thin and had ears, and this worked to the advantage of the prostitute. Her *shinzo* and servants were not duty-bound to keep their mouths shut. Even when Edo's population passed a million, the rumors from Yoshiwara spread south like fire in a Japanese house built of dry wood and paper. There was nothing Edo folk would gossip about more than when the gorgeous Girl X from House Y had rejected Lord Z, the great daimyo from one of the northern provinces. And imagine! Later the very same evening, she gave audience to a handsome young coal merchant! It was such stories from real life that made life in Edo worth living.

An auspicious series of rejections of influential men would increase the allure of a certain prostitute, especially in the eyes of the young, sexually self-confident suitors who thought themselves to have a far better chance of being accepted.

According to a guidebook from the mid-1700s, a visit to a high-ranked but still inexpensive prostitute cost three silver coins to the brothel owner, two to his wife, two to the girl's escort, and one half to her *shinzo.* The client also had to pay at the teahouse by the main gate, buy refreshments and food for actors and musicians, and treat the friend he had brought along for company. In terms of present-day monetary values, a stylish, honorable, but not necessarily extravagant visit cost the equivalent of at least $2,000 U.S.

Only a fraction of that price went to the girl the men were courting. She often went to bed hungry, for etiquette forbade her to eat in the presence of her visitor—she could only feed him. When he finally departed, her servants frequently had eaten all the leftovers. And the whole time, there were so many, many others who wanted a share of the money and the tips: oarsmen, palanquin bearers, escorts, chaperones, entertainers, seamstresses, and hairdressers. Yoshiwara was composed of a hierarchy of services, all important to preparing and implementing the great encounter of love. Despite the apparently astronomical earnings of the high-class *tayu*—they were the most coveted and best-paid professional women in Japan—they regularly, after some years in Yoshiwara, ended up deeply in debt.

Of course, price differed even in Yoshiwara. A customer who cut down on everything might get away with spending $150. Out on the streets of Edo, one could get sex for a lousy $10. The intoxicating magic of Yoshiwara was due not to sex but to absolute female beauty, absolute manhood, and absolute happiness. Absolute financial ruin was a likely result for those who became totally besotted.

The best-schooled, best-trained, and most well-off men in Japan wended their way to Yoshiwara to meet the country's most beautiful women. Surely they had a fair chance to meet that greatest love of all. An anonymous *yamato*-bushi poem echoes the transience of existence and the courtesan's sadness at the brevity of her period of popularity and the couple's mutual love:

> *Gallantry and love affairs*
> *are only when we live.*
> *We will die at last, will die.*
> *Come let us drink our fill, carouse,*
> *we, who know no tomorrow.*

In some extremely exceptional cases, a *tayu* was bought out of the brothel by a former client and married him. He had to be from the merchant class. Over the centuries, the planned political marriages and the codes of honor among daimyo and samurai allowed for less sexual and emotional pleasure in marriage. It became correspondingly easier to develop warm feelings for a charming, graceful, and elegant prostitute whom it was inconceivable to marry. A loyal *shinzo* might for a short time help a lover who had run out of money to find a way into his beloved's quarters. This was only a short-term solution, and there was nowhere to flee a transparent, well-organized society like Japan's. Lovers on the run had nowhere to hide.

True love was destined not to last. It would lead the lovers into bottomless debt or an even worse fate. The history of Yoshiwara is one of tragedy in the midst of luxury, of grief and despair in the midst of highly evolved decorum and etiquette.

*   *   *

A highly priced prostitute's success depended to a great extent on her accomplishments as an actress. But the game of love is intricate. In Yoshiwara it was pursued intently by most male visitors—and many courtesans too, despite their love-avoidance training. Often the prostitute met at least one man among her gentlemen callers whom she considered her equal. Edo's playboys made sport out of their search for whether a man was the real favorite of a particularly popular *tayu*.

A clear sign was if she had her favorite's name or code name tattooed on her body. Tattoos were regarded as inelegant, but the custom proliferated due to its symbolic value. Some girls attempted compromises with tattoos in invisible places, such as between their fingers.

Just as the samurai had been educated as warriors from early childhood, the *tayu* were trained to be loved but to hide all feelings. A *tayu* who showed infatuation was mocked and harassed or even tortured. She was also denied the right to meet the man she had fallen for, usually a young samurai, who for his part was in danger of being disinherited and deprived of his position in society if he showed similar emotions.

From the late 1600s on, lovers demanded increasingly painful proofs of the depths of each other's feelings. Some men asked a prostitute to remove a nail while he watched. The next request could be for the removal of a fingertip. Many girls did this, despite the fact that their female guardian and *shinzo* always tried to dissuade them, well aware of how it decreased the value of their main source of income. Besides, no woman had more than twenty fingers and toes, and the symbolic effect weakened with every digit she removed.

The knife is a well-known love symbol in Japan. Homosexual samurai usually stabbed one another in different parts of the body as double evidence of masculinity and love. *Tayu* prostitutes with samurai lovers did the same. One *tayu* from the early 1700s watched her lover stick a knife in the sinew of his elbow to demonstrate his tolerance of pain; then she grabbed the knife and stuck it twice into her private parts, right to the bone. She was close to death for three months.

The only honorable way out, and the only proof of true love, was the mutual hara-kiri, usually performed with a sharp barber's knife. It was simple enough for two lovers to cut each other's throats or slice through their abdomens. The registries of deaths from Japanese temples contain an incredible number of double suicides. Next to the samurai no group committed hara-kiri so frequently and elegantly as did the high-class prostitutes. Very often a samurai and a *tayu* did it together.

Between 1690 and 1720, the rate of suicides—particularly the double hara-kiri of a prostitute and her lover—developed into something of an epidemic. Chikamatsu Monzaemon, who has been called Japan's Shakespeare, demonstrated this with shocking clarity. He was born into the samurai class but chose to become a playwright. He authored thirty-nine Kabuki and more than a hundred other dramatic works. *Victorious Kagekiyo*, from 1686, is a historical play in the ancient high style: with subtle irony, it shows the victory of the famous warlord paling in light of the tragic suicide of his mistress, Akoya.

In his own day, Chikamatsu's plays were normally performed with puppets steered by an especially talented chanter, or *Kaga-no-jo*. Their growing audience of *chonin*—commoners—made Chikamatsu's dramas beloved by the whole Japanese nation in a way inconceivable in earlier times; even more so when his male protagonists changed from heroic young daimyo or samurai to sons of the merchant class, while the heroine increasingly was a prostitute, often of the middle or lower ranks. Chikamatsu also abandoned history and began to choose his plots from contemporary life, simplifying and ennobling these true stories into art and challenging the balance between low and elevated style, laughter and tears.

Chikamatsu's love affairs pass as swiftly as a dream, as slowly as a lifetime, while a mildly thundering temple bell demonstrates how two lives flow ineluctably away. His personal style is unmistakable, but his stories were authentic tragedies his audience already knew very well. Twenty-four of his later plays were based on contemporary love stories that both in reality and on stage end with the suicide of one or, more often, both protagonists. In play after play, Chikamatsu demonstrated a chance meeting in a brothel destined to end in tragedy, as he pointed out in the following passage from *Love-Suicide at Amijima*:

> *I shall kill you, then myself.*
> *Our fault a foresight not enough*
> *To fill the tiny shell of the Shijimi Bridge.*

Short our life here. As the autumn day
In this world we could not be together,
In the next and every one to come
We shall be man and wife.

Down through the generations, Chikamatsu's most widely known and performed play has been 1703's *The Double Suicide at Sonezaki,* based on events
from the previous year. Ohatsu, a prostitute, is in love with a young soy
sauce salesman, Tokubei. His uncle, who owns the soy business, wants the
boy to marry his niece. Tokubei's stepmother has accepted the alliance;
she wants the dowry in the family. Tokubei cannot stand the thought of a
life with his obstinate cousin and breaks the marriage contract, whereupon
his aunt demands the return of the dowry. Unfortunately, the young man
has already lent the money to a deceitful friend who denies everything and
brings down the innocent lad. Battered and disconsolate, he seeks sanctuary at the brothel, and Ohatsu hides him under her veranda chair as the
false comrade and his cronies come to continue the beating.

The evil friend directs unfounded accusations at the poor Ohatsu.
Tokubei makes a desperate attempt to defend the honor of his beloved,
but the girl keeps him trapped under the chair by holding her foot against
his throat.

Dew step by step
vanishing
dream of a dream is sadness.

The young couple, like the audience, has been aware of impending death
since they first fell in love. Late that night they steal away to commit double
suicide in the woods near the local Shinto temple.

In terms of the conventions of Japanese culture, Chikamatsu's play
was tragic, perhaps, but also absolutely realistic.

Lieutenant Pinkerton was no samurai; he belonged to a foreign culture and
a later era of Japanese history. But *Madama Butterfly's* Cio-Cio-San may be
understood much better in light of Yoshiwara.

In 1853, just after the American and European punitive actions against China during the Opium wars, Admiral Perry's "black ships" dropped anchor in Edo Bay. He left in peace but promised to return in greater strength a year later. The Japanese realized what he meant, and over the next fifteen years, both the shogunate and many of its most dominant cultural institutions fell. Posterity called the period the Meiji Restoration, which may place too much emphasis on the reinstallation of the emperor. From a global perspective, it was most important that Japan was opened up to the West and to the influence of the U.S. and Bismarck's Germany. From a Japanese point of view, a modernizing generation within the armed forces and the bourgeoisie came to power. As Edo became Tokyo, the glamorous Yoshiwara decayed and, after some decades, was hard to distinguish from any red-light district in the West. Anybody with elite roles in Yoshiwara reappeared in modern establishments in Tokyo. The former specialists in the world of ceremony and entertainment, the geishas, would for a period take over the top of the sex-industry pyramid, but after World War II, they returned to ceremonial functions, remaining outside society, often as mistresses or second wives of rich businessmen.

The West may understand Madame Butterfly's suicide as a parable of the defeat of traditional Japan. By 1903 hara-kiri had gone out of fashion as an act of love. The sophisticated classes looked upon love with irony; the new Japanese ideal was the total lack of emotion, the withdrawn *tsu*. In Europe, Cio-Cio-San and her fate were much more compatible with the full-blown sentimentality of neo-Romanticism. Even if the Japanese had repudiated all former sentimentality and warmth of feeling, neither masochism nor hara-kiri had been extirpated from their culture. That was to be fully proved during World War II.

E I G H T E E N

T H E   P E N E T R A T I O N
O F   A F R I C A

T he white man's whorehouse" was the slogan Frantz Fanon, the revolutionary from Martinique, used to describe the third world in the years after decolonization, and his formula can easily be applied to both Southeast Asia and North Africa. It seems less suited for sub-Saharan Africa, where prostitution arose later and originated with a black African market.

The Mediterranean and West African worlds have been aware of each other since antiquity. The Romans introduced an old African term—Guinea—to name the western part of the dark continent, the hinterland south of the Sahara Desert. The Arab name Sudan was adopted for the area stretching from Timbuktu to Upper Egypt, where Islam would become dominant, with the exception of the Horn of Africa, which partly held fast to the Coptic Christian faith. That region would continue to be named by the Hellenic word for the land of the blacks—Ethiopia. Three groups of peoples, both ethnically and linguistically distinct, had been populating the sub-Saharan continent. The ethiopides, or nilotes, slender, often tall peoples often referred to as brown Africans, dominated the east from the Horn of Africa and farther south. The southwest was originally inhabited by smaller peoples speaking languages of the Khoisan and related linguistic families, known under names such as Hottentots, Bushmen, and Pygmies. The black Africans speak languages of the Niger-Congo group and had their roots in West Africa's coastal lands and inland. A series of migrations east during the first millennium B.C., then farther southeast, would at last make the blacks, or Bantus (named after the most important linguistic subdivision), dominant. Both the taller nilotes and the many smaller peoples were minimized in numbers and cultural importance, while most parts of the continent achieved a greater standardization of culture.

The Bantus passed Lake Victoria only ten centuries ago and had not reached the most southern parts of the continent when Vasco da Gama circumnavigated Cape Horn.

How far back in time prostitution has existed south of the Sahara is complicated because we lack indigenous written sources and must build a picture from European travelers. Relatively recent research has supplemented these European sources as African oral tradition has been committed to the printed page. But in societies strongly marked by social change, verbal transmission is subjected to particularly scrupulous criticism.

Europe obtained an overview of the whole coast of Africa only five hundred years ago. In 1497, Vasco da Gama rounded the Cape of Good Hope. Cape Town was founded in 1652, whereupon Dutch settlers and Portuguese merchants settled permanently at the southern end of the continent, while most other Europeans limited themselves to coastal trade.

European merchant ships anchored regularly along the Guinea Coast on their way around Africa to the Orient. They conducted trade with local chiefs who normally sent boatloads of women out to merchant ships as symbols of hospitality. They did not board the ships to sell sex, but they did provide gratification to the captain and his people. These women were wives or slaves of the local high chief; in their capacity as hostesses, they were expected to make the foreigners happy and remain on board until the chief had finished his trading.

As far back as Africans and Westerners can recall, Africa has seen the enslavement of debtors as well as war captives, just as in the Mediterranean and Arab worlds. In household and village, the slave had to carry out the heaviest and most unpleasant work. Slave owners might sexually mistreat exceptionally attractive female slaves, but in general, the Africans preferred sex with free women. To itinerant merchants, the status differences among the native women were less important, and on the Arab plantations of Zanzibar, it was normal to offer free sex with female slaves to all visitors.

Around 1700, the Dutch East India Company established a large house of female sex slaves in Cape Town, primarily for its own employees. But whenever there was a surplus of women, paying sailors and local residents were accepted, since that brought additional profit. The women in the house would hardly be called prostitutes, since they were slaves who did not receive any payment. But the institution can be called South Africa's first bordello, since customers paid for every single trick.

At this time, the slave trade between Africa and the European colonies in Brazil, the Caribbean, and North America was growing, due to the need for controllable labor on the plantations of the New World. The slave trade reached its apotheosis in the late 1700s and was abolished during the 1800s. An unending number of lives were marked by force and violence, starvation and want, as people were transported across the Atlantic and the survivors were forced into slavery. The ripple effect for the African chiefs who triumphed in limited wars and raids, and sold prisoners of war to slave traders, was a consolidation of larger African principalities—in West Africa, along the Guinea coast, and in Buganda, Congo, and Katanga.

During the 1700s, slave traders and other merchants explored the interior of Africa. As they ascended the rivers, they reported on the existence of sexual relations resembling prostitution. Some adult women were apparently free women who offered themselves sexually to whomever they wanted. Often in a village there would be two or three such women who haggled in public over prices for their services. They were content, self-assured, and well dressed. But the women did not keep their earnings—they went to the local prince, their chief and employer.

In the early 1800s, Europeans observed free women out every evening in the markets of the Nupe king in Nigeria, made up, wearing jewelry, and finely attired. Ostensibly, they were selling kola nuts, but after having laughed and haggled with the men for a while, they disappeared. The foreign visitors reported that when the intoxicating effects of the kola nuts came over the men, the women would minister to them in their huts. Along the Volta River, a woman dissatisfied with her husband could escape to a neighboring village as a free woman, and each arrival was celebrated. The men who wanted sex would negotiate directly with the woman or through a young male relative. Any husband who required his wife to return to their village compensated the village where his wife had been living. If she refused to return with him, she had to travel on to another village, where the drama could repeat itself.

Along the Guinea coast, some men began to obtain more wives than they needed for farming, to use them for the seduction of other men. Ancient tradition gave a husband the right to fine or force labor from a man who seduced his wife. While, in the olden days, this had been compensation for lost honor, it now became a way to accumulate capital. As more men sought out wives in order to prostitute them, fathers and brothers increasingly assessed value according to female beauty, rather than family relations and working capacities.

Along the lower parts of the Congo River, white travelers have reported that local chiefs offered their wives for sex in exchange for cash just as long as there have been reports about the slave trade. No tradition can be documented past the first European visits to the banks of the Congo. The kingdom of Buganda lay for centuries beyond traditional European influence, but we have European reports from the early 1800s about free women even there. They set themselves up under the protection of the king's or local chief's *kabaka,* but they entered short-term relationships with different men, exchanging cooking, household care, and sex for food and gifts. A free Bugandan woman could leave a man's house the moment she met a more attractive partner, and such women were held in high esteem. From the east and southeast coast would come reports about young men willing to have sex for money from itinerant men of either color.

More recent accounts—from oral history projects begun in the 1960s, with decolonization—confirm most of the stories written down by Europeans one or two centuries earlier. African polygamy has a long and liberally practiced tradition. Jealousy cannot have been rampant among men with many wives: nor does it seem to have been difficult for a woman to evade marriage or leave a husband with whom she did not get along. No witnesses give a clear indication about the sale of sex on a short-term or one-night basis. It seems more likely that an inherent but subtle promiscuity among Bantus gradually developed into prostitution due to the influence of the Arab and the European worlds.

"It is something they call love. We do not understand it at all. From the moment the Europeans started to preach about it, everything began to go wrong," one old Mfengu man complained to a British civil servant in 1883.

The missionaries arrived in Africa with the strict mandate that slavery had to be combated in a planned manner. But they went on immediate frontal attack against two other institutions, polygyny (in which men take several wives) and bride-wealth. Seeking all direction from the Bible, they were unable to question whether these institutions might represent challenges or safeguards for the women whose salvation they wanted to ensure.

African marriage ensured stable family relations, not true love between individuals. *Lobola*, the most common Bantu designation for bride-wealth, gave a wife's relatives a material interest in the safeguarding of a marriage. If it fell apart, the wife's relatives had to return cattle or goats to the groom's family. Bride-wealth differed from the sale of sex, as anthropologists have pointed out again and again, characterizing the institution as a life insurance whereby the children gained membership in the clans of the father and mother.

In precolonial times, a man with many daughters could become rich, especially if he earned a living from goats and cattle, since livestock were most frequently used to pay bride-wealth. But at the end of the 1800s, farmers had problems when the worst cattle pest in history hit East Africa. By 1899, the herds were reduced by about 90 percent, and people died of famine. Twelve years later, another epidemic appeared, with further outbreaks following one year after.

The cattle plague and the resulting decrease in population almost forced the institution of marriage to defy the boundaries of clan and tribe, as families sent both sons and daughters to the towns to raise capital for new herds. A daughter might have been exchanged for a whole herd in better times; some girls might manage the same through prostitution. The sons would traditionally take over the herds. Now they could make money in the cities, but much less than their sisters.

Africa's polygamy was conspicuous. It was most prevalent in South and West Africa; in the east, it was exclusively chiefs who had many wives. Although most men had only one wife, the few with many were noticeable. A poor, sick, unfortunate, or otherwise deviant man would not marry; he would remain in his family as a helper. But white travelers rarely noticed this phenomenon. By the beginning of the colonial years, the expansion of polygamy was among the most obvious proofs of growing social stratification. By 1900 every third African male had multiple wives. But the average man, with two and a half wives, was not to be found. Princes and chiefs had many, while an ordinary farmer who kept goats or cows would have to be very well off to have more than one wife. Two wives gave high status but required economic and administrative talents. After having acquired the means to pay the bride-wealth, the husband had to have chores for all the women in the household.

African polygamy was neither a woman's prison nor a paranoid defense of a man's sperm, as it tended to be within the Ottoman and Arab worlds. Princes and chiefs might treat some wives more like friends, guests, or business associates. Polygamy established kinship and alliances with other lines of descent, protected women from sexual harassment, and lowered the number of pregnancies and the high risk of infant mortality. A man under this system would provide protection to all widows and children in the event of his demise.

Polygamy expanded among farmers and cattle keepers, together with increased commerce within agriculture, which favored a man who could mobilize labor power in the form of wives, children, and unmarried siblings. But during this period, Christian missions were on the offensive. They struggled hard against polygamy and refused to baptize men with more than one wife, or the children of those marriages. The first black African bishops understood that it would be wise to nuance such a policy, but they lost on all fronts. Farmers and cattle keepers who had adopted the white man's religion were less able to progress socially and economically. Those who held on to their ancestors' religion or Islam had a competitive edge, because their many wives would secure them a remunerative agricultural enterprise.

The missionaries could hardly have understood to what extent their campaign against polygamy weakened the competitive edge of Christian Africans in capitalistic agriculture. To some extent, missionaries must have seen the consequences in another parallel struggle—against the recently developed prostitution.

As a result of the missionaries' struggle against polygamy, the number of socially superfluous women increased drastically. What were they to do? The missionaries advised them to seek their fortunes in the city, secure in the belief that God would raise His hand to protect His new black children. They strongly urged the women to seize the day, leave the village, and become independent; they iterated repeatedly that men and women were the same in the eyes of God. As they explained about Jerusalem and its pearly gates, they surely didn't have in mind prostitution in Nairobi, Dar es Salaam, or Lagos. But in the new African cities, there were almost no industries providing good money to women, apart from prostitution. Up to half a century later, a great number of African prostitutes would point to the mission stations as the factor that triggered their decision to move to the city where they later became prostitutes.

In a couple of scandalous cases, the missionaries promoted prostitution directly, for example, at the Wesleyan mission in Dahomey. In 1874 it came to light that Pastor Peter Bernasko had been running the coast's best brothel for twenty years. Bernasko combined his mission station with his trade in palm oil, but he had become an alcoholic during his years in Africa, neglected the mission's tasks, and fathered twelve children with native women. The oldest daughters were at work in the brothel when the scandal erupted.

In 1902 the British military expert Richard Meinertzhagen discovered a remote mission station in Kenya, run by three Italian priests. He was first astonished by the exceptional youth and beauty of all the African Christians who took the holy communion. Actually, they were undertaking religious and sexual education at the same time. An iconoclastic Brit residing at the station explained the local theology to the clueless Meinertzhagen. No young boy or young girl could find salvation for his or her soul without regularly sleeping with a priest—who, they were told, contained part of the deity. But African missionaries generally were such paragons of virtue that they ended up in more splendid isolation from other Europeans than they did on any other continent.

In East Africa some young women converted from Christianity to Islam upon arrival in the city; in Muslim eyes, she who had a child out of wedlock was not automatically a bad woman, as most Christians contended. Moreover, Islam allowed women to take control of their own property.

Over the decades, as prostitution increased, a number of unmarried African city women who had previously used all their earnings to buy land and livestock for their fathers or brothers in the provinces now began to work for their own future. In this sense, the missionaries were right when they said women had better opportunities in the cities.

In the second half of the nineteenth century, the European powers scrambled for control of Africa. France and Great Britain had innumerable bases; the Germans had a number of smaller strongholds in the west, southwest, and Tanganyika, in East Africa. King Leopold of Belgium had huge holdings in the Congo; the Portuguese dominated Angola and Mozambique; and in the end, even Spain and Italy enacted colonial operettas, with little tangible gain except to plant their flags in African ground and their names on the newly drawn map.

The Bantus of the south had been fighting one another for a long time and had expended so much energy that the military advance of European powers was facilitated, along with the their regimes of law and order. The city-states in the Niger Delta were the most complicated to subdue. But the local ruler of Timbuktu was overthrown in 1893; the sultan of Sokoto and his Fulani army were finally defeated in 1903. Just as they campaigned to defeat small native principalities, the colonial powers fought among themselves, until the British and the French gave up their conflicting strategies against the Mahdi of the Sudan in 1898, and the armies of both great powers then dug themselves in at Fashoda, in the Nile Valley. A year later, the boundary line between the spheres of influence was drawn at a negotiating table, without the distracting presence of Africa's own dark princes. A short encore occurred in the form of the Boer War, between 1899 and 1902, but only the British and the Boers were involved. When all the battles had died away and all the borders were drawn, the only remaining prince in Africa was the Christian emperor of Ethiopia—who, perhaps because of his faith and certainly because of his diplomatic contacts with Europe and his spies, was able to scrupulously follow the Europeans' game—and eventually to beat them at it by playing them against one another.

In these same years, prostitution spread over almost the whole continent, following on the heels of the colonial armies and in pacts with the expansion of colonial administration. The construction of the Suez Canal and many railways drew large groups of black workers away from their tribes; neophyte women prostitutes abandoned agriculture and followed the men.

When the infrastructure was established, the railway functionaries, soldiers, and businessmen arrived to replace the construction workers. Any woman with sex to sell would have a continual supply of customers. The gold mines of Witwatersrand, at Johannesburg, opened in 1886 and became Africa's Klondike. Bantu workers were drawn in from the whole of southern and eastern Africa. Large contingents of manpower were also recruited from China.

The railway line from Mozambique to Johannesburg was finished in 1895. This not only made it easier to get the arriving workers to the gold mines, and the tools, equipment, and weapons to South Africa; it also gave white prostitutes much greater access to Johannesburg. Seven hundred fifty extremely beautiful Jewish women stepped off the first train into the storybook city. Seventy thousand men stood as if paralyzed: A host of divine angels had suddenly blessed the exclusively male mining society. More girls followed on the next train. The gold city quickly had 133 brothels, and the white prostitutes gave the black women a run for their money.

The East African railway line from Mombasa to Lake Victoria was under construction from 1896 to 1901; when it was finished, it put an end to boat transport and increased trade—including the sale of produce—and the further establishment of mines, bureaucracy, small industries, and brothels. Food, tools, equipment, weapons, and luxury goods could be sent in cheaply from the coast. This changed the nature of animal husbandry and agriculture among all African peoples and tempted European settlers to establish themselves. The exchange of sex for cash became more and more common, even in remote station towns. These transactions were new to most of the young African males and females, but they quickly became accustomed to it.

Thus prostitution in the cities grew, along with the other signs of the forward march of white civilization. The development was parallel, with prostitution encouraged by the development of society. But this was not always so easy to see at the time. Many Europeans were aware only of the arrival of sin and were greatly astonished by it.

However, hardly anyone blamed the Africans. Europeans thought of them as living in a state of innocence, tens of miles outside the cities, and missionaries continually reported how all black hearts opened themselves to God. Sin must have come to Africa from somewhere else. A great many blamed "the Orientals." In 1899 an elderly British civil servant, Sir Frederick Jackson, described an Indian construction camp in Kenya as "packed with prostitutes, small boys and other accessories always required by the bestial Orientals, as is widely known, for their sinful lives."

It seems self-evident now that the European lust for money brought out Asians and Africans on long tours of labor to the newly established cities, mines, and plantations. The Asians traveled as ships' cargo; the Africans migrated in smaller groups by railway, and many on foot. The result was that the workers were isolated from traditional methods of finding lovers or sex partners, so prostitution and homosexuality flourished. If anyone was to blame, it was the white entrepreneurs, but the white men of that time preferred to accuse the lust of the yellow men and the bestiality of blacks.

Thousands of Chinese coolies arrived at the gold mines of Johannesburg. This gave rise to a new and surprising argument in the sex and morality debate in the London newspapers, where it was alleged that the Chinese "had taught the Negroes to become sodomites." The rumor spread in the South African colonial administration to London, and the more who heard it, the more troubling it became.

The worry began with a well-intentioned letter from a zealous young Anglican priest in Johannesburg by the name of Francis Alexander. He had obtained his information on the good authority of a countersignee, a mission helper who carried out his work among mine laborers, an odd moralistic Boer by the name of Leopold Luyt. Chastened, London decided to accept the allegation as the truth and established a public commission to determine the extent of the problem. The Colonial Office demanded full discretion and reiterated this when the report was ready in 1906.

The director of patents for Transvaal, J. A. S. Bucknill, was appointed leader of the commission. He would prove a happy choice, for he was tremendously levelheaded. Bucknill's report is distinguished by its clarity of expression, sharp analysis, and precise description. From a present-day perspective, this strengthens his credibility and makes the report a unique source for historical research. He stated that it was correct that younger boys, both Bantu and Chinese, received payment for sex with older workers in the gold mines of Johannesburg. But was this really so very surprising? At the most, 7 or 8 percent of the workers could be said to be male prostitutes, and for most of them, it was simply a handy extra income. "But I find it impossible to conceive that there is more sodomy down here than at home in London," Bucknill concluded. He also clarified that most of the Chinese boys who prostituted themselves were not mine workers but rather barbers and actors in the small local Chinese theaters. Among the Bantus, the youngest and most handsome took a little money in return for assisting their elders sexually. Bucknill insisted it would be wrong to assert that one was dealing with an "infectious" sin. Indeed, the Chinese preferred boys with a Chinese appearance; the Bantus without exception chose boys of their own race, and a great many used only boys from their own tribe.

Bucknill expended great energy collecting medical information among the best physicians in the area. Among both Bantus and Chinese, the adult men always were the sexual aggressors and the ones who paid. The young men who took a passive role during the sex act were expected to act a little effeminate or at least to tolerate rough verbal treatment. The young Bantus were referred to and addressed as "dirty young brides."

It was widely known in London that sodomy was a custom with a long tradition among the Chinese. Sexual practices among Bantus and Chinese must have different and independent traditions, lectured Bucknill. Whites who had lived for a long time in South Africa knew that sex among men was practiced by Bantus from the east coast, along the Zambezi and beside Lake Malawi. "But," pontificated Bucknill, "I personally have never heard of this among Zulus and Swazis." Homosexual Bantus practiced intracrural sex, between the thighs, which strictly speaking shouldn't be classified as sodomy. The Chinese consistently practiced anal penetration. Yet there was almost no registered rectal syphilis among the men of Johannesburg.

In defense of the "Chinese catamites," the term in use for young male prostitutes, Bucknill pointed out that they all behaved very discreetly. The most feminine quite often played female roles in the Chinese theaters. As to whether prostitution was the term for what was going on, Bucknill felt it was appropriate only regarding the Chinese. Among the Bantu workers, permanent, warm relationships seemed to develop so easily that Bucknill preferred to call them temporary marriages. He could, however, assure the authorities that no permanent sexual relationships in the mine society had led any Bantus to bring male "wives" back to their home villages.

Bucknill concluded coolly that the most negative thing he could say about homosexuality in the mines was that it limited the market for black female prostitutes who had established themselves some distance from the mines. These cheap female prostitutes were afflicted with venereal diseases. One negative factor could be said to compensate for the other.

London was calmed by this exhaustive and down-to-earth description, and the report led to only a few insignificant precautions. Five or six Chinese theaters were closed, and fifty or sixty openly "feminine" Chinese men were deported. No countermeasures were taken against the Bantu workers. Bucknill's solid report surely prevented the British authorities from overreacting upon their first official encounter with nonheterosexual prostitution in Africa.

When the British took over Cape Town in 1807, they immediately provided white prostitutes for their countrymen, installing them in the huge brothel that the East India Company had run with black slaves. Inside this large bordello, independent prostitutes taking their own profits would gradually replace sex slavery. Most of the British preferred white women and willingly paid the much higher price. Newly recruited white women prostitutes maneuvered considerable numbers of black women out of the brothels, particularly in Cape Town. The few black women who remained enjoyed better earnings and working conditions than any other black women in Africa, since they worked side by side with white colleagues. The majority of black prostitutes, however, had to seek new markets in the hinterlands. But they, too, had become acquainted with the finer points of the sex industry and could teach others. Rumors of easy money through sex began to vibrate across the whole continent.

In the early 1900s, one ripple effect of the Boer War was an upswing in prostitution all over South Africa. Increasing numbers of white girls, most from France and central Europe, were put at the disposition of white soldiers, along with the black girls who managed to stay in the market. Soon Johannesburg became one of the world's real sex metropoles. No other place on the continent saw so many unmarried men assembled in one city. As there was big money circulating, the prostitutes continued to stream in.

World War I—often called "the Germans' war" in Africa—gave prostitution another boost, particularly in East Africa, where the war had the greatest impact; it was in this region that the Germans had their most important base. At the turn of the century, the authorities running British East Africa had no need or desire for many white civilians in their jurisdiction. But with the war, everything was changing, and British East Africa became an expanding colony—with its largest city, Nairobi, in a state of constant growth. The idea of racially segregated quarters gained ground, largely because Nairobi was developing a culturally mixed population with British and other Europeans, Indians, and brown and black Africans from Maasai to Bantu, along with Muslims, Christians, and "heathens," both circumcised and uncircumcised men.

The ratio of men to women was soon ten to one in the African population, but the deficiency in the numbers of women was significant among the Europeans and the Indians as well. Consequently, prostitution spread as never before. Women employed as domestics or in the small-business sector sought extra income by carrying a sack when they walked through a work site of Europeans, Indians, or Africans. Quite often it appeared as though they were heading off to plant beans. But any male with a sharp eye understood that the sack would serve as a mattress.

The most widespread form of East African prostitution was the one-night home visit. Large contingents of men lived packed together in barracks with wretched hygienic conditions. When single black women established themselves in relatively large, clean apartments, it became all the more tempting to pay them a visit. The women were willing to cook, wash, and look after the men, both before and after sex; some also washed their clothes. This domestic care for exhausted workers would later be known as Malay prostitution.

No posters or red lights showed the way. These women trusted the men to recommend them to one another. The women seemed to get things the way they wanted. A man should knock politely on the door and carefully ask if the woman lived alone, and that no other man would enter and beat him up if she were so kind as to allow him in. The bill would be settled when the session was over, late in the night or early the next morning, as if the man had been to a restaurant or hotel. Before departure, he received an itemized bill. Old-time Nairobi prostitutes have become legendary for their detailed statements of account. Food and drink, washing, consoling, love talk, and sleep were listed as separate items on the bill.

This variety of prostitution was discreet in every way. A customer who protested about the bill could leave unpunished. What the women wanted least was trouble in an apartment for which they paid a high price. As long as they never openly showed their neighbors how they earned their money, they were treated with respect. Indian and European clients were in a minority compared to the Africans, but they were much sought after by the house owners, because they paid better and disappeared faster.

In the early 1900s, there was male labor migration—soldiers, railway personnel, and miners—over virtually the whole continent. The prostitutes normally worked locally, in a very narrow radius of activity. A woman from Uganda could perhaps become a prostitute in Nairobi and contemplate traveling to Mombasa or Dar es Salaam, scarcely any farther. Almost all worked for themselves, and very few agents or middlemen demanded a share of the profits.

West African and Nigerian prostitution has been less thoroughly researched than its eastern and southern African counterparts. It is nevertheless evident that prostitution spread out over the whole of Africa at about the same tempo, despite the cultural differences between tribes. Maasai women did tend to drop out of prostitution as soon as they had obtained livestock, and they never seemed to take the money as seriously as women from other tribes.

The majority of prostitutes in Nairobi were Kikuyu, the dominant tribe in the districts around the city. The city's male population was a lot more composite; the Kikuyu were only a large minority. The complex composition of clients led to different strategies among the prostitutes. A few seemed to feel there was safety in clients from their own tribe, but the majority of Kikuyu prostitutes stated that men from their own tribe were "more tiresome." To receive a client from one's own tribe involved a discount, and many Kikuyu prostitutes found their men to behave more violently toward them. Quite a few women developed tricks to hide their tribal origin, and they would be careful to avoid a customer related by kinship.

A number of prostitutes from tribes that practiced circumcision found it difficult to serve uncircumcised clients and referred to them as puberty lads. An uncircumcised woman receiving a circumcised African might be threatened violently. While prostitution was a new phenomenon in Africa, sexuality is as old as time itself, is marked by generations of myths, and is driven by traditions and emotions far beyond all commercial acumen.

While African prostitution geared to native men exploded, an increasing stream of white prostitutes found their way to the brothels of the large cities. Together with the prostitutes arrived increasing numbers of chaste white women who intended to marry white settlers. These factors minimized all contact between European men and African women, both sexually and socially. When the British took over Cape Town in 1807, 10 percent of the European men were married to women who were Asian or of mixed race, and 3 percent had wives of unmixed African blood.

Local mistresses were less acceptable in Africa than in most other parts of the world where Europeans established colonies. The British and Dutch had been resistant to sex with dark or brown partners. Through the whole of the 1800s, the missionaries fanatically opposed the mixing of races. An African woman might be a convert, baptized and filled to the brim with Christian faith, but very few missionaries liked to consecrate her marriage to a white man. Nevertheless they blessed some such marriages. Later, this became impossible.

Some explanation for the aversion to miscegenation among the British and the Dutch is to be found in the Protestant religions; more stemmed from a deeper level. Few British or Dutch felt physically attracted to people with dark skin, while the Portuguese eagerly sought out black partners, both women and men. For their part, the French actively conducted propaganda for mixed alliances, and "temporary union with a carefully chosen native woman," as L. G. Binger, director of the Africa Department of the French Colonial Administration, expressed it in 1902. Indeed, the greater the number of such alliances, the stronger would be the Gallification of West Africa. This was the official policy of France. But the Brits were not interested in making Africa British; their goal was to maintain what they considered to be civilization among their own.

Richard Meinertzhagen, the British military adviser who visited Kenya in 1902, was shocked, not only by the Indians and Africans in Nairobi but also by his own countrymen: "One drinks like a fish, one prefers boys to women, and is not ashamed. . . . Nearly every man in Nairobi is a railway official. Nearly every one of them keeps a native girl, usually a Maasai, and there is a regular trade in these girls with the Maasai villages. If a man tires of his girl, he goes to the village and gets a new one, or in several cases, as many as three. And my brother officers are no exception."

In Salisbury, Rhodesia, British etiquette and morality were valued more highly than in Kenya. It was a "more white" city, with the local African population living in outlying areas. Salisbury considered itself a white outpost on a black continent. In 1910 there were about five hundred unmarried white men in Salisbury. British women would have been very offended to see any of them with a black mistress, so they contented themselves with the city's only brothel, which housed almost all the city's twenty-five European prostitutes—mostly Jewish women from England,

France, and Eastern Europe. The more white women arrived in the colony, the more scrupulous were their efforts to freeze native-born women out of good society. African women were seen as primitive and uncivilized based solely on their physical comportment.

While the objections to sex between European men and African women were strong, the prejudice against intermarriage with Africans was even stronger. Very few children were born as a result of mixed marriages. Both servants and slaves were utilized in the white penetration of Africa. The Durban police chief stated in 1903 that scarcely over 10 percent of the black domestic servants in the houses of whites "avoided having their lives ruined." Upright citizens preferred Zulu boy servants, but even this led to considerable heat and loud discussion. Private correspondence of British women from the early 1900s is rich in erotically colored visions about these boys. Yet there seems to have been hardly a single situation where a black boy became involved with his white mistress in a way that caused public scandal or led to police reports or prosecution.

The 1903 Morality Act of the Rhodesias stipulated two years in prison for any European prostitute discovered with an African client, while the African client was liable to a sentence of five years. A male European suspected of having sex with a male partner of another race normally would not be prosecuted. Such a relationship never resulted in children and did not threaten to force itself upon polite society. Certain men did try bringing their African mistresses into white society, but such efforts met with minimal success.

At the beginning of the 1900s, men with dark-skinned mistresses or wives were sustained in the periphery, the far-off corners of British Africa. There were rumors about white men in remote valleys who lived in lonely splendor with veritable harems. This gossip is a good indicator of the British imagination but is far less reliable in describing African realities. However, as polygyny continued to be the norm among well-off Africans, some of the few British who identified with the native style of life did adopt the tradition as well.

A series of public scandals and newspaper and parliamentary debates pushed their way to the center of the puritanical circles of British settlers. One characteristic affair started as a local fight between neighbors in Kenya in 1908. A settler named W. S. Routledge and his wife attempted to "rescue" an African woman from their British neighbor.

Of course, the man in question was not "normal." Nor was his wife completely as she ought to have been, according to Mr. and Mrs. Routledge. Their neighbor, Hubert Silberrad, openly lived in sin with three Maasai girls—Niambura, Wameisa, and Nyakyena. When his neighbors first complained about this arrangement, Mr. Silberrad smilingly explained that all his wives were honestly and honorably paid for with the number of goats appropriate for wives in that area. But "Massa" and "Missus" Routledge were opponents of polygamy and bride-wealth and felt justified in their belief that the youngest girl seemed a little unhappy with the marriage that her parents had arranged. The Routledges rolled into action.

Hubert Silberrad used neither power nor violence in his household, but three women can create their own internal dynamic. It seems that the youngest wife was not paid sufficient attention. The fact that all three girls were teenagers received no media attention whatsoever. The bride-price and polygamy were provocative enough in themselves.

The local civil servants in Kenya, including the governor, Sir James Hayes Sadler, wanted to play down the whole affair. Private investigators interviewed the girls and their relatives with soothing results. But the Routledges did not give up before the issue finally bulldozed its way up through various levels of the bureaucracy and reached both Parliament and world media: "British Colonial Office Discovers Fornication with Negresses—and Polygamy." The Parliament could not let such a matter lie. So ended the story about the last Brit who had contracted a decent African marriage. When he was forced underground, Mr. and Mrs. Routledge became heroes in the eyes of the British media.

J. E. Stephenson is among the most famous figures in South African history. He had become almost legendary—before a media storm broke loose. But Stephenson showed himself to be so intelligent and timely in his reaction that he escaped all British moralism. His contemporaries said that Stephenson "could well have been governor." For several years, he lived as a first-class British civil servant in Rhodesia, with an Ngoni woman at his side, and no one became discomforted. Stephenson had fathered a son by this woman, and when the son turned sixteen, his father decided to bring him along to Salisbury on an official errand. On his way to the capital, he learned that his superiors—and their wives, especially—had expressed themselves in acrid terms about seeing a half-grown son of mixed blood in their homes.

Stephenson reacted spontaneously, taking leave from his duties and moving to a far-off valley, where he continued his life independent of British administration. He became a pioneer in the development of roads and infrastructure across northern Rhodesia, which in turn opened the way for the development of copper mining. Stephenson had removed himself from public life once and for all; despite his British political sympathies, he lived like an African. But because he made a great contribution to the country and never openly provoked either British women or any public institution, the authorities left him in peace. The local African population regarded him highly, referring to him by the honorary title Chirupula. Stephenson later took additional wives in the African manner; he lived a very long time and contributed to social changes and—through his own profligacy and the health and economic reforms he championed—the population increase in his part of the world. During the "Germans' war," Stephenson took an active part on the British side, and throughout his later life, he kept in contact with and enjoyed the respect of men in the British administration, above all, those in commerce. Still, no British "missus" would receive him. It is highly probable that he detested them as much as they did him.

Things turned out rather differently for Hubert Silberrad. His case had created a scandal in the British press, and he was a man of little standing and schooling. Almost all respectable British people of his time agreed that he should be dismissed from public service. For years afterward, the searchlights were out over Rhodesia and Kenya, looking for British public servants living with native women. At least seven men lost their postings.

However, nobody tried to prevent a British male from having sex with an African woman, nor to punish a man who fathered a child of mixed blood. What was considered outrageous was not the sex but the display of love or respect for a black woman or black children. Woe betide the Briton who openly took responsibility for mixed-race children. Why? Because miscegenation was atrocious and could not be tolerated. That an African woman and her relatives could possess family pride or a sense of honor was an incomprehensible notion for the British of 1910. After 1920 virtually no British person in Africa was seen in public with an African woman at his side, for at least forty years.

NINETEEN

NANA AND HER TIMES

A woman clad only in silk undergarments and high-heeled shoes stands doing her makeup. She holds the lipstick in her left hand, the powder puff in her right, and wears a ring on one finger; her little finger sticks up bravely and stylishly in the air. A thick gold bracelet is in the process of sliding down her naked white arm.

Édouard Manet's masterpiece of 1877 leaves no doubt about what profession is being represented. Those who do not grasp the fact immediately are given the additional assistance of a crane painted on the background wallpaper—*une grue,* or crane, being French slang for "prostitute."

A gentleman in a silk top hat and evening attire sits and watches the woman from a velvet-bedecked sofa. She knows full well that he is aroused by the challenge of her backside. But her glance is in another direction, as though to another man we do not see. This man, who almost represents the painter's point of view, is enjoying his view of the woman. She also admires herself. She is an independent woman, but she is not completely free. Her ability to shift from one client to another is dependent upon her physical attractiveness.

The woman in the painting is called Nana. Manet named her after a prostitute he had read about in the work of the writer Émile Zola. The whole of literary Paris was talking about Nana while Manet was working on his painting.

"She distinguishes herself from all other merchants, no matter what goods or other saleable services are on offer, for the prostitute is all things at once." The German philosopher Walter Benjamin wrote this of the prostitute who so frequently figured in Charles Baudelaire's lyric poetry from the 1850s and 1860s. The painting of Nana is a touch too delicate to be illustrative of Baudelaire's poetry, but her expression is of the big city that Baudelaire's lyrical lines bore witness to. The professional prostitute of the nineteenth century developed the urban expression before anyone else. Nana is both inviting and calculating, aloof and frank, filled with distance despite all the intimacy.

Nana is young, lively, and dressed in the uniform typical of many of France's prostitutes around 1880, particularly those who worked in the brothels. By that time it was common to see white, pink, or black fishnet stockings, low-cut high-heeled shoes, and a transparent half-length peignoir of tulle—that is, if one had not progressed to corsets and panties. In the brothels that catered to a bourgeois upper-crust clientele, rings, bracelets, and neck chains were also part of the adornment. Manet did not have to show us a client all decked out in evening dress, white tie, and top hat to indicate that Nana was a cut of meat of the highest quality. Perhaps Nana was one of the most costly goods in the whole of the Parisian world metropolis.

"You have all been more or less her lovers, but none of you can say that she has been your lover. She can always get you, but you can never get her." This is how the decadent young Blondet spoke to his friends about a very beautiful prostitute whom he had encountered at the Paris Opera. This woman, Esther, was the heroine of Honoré de Balzac's novel *Splendor and Misery of the Courtesans*.

As a challenge to Blondet's belief, Balzac let Esther meet her love in the form of the handsome but poor aristocrat, the tender Lucien de Rupembré, one of world literature's great romantic heroes along with Tristan and young Werther. In Balzac, true love trumps commercial sex; his main message was the triumph of romanticism.

Nonetheless, Esther's life fell to ruins, much to the sorrow of Lucien and the reader; apparently, also in opposition to Balzac's demonic master of intrigue, Vautrin, and his aim—to rehabilitate Esther and give her a secure and happy future with Lucien.

Alexandre Dumas based Marguerite Gautier, the main character of another novel from the same period, *The Lady of the Camellias*, on one of the actual Parisian courtesans: the "goddess" Marie Duplessis, who had affairs with civil servants, officers, diplomats, and artists such as Eugène Sue, Alfred de Musset, Franz Liszt, and Dumas himself. Just as Marie Duplessis in real life died far too young, so, too, did Marguerite Gautier.

Dumas's novel was immediately presented as a stage drama, and Giuseppe Verdi created the opera *La Traviata* two years later, which made the lady of the camellias immortal.

Émile Zola also wrote about a great courtesan, or what we now call a demimondaine. But when Zola's heroine, Nana, goes down the drain, the reader feels that at last the world has been freed of a female angel of death, a deadly threat to humanity, a monster of a harlot.

Émile Zola introduced this terrifying woman toward the end of *L'Assomoir.* Two years later, she became the main character in his next novel, which also carried her name. Édouard Manet most certainly meant his painting to refer to the figure in Zola's novel. But one cannot possibly say that it is Zola's Nana we see—nine out of ten art historians are in agreement on this point. The Nana whom Manet shows us is no monster, while Zola's literary character was as monstrous as conceivable—the coquette who clambered out of the gutter to take revenge on the ruling class, and place men of all social classes at her feet, crushed, destroyed, and ruined. Nana was both Venus and Amazon, love goddess and avenging angel, erotically seditious and socially threatening to any man within or without Paris.

Zola told us with dread and warning that the love and admiration of all the men in Paris was not sufficient to prevent Nana from being overwhelmed by boredom. She sneaked into a Paris bordello dressed as a man in order to spy on her colleagues; she then took a lesbian lover in the hope of finding authentic love. Nothing helped. Maybe it was because the whole world craved physical contact with her that Nana developed into "a destructive force of nature who corrupts Paris between her snow-white thighs." When such is the state of affairs, the writer must indeed let her come to no good end. The novel *Nana* is a masterpiece of decadence, closing with a detailed description of smallpox destroying what was formerly an extremely attractive female body. The stink of putrefaction was so intense that the comfortable drawing rooms of the French bourgeoisie were contaminated for decades to come.

The nineteenth century's doctors were more hostile to sexuality than doctors of the previous century. They struggled against masturbation and advised women not to have sex more frequently than once a month. The myth of motherhood dominated, something that made it unseemly for a woman to take pleasure in sex. On the other hand, the doctors advised men to have sexual intercourse every fourth day, maintaining that any woman who enjoyed her sexual life would be easy prey to venereal diseases: Sexual pleasure was as dangerous to a woman as masturbation was to a man. Thus it was that these medical practitioners contributed forcefully to an upswing in the sex trade.

The Parisian police estimated in 1860 that there were around thirty thousand prostitutes in the city, although only six thousand of them were registered. In the following decades, the numbers increased dramatically. London could compete with Paris in terms of numbers of prostitutes, but France became the major country of the sex industry. In Paris and the region between Cannes and Marseilles, there were more than fifty police-registered prostitutes to ten thousand men, or one public woman for each two thousand men between the ages of fifteen and forty-nine. The French police estimated that there were over five times as many unregistered women. The registered women had many clients every week. There are good reasons to believe that French men, married or unmarried, had a lot more sex with prostitutes than between their conjugal sheets.

The reasons are clear why the theme took such a central place in the literature of the day. Many others besides Zola and Balzac introduced us to prostitutes. Even the very moral Victor Hugo dealt with them; we also find them in Eugène Sue, Paul Alexis, Gustave Flaubert, and Alphonse Daudet. The brothers Edmond and Jules Goncourt in particular describe hedonistic and unstable women. Guy de Maupassant writes humorously and sympathetically about whores of all age and weight classes; after *The Lady of the Camellias*, Alexandre Dumas the Younger went on to incorporate the modern pimp—in a French suit, of course—into world literature with the book *Tue-la Monsieur Alphonse.* Joris-Karl Huysmans described whoremongers and petit bourgeois functionaries who married prostitutes. The intense lyrics and imagery of Charles Baudelaire, Paul Verlaine, and Alfred de Musset also dealt with prostitution. Huysmans's *Marthe*, the brothers Goncourt's *Elisa,* and Eugène Sue's "Flower Girl Marie" became almost as famous as Nana and were much better liked. The most humorous whore in world literature is de Maupassant's Boulle de Soif. The most tragic and best known of all literature's demimondaines was Dumas's Marguerite Gautier, who died with the novel about her working sister Manon in her lap.

This favorite of French themes affected writers in other countries. In the U.S. it was lightweights like George Foster, Osgood Bradbury, and

Henry Williams who first took up the glove. In Scandinavia, authors showed their dependence on French literary trends for over two decades in their portrayals of a number of minor characters, but they left it to the painters to emphasize prostitutes directly. By the time Norway's Amalie Skram reached out to the Scandinavian countries with her character Lucie, Americans such as Theodore Dreiser and Stephen Crane were writing *Sister Carrie* and *Maggie*. Russia's whores were made immortal by Dostoyevsky. His Sonja from *Crime and Punishment* sold her body to help the poor and the starving; she was a true Mary Magdalene who rekindled faith in the novel's main character, the socially engaged and philosophically confused murderer Raskolnikov.

French writers described more, and more beautiful, coquettes and demimondaines than did anyone else, but the most pious whore in world literature had to rise from the deep heart of Russia.

The brothel girls, flower girls, and seamstresses of Manet and Renoir, and Toulouse-Lautrec's bawdy women, are accepted as the beginning of the modernist phase of Western painting. The female prostitute was the symbol of modernity for the French avant-garde.

Manet's *Nana* stands even today as the best-known prostitute painting in art history. An 1863 prostitute painting from Manet's preimpressionist phase, *Olympia*, however, became a great scandal of the art world. Paul Cézanne took prostitutes for himself in great numbers. In all, he himself painted *Olympia* three times, as a commentary on Manet's painting. Toulouse-Lautrec never let the motif rest. Anatole Vély and Gustave Courbet painted prostitutes, as did Jean Louis Fourain, Eugène Girard, and Henri Gervex. Eva Gonzalès, Auguste Renoir, and Edouard-Theophile Blanchard preferred seamstresses and barmaids who took in supplementary income by prostitution.

Caricatures and cartoons, sketches and etchings of Louis Morel-Retz, Victor Morland, and Jean-Louis Feraud also contributed to the prominence of prostitution in French art history of the nineteenth century, exactly as in literature. But prostitutes were painted in other countries during the transition from naturalism to impressionism. In Germany this applies particularly to the work of Max Liebermann, in Sweden Anders Zorn and Ernst Josephson. In Norway two oil paintings by Christian Krogh, *A Meeting* and *Albertine in the Police Doctor's Waiting Room*, stirred up a political and moral debate that no painter has ever experienced in this distant corner of the modern world. This was due mainly to the political statements implied in Krogh's paintings. Prostitution as a theme of the time was accepted, demonstrated by the fame obtained by Hans Heyerdahl's paintings *Champagne Girl* and *Black Anna*—two sadly contemplative statements that confirmed prostitution as a theme of the time. Edvard Munch would take up the theme several times, first in *Heritage, Christmas in the Brothel,* and *Rose and Amélie.* Later, in a whole series of paintings known as *The Green Room,* a specific room in a German brothel by the name of Zum süssen Mädel became his point of inspiration. It is reasonable to assume that professional whores haunt many of Munch's madonnas as well.

French painters have created the most beautiful prostitutes imaginable, with Henri Gervex's Rolla maybe at the very top, while some of Edgar Degas's fat whores were more ugly than anyone in real life.

In Balzac's novel, Nana, the queen of the demimonde, could dominate a horse race at Longchamps simply by costuming herself and arriving in a landau coach so refined that all the women of the elite class blanched. One of the racehorses bore Nana's name, but no respectable man or woman dared bet upon it. Nana met her clients in her own elegant residence. Women in real life who conducted their lives like the fictional Nana were classified—at least by the authorities of northern Europe—as privately dwelling public females. The Norwegian Hakon Boeck spoke from direct knowledge of all the cities of northern Germany and Scandinavia when he pointed out the differences in age, beauty, and health between prostitutes in private apartments and *puella publica,* the brothel girls. In France, prostitution was far more subtly divided, more specialized, more segmented by class, and more open to satisfying a variety of tastes and desires. In a *maison de rendezvous,* rich clients could maintain an illusion of being in a home that could double for their own. They got commercial sex in homey comfort, in almost the same conditions found among the petite bourgeoisie. One paid not the girl but an outsider, an agent, and the man could behave more gallantly. The *maison de passe* was the name for the unregistered small hotels where girls took clients from the streets and restaurants. A *maison de tolérance* was the standard name for an organized brothel; these places encompassed all prices and standards, from the king-size bed with marble and draperies to the iron bed or the mattress on the floor.

The grand proportions and the frescoes on the wall would lead us to believe that Manet's Nana, with her jewels and bursting good physical health, is observed at work in a first-class brothel. But in Paris, girls of her class would probably earn even more than her colleagues in northern Germany and the Scandinavian countries, where the luxury brothel never came into existence.

Zola's literary heroine came from working-class conditions; many other prostitutes in literature were from seamstress backgrounds or worked as serving girls until they ended up in prostitution. In reality, the social background of prostitutes was a lot more varied. The police registries from Marseilles in the 1880s show that the girls came from nearly all classes and strata. The greatest number had fathers who were craft workers or small businessmen, but within this category, the variations were large. Few came from village life, only five hundred out of three thousand. A total of forty were daughters of fishermen, and five had goatherds for fathers. Could it be that the old stability of life on the land provided the best security against the drift to prostitution?

The majority of French prostitutes were second-generation province-dwellers; they had fathers who were lower-level officers, railway employees, policemen, workers in the building and metal trades, or stevedores. Unbelievably enough, there was a total of thirteen prostitutes in Marseilles who were the daughters of teachers, a group both counts and commoners—as well as physicians—expected to find on the summit of virtue. Four women were daughters of lawyers. And the daughters of clergymen? There was little pursuit of this line of inquiry in Catholic France.

Edgar Degas was the foremost French brothel painter. He not only painted prostitutes with and without clothing, in cafés in the evening, or on the streets of Paris at night, he was even commissioned to make decorative paintings for one of the really luxurious bordellos in the quarter around the Paris Opera.

The interiors of these establishments could have competed with the opera itself: gold, velvet, and marble everywhere; a big bed, open on three sides and bedecked with pillars and draperies; mirrors on several walls, and perhaps the ceiling as well. Bronze statues of fauns and celebrants of Bacchus were meant to call up one's erotic fantasies. The light was filtered and arranged in intimate and fantastical displays. Silence and discretion dominated. Clients arrived and left without seeing one another, without heed to the women other than she whom they were to meet, perhaps a woman they had noticed with their binoculars at the opera earlier in the evening. Toulouse-Lautrec immortalized the atmosphere of the most elegant bordello in his painting *Salon.* The painting shows the rich sensuality of such an interior. It does not depict a single person; there is no skin to be seen. Still, one knows at once where one is, standing before a whole interior redolent of women, bodies, and expensive perfumes.

It was not possible to distinguish between the most costly brothels in Paris and the villas and luxurious urban estates. The clients were accepted by recommendation or arrived via an exclusive travel guide. At more modest places, one might find a red lantern, subdued lighting on the staircase, suggestive paintings, or a woman outside making it clear to the prospective visitor that he had come to the right place.

Many brothels allowed clients considerable sexual freedom. Certain clients wanted the girls, at least by way of introduction, to wear bridal gowns or nuns' habits. At better establishments, it was possible to ask for two girls at the same time. If the client wanted to confine himself to watching the two women together, there were voluminous black velvet draperies, black satin sheets, and discreet lighting designed to emphasize the whiteness of the women's bodies. Torture fantasies or sex with a Great Dane were among the services offered by specialist establishments. In expensive and exclusive brothels, it was no problem if a client preferred men to women; this was arranged with the utmost of discretion. A woman would follow the man up to the room, then disappear for "a young man of her acquaintance" to take over, in either an active or a passive role, according to the client's desire.

In 1879, Degas finished *The Madam's Birthday,* which shows a festive occasion inside a brothel, with the madam seated at the middle of the painting, clad in black. The girls dance and laugh around her; they have brought presents, and some kiss or caress her back and shoulders. There are no traces of client-oriented calculation in anyone's face, and no internal competition. The girls wear necklaces, pink stockings, and high-heeled shoes. Otherwise they are naked. Maybe the painting's charm derives from its loose and girly atmosphere; it is unlikely that most French madams could have been as beloved and maternal as the central figure in Degas's painting.

Most of France's *maisons de tolérance* were secluded houses where the prostitutes lived and ate under strict discipline. Although the interiors reflected the clients' price bracket, the inner orders were similar. The institutions had many features in common with nunneries. This was one among many reasons that the term *abbess* remained in use as a synonym for the brothel hostess. The French police and French doctors were in agreement that great demands be placed on the madam. "She must have strength and power, moral and physical energy, natural authority, something almost masculine about her," it was maintained in the well-known Parent-Duchatelet study, which attained almost the character of a regulatory handbook for brothel life.

A madam had to keep order in her house and over her girls, and to prevent them from developing relationships with men outside the brothel, particularly with an Alphonse, a pimp or lover of the type used by unregistered prostitutes. The madam should also be unmarried. A man in the house would put things out of balance in relation to the patriarchal authority that the doctors or police felt they should be accorded.

It was very common for a brothel hostess to have children, but they were not admitted to the brothel. They were sent away to boarding schools, most ranking a lot higher up the social ladder than their mothers.

Within the brothel, the madam had other "children" who required daily upbringing: the girls. Every time "Maman" came into a room, the girls had to stand up and perhaps even curtsy. Mealtimes were regular, and the dishes were good and nourishing. Maman kept the mealtime atmosphere one of middle-class respectability.

Because the girls worked at night, they did not get up until ten or eleven. The first part of their day was normally devoted to bathing, caring for their appearance, and doing their hair. After lunch they filled the endless hours playing cards and betting—or reading novels. Some brothels were equipped with gardens where the girls could relax or play ball; otherwise, they lived in conspicuous seclusion from the surrounding world.

Perhaps the boredom was one reason the girls did not stay for long. Brothel prostitutes seldom stayed in the business over four years. Some continued to work on their own or became waitresses in restaurants, with prostitution as a sideline. The majority went back into society. There was a high turnover in the trade, a fact that stood in sharp contrast to the nineteenth century's ideology that prostitution was a safety valve, its own society beyond civilization.

The bulkhead between the bourgeois and the sinful worlds was much less firm than the police, moral propagandists, and most clients realized. The majority of prostitutes wended their way back into proletarian or petite bourgeoisie life as wives and mothers; those who had only lived in a brothel could more easily camouflage their past.

None of this should suggest that life in the brothels was ideal. French novels are most unrealistic in depicting life inside the brothels. In *Maison Tellier,* de Maupassant describes girls who pretend to be going to church when they are actually going out dancing, and girls who lower themselves from the upper stories of the house with white bed linen in the best boarding-school style. Their existence was a lot less cheerful. In 1867 the girls sitting in a brothel at Parthenay, between Poitiers and Nantes, set fire to their home to gain their freedom. This revolt was no isolated accident, as later research has demonstrated. The girls did not go to church. They got holidays or visits home only under exceptional circumstances, and usually only a few were allowed. These were mostly the mature girls who had been in the business many years and were more like daughters to the madam. One older prostitute explained that she had been allowed two visits to her home city over the course of seven years.

Holidays were even celebrated at the brothel, as when the madam had her birthday. There would also be a celebration whenever two best girlfriends decided to "marry," an indirect concession to the brothels' lesbian subculture. Such marriages were also functional, since for the clients who wanted two girls at once, it was preferable to have girls who were already physically intimate.

The critics of prostitution found such relationships particularly offensive; even the leading French expert on the issue, Parent-Duchatelet, devoted lengthy passages to critical discussion on lesbian relationships in the bordellos. In the hospitals where venereal diseases were treated, and in the prisons, lesbian relationships were severely combated.

After dinner, around seven o'clock, the girls got dressed. Most of them ended up in costumes, much as in Manet's picture. The men's sexual ideals had more in common than did their pocketbooks. French whoremongers of 1880 liked the same thing, whether they were rich businessmen, poor waiters, soldiers, or sailors.

At the Folies-Bergère, a bar girl is standing among cakes, pastries, and bottles of liqueurs and champagne. She has a faraway look in her eyes, her hair is upswept, and around her neck hangs a medallion from a tight black silk ribbon. In each ear is a gold ring. The wall behind her is covered with a mirror that reflects a more outgoing colleague who is bent over in conversation with a man wearing a mustache and a hat. The picture is full of erotic ambivalence: Is the one woman willing and the other not? There is no doubt that commercial sex is a component of the picture. But to what degree? Can one say that Manet in this, the last of his greater paintings, has again in 1882 depicted prostitution?

The Folies-Bergère was the largest and best establishment of its type in Paris. By the beginning of the 1880s, there were a lot of equivalent places lower down the price scale. Were they bordellos? These places looked like ordinary restaurants where one sat down to have a drink of beer. The seduction was gradual. The barmaid came over to the table, served herself, and challenged the customer to drink up. After a period of flirting, she might explain that she herself is "an item of consumption." Many of the girls profited from the sale of drinks, or received a bonus for good sales. Those who managed to interest a client in sex took him off the restaurant premises, usually to a small hotel down the street or a room not beyond the second or third floor in the same building, much as would have occurred in an ordinary bordello.

The number of police-registered prostitutes in France was lower in the 1880s than it had been for many years. French men had in no way stopped paying for sex, but opposition to the meticulous regulation of the business had finally had results. Times were also changing, and many clients wanted to meet the prostitutes in more open relationships. Perhaps some of the girls also wanted more freedom and the right to choose customers.

Restaurant and cabaret prostitution distinguished a new generation of sex workers. This new form of prostitution took a large portion of the market away from the traditional brothels. In 1888, Gustave Macé wrote that from time to time an elderly madam converted her establishment into a restaurant or cabaret because she could no longer stand the many interferences by the police and health authorities. Plus, sometimes the client felt good when the prostitute gave the impression that he was seducing her. Another contemporary observer wrote, "One gets the impression of both real conquest and real love—they smile, they talk, they enjoy one another. The illusion of independent choice is in the process of ruining the prestige of this diversion's lowest establishments."

A whole generation of French youth had by this time grown up with books that dealt with love between women prostitutes and young poets or students, so it was not strange that they began to believe such things could happen to them. In any case, the fact that two young people, who could spend a night or some hours together, could mutually choose each other must have felt like an emotional improvement for both partners.

Nana's fame as an archetype of prostitution in both a popular novel and a world-famous painting was unsurpassed. Yet as the years passed, her name had little influence in France's brothels and cafés.

Paulette, Brunette, Blondinette, Odette, or Arlette is what they preferred to call themselves, these girls one met in a French whorehouse at the fin de siècle. Very few used their own baptismal names—Marie, Jeanne, Louise, Joséphine, or Anna.

Brothel girls were considered more flighty, childlike, and capricious, more clothing-mad, more crazy over flowers than ordinary girls. Brothel girls were also ostensibly more religious and romantic.

Reading proficiency among French prostitutes was exceedingly high: Only 10 percent were illiterate. They had free time in the afternoons, and romance novels were a very popular pastime. Now that so many books had come out with French prostitutes as heroines, these likely found their way on the prostitutes' reading lists.

The most frequently used of artistic names was Carmen, which the brothel girls had taken over from Prosper Mérimée's novel, which later became Bizet's opera. Other artistic names were found in the melancholy novels of Hugo, Dumas, and Abbé Prévost. The bordellos were filled with girls who called themselves Mignon, Manon, Camille, or Fantine.

Strangely enough, many of them also liked exotic Russian names like Olga and Sonja, though to attribute this to the reading of Dostoyevsky is less probable.

Although most girls had read Zola's famous book about Nana, it had awakened such a commotion that none of the brothel girls took over her name. This was a wise decision. There could not have been very many nineteenth-century clients whose passions would have been ignited by the memory of France's most demoniacal harlot.

TWENTY

MORAL CRUSADERS

C hrist in female form, descended to Earth to save us from all misery. The thought hit me at the sight of her, and has never left me since." This is how a disciple, in 1871, summed up her first meeting with Josephine Butler, one of history's most energetic, persistent, and famous opponents of prostitution. After Queen Victoria and Florence Nightingale, she was perhaps the best-known woman of Victorian England.

Josephine Butler might have appeared shy, but a letter from her could cause political chaos among the governors of the British Empire in India and parliamentarians in distant European countries. She could mobilize half the world to her cause, and did so when necessary. Anyone who received a letter from this formidable lady therefore would read it thoroughly.

"As she approached the lectern she looked at us with a glance filled with eternal sadness, as though the weight of the words sin and despair pressed down on her slender shoulders alone." This slightly built woman was always clad in the latest fashion, becoming without being provocative, appealing without being forward; she knew how to cast a spell over vast gatherings of both men and women. She would stare into the audience with infinite sorrow while slowly and dramatically exposing how everything was connected—the decadence of the ruling class, police corruption, and all of the world's dishonest, lowly male behavior toward innocent women, in private and in public. According to her, prostitution was the great social evil, the problem above all others that the world had to fight. Those who heard her lectures were never in doubt that what she preached was the truth.

She was born wealthy, in 1828, to a mother of Huguenot descent and a father descending from the Border barons, cousin to Earl Grey. They raised Josephine a Protestant. At the age of twenty-two, after a period of religious discontent, she met George Butler, a highly regarded thirty-year-old Cambridge scholar. She moved with him to Oxford, where she gave birth to two sons and established herself as a provocative presence among the celibates of academe, assisting her husband in his research and once hiring a girl who had served time for infanticide to work as her maid. In 1864, after a move to Cheltenham and with a third son and a longed-for daughter to care for, tragedy struck—the five-year-old girl fell over a banister and was killed. After this, Josephine searched far and wide for people with "grief much deeper than my own, people more unfortunate than I." That same year she burst onto the stormy political scene as an abolitionist. Once the antislavery battle was won, she looked for another, equally important issue.

A missionary cousin put her in contact with the poor of Liverpool. A couple of prostitutes took her with them on their nocturnal wanderings in the port area where they earned their daily bread. This experience shook Josephine Butler to her core and helped her find purpose in life. In 1869, at the age of forty-one, she was already nationally known as she accepted the leadership of a Ladies' National Association for the Repeal of Contagious Diseases Acts. That year she published her first pamphlet, entitled "Women's Work and Women's Culture," an open attack on the venereal-disease law that Great Britain had just ratified. As her reputation grew, she soon had the whole country and perhaps half of Europe divided between adherents and enemies.

At the height of her influence, the beautiful, gracious Josephine Butler regularly traveled to Germany, Italy, and France; her husband, now principal at the Liverpool College for Boys, always waited faithfully for her at the railway station when she came home, worried to death that she had caught a chill. Josephine Butler always stressed that a woman's place was in the home, as mother and housewife. But in her own family life, it was the opposite. "We must liberate the world's daughters, for motherhood is the most sacred state in the world," she repeated tirelessly.

In 1874 the World Organization for the Struggle Against State Regulation of Prostitution was founded, with Josephine Butler as secretary-general and de facto leader. *A Letter to the Mothers of England*, her first book, published in 1891, took on the issue of prostitution among minors and put the question of the age of sexual consent at the top of the political agenda in several countries.

Josephine Elizabeth Grey Butler's family tree shows that her uncle Lord Charles Grey had been foreign minister and prime minister in a Whig government. Her aunt Margaretta Grey was an old-time feminist in the spirit of the Enlightenment who had sneaked into Parliament dressed as a man; she was a gutsy woman known to slap men she disliked in the streets, using her pocketbook or her parasol. Josephine resembled both, but she pointed out that she was on the side of "honest working folk ... and the unprivileged, who possess no words beyond 'how come' and 'jeez' ... " She did not, however, have regular personal contact with workers and prostitutes. She was a woman divinely called to become a prophet.

The chief medical officer of Kristiania, Norway, wrote in 1881 that stopping prostitution would be like "Unplugging the Outflow of a Sewer, whose stinking Contents rapidly seek other Ways out, and then through a Quantity of inevitable Leakage, where the Environment becomes infected." Napoléon Bonaparte, for his part, maintained that prostitutes were necessary, for without them, ordinary men would accede to their base instincts and accost respectable women on the streets.

The Norwegian doctor and the French emperor were in agreement about a lot—not only that commercial sex was necessary but also that it had to be regulated and supervised by matrons, policemen, and doctors. France pioneered the regulation of prostitution. The French technical term was *réglementation,* while the Scandinavian was *reglementering,* and *statutory regulation* was the proper British term. The French doctor A. J. B. Parent-Duchatelet became world famous as the Newton of veneral disease; he later also became the founding father of the statutory regulation system. In 1835, he published a two-volume work on prostitution grounded in meticulous studies of twelve thousand prostitutes whom the Parisian police had under surveillance between 1815 and 1831. Parent-Duchatelet drew well-measured conclusions about the women's social background, marital status, clandestine births, literacy, and emotional life. His work was an argument for *réglementation.* By these means married life was protected and venereal diseases believed to be under control.

His writings were commented upon all over Europe, whereupon similar systems were implemented in London, Glasgow, New York, Brussels, Antwerp, Berlin, Hamburg, Milan, Rome, Kristiania, Stockholm, and

Copenhagen. The meticulous Dr. Parent-Duchatelet stated that his investigations did not cover all strata among prostitutes and that he knew very little about the *femmes galantes*, the demimondaines whom the literary and artistic worlds praised, loved, painted, and wrote about—simply because the French police had not gathered information about them.

Parent-Duchatelet demonstrated the slippery overlap between sexual criminality and general poverty in Paris. Few women he wrote about had experienced a sudden plunge in social standing, and few had ended up in total misery. He also noted that prostitutes in no way lived outside society. For many French prostitutes, the sale of sex was a phase of life. After some years in prostitution, most of them married or went into another line of work. But during their prostitute years and in later life, most of these women lived at approximately the same low social status.

No other police corps in Europe had collected material like what the French police had provided through decades of painstaking supervision of the sex trade. Nor could any other prostitution researcher demonstrate the same scientific enthusiasm as Parent-Duchatelet. Physicians around the globe would utilize the French findings, but without a comparable level of veneral disease research their strategies were both more pragmatic and brutal than Parent-Duchatelet would have dreamed. His observations on prostitutes' social status were ignored; his thorough but critical discussions of sterility, frigidity, and physical decadence were taken out of context and presented as facts applicable to all prostitutes.

French statutory regulation was copied, and Parent-Duchatelet's studies were read all over Europe. Belgium, the Netherlands, and Poland were the first to follow the French paradigm. Italy's many small states copied France one by one, and the system was standardized after Italian unification. The midsize German and Scandinavian states also looked to France. Norway mechanically copied the French models when the public statutory regulation was implemented in 1840. But in the Scandinavian and German states, the police were given wider powers than in France. In some northern cities, they insisted on the registration of prostitutes who lived privately, but were less interested in the brothels. Stockholm started a struggle against organized brothels, while Gothenburg, Copenhagen, Bergen, and Kristiania only made them subject to statutory regulation.

Great Britain had always been less keen on regulation than the rest of Europe. But new studies from the 1830s and 1840s forced the British to analyze statistics on numbers of prostitutes and cases of venereal diseases, and they finally understood that they had more venereal disease than any other country. London instituted a police force with broader powers. New laws were implemented between 1864 and 1867 to fight venereal disease, first in port cities like Southampton and Plymouth, later in London, and finally throughout the whole British Empire. This series of statutes came to be known as the Contagious Diseases Act.

Everywhere statutory regulation was introduced, the number of prostitutes declined, while those who continued in the business appeared more attractive and contracted fewer venereal diseases. The Rescue Society homes in London and other cities received more clients and larger donations. From Great Britain, where earlier conditions had been completely chaotic, now came reports that were almost exclusively glad tidings, though in fact the whole nation, including most physicians, was kept in the dark about any information that could disturb the overall message.

By 1870 all of Europe, including the colonies, had adopted French *réglementation*. With the exception of the U.S., China, Japan, and the Arab world—and some provinces at the edges of Europe and its colonies—regular medical checkups and the registration of prostitutes had become a worldwide norm. The speculum, an old French gynecological instrument, was put to use all over Europe and in parts of Asia and the Americas. Marseilles and Dresden checked prostitutes on a weekly basis, Prague and Madrid every other week. Other cities adjusted their inspection to the different classes of prostitutes. Those who had many daily clients were considered eight-day girls and had to be checked more regularly than fourteen-day girls, who took fewer, better-paying customers and correspondingly had better general health. Some few had the privilege of reporting to the police doctor almost as discreetly as when they met their clients. In the 1870s even Kristiania referred to its elite prostitutes as "Females with private Visitation" in the police register, and police and medical doctors all over Europe admitted the quality difference between "the finer ones" and "simple prostitutes."

"I am an unqualified Supporter of the Control System, and this in its sharpest possible Form. I cannot find other than that the Woman who publicly enjoins her Body be sold as whatever Price can be fetched, to whomever she sells herself, must be subjected to the same Gaze as any Shopkeeper who sells goods that can be dangerous to the Health." Thus did a leading Norwegian physician in 1870 summarize the worldwide opinion of his profession. Between 1865 and 1890, a unified international body of medical opinion supported the statutory regulation system, while medical congresses in Paris, Florence, and Düsseldorf proposed resolution after resolution in defense of regulated prostitution. Within the police and military forces, there was an equally broad agreement that regulation was the only solution to the related problems of sexual immorality and venereal disease.

Amid all this progress, was it possible that Parent-Duchatelet's system sometimes was practiced too rigidly? Or that the police were given too much authority? Parallel with the good news about the decline of venereal disease, reports began to appear about innocent young girls newly arrived from the countryside, and about servant girls who were out on the streets too late at night, being arrested and brought to doctors and the police only because they looked like they ought to be registered as prostitutes. How many innocent women had to be unlawfully charged before the system was threatened?

Just when regulation had become a worldwide norm, a war broke out, and a crusade was mounted against the system medical and juridical leaders had established. The 1880s saw its downfall. In a few years, with Josephine Butler in the lead on behalf of Christian and moralistic men and women all over Europe, prostitution was transformed from a question of practical, medical, and health policy to a deep personal problem that involved outlooks on morality and the treatment of women.

Statutory regulation would be replaced by a new era of moralism, abolitionism, and feminism, ambiguous developments with conflicting side effects.

The British Christian moral reformer William Tait made this pronouncement in 1840: "No poor youth can take so much as a step in the city at night without encountering overtures. . . . From his boyhood days onwards, step by step, he becomes exposed to formidable temptations from the city's women, such that his whole life becomes a continuous struggle against all this sin." Given such conditions, it came to the point where even the most innocent become corrupted and seduced: "All authority is paralyzed, while immorality spreads at a frightening pace."

In Protestant Christian circles of the mid-1800s, there was a resurgence in the belief that love within marriage was a fundamental force that affected all aspects of civil society. Faith in love was a Christian variant of the romantic currents running through art and literature at that time. Those who believed in heartfelt love condemned the rational marriage of the ruling class, with its unfaithfulness and lack of the loving family life supposedly characteristic of the lower classes.

The solution to everything wrong in society was to strengthen family in society, so marriage could become an "eternal institution based on mutual love ... determined to last until all eternity." Unfaithfulness was destructive to both partners in a marriage, an absolute threat to this "sacred and invulnerable union." Since God had founded marriage, unfaithfulness was also a threat against good society. One should defend love privately and in one's own marriage and relationship with God; and one should defend true love and virtue by participating in public debates that aimed for a good and Christian society. Prostitution represented infidelity in its most unvirtuous form and worked to undermine love, virtue, and all morality.

The new Christian opinion makers regarded prostitution from an entirely different point of view than the doctors, lawyers, and military. Prostitution was not a question of regulating venereal disease and the physical boundaries of immorality. What this issue was all about was plugging a moral leakage from which the whole society was thought to be suffering.

A number of Victorian men blamed the women for the corruption and depravity of morals: "From the moment a woman has climbed down from the pedestal of innocence she is ready to continue with any sort of criminal activity," wrote the moral reformer J. B. Talbot in *The Miseries of Prostitution*, from 1844. Individual moralists wanted to prohibit all prostitution and punish all prostitutes. "No Compromise with Whoredom" was the radical slogan. Only punishment and the imprisonment of prostitutes in Magdalene homes would put an end to prostitution.

Only the most extreme opponents of prostitution thought that its complete suppression was possible in the short run. Those who were better at sniffing the political winds understood that the first goal had to be the repeal of the statutory regulation system, which they felt implied approval of immorality. As the morality movement developed into an international network after 1875, it started a goal-directed campaign against the regulatory system, a well-planned and well-organized struggle based on political alliances.

Male opponents of prostitution often accused female prostitutes of being worse moral vessels than their clients. Such women represented something primitive and animalistic as they "devalued the highest Life Functions of Humanity to just a few Crowns and Pence, Fineries and Amusements," as law professor and chairman of Norway's Society of Morals, Bredo Morgenstierne, put it in 1882. The other half of the equation, the male client, had really been thrown into a situation where he lost control of "the Natural Impulses which are Man's strongest." People's healthy common sense was evidence of this, said Morgenstierne. The popular opinion also "always judged more severely Those who prostituted themselves than Those who were merely reckless." The trade unions expressed the same message in different words: "Seize the Day, Workers, in the Defense against Prostitution."

The morality movement became a worldwide phenomenon. Its adherents also combated pornography by calling on writers, booksellers, and publishers to stop any publication with pictures of nudity or erotically suggestive illustrations. In addition, the movement opposed birth control and homosexuality; considered masturbation a harmful abomination; and combated all intercourse outside the bounds of marriage. It also combated other immoralities, such as alcoholism and gambling. But the movement's most central goal—aside from its war against prostitution—was to raise the age of sexual consent, which stood at twelve in most countries.

The White Cross Army, a typical international youth movement of the day, wanted to improve morality among young men of the working class. White Cross aspirants had to promise, with their hands over their hearts, that they would treat all women with respect, save them from all suffering and temptation, take measures to keep themselves pure, eradicate bad language and ugly comportment, and contribute to moral purity just as much among boys as among girls.

The morality movement was known for going into action, and not least on behalf of Christian soldiers and missionaries. Indeed, sin was criminality and had to be combated by all possible means, no matter what the police said and did, as Catherine Booth of the Salvation Army said. New York's Judge William Travers Jerome, who was a fanatical opponent of sin and debauchery, closed fifty brothels and seventy gambling dens in the city: "I know the law! The police are not prosecuting the matter. So the good citizens have to take action!" The judge was greeted by a backlash of public opinion for his unorthodox behavior. Even though most of these establishments rapidly reopened, Jerome was shortly after appointed state prosecutor, proof of the general support he enjoyed.

There were many strands to the great morality debate. The supporters of statutory regulation and the moralists argued forcefully against each other over prostitution. Male and female activists disagreed with regard to living together outside marriage, but they stood together in the debate on pornography and prostitution.

That prostitutes never expressed their opinion is what one might expect. It is a bit harder to believe that very few thought about giving the women a voice in the matter, with the exception of the bohemian painters and novelists. In depicting prostitutes in paintings and novels, to some extent they managed to expose the intractable nature of a society in which prostitutes represented a radical break with convention. Privately, many of the artists and intellectuals had intercourse with prostitutes, used them as models, and supported them economically. But their view was that all forms of love should be free, and they wanted upper-middle-class women to live just as freely as prostitutes. Those bohemians who were familiar with socialist or anarchist thinking maintained that prostitution would disappear with the increase of sexual freedom for all. And in a society with weak family ties and free love, the state would have to take care of the children.

Female socialists and anarchists of the day hardly belonged to any traditional positions in the debate; they approached the prostitution question in more realistic terms. The anarchist Emma Goldman defended open prostitution as a solution to want, and sold her body in service to her cause for some years. Clara Zetkin, the German socialist leader, brushed aside all moral arguments against prostitution as "the empty chatter of bourgeois women." In her correspondence with Vladimir Lenin, she criticized him for naive moralism. Zetkin's unique class-conscious criticism of most feminist approaches to prostitution and other issues was expressed in her 1889 book *Die Arbeiterinnen—und Frauenfrage der Gegenwart* (Working Women and the Woman Question Today). Her starting point was working women's need for their own income. Without real and well-paid work for women in the crafts and industries, she felt, any discussion for or against prostitution was pure nonsense.

"It is men, only men, from beginning to end, that we get to deal with. It was in order to make a man happy that I sinned for the first time. Since then I have gone from man to man. Then the police come and lay their hands on me. And it is men who investigate us, cure us and soil us all over again. And again in the institutions it is men who come and read the Bible to us, pray for us. We never get out of the hands of the men," complained a bitter prostitute in a letter to Josephine Butler. Gradually, the prostitution debate became influenced by feminism. An important argument in the struggle against regulation would be advanced in the name of gender equality. It was considered unfair that all supervisory initiatives were aimed at women. All the consumers of sex were men, but they were not pulled in for medical checkups or taken by force to hospitals.

In 1873 the former prostitute Harriet Hicks was dragged before the court in Plymouth. The judge asked if she was still a prostitute. "Today," she replied, "I only prostitute myself with the man I am married to." The answer worked in her favor, but it shows that her times were marked by conceptual confusion. What does it actually mean to be a prostitute? A great many believed that any woman the police had characterized as being of easy virtue was a prostitute. But if one were to take seriously the arguments of the police, one would admit that included any woman who went around unescorted or after nightfall, especially if she dared to use a bit of rouge.

Increasingly, the feminist opponents of police supervision brought forward examples of innocent women who were victims of "perverse" doctors and policemen. The medical examination was compared to a rape. Above all, this reflected the confusion of ideas marking the Victorian era. But there is also more than enough evidence about policemen who helped themselves to sexual services from women that the police doctors had just examined.

"On the Forced Introspection of Women by the Oligarchy That Calls Itself Doctors" was a characteristic pamphlet from England in 1870. Doctors, said the pamphlet, had enjoyed dominating and humiliating women from time immemorial; the police relished the task of hunting them down and punishing them. One suicide following a medical examination caused the newspapers to take a broad interest in the case. Freemasons, trade unions, and religious sects went on the attack against police raids and medical examinations as being un-English.

Actually, it was sufficient for the police to think a woman was a prostitute to order her in for supervision. Young officers competed to patrol the streets of a prostitution district. It was not even necessary to observe a woman alone on the street. Suspicion of irregular gentlemanly visits was enough to take in for a medical examination. This gave the local police enormous freedom to take a closer look at girls they fancied.

As the gender issue gained increasing importance, Josephine Butler would partially break with the men in the morality movement. She established her own organization, the Ladies' National Association for the Repeal of the Contagious Diseases Acts. She used different arguments in defense of women in the debate about forced statutory investigations. Several times she maintained that men in homosexual relationships had contracted venereal diseases that they gave to women prostitutes. It was reported that seventy men of the British Navy who had not seen a woman for a year were infected with venereal diseases. Butler's polemic maintained, "That coward of a doctor made them point out which women had been the cause. Too ashamed to admit that they had infected one another, the sailors had of course pointed to the first and best woman they found." It was easy to argue from both female and male perspectives that the regulation system caused attacks on many women. From the medical-administrative perspective, it was felt there was no alternative, and no better medical technology. But as moral and religious arguments and women's political agitation came closer together, they began to weigh more heavily than all the pragmatic and medical argumentation.

Josephine Butler and her disciples often asserted that prostitution ought to be regarded as a form of slavery. They based their argument on a vague analogy—all prostitutes were ostensibly subservient to brothel keepers or pimps, and as such, they were slaves to their clients. If the analogy were to hold, the women would have to be locked up or at least not be able to spend the money they earned. The fact that Josephine Butler had her political

schooling in the abolition movement explains her choice of words but
doesn't make the concept any more precise.

William T. Stead was one of Butler's foremost coworkers. He was
just as piously convinced as she was that prostitution was the world's greatest evil, but he lacked her charismatic presence and her high personal
morality. To W. T. Stead, the cause was so noble that he did not have to
consider the means he used to achieve his ends. He was a media household name, in our present-day sense of the term, and wrote and edited a
series of newspapers simultaneously. In issues involving the British Empire,
he wrote for the Quaker newspaper *The Sentinel,* while he reached the broad
British public through the *Pall Mall Gazette.* The paper's foremost issues
of the 1880s were prostitution and the age of sexual consent.

In the 1870s there were rumors of young British girls working in French
and Belgian bordellos. The term *white slave trade* triumphed from one British newspaper headline to the next, from one piece of pulp fiction to the
next. Finally, a British police investigator sat down to research the rumors
and made his findings known to a restricted circle of police employees and
civil servants. He had found that over a period of five years up to 1880, thirty-
four young girls had left England to work in brothels on the continent, all
traveling under their own initiative. Most were seventeen or eighteen, three
were fifteen, and one was fourteen.

We do not know for sure whether W. T. Stead knew about this police
report. In any case, his newspaper articles gave a much less sober-minded
picture of the situation; he thundered on that large numbers of the British
prostitutes were very young, and that young maidens were being sold to
foreign brothels. If the press did not have sufficiently gruesome facts to report,
they could be produced, as the history of the press amply shows. W. T. Stead
would go far in the service of his good cause, and if his articles in the *Gazette*
had not made him famous enough, he surely received world fame when they
were collected into a book entitled *The Maiden Tribute of Modern Babylon.* With
the help of a purely journalistic stunt, Stead was able to "prove" that it was
possible to "buy" a thirteen-year-old English virgin and "export" her to
France. In this way, Eliza Armstrong and W. T. Stead became world famous.

Stead's campaign in the *Gazette* may well have ensured that the age
of sexual consent was raised to sixteen, first in England and then in other
countries. But there are many indicators that the change in the statute

would have taken place anyway. Be that as it may, did W. T. Stead's goals justify the publication of erroneous information? Stead's moral agenda and fighting spirit carried him far away from acceptable ethical standards.

When the parents of the abducted Eliza Armstrong finally discovered that the writer had actually tried to prevent them from getting their daughter back, they availed themselves of an attorney who was able to unravel Stead's role in the whole series of events. The journalist had been involved in both placing an order for a British maiden and arranging the "export" that he thereafter "exposed." Stead ended up with a short prison term. But his newspaper, which had financed the exposure of the case and earned well from its subsequent increase in circulation, went scot-free.

W. T. Stead may have acted with good intentions, but was he operating with appropriate reason and dispassion? Phlegmatic commentators of the day considered him a bit of a sexual fantasist who grew desperate in his struggle to keep the bridle on his own wild imaginings. Contemporary reports describe W. T. Stead as conspicuously radiant and at times agitated and argumentative. A woman journalist wrote that she felt that this man "sweated semen through his skin" every time he began to talk about his pet subject—sex with children. At any rate, after a few months, Stead was released from prison and continued to have great renown in his own circle. Nonetheless, fate dealt unkindly with him: He perished at sea on the *Titanic* in 1912.

Certain experienced whoremongers who were contemporaries of Stead would publish memoirs with descriptions of their sinful youth in the brothels. It is understandable that many found such books objectionable, but they provide an interesting backdrop to Stead's journalism. In the eyes of all these writers, English brothel girls were distinguished negatively from all other nationalities. They were known to be vulgar, violent-tempered, running to fat, prone to drink, and unwilling to deviate from the missionary position. Thus, the international demand for English women was extremely small, even when the girls were young and pretty. There were few underage British prostitutes in other countries and very little demand for them. The one abducted teenager the world became aware of was a construct of the press. It was therefore rather ironic that the company publishing the *Pall Mall Gazette* continued to get credit for raising the age of consent in Great Britain.

*   *   *

Surprising political alliances formed all over the world in the struggle against regulated prostitution. During the 1880s, the women's organizations, workers' associations, and humanitarian and Christian organizations all made resolutions, demonstrated, and sent their demands to their respective governments.

The cumulative effect would be the repeal of the system. In the final two or three years of the 1880s, regulated prostitution was done away with in country after country, more abruptly than it had been implemented.

Britain's leading politician, the liberal but puritanical Scotsman William Gladstone, served four terms as prime minister and led the opposition. For years Gladstone maintained a friendship with an intelligent ex-prostitute of his own age, a Mrs. Thistlethwaite. Despite his exalted status, Gladstone had been out with her on nocturnal salvation missions aimed at prostitutes. One of Josephine Butler's disciples, Mary Hume-Rothery, worked especially hard to get Gladstone to understand precisely what happened when a police doctor sent a "spying tube up into a chain-enslaved abdomen."

In purely physical terms, the medical examinations were very unpleasant—and plainly hated, even by experienced prostitutes. Many prostitutes said that they felt the doctor was almost "taking revenge" on them. The high tempo of the examinations—up to thirty patients an hour—did nothing to augment the women's sense of human worth. It soon became a central argument in the propaganda of the abolitionists that the doctors' examinations were "unnatural," "voyeuristic," "brutal," and highly degrading for any woman, whether she was a private patient or a prostitute. "I personally would rather die than experience this," said Josephine Butler in one of her incendiary speeches. "It would have been a great advantage for our country if this technological innovation had never been brought over from France," said a prominent British politician.

In 1879 the British House of Commons set up a commission to look into the continuation of statutory regulation, all while the debate was raging to greater and greater heights. William Gladstone became completely convinced by the abolitionists. In the end, there was also a majority in the House of Lords: In March 1886 the British laws concerning venereal disease were repealed. In July 1888 the supporters of regulation suffered a partial defeat in Italy. The police lost their wide discretionary powers with individual prostitutes but, as before, supervised the brothels. Even at the very heart of regulation, France, changes came in 1888. The new French system has sometimes been described as neo-regulatory. To a considerable degree, such a concept conceals how radical the changes were at the time. Nonetheless, French doctors continued to examine prostitutes more frequently than did the British. The syphilis argument was still of importance in France, even though all obligatory supervision had disappeared.

Norway's last three brothels closed in 1884. In midsize cities all over Europe, the same thing would happen; the trend was visible even in France. It looked as though the time of the bordellos would soon be over. But prostitution continued in other establishments. The meticulous police supervision and the abolitionist movement contributed to this development, each in its own way. Across the whole society, a need was coming to the fore for freer personal relations between the sexes. This also implied the need for freer prostitution in the restaurants, beer cellars, and dance halls.

The fall of statutory regulation led to fewer brothels but more hidden prostitution, which in turn weakened contacts between the prostitutes and the health services. The most negative result was a stark increase in venereal disease from the late 1880s. In the 1890s syphilis spread at unprecedented rates. Most of the world's physicians had daily practical experience that made them consider this a truly ethical dilemma. Very few within the morality movement ever realized that they had caused new problems.

The leaders of the moral sisterhood had a remarkably similar background, as Christian, well-married, or rich widows well connected to their country's leading political families: Emilie de Morsier and Caroline de Barreau in France; Georgina Crawford Saffi and Anna Maria Mozzoni in Italy; Elizabeth Cady Stanton and Carrie Chapman Scott in the U.S. While their Christian faith provided strength and energy, their powerful families gave both practical help and political support.

None of these women went regularly to the opera or arranged debutante balls, but they all had relatives who did. Some incongruous figures nevertheless stand out among their sisters. Elizabeth Wolstenholme was no practicing Christian; she lived in sin with Ben Elmy "to the great harm of the cause." The cigar-smoking divorcée Emilie Venturi was as unique in England as the unmarried and mannish Aasta Hansteen in Norway.

All these moral women were politically liberal in matters that had to do with women's suffrage and gender equality, but their outlooks did not extend to love and sensuality, where they placed strong, indeed absolute, demands. The morality debate gained some of its intensity because these women arrived on the scene with double demands for love in marriage and public condemnation of immorality in society.

The moral crusaders won the first battle in their war against prostitution when regulated prostitution—and thereby all publicly accepted immorality—came to an end. Though venereal disease increased, as did the number of prostitutes and destitution among them and their children, the moral crusaders did not want to evaluate their actions by the results. If only one could bring an end to prostitution, the world would become a Protestant utopia, and "the principle of original sin will then be pulled from the earth by its roots," concluded Butler in one of her speeches. "Then and only then will justice be restored on earth!"

Josephine Butler was a woman of her time. She was scarcely a new Jesus, though she won an important battle in her struggle against prostitution. She lost the war, but she still has many disciples, and the faithful believe in her doctrine even today.

TWENTY-ONE

SEX IN THE WILD WEST

Kitty LeRoy met her fate at the Lone Star Saloon, in the room she rented on the floor above the dance hall. The year was 1878, the place Deadwood, South Dakota.

Kitty was shot by the current man in her life, Sam Hurley. It was not her profession that had made him jealous, the newspapers assured their readers. Prostitution was far too common in the largely womanless and lawless West. No, it was the rumor that Kitty had reestablished regular unpaid contact with a former husband from her time in Texas.

Several people had seen Sam arrive at the Lone Star Saloon with a six-gun in his belt. Even more people heard the shooting. Sam had challenged the Texan to a duel, but to no avail. Then he had snarled to a black waiter that Kitty's number was up. And since no one had seen Sam come down, it came as no surprise when they found two bodies in Kitty's room.

The saloon owner and madam washed, powdered, and tidied up the corpses so they looked nice and sexy amid firearms and pools of blood in the photographs. It was good publicity, though the career of the twenty-eight-year-old jig dancer was definitely over. Kitty had danced and whored from Michigan to Texas, from California to Denver, leaving one child and three husbands along the way. Who knows how many others she had besotted.

Kitty LeRoy is not a Hollywood caricature. Her story was documented in detail and was in no way unique. The Wild West was a violent society. Where weapons abound, they are liable to be used. Not only were large numbers of whores killed, many of them shot their clients, lovers, and colleagues. The tall blond Swedish Nina, who dressed as a man when she wasn't working, shot a customer in a Denver saloon in 1882, but was acquitted for self-defense. Few were that lucky. Mattie Lemon got away with ten years for shooting a client, since she was only twenty-two. Fastest on the trigger were the black girls streaming into the sex industry after the abolition of slavery in 1865. Belle Warden had reached the status of madam when she shot a customer in Denver—but she was adult and black and, unlike Mattie Lemon, got imprisoned for life. On film, we never meet amply proportioned black madams or huge, vengeful Scandinavian blondes with smoking six-guns. In the movies, most prostitutes are sweet little things, friendly and acquiescent, and they wear frilly panties under skirts that they willingly roll up: "We're just one big, happy family," says the madam in *The Cheyenne Social Club* to an old cowboy, alias James Stewart. Here a brothel was depicted in such an idyllic light that it was hailed as "a sex film for the whole family."

The first white settlers reached North America in the early 1600s. The way west became a struggle to put an untamed country under the plow. The Brave New World had to detach itself from Great Britain, purchase French Louisiana in 1803, and go to war with Mexico in the 1840s before the surge westward commenced. Then all public attention focused for a while on separatism in the old settlements in Virginia, Georgia, and Carolina, and the Civil War that followed. The subsequent twenty-five-year period was the heyday of the Wild West. A northern and a southern railroad across the continent secured twice the amount of territory settled previously, territory that could be transformed from borderlands and hunting territory into permanent settlements. By 1900 it was all over. The former Wild West entered the twentieth century with electricity and telephones, and in time with roads, cars, and Hollywood versions of its history. The nation was quick to put the frontier experience behind, but it has kept the mythology alive like a youthful infatuation.

The Wild West was a masculine society, though women did exist: settlers' wives, fine ladies at the ranches, teachers, and missionaries. A few ranch owners had well-educated, Christian-minded, and in some cases attractive daughters. It was not for everyone to experience close contact with one of these rare creatures. H. C. Cornwall, contractor and co-owner of some new coal mines in Irwin, Colorado, kept a diary in the early 1880s, when property prices were rising and miners, shopkeepers, and gamblers abounded in the town. His notes are both entertaining and informative. At a charity ball in Irwin, five respectable ladies danced side by side with the notorious Durango Nell, Timberline Kate, and their professional sisters.

Irwin's only guaranteed virgin was the mine doctor's eighteen-year-old sister-in-law. She could lower her eyes, recite poetry, and cause the hearts of yearning young men to pound. There were hundreds of unskilled laborers in the mines, but only forty with romantic notions strong enough to fight for the one available pillar of virtue. They behaved as well as they could. None of them went to a whorehouse. Oh, no—they were too busy grooming themselves, putting on their finery, and getting ready to visit the Chosen One. She received them all on a sofa, six at a time. The doctor's wife sat behind a potted palm at the opposite end of the room, watching the clock, carefully limiting the audience to ten minutes per group.

Unbesmirched middle-class girls were not easy to find in the Wild West. There were plenty of laundry girls, seamstresses, and shop assistants who could not play piano or embroider. The saloon hookers and dancing girls seemed to be everywhere in the West, but their profession required them to be seen. Actually, only one in ten was a prostitute.

The population was also smaller than we tend to believe. While the U.S. population more than doubled in the period and soon was to pass ninety million, only five million settled in the enormous Wild West. Most growth was due to fresh immigration from Germany and Ireland, then from Scandinavia and southern and eastern Europe. Immigrants from China, Japan, Mexico, and the Pacific Islands entered on the West Coast. Some newly immigrated women were prostitutes. According to the police physician of Kristiania, Norway, twenty-five "public women" migrated annually to the U.S. from this relatively small city. Some set out for the border areas, where there was only one woman per five men, but among those who were prostitutes, most had been in the country several years before trying their luck in such exposed areas. The possibility for an unmarried woman to find a husband was high, but the temptation to prostitute oneself was nearly as great. Like Kitty LeRoy, quite a lot tried both.

In Arizona, the following notice was hung up in January 1882, signed "Doc. Linton, Sheriff":

> All women of dubious character in the fair city of Tombstone must continue to confine themselves to the shady side of the street. This applies particularly to Amazon Amy, Big-Nosed Bertha, Bubbles Berrick, Footsie Ferrel, Formaldehyde Flo, Coal Oil Katie, Fifi L'Amour, Tuberculosis Tessie, Toothy Jane, and twenty others. You all know who this concerns. If any of you are seen on the sunny side

of the street, there's a quiet place waiting for you—jail. The alternative is to leave town for good. At any rate that would be good for Tombstone.

The West had few public officials beyond the local sheriff. There were no population figures and little record of newcomers, certainly not of prostitutes. But the women who ran saloons and brothels, important sources of tax revenue, were included in documents of many kinds. We know their employees, the prostitutes, first and foremost to the degree that they came into conflict with the law, when they died, or when they put a child in the graveyard.

Wyoming, a sparsely populated state in the northwestern prairies, had one small railroad town, Cheyenne, where the profession was included in the census of 1880. The would-be state registered seventy-one women prostitutes out of a total population of ten thousand. All registered prostitutes lived in Cheyenne. The census takers didn't include the Indian prostitutes or the married women who earned extra income from sex. In the more heavily populated Texas, there were more prostitutes. In the cattle town of Austin, the sheriff arrested 240 named prostitutes between 1876 and 1879—for murder, drunkenness, fighting, and bad language. If we assume that half the prostitutes stayed out of trouble, this figure allows for one prostitute per ten inhabitants, more than were found in an average town of Austin's size.

In San Antonio, Texas, and around the Mexican border, most prostitutes in the nineteenth century were Hispano-Indian. Many in California were from China and Japan. Every fourth prostitute in the Wild West was a former black slave. Historians have found scattered evidence of male prostitutes in brothels and military camps, but all were transvestites and may have managed to keep their sex concealed. Nakedness was the exception, not the rule, among prostitutes in those Victorian times.

The total number of prostitutes was somewhere below two hundred thousand women and a few men. Whores of the Wild West were tough, poor, and unglamorous compared with their professional sisters in the civilized South and East; they died younger, contracted more venereal diseases, and were involved to an almost incredible extent in drunken brawls, violence, and murder.

François Boucher's *La Toilette* from 1742 exudes domesticity and the innocence of its young subject. Most of the better bordellos of eighteenth-century London and Paris projected an intimate atmosphere and sought out girls with healthy skin and immaculate manners (Louvre, Paris).

The implicit presence of the voyeur in pornography became literally evident in the art of the eighteenth century. In this illustration for *Fanny Hill* (by Borel and Elluin for the 1776 French edition), Fanny spies on an older brothel hostess who has paid for the fiery nineteen-year-old's enhancement of the couple's encounter (British Museum, London).

Two of impressionism's most famous prostitution paintings are Edouard Manet's *A Bar at the Folies Bergère* (top) from 1882 (Courtauld Institute Galeries, London) and Edgar Degas's *The Madam's Birthday* (bottom) from 1879 (Musée Picasso, Paris).

"Prostitution Exposed," from New York, 1839, a tract against prostitution, but also first and foremost a guide for clients of the trade. The publication contains detailed descriptions of establishments and names and addresses of prostitutes (Leo Hershkowitz, private collection).

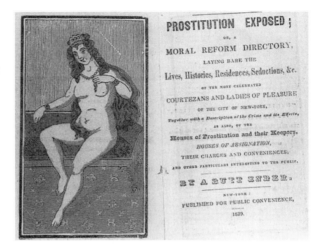

The health certificate for one "Della" from New York, 1901. The certificate attests to the fact that Dr. S. Rothenburg has found her to be in good health (New York Public Library/Astor, Lennox, and Tildens Foundations).

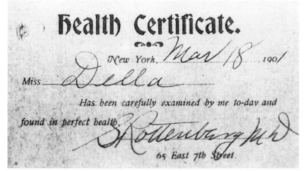

A dance at the largest brothel in Abilene, Texas, depicted vividly in a drawing from Joseph McCoy's history of the cattle trade (Kansas State Historical Society, Topeka).

A young *karayuki-san*, or prostitute, in Singapore around the year 1910. Her hair has been let loose, and we see the girl's profile in the mirror on the table (Collection of Gretchen Liu/National Archives, Singapore).

A Jewish woman purchased in Poland or Russia. The girl appears willing, her relatives skeptical, in this 1902 illustration by Eugène Grasset for Anatole France's *The Jewish Whore Merchant* (John Lewis: *The Twentieth Century Book,* New York, Van Nostrand Reinhold, 1954, 1984).

Aging French *fille publique* before World War II, photographed by Eugène Atget in Paris (Museum of Modern Art, New York).

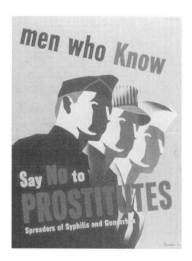

Posters commissioned by American health authorities at the beginning of World War II, designed to alarm and frighten (Olafia-Klinikken, Oslo).

The majority of Japan's military prostitutes were Korean girls; however, here some of Japan's own daughters freely reported for service to their emperor and homeland in 1942, unaware of the wretched duty that awaited them (*Dong-A Daily*/Meiji-Shobo, Tokyo).

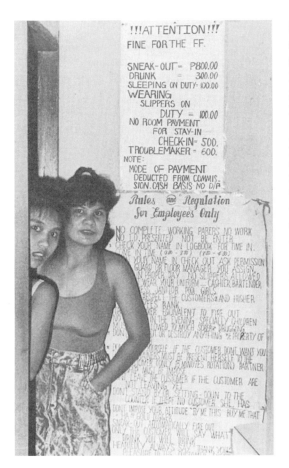

Left, military orders and discipline were features of the sex bars in Olongapo (Saundra Pollock Sturdevant and Brenda Stoltzfus: *Let the Good Times Roll*, New York, The New Press, 1993). Below, members of the English Collective of Prostitutes, Britain's largest prostitutes'-rights organization, reveal themselves semi-anonymously to the British press in 1982 after twelve days of church occupation in protest of police violence and racism (Gigi Turner, English Collective of Prostitutes, London).

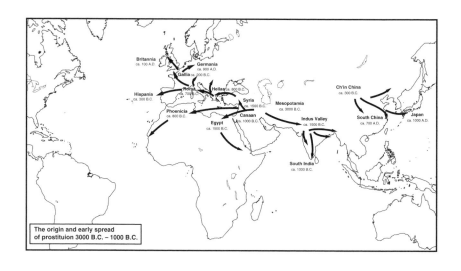

Britannia ca. 100 A.D.
Germania ca. 900 A.D.
Gallia ca. 200 B.C.
Roma ca. 700 B.C.
Hispania ca. 300 B.C.
Hellas ca. 800 B.C.
Phoenicia ca. 800 B.C.
Syria ca. 1500 B.C.
Mesopotamia ca. 3000 B.C.
Canaan ca. 1000 B.C.
Egypt ca. 1500 B.C.
Indus Valley ca. 1500 B.C.
Ch'in China ca. 300 B.C.
South China ca. 700 A.D.
Japan ca. 1000 A.D.
South India ca. 1000 B.C.

The origin and early spread
of prostituion 3000 B.C. – 1000 B.C.

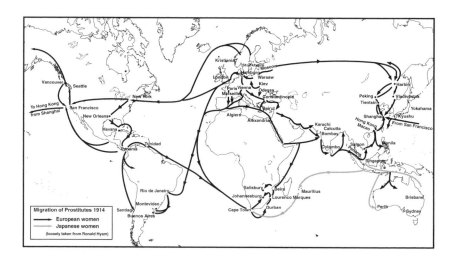

Kristiania
Stockholm
Moscow
Vancouver
Seattle
London
Hamburg
Warsaw
Harbin
Paris
Vienna
Kiev
Peking
Vladivostok
New York
Marseille
Odessa
Constantinople
Tientsin
Yokahama
To Hong Kong
from Shanghai
San Francisco
Beirut
Shanghai
Kyushu
New Orleans
Algiers
Karachi
Hong Kong
Macao
From San Francisco
Alexandria
Calcutta
Bombay
Havana
Saigon
Manila
Trinidad
Panama
Colombo
Penang
Singapore
Rio de Janeiro
Salisburg
Seira
Mauritius
Johannesburg
Lourenço Marques
Brisbane
Montevideo
Santiago
Cape Town
Durban
Perth
Buenos Aires
Sydney

Migration of Prostitutes 1914
European women
Japanese women
(loosely taken from Ronald Hyam)

But the girls seemed to be everywhere, and they worked hard. Brutal living conditions made instability a norm. The only social body attempting to help was the Sisters of the Good Shepherd, but without much success. The girls could have done with more advice and support; only one in ten could afford legal assistance. Few managed to put aside some of their earnings. It would have been hard to get better pay, since most of their customers earned less than the day's national economic boom led us to believe.

The prostitutes who did not die young sometimes ended up as madams or abortionists. The first did best. As the years passed, many chose life with a husband and children, if they were able to get pregnant again after many abortions. The trouble was that their husbands tended to be among the frontier's most disadvantaged: railroad workers, miners, and cowboys. Many had a criminal background and forced their wives to continue prostituting as a second income.

In spite of abortions and violence and poor income, prostitutes often ended up as the foremothers of later generations of the West. This significant fact would embarrass Hollywood directors, but it does come to light in some of the very best western films featuring whores—for example, in the final scene of *Stagecoach*. This story has been filmed a number of times, but the classic is John Ford's 1939 version, featuring a young John Wayne and Claire Trevor. The stagecoach creaks and rumbles south through New Mexico, full of shady characters, and as it and the film roll on, most viewers fall in love with both the Ringo Kid, who is on the run, and Dallas, the whore who has been chased out of town. That two such misfits would ride into the sunset together—any member of the audience with his heart in the right place might let loose a tear as the drink-sodden, penniless Doc sums it up: "These two, at least, have been saved—from civilization!"

Native American women enjoyed considerable freedom in the old days. It was considered an advantage if a woman was not a virgin when she chose a husband. A rich song tradition among the Papagos praised free women. The Navajos let free women set up their tents and entertain the men they wished. Effeminate men, or *berdaches,* also put themselves at the disposal of lonely members of the tribe. Native American women in the South and

West were promiscuous during great feast times, then they left their husbands' house and offered themselves to others for some days.

At the sight of Western ships, Californian Indians of the early 1800s brought their wives to the beach and offered them to the sailors. Afterward, man and wife went home with a surplus. In the deserts of Mexico, Texas, and Nevada, internal prostitution existed in several tribes; the Sierra Tarasca older women always knew the young women who were available to unmarried men from the tribe, set up agreements, and got their share of the pay.

Hollywood has a long tradition of assigning Indian girls as lovers or temporary wives of solitary hunters on the fringes of civilization. Here the movies can be quite realistic and historically correct. For centuries the Native American way of life was accepted—indeed, respected—by white hunters in the borderlands. Hunters and fur traders had no difficulty adapting to the indigenous and often directly negotiated marriages *à la façon du pays*, as the French said. The Native Americans felt they gained something from contact with foreigners via the hospitable lending of women.

But the tune changed as the missionaries arrived and began to accuse the natives of immorality and prostitution. The pioneer women in the Protestant settlements would soon ally themselves with the missionary point of view. Thus Indian women gradually lost the respect they had enjoyed from white men before the arrival of modern agriculture, and more white settlers. Marriage between Indians and whites disappeared over a few decades, while prostitution grew.

The U.S. military forts were established as outposts between agrarian civilization, Indian reservations, and the remaining wilderness. The soldiers were supposed to secure the Pax Americana whenever it was threatened, but they maintained broad contact with the local tribes who could move freely in and out of the forts to sell their various wares, including sex. There were some white females inside the forts, too, generally wives of soldiers or officers, or cleaning ladies and cooks. Nevertheless, Indian prostitution was the most important sexual stimulation for the boys in blue. Brothels near military forts in the South and West often looked like farms but offered girls of the Navajo, Maricopa, and Yuma tribes to soldiers. It would be very exceptional to encounter a Sioux woman, however. Hardly any Native American girls were truly professionals; the natives sold their bodies occasionally; and few contracted venereal diseases.

In times of crisis, the native men would withdraw from the forts, warriors such as they were, while their women remained, in hopes of earning some reserves from soldiers. The need for money increased in proportion to the risk that their husbands would be killed.

Sex for money between soldiers and Native American women seems to have been too complex for Hollywood, so the movies continue to show soldiers fighting the Indians—stalwart, eyes front, without any considerations for the Native Americans. Especially in the Southwest, native girls ended up as more permanent or occasional prostitutes. Many generations before the first prejudiced missionary or settler's wife decided to accuse Native Americans of immorality, old men of all tribes had blamed the white man for ruining the young men of the tribe with alcohol and deluding their young women into selling sex for money.

In *Gone with the Wind*, Hollywood gave its all-time sweetest portrait of a brothel madam. Belle Watling is the full-blooded, warmhearted, and sensitive woman whom Rhett Butler, played by Clark Gable, once almost loved. He still visits her when he is in despair, or if Scarlett O'Hara, portrayed by Vivien Leigh, disappoints him. A man like Rhett Butler could have gotten the treatment he wanted free of charge from Belle, or from others, but that was not why he came. He wanted sympathy and advice.

We never meet Belle interacting with girls in the profession, just with Butler and women from the upper class. However, she is depicted so vividly and possesses such wisdom that no one would doubt she must have treated her own employees with compassion. In one scene, Belle reveals that she has a grown-up son she seldom hears from, and a daughter she will never have a chance to see, though she has invested a great deal of money in their upbringing. Hard work has given the madam worldly goods and wisdom but scarcely any happiness.

Belle Watling lived in Carolina, in the old southern states, where old-fashioned good manners were a way of life among whores and madams. It is not unthinkable that the odd nice little whorehouse may have existed in the Wild West. "There is nothin' dirty goin' on here," sings Dolly Parton in the film *The Best Little Whorehouse in Texas*. Perhaps we ought to believe her. Dolly is the madam at the Chicken Ranch Brothel in Gilbert,

Texas, and must defend her business from being closed down by Sheriff Ed Earl, alias Burt Reynolds. But in most western whorehouses, you would find prostitutes of the coarsest caliber and brothel keepers who were not particularly interested in taking care of troubled girls.

In the little town of Boise, Idaho, in the cold Northwest, the local police demanded $30 a month to permit the operation of a brothel in the 1870s. Agnes Bush and her colleagues Jean Gordon, Nona Dee, and May Bradbury shared the cost, each supervising her own girls. Agnes had fourteen working for her, while the least established madam had four.

Madam Agnes owned a fairly large fine house with six rooms upstairs. In addition, she rented out some dilapidated huts in the alley behind. Those whom Agnes allowed to stay in the main house paid $20 a week each for board and lodging. In the 1870s the girls could earn between $3 and $7 from one customer, so three or four a week meant a profit for the girls and their madam. It was worse for those who had to ply their trade in the small huts at the back. First they had to pay up to $50 a month in rent, half of which went straight to Agnes, who moved the girls around as she saw fit. If they became less popular with her or the customers, they were sent straight to the huts. If they had not put some money aside by then, there was no way they could do so later. They could not expect any help from Agnes.

The deeper one penetrated into the Wild West, the more distant became the fairy tale of kindhearted madams and whores with a heart of gold. Even in the few "good little whorehouses" in the golden age of Texas, conditions were more dismal than one would find in western movies, and working conditions were far worse than in brothels of the East.

But it was not Hollywood that first painted a rosy picture of Wild West prostitution. The whores of the time began doing so themselves. The most famous of them all was Calamity Jane—Martha Jane Cannary. By the age of twenty-four, she was already ravaged by drink and hard living, if we are to judge from pictures. By then she had danced and whored from town to town for eight stormy years, from Cheyenne, Wyoming, to Hays City, Kansas. Then she became famous via her alliance with James Butler—Wild Bill Hickok—another living legend.

Calamity Jane survived Wild Bill, and her reputation as an eccentric grew. She began to wear men's clothes and deviated more and more from a traditional woman's role. For years she gave interviews to new generations of journalists. Hardly any of them had sense enough to compare the stories she served up from one year to the next. As Calamity Jane grew into an American national monument, she contributed to the mythology of the Wild West. Hollywood's filmmakers did not have to construct the myths of the Wild West's hookers. They had them served up on a plate.

TWENTY-TWO

IMPERIAL VIRTUE

The press was there to greet Lord Roberts as he stepped ashore on his return to England in May 1893. There was a hail of questions. Roberts had just retired as commander in chief of the British forces in India, the jewel in the crown of Imperium Britannica. It was natural for him to believe that this was the reason why the newspapers were out to greet him.

Frederick Roberts was still bronzed by the sun of India, lean, with piercing green eyes. He was one of the great sons of the nation, lionized for the first time during the Sepoy mutiny of 1857, when the British dominion over India almost collapsed following an uprising among Indian soldiers, supported by a variety of princes and maharajahs in India's northwest. Young Roberts reached national fame as "the brave Lieutenant Roberts from the struggles over the Shah Nahaf Mosque in Lucknow." In the following years, he was promoted through the ranks to general; he was raised to peerage and had recently been awarded a lordship. As Sir Frederick Roberts, he had led the march from Kabul to Kandahar in 1879, yet another heroic deed. Many men of influence shared the belief that in a few years' time, Lord Roberts would be sent back to India as viceroy.

But alas, it was not the forgotten wars and old military feats of derring-do that now preoccupied the British press. The newsmen waiting for the ship to dock were burning to ask questions of current interest: "Is it true that British military officers are systematically offered prostitutes in the military camps?" Roberts replied with the clipped precision of a soldier: "I deny this. This is not true." He showed his first signs of hesitancy when asked if syphilitic women were compelled to stay in hospitals. "It is true, and moreover desirable. But I have little concrete knowledge of this!"

One newspaper, the *Christian Commonwealth,* quoted his statements in a format that would subsequently be used as citations in most of the English press. W. T. Stead made sure of this. "An army chief who does not know what is going on in half a dozen of India's greatest military garrisons, can hardly be the man we thought he was" was the sly conclusion of the *Christian Commonwealth,* in an article signed by W. T. Stead.

What Lord Roberts did not know was that two American women, Elizabeth Wheeler Andrew and Dr. Kate Bushnell, had been on a three-month inspection tour of India's military camps in 1891. They had visited brothels and hospitals and interviewed prostitutes. In 1886, Great Britain had repealed its laws concerning initiatives against venereal disease and the public supervision of prostitution. The change was implemented in India two years later, and many were interested to find out how this had been followed up. Immediately before Lord Roberts's return, the two American women had testified before a public hearing about their findings. It appeared to them that prostitution in India, a system with a long tradition, continued to prevail.

The British press in India duly took up London's news items. *The Tribune* of Lahore wrote that Lord Roberts's future career was presumably now at stake. In London, W. T. Stead made sure this was referred to in bold type. In one of his own papers, *The Sentinel,* he maintained that the risk of having an incompetent viceroy had now been averted.

There may have been a certain degree of truth to the British press's conclusions that the military authorities in India had not contributed much to enforcement of new British sexual policy. "The natives of India live in accord with old customs and traditions. This makes it difficult to push them into abrupt changes," explained Lord Roberts in his first semiapologetic letter to the press. But in the Great Britain of the 1890s, this argument would not fall on sympathetic ears. There, it was considered correct, proper, and plainly democratic that political decisions taken by a bare majority in London should be implemented on a continent many times greater, on the other side of the globe, in a part of the world marked by other languages and religions, and with several hundred million inhabitants who had absolutely no inkling about something that was, at most, of incidental interest in London's moral circles.

It is useless to pretend that our life was a normal one. Ours was a one-sexed society, with the women hanging on to the edges. And every man who pursued the physical aim of sexual relief was in danger of

developing a cynical hardness and lack of sympathy. Of those who tried
sublimation, some chased polo balls and some chased partridge, some
buried themselves in work, and all became unmitigated nuisances. And
some took up the most unlikely hobbies, and some went to diseased
harlots, and some married in haste, only to worry over who was now
seducing their wives in the hill stations where they had seduced so
many other people's wives. And a few homosexuals followed their own
secret star with comparative comfort in that large and easygoing
country.

With these words, John Masters summarized life in the good old days of
British India.

India was not a country but a subcontinent. Between the Suleiman
Mountains and the Karakorum in the northwest, throughout the Deccan
Peninsula to the south and Burma in the east, Buddhists, Hindus, Mus-
lims, Sikhs, and Christians lived side by side with a variety of tongues, in-
cluding English, Punjabi, Bengali, and a whole raft of Dravidian and
Tibeto-Burmese languages.

The British East India Company established itself in Calcutta and
Bengal in the 1600s and 1700s in collaboration not only with the mughal,
an enigmatic Muslim emperor in Delhi, but also with hundreds of maharajahs and local princes. From coastal colonial enclaves, Portugal, Holland,
Denmark, and the archenemy, France, conducted separate trade. In the
interior, the East India Company and the British government twisted their
way into control through battles and agreements. The British army proved
its superiority in the wars against Maratha princes, Sindh, and Punjab. In
1857 an uprising among the Indian soldiers in the British army, the sepoys,
resulted in another bloody war. Later, this sepoy uprising would be viewed
as the starting point of Indian nationalist politics. But for another century,
India was considered the loser and was placed directly under the Crown
in 1858. The governor-general in Calcutta received the title of viceroy,
while Queen Victoria was unilaterally declared empress of India in 1877.
India still did not become fully British, since two-fifths of the continent,
the less fertile and more sparsely populated parts, remained self-governing
principalities, although at least one British adviser was required in each
state. All in all, there were 675 principalities. The largest—Mysore,
Kashmir, and Hyderabad—were roughly the size of Ohio and much more
populous. Some maharajahs were rolling in money. The smallest princely

states, on the other hand, were the size of an average American munici-
pality and ruled by dismally poor rajahs who struggled daily to feed their
only elephant and keep up the appearance of princely dignity.

No individual British governor or Indian prince could set the tone
in the metropoles of Madras, Bombay, or Calcutta: These cities swarmed
with sailors, smugglers, and adventurers, together with rich and poor
merchants from every corner of the earth. Most Eurasians, or European
educated Indians, the Babus, preferred to live in the cities. But though many
had received good educations in Europe, their salaries in India remained
low. In restaurants and beer joints, Hindu lads and British girls served
customers side by side. No Indian female took up such jobs. White girls
took the positions without challenge until, in the 1890s, it dawned on the
British authorities that the virtue of the empire would suffer when white
womenfolk served menfolk of brown and mixed race. White waitresses had
to be stopped to protect and respect the empire and the white race.

Prostitution was something else. Whether in hues of white, yellow,
or brown, it blossomed all over Madras and Bombay. There were more
than thirty thousand prostitutes in Calcutta alone: Hindu, Muslim, British, French, Jewish, and East Asian women. The local missions tried to do
battle with this evil, and did so most ardently wherever white women were
involved. In the 1890s the Bombay Midnight Mission patrolled from seven
in the evening until three in the morning. Activists from England and the
Netherlands, together with Christian Indians of mixed race or outcasts,
went around reading aloud Bible verses, shouting hymns at the tops of their
voices, beating upon doors, and smashing the odd window, all in the hope
of disturbing a sinning seaman and his paramour. In contrast to the situation in England, no missionary or Salvation Army officer tried to save or
reeducate the prostitutes.

Hindus and Muslims were never part of actions against prostitutes
or their customers, although they themselves occupied the red-light districts in the daytime. Nevertheless, for visiting Indians, these quarters of
the city became tourist attractions. Here, it was easy to observe the differences between European prostitutes and the traditional prostitution they
knew from small towns and villages in the Indian hinterlands.

There were no white planters or independent farmers settled in India.
All agriculture was Indian. Foreigners engaged in mining and control of
the trade. From the 1850s, a wide railway network linked the big cities and

opened up the interior. As a result, one could encounter Salvation Army officers and white adventurers of both sexes high in the mountains and along the most distant coasts. In every single Indian town, wrote Rudyard Kipling, there would be two or three Englishmen who were born there. Careful observation was needed to distinguish them, "for they too had become brown all over." There were more than a hundred thousand British in India whose lifestyle was not determined by those who set the moral tone in the circles around the viceroy, or the governors who personified correct British behavior and represented the British Empire.

These representatives of the empire lived in an elegant and civilized manner, as if they belonged to the aristocracy of their homeland. In truth, very few of them did, although those at the top tended to be raised to the peerage over the course of their careers. Without shame or irony, they called themselves the master race and lived in British enclaves near but well insulated from the cities. They were wealthy merchants, officers, and civil servants interspersed with the occasional doctor, teacher, or High Church missionary. In these imperial enclaves, over a third of the men lived with their wives, many of whom were veritable dragonlady memsahibs, plus children, governesses, and various stray relatives. Every daily routine followed proper British standards: One took tea at five o'clock, believed in God, toasted the queen, and dressed correctly for every occasion.

"The greatest mistake the British made was to bring their women to India." We have numerous statements like this, made by Indians as well as Britons, and reiterated from Kipling to Conrad. The Britons of the eighteenth century seldom brought their wives and families to India; the memsahibs did not become historically important until the latter half of the nineteenth century. It is hard to find any social group as condemned, and perhaps even maligned, as the memsahibs, the protagonists in the development of the British Empire's corpus of etiquette and morality around the turn of the century. They were the scapegoats for the racism that marked relations between Britons and Indians. They were also, according to contemporary accounts, a class of women devoid of curiosity or lust for adventure, yet they were filled to the brim with prejudices and trivial interests. Their concerns spanned a compendium of topics, from flower arrangements, through gossip and flirtation, to bridge. Their behavior showed its worst face to servants, Indian women, and the few Englishmen to express sympathy for the natives. The memsahibs nagged and carped about such men in a tasteless mix of racism, moralism, and megalomania. But that was the way it was. These women were, after all, small-town girls who all at once had become the ladies-in-waiting to the empress—abroad.

In the 1880s the memsahibs had become so numerous that they could demand cultural and racial purity in social relations. But in Kashmir, northern Assam and Burma, or toward the Goan coast, in isolated valleys or coastal regions where conditions were too rough, too cold, too humid, or too hot for the memsahibs, Englishmen could go on living as British gentlemen had lived in the 1700s, with an Indian wife, or a *bibi,* as the Indians respectfully called such women. Even the governors lived in this manner. This explains why there were at least three hundred thousand Eurasians in the country by the end of the nineteenth century, many of them well educated.

Nevertheless, love relationships and racial mixing continued. Children were "a hideous race, who had taken over nothing but the worst features of the Indians, and none of our good qualities," as the memsahibs usually put it. The very existence of so many Eurasians created palpitations of exasperation in the breasts of the memsahibs, and tortured their leader, the man who became viceroy of India in 1899, Lord George Nathaniel Curzon.

Curzon was horribly virtuous and moralistic; he preferred to be only betrothed as long as he possibly could, and managed to stretch out this status for an eternity before he submitted to matrimony. Everybody whispered about how he had been kissed at Eton, while he, in public, explained that he found celibacy most practicable. He would never be one of those who sullied his race, but neither would he expand it.

The viceroy became just as exasperated as the prudish memsahibs every time he got wind of Brits practicing race-damaging animal behavior with the natives. Such a rumor would be enough to delay or put a complete stop to the career of the man concerned: He would rapidly be reassigned to a less attractive post. Respectable Britons broke all contact with these men out of consideration for the virtue of the empire and the empress—and the vice-queen, as some few called Curzon behind his back.

"A lieutenant is always a bachelor, a captain may get married, a major ought to, and a colonel must" was the saying in the British army. In practice, an officer was never married before thirty, seldom before forty; a considerable number of stiff-backed colonels and even generals managed to hold on to their bachelorhood throughout their lives.

The vast majority of the imperial army's elite officer corps was composed of young unmarried men. In all, about a thousand well-groomed, cultivated, racially pure British gentlemen were in place to defend the empire, God, virtue, and the queen. But they could not live without a love life altogether, and since Indian lovers were totally socially unacceptable after 1900—thanks to the coalition between Lord Curzon and the memsahibs—the young men had intense flirtations with the younger among the wives, and discreet visits to prostitutes.

Detailed information about these love lives came to light with a series of erotically oriented memoirs that many once-lusty gentlemen brought out with geriatric but uninhibited smacking of the lips: *Love Adventures in Hindustan, Black Diaries,* and *My Secret Life* represent a literature rich in variety. The critical reader must take account of some obviously fanciful passages and a certain degree of old men's virile overindulgence. But altogether, the memoirs provide solid evidence about how secrecy gave rise to deviations from the path of virtue by almost all the outwardly staid civil servants and officers, a degree of deviance more immense than the wildest dreams of any contemporary gentleman in Europe.

The memoirs explain how easy it was for three or four young officers up in the highlands to hire five or six of the most expensive prostitutes for days. Bombay's well-educated officers and doctors would organize weeklong orgies in which they undertook close comparative anatomical studies of prostitutes of various nationalities, and awarded the women what they considered appropriate grades. Most of the memoirs also openly discuss flirting and relationships between officers, and relationships with young Indian, Singhalese, or Burmese boys independent of, or concurrent with, their heterosexual exploits.

The memoirs describe "poodle hunting," or the constant competition to seduce the attractive wives of officers. Obviously not every memsahib was a total dragon, at least as seen through British eyes, and many of them were considerable flirts. Infidelities could make time pass more quickly for those living a life in the colonies that was otherwise notable only for its boredom. If children were to result, they would at least be racially pure.

However, the British could not live in complete social isolation, no matter how much the memsahibs might have desired it. The complex administrative structure of the empire, with all its princely enclaves, required minimal interaction with full-blooded Indians and people of mixed extraction. It was simply not possible to turn down all invitations from the local aristocracy, and sometimes it was necessary to invite them in return. "The maharajahs had to be considered part of the ruling class, but in no way part of the ruling race," Curzon would point out with utmost precision.

The Indian maharajahs and princes controlled a great deal of land, and some of them possessed huge fortunes. A considerable number had received European educations. But this did not cause them to behave like the Brits. On more than one occasion, members of their ranks had expressed their homosexual preferences, and this in public. A Briton would never speak of such a thing. The princes thereby threatened the British self-ascribed order of social precedence. Indeed, the British race's God-given dominance was at stake every single time a young maharajah made eye contact with a British maid.

Lord Henry Hamilton, who served as prime minister for India, criticized the hyper-British Curzon for treating the Indian princes like schoolboys. "But that is exactly what they are," replied Curzon, who used every means available to prevent the marriage of the maharajah of Patiala to a British miss, Florry Bryan—all in vain. Shortly afterward, the rajah of Jind celebrated his own nuptials in a more discreet manner. In this case, the bride was Dutch. There wasn't a single representative of the Crown among the guests.

The European literature, music, and art of the late nineteenth century developed a far more curious attitude toward India and its culture than that of Curzon, the memsahibs, and other representatives of Britain, with their indomitable moral approach.

Temple prostitution was still widespread in India during the nineteenth century, despite the fact that several Muslim rulers had tried to put a stop to it. India's temple dancers, the *devadasi,* experienced a romantic world fame. Continental Europe was especially interested in the *devadasi,* who in poems and songs were better known as *bajaderas,* derived from the Portuguese term *bailadeira.* Jacques Offenbach made a *bajadera* the heroine of an operetta, which became a success even in London. In an 1860s lecture to London's Anthropological Society, Dr. J. Shortt maintained that Indian *devadasi* were "beautiful enough to satisfy the foremost connoisseur's critical glance."

A nautch, or Indian ballet performed by *devadasi,* was a traditional part of grand celebrations among India's aristocracy. After dinner, a prince would entertain his guests with Indian ballet, and after the performance would offer the ballerinas for individual nightlong amusement as an expression of his hospitality.

Indians of all classes considered nautches graceful, beautiful, and sensuous, and those visitors who were curious about and open to Indian culture found the temple dancing impressive. The prince of Wales, Albert Edward, was entertained on his visit to India in 1875 and expressed his gratitude and enthusiasm for Indian ballet, performed by *devadasi* from the country's foremost temples.

The memsahibs were, for a long time, like India's aristocratic women, not present at such gatherings. As some British women came to be entertained by Indian ballet, the memsahibs collectively pronounced this, like so much else in Indian culture, offensive. Male representatives of the empire would gradually adapt to the new times and claim to find Indian dancing boring, monotonous, and inelegant.

In 1890, Queen Victoria's grandson Albert Victor paid a visit to India. Like his father, he expressed an interest in Indian dancing, and got what he wanted. But times had changed. It was now considered tasteless to entertain a British prince in such an unseemly manner. The Anglican High Church in Calcutta set the tone as the bishop composed a sharp protest to the viceroy, Henry Charles Petty-Fitzmaurice, Lord Landsdowne, a farsighted and tolerant man who himself had attended the presentation. He reassured the bishop that everything had been of pure and ceremonial character.

This was a provocative speech for those who wanted to view Indian ballet in a more moral light. *The Sentinel* and its editor, W. T. Stead, would follow up on this single event endlessly. Two years later, the newspaper pointed out how a certain Dr. Miller, rector of the Christian College of Madras, "a missionary of the sort who mingles with the upper classes," had participated in the preparations for the prince's royal tour. What made this even more unpleasant, wrote W. T. Stead, was that "such dances are performed by prostitutes, and their songs are of a highly frivolous character." The British editor, who had neither been present nor learned to speak any of the Indian languages, concluded: "Both their forms of expression and the movements of their bodies had been unequivocally obscene. Most of the girls have ties to heathen temples and call themselves the slaves of the gods." The viceroy had maintained that these women were artists, and that they had a ceremonial function, "but," concluded *The Sentinel,* "when it comes to the men who get to see them, we can vouch for the fact that they come to commit sinful acts only hours after having witnessed such dancing."

India had developed its own morality movement during the 1880s, ethnically Indian but strongly influenced by British Victorian moral attitudes. *The Hindu* was the leading organ of this movement. The editor of this newspaper, Subramanya Aier, wrote open letters to Lord Wenlock of Madras and Lord Landsdowne in Calcutta, demanding that they publicly boycott all social gatherings in which Indian dancers participated.

Landsdowne, who was often lively in expression, answered right away that he was not in the habit of carrying out research into the morals of British actresses and ballerinas when he attended the theater in London. He intended to comport himself in the same manner in India.

When Lord Curzon became viceroy, it all became a different dance; indeed, there was barely any dancing at all. The united front of British memsahibs, Christian missions, moralistic Brahmins, and the prudish Curzon would cause some changes, particularly in northern India. However, it in no way extinguished prostitution, which merely lost many of the religious and cultural contexts that had given the prostitutes status in their local society, and security within the temples when they grew old. In southern India temple prostitution and dancing had always been more widespread, so things continued to follow the same old grooves there, even during Lord Curzon's years as viceroy. By now it seemed the British had lost interest in attending Indian dances or exploring Indian temples.

In 1905 yet another crown prince, George, went to India on a royal tour. He would later become both emperor of India and king of England. But he was not to experience a single example of the thousand-year-old dance culture of India. Instead, he received entertainment tailored after a new German fad—muscular poses and the lifting of heavy weights by India's strongest man, a faithful copy of the German Eugen Sandow.

*   *   *

"The soldiers come from the social classes that are least used to self-control. They have a natural tendency to marry at an extremely young age. But in India we gather great numbers of such men, we treat them better than what they are used to, give them enough hard work so that they come into good physical condition, but we refuse to allow them to marry. It is a great deal to demand that men who are submitted to such conditions be expected to behave with monastic discipline."

This statement by the British military district chief of Ahmedabad reflects a typical officer's attitude. It was one thing to expect discipline, modest comportment, and sexual abstinence of the university-educated young doctors and civil servants. But it was impossible to expect British behavior from common soldiers from the lower social strata.

The soldiers were the largest and most important group of British in India. Early in the nineteenth century, there had been forty thousand British conscripts in India, but there were six times as many indigenous Indian soldiers, or sepoys. Following the uprisings of 1856 through 1858, the ratio of races was changed, with an increase in the number of British soldiers to sixty thousand, and a halving of sepoys. By the 1890s, there were eighty thousand British soldiers in India and double as many sepoys.

"For a young man unable to get married, and not having the higher education that is necessary to teach himself to suppress the natural instincts of physiology, there are found only two forms of gratification: masturbation and commercial sex. The first solution destroys both body and mind; the second solution can lead to venereal disease," explained Bombay's chief surgeon, Dr. W. J. Moore, in 1886. There was a third way out; but both doctors and officers evidently felt that homosexuality was more damaging to the conscripts than to the civilized officers; it was, after all, an unmanly threat to military discipline.

The soldiers lived in segregation from the surrounding society; they remained indoors during the hottest part of the day and had a great number of idle hours when the political situation was stable. Consequently, they needed distraction. The cheapest and simplest entertainment was found in the local Lal bazaars that sprang up around the military barracks. There one could find prostitutes from neighboring provinces, Burma, and Ceylon, or boy prostitutes, if that was preferred. The Lal bazaars provided relaxation and attention and psychologically stimulated the soldiers as men and thereby warriors. The system had only one drawback—disease.

There had been Lal bazaars in India as long as there had been British soldiers. At the beginning of the nineteenth century, comparisons were made between the social conditions and the amount of sexually transmitted disease around the various military camps. Kanpur and Mirat, two military posts close to Delhi, had particularly low incidences of disease. At these camps older women were paid to look after prostitutes with sexually transmitted diseases, to give them medicines and keep them away from the soldiers until they were well again. Hospitals for those with venereal disease were opened in Agra and Muttra. Similar schemes spread to all the military districts as doctors and officers learned from one another, although the system did not develop without acrimony. The bishop of Bombay issued a statement saying that it was frightful of the military authorities to remove the risk faced by those who sinned.

The British had thus developed procedures concerning prostitution in India many decades before the notion reached England in the 1860s. In 1855 prostitution in each of India's seventy-five military districts was organized and supervised. The women lived in their own houses or in tents that were superior to those issued to other civilians who provided services to the armed forces. The minimum age for prostitutes was fifteen. Sixty to a hundred prostitutes per bordello—which yielded an average of something like fifteen British men per woman, or forty-five men per woman if the sepoys were included—assisted the forces. The women were subjected to regular health checks and, after 1865, were sent to hospitals for the treatment of venereal disease.

Unlike the officers, the conscripts seldom wrote memoirs when they grew old. Frank Richards was one of the few who did, portraying military prostitution in lively colors. It was "acceptable, almost expected" that a healthy and vigorous man could not abstain from women, but Richards swore he knew some who did. It was impossible to move around outside the barracks without hearing shouts about "jiggidy-jig," the contemporary slang for sexual intercourse. The military brothel in Agra was situated across the road from the Anglican Church. Anyone who stood in the middle of the road could hear the parson preaching on one side and the girls squealing on the other.

Everybody knew the story about the elderly low-caste prostitute who had stationed herself for years outside the viceroy's audience hall in

Calcutta. One day she announced the time had come for her to retire. By
then she had been in the trade for thirty-six years. To mark the day of her
retirement, she provided free service for five hours. Almost sixty men were
said to have made their intimate farewells.

Certain military camps had separate bordellos for the sepoys. In other
places, the sepoys were told to stay away from the British bazaars and find
themselves girls outside the camps. Normally, they slipped in whenever
there was room, particularly early in the day. But there is a lot to indicate
that the sepoys were not very interested.

The military doctors began to notice early on how few sepoys fell
victim to venereal disease. It appeared to some doctors that they were almost immune. Did it have something to do with race? Some argued that
the Hindu caste system led to such a complex partner selection that it less-
ened venereal infection. Muslims and Sikhs did not drink alcohol, while
Muslims were circumcised and in all ways cleaner than the British. Maybe
the sepoys practiced different sexual techniques, suggested some puzzled
doctors. Or perhaps they knew intrinsically to stay away from a woman
who was infected.

It is quite strange that the British doctors never emphasized another,
significant difference. Three out of four sepoys were married men, while
the British soldiers were bachelors. Of course the wives of the sepoys frequently lived far away, and prostitution was widespread in India, but it
must be considered a serious failure of imagination among British doctors
that none of them considered the possibility that Indian men could be faithful to their wives and stay away from prostitutes.

Occasionally British soldiers would enter permanent relationships
with local girls, most in Buddhist regions like Ceylon and Burma. The military authorities systematically opposed this practice, as they did not want
to be saddled with the offspring that would follow. Permission to marry
was granted only in exceptional cases. Within the camp, the officers took
male and female orderlies as wives and lovers, a privilege that gave these
happy few a better opportunity to put aside money for the future.

Sexual violence was not tolerated in India. The British military police took immediate action if Indian prostitutes felt they had been handled

violently, or if the customer had avoided paying the normal price of a rupee. Today it is natural to view these regulations as a sign of legal protection for Indian prostitutes; but in England in 1893, it was interpreted as the sanctioning of immorality.

The seventy-five hundred military prostitutes in the Lal bazaars made up barely a couple of percent of the whole sex industry. Indian prostitution was completely independent of the British and other foreigners. Temple dancers, aristocratic courtesans, independent village girls, and big-city brothels could be found in every corner of the Indian subcontinent. Any soldier who moved outside the camps would easily find more beautiful, younger, healthier, and cheaper girls. Soldiers on leave had no problems finding the red-light districts in Madras, Calcutta, or Bombay. The British authorities tried to establish medical help in the large cities, where they built hospitals for treating venereal disease and brought in prostitutes for checkups. But these initiatives were more complicated to carry out, and providing care for every prostitute would have been an almost insurmountable objective.

Instead, the authorities focused on venereal disease in the known haunts of Europeans. In Calcutta it was freely admitted that they had only the capacity to register and treat the prostitutes in these areas. In Madras and Bombay they phrased the program more diplomatically to hold their critics at bay. In Bombay some initiatives must have been quite effective. The captain of the H.M.S. *Dragon* had complained on a series of occasions that his sailors came aboard after a couple of weeks in Bombay with so much venereal disease that it was difficult to get the old tub out of the harbor. In 1884 he radiantly reported that his crew had withdrawn six hundred pounds sterling when they went ashore, and had enjoyed themselves as usual, and returned with only two mild cases of gonorrhea.

Syphilis and gonorrhea were unimportant diseases compared with malaria, cholera, dysentery, and the other infectious diseases that brought about many more deaths and much more suffering. The European-educated doctors, often Eurasians or Bengali *babus*, asked why health initiatives against venereal disease had such high priority. In their eyes, this was another proof that the British were only concerned about their own kind.

*   *   *

When the London society began to discuss prostitution in India in the 1890s, it focused on the Lal bazaars outside the military barracks. The Christian journals referred to those girls as "harlots licensed by the state."

Alfred Dyer from *The Sentinel* undertook a fact-finding tour of India's military camp brothels. He found it particularly odious that the military authorities had installed lights around the tents, secured a good water system, and purchased furniture. This was proof of how the military authorities had done everything in their power to make attractive these dens of iniquity. Dyer would also triumphantly cite a letter in which a medical inspector from Faizabad advertised for younger and more attractive prostitutes.

In the "good old days" of 1870s, the rate of venereal disease among British soldiers in India stood at 270 per 1,000 soldiers annually, which was just a little higher than in England. But few doctors dared to draw public attention to the differences between English and Indian numbers and comparable statistics for venereal disease among French or German soldiers, where the rate was 44 and 27 per 1,000, respectively.

Reportage from India would play a significant role in England's morality movement. But even though an echo of the London events normally reached the British press in India, it came as a shock to the military authorities when the British regulatory system fell. The venereal hospitals were made optional, and all obligatory supervision was wound down while the registration of prostitutes came to an end.

Of course, this by no means brought an end to prostitution, and London would become increasingly terrified by the morals of British soldiers and by the dissonance between these and the moral fervor at home. But there can be no doubt that the change of laws had tremendous consequences. In 1892 the annual infection rate in India had soared to 438 per 1,000, against 203 per 1,000 in England. In 1896 it was 522 per 1,000. The empire's soldiers were hospitalized and treated for venereal disease every second year and had more syphilis and gonorrhea than all other diseases together. By the mid-1890s, more than two thousand soldiers were dying from venereal disease every year, most of them after repeated treatment in India and a trip back to England for third-stage syphilis. This horror could be explained in many ways—by India's evil temptresses, by the animal nature of the soldiers, or by a seriously wrongheaded British policy. In any case, it was virtually destroying the honor of the empire.

The press campaign against military prostitution in India, with the omnipresent W. T. Stead at its head, did achieve complete success on one point: Lord Roberts would continue his military career in South Africa, but he would never follow Landsdowne as viceroy of India. Even Curzon wouldn't solve the moral decay that London felt had befallen the Indian portion of its empire. In the eyes of the moral crusade, this became a total fiasco. India had to reintroduce all the supervisory initiatives of former days; there was simply no other way. But in the 1890s, this probably would have been impossible without thoroughgoing support from British women.

In the end this had its social base far above Curzon and the memsahibs. God bless Lord Henry and Lady Alice Hamilton, the prime minister for India and his sweet wife, who had the necessary connections. In 1897, London met with an apparently spontaneous initiative that saw a substantial part of the petition made public. One princess, several duchesses and countesses, and a number of baronesses, including Florence Nightingale, advised the British government to reimplement medical inspections of prostitutes in India—above all, to save lives. The ladies pointed out that it was at least as important to supervise British men as Indian women. At last, by 1901, the rate of infection in India had fallen to 276 per 1,000. By 1909 it was down to 68.

India's syphilis rates had a powerful impact, so powerful that it divided Great Britain's women over the question of prostitution. The realistic approach had shocked London. It was seen as a symbol of double-standard morality, though this was nothing new to the soldiers or the Indian prostitutes. The soldiers did not become more virtuous; nor did the officers or the prostitutes. But they would live longer because they received medical checkups and medicine. And thus they kept themselves healthy and strong until the next fall of man.

TWENTY-THREE

TANGO!

Europe had created a terrifying picture of Buenos Aires by the early 1890s—a cesspool of sin, where slave dealers imported shiploads of kidnapped European virgins who were forced to appear half naked in the brothels. And there they danced the tango!

The tango's victory tour of the world started around 1910. It was the most suggestive dance anybody had seen. As described by Ezequiel Martinez Estrada, one of Argentina's foremost essayists: "It is danced from the hips to the feet. From the waist upwards, the body does not dance. It is rigid, as if the lively legs carried two bodies asleep in embrace. It is a monotonous and expressionless dance, with the stylized rhythm of coupling." The dance appeared to be a symbolic representation of a sexual encounter where the man dominated. In reality, Estrada argued, it reflected the man's weakened position in the modern world. The tango contains little sensuality; it imitates machinelike sexual copulation, commercial sex without pleasure. The tango does not dishonor the woman by giving her a subservient role. It brings shame on both sexes by showing that men have become just as victimized by the sexual act as women who are for sale, concluded Estrada.

It is true enough that the tango emerged in the brothels of Argentina and Uruguay toward the end of the nineteenth century and was performed with visible body contact. That gave a certain credence to the belief that among all the dances in the world, this was the one that most resembled prostitution. The tango wave would also be an expression of brothel culture: Lyrics, music, and dance all reflected the conditions of the prostitutes' lives. The moral debate in Argentina would follow the tango from the brothels to the dance halls, and change its main theme from the pernicious influence of prostitution to the evils of the tango.

* * *

Argentina means the Silver Land; it is Latin America's whitest country, radically different from Brazil or Cuba, former destinations of the black slave trade that today have a substantial black population. Argentina also differs from Bolivia, Colombia, and Mexico, where mestizos and Latinos—mixtures of Spaniards and Indians—make up the majority.

During the early Spanish immigration, few Indian tribes lived in Argentina. In the north, cotton and tobacco were cultivated, but the country was still largely uninhabited as conditions became ripe for mining and agricultural expansion, cattle industry, and sheep breeding on the pampas in the south and west. These enterprises needed young, adventure-loving men, and a new wave of migration commenced. Men poured in from Italy, Britain, Spain, and central Europe, just slowly enough to preserve Spanish as the national language. With the exception of the language, the country became more similar to Australia and South Africa than to other parts of South America. But Argentina quickly developed an enormous deficit of women, which in turn encouraged adventurous girls to seek their luck there.

Buenos Aires is strategically situated in the river basin of the Rio de la Plata, and it soon became the center of the continent's railroad network. As both male and female travelers poured through this transit hub, the city became a major detention point—if not the final destination—of female immigrants. Between 1869 and 1914, the population increased from 180,000 to 1.4 million, which made it the biggest city in the Southern Hemisphere.

Although the canneries and harbors encouraged internal migration to the capital, immigration was the prime reason for the city's growth. No other country of the time had a population ratio between men and women as unbalanced as did Argentina. This was good news in Europe, where money was made by anyone helping girls to get there. But few business-men invested capital in jobs for women, and the men who found work in the Argentinean countryside did not often visit Buenos Aires to hunt for a wife. Meanwhile, the women remained in the capital.

It is far from the truth that all the European girls intended to prosti-tute themselves or actually did so. Many more girls learned to sew and wash than to dance the tango. A few girls were actually kidnapped, but the hysterical rumors about the white slave trade give far better evidence of Europe's fear of disrupted family ties and independent female migration than of turn-of-the-century criminal behavior. Young single men could seek their luck, but if unmarried women migrated, they would either be sexually abused or end up in a marriage their families could not tolerate.

In spite of all the dire warnings, more than a hundred thousand single girls left overpopulated, crisis- and conflict-ridden Europe for Argentina. A lot of them became prostitutes, many for only a few transitional years; among these, a significant minority had been prostitutes in their homeland. "They keep on going to Buenos Aires as if they expected to find gold in the streets. Out of my house alone, I lost fifteen girls in four months. It must be as good as they say, because they don't come back," said a French brothel keeper.

After the turn of the century, the sex industry in Buenos Aires flourished. Sixty percent of the registered prostitutes were born abroad. The proportion of European girls in the brothels was far greater than in the unofficial semiprostitution at the dance halls and nightclubs that sprang up in this period.

By the late 1800s, any man of initiative who could get a piano or a small band and permission to sell alcohol could attract a broad male clientele and earn good money. In Argentina, as in southern Europe, people danced not only in cafés and dance halls but also in marketplaces and circus tents. Soldiers and sailors, country lads in town and poor immigrants, handsome hunks with tarnished pasts and bad intentions could be encountered along with genuine upper-class boys. The girls were far more homogeneous. Drinking and dancing in public places did not belong to the social repertoire of respectable girls. The girls on the town were semiprostitutes or girls of low repute. Many received money just for showing up at dance halls. A man who wanted to dance paid for the service. This was not prostitution but a related sign of the woman's economic subservience. If no man asked the girls to dance, or if the floor was empty, they would dance with one another. In both southern Europe and Latin America, men would do the same, mainly to save money. There was no hidden homosexuality. As with most forms of dancing, it enabled the exhibition of one's body in a flattering way. The idea that dancing was erotic foreplay was widespread, with good reason. The problem was that sex had to be paid for, while dancing was free. Dance halls and cafés were easy to find. Drinking was cheap. For many, dancing and dreaming yielded satisfaction enough. As centers of entertainment, the dance halls gave the brothels a run for their money. The Buenos Aires police commissioner Francesco J. Beazley wrote in 1897 to the minister of the interior: "Small bars serving drinks on the sidewalk and the fashionable cafés with stages, bands and indoor service are ruining the market for all the city's lawful brothels. Now there is nothing to prevent young girls of about fifteen from dancing, and waitresses from drinking with the guests."

The dance halls were never designated as brothels. Nevertheless, the sex deals negotiated there would soon outnumber those in the brothels. All the girls needed money. As the tango conquered the dance halls of Argentina and other parts of the world, it undermined brothel prostitution to some extent. It also encouraged modern and more cynical attitudes to sex and love.

The first phase in the history of the tango has been called the brothel phase. The lyrics had little significance. The dance was most important, and while the dance halls were in their infancy, dancing the tango was confined to the brothels. A tango from 1888, "Dame la lata," refers explicitly to the prepaid dance token a customer gave to a dancing girl whose company he wanted to enjoy. Early tango lyrics mention brothels, madams, and dance halls, but the singer often points to his venerable worn-out mother, earning a pittance at the factory or from cleaning jobs in a remote suburb, as contrast to the girls who ask for money instead of love.

Around 1910 the tango had spread from Argentina. A new term, *tangomania,* was coined to explain the almost hysterical popularity of the dance in Paris, where no one bothered about its origins or moral implications. This caused even greater anxiety in conservative circles. Pope Pius X issued a stern warning against the sinful new dance, while both the German kaiser and the Austro-Hungarian emperor banned their soldiers from dancing the tango in uniform. But no one could stop the obsession with this dance.

The dancing of the tango would evolve along different paths in Europe and the U.S., as the bourgeoisie attempted to expunge the vulgar sexual associations from the dance. Irene and Vernon Castle were the most famous ballroom dancers in the U.S. during World War I and performed at New York's showy nightclubs. The Castles maintained that the tango had to be practiced often but with only one partner, to keep it civilized, gentle, and graceful. Vernon wore a dinner suit, while Irene exposed less of her legs and back than the tango pioneers in Argentina's brothels. Sometimes the Castles claimed that the tango had originated in Europe, on other occasions that "they had learned it from an Argentinean diplomat at Maxim's in Paris."

Argentina's upper classes cleaned up the tango in their own way. It was brought from the brothel to the ballroom in 1912 by an Italian baron who hired tango dancers for a society ball. Shortly thereafter, Buenos Aires was overrun by professors of the tango who provided morally impeccable private lessons at home, while the music of the tango echoed through the most esteemed restaurants. As the elite of Buenos Aires took over the tango, formal attire became an absolute must.

As the tango's social status improved in the years following World War I, its lyrics also became much more acceptable; the voice of the tango changed from a suffering victim of social deprivation to a spectator and commentator. It became easier to relate to the stories of loose women and prostitutes, for the tango stories were still theirs.

The foremost interpreter of the tango, Carlos Gardel, achieved spectacular popularity. He was from a poor background and knew the lives and fates that, as a singer and writer, he conveyed to the Spanish-speaking world. Carlos Gardel would become Argentina's most legendary figure, but for Evita Perón. Both of them were the stuff myths are made from, and both were perfectly suited for the music, the lyrics, and the philosophy of the tango.

The paradox of the tango, in lyrics and performance, lies in the fact that the men who sing and seem to dominate the dance have lost control over women. The tango texts from the dance's golden age have been subjected to detailed analysis. This era stretches from Carlos Gardel's first recording in 1918 to 1935, when the young singer tragically died in an air accident. Most golden-era lyrics depict modern women who wear trousers, smoke cigarettes, and drink whiskey. Sometimes they are prostitutes; at any rate, they consistently deceive their men. "I am a bull, but tamed and castrated" is a characteristic expression of these men's feelings. The women are sexually unrestrained and do not wish to be mothers. They let rich men pay for their clothes and apartments and leave poorer men who love them seriously. These facts overwhelm the tango singer, who longs for the simple life of his childhood and his mother. Fathers have no place in tango lyrics.

The lyrics of Gardel and other tango lyricists reflect men's feelings while they deal with women's fates. But the depiction is not one-sided; in some lyrics, the man's voice is aggressive, in others aggrieved. Tango lyricists not only employed the street language of Buenos Aires to castigate women—they also depicted these women as victims, seduced and cast off, exploited by *bacanes* (rich lovers) or *apaches* (gangsters) or *cafishos* (pimps).

Before the 1930s, it was rare to hear a woman singing the tangos. When female singers had success, it was with moralistic tangos. It was not permissible for a young woman to criticize her lover. She could, however, reprimand her father or brother. At a few of Argentina's chicest entertainment venues, female vocalists were allowed to sing the real tangos, but dressed in glamorous tuxedos. Only when women played the roles of upper-class men could they sing men's songs.

The popular tangos often began with an introduction, addressing Señor Commisario. The singer has a complaint to make; he has been dumped, tricked, perhaps he has even seen his wife deceiving him. In the 1930s, after a period of transition on the radio, women were allowed onto the record market with genuine female tangos. Their complaints were ironically based on old tangos and addressed to the same chief of police, now with the opposite message: "Señor Commisario, give me another husband, because the one I have won't sleep with me!"

"Julian" became immensely popular. It had to be sung by a woman in women's clothing. Julian is the man whom the female tango singer complains about. He has left his woman and his child, but not because of a new woman. He has dedicated his life to dancing the tango. Should this be read as a sign of beginning male prostitution? Homosexual themes were known in plays and novels from the age of the tango. In all literature of the period, homosexuality was severely punished. At the end of the play or novel the heroine would shoot the man or men who had betrayed her and her sex. But the lyrics of "Julian" do not provide the smallest hint of what truly led him away. To lay the blame on the tango itself gives rise to an ambiguity that titillates the imagination. Perhaps this was why the song became so genuinely popular. But it could also be argued that this tango lost some of its force with its resistance to a theme that would have better suited its jealous logic.

All the men of the tango are jealous. Nevertheless, they are innocent, compared to women. Scarcely any woman in a tango lyric is a virgin; but as the years passed, the number of outright prostitutes dwindled away, while the number of liberated women increased. There can be no doubt that the lyrics reflected a historical development in Argentinean society.

The contemporary pulse of the tango is as true as any heartbeat. But their description of prostitutes' fates in real-life Buenos Aires are far from true. Immigrant girls dominated the brothels and dance halls, and one in ten was Jewish. But in the tangos, foreigners hardly exist. All girls are named Margarita, Conchita, Linda, Consuela, or Anita—never a Raquel or Esther—and they are all born and bred in Argentina, usually in a suburb of Buenos Aires.

Argentina is a country in love with myths. In all its melancholy, the tango camouflaged a social truth that many considered problematic, and instead established a nationally acceptable mythology around sexuality and prostitution.

Within the plethora of myths surrounding Evita Perón, there are the rumors that she started out as a prostitute. This unknown, ambitious, and sensual president's wife *must* have been a whore; how else could one explain her power over men? Latin American myths never believe prostitutes to be emotionally involved with the men they go to bed with. Instead, like witches, they transform all their pent-up emotion into a secret, mystical power.

Catholic and conservative circles in Argentina were filled with people who wished to view prostitution and Perónism as parallel, almost mutually dependent expressions of moral decay in the modern world—indeed, the work of the devil. But Evita had not been a prostitute. It was not something in her past that explained why unionized prostitutes supported the Perónist movement or why Juan Perón reopened Argentina's brothels. Evita was a modern woman, an archetype of her country in the modernization phase. That was why she grew so fond of dancing the tango. That was why she became so popular. And that was why she became so interested in sexual information for prostitutes and promoted the increased control of venereal disease.

Eva Perón was born poor and out of wedlock and learned early to be independent and exploit her sensuality. This placed her on a par with the tens of thousands of young women who came to Buenos Aires from the countryside or from abroad. Not all poor girls became prostitutes; likewise, not all women with power over men sold their bodies. Evita's life was nevertheless like a tango: quick, controlled, and sentimental.

TWENTY-FOUR

OTTOMAN FOOTNOTE

O ne of the most mournful processions of fallen grandeur that passed through the streets during these days was composed of the inhabitants from the ex-sultan's harem. These unfortunate ladies were of all ages between fifteen and fifty and so numerous that it took thirty-two carriages to convey them," reported Francis McCullough from Constantinople in 1909. It was the end of an era, a time when old institutions died and truth behind myths was revealed. "The Seraglio remains among the very few places on earth that no Anglo-Saxon or American foot has trod. As the Pole used to be for the explorers—as Everest still is for mountaineers—so have the harems been for tourists," wrote Sir George Young.

While, until that point, the world had lacked facts, myths had flourished. Antoine Galland's early-1700s version of the *Arabian Nights* defined the European imagination of harem: Vicious sultans, aroused by aphrodisiacs and titillating music amid cool fountains, were exposed to heavily perfumed, sex-starved beauties and fat, black eunuchs intriguing against one another to best serve the pleasures of their Ottoman lord.

The Ottoman Turks conquered Constantinople in 1453, and during the mid-1500s reign of Suleiman the Magnificent and his successors, they established an empire that reached the doorsteps of Venice and the German-Roman emperor in Vienna. The Ottomans held Moldavia, Greece, the Crimea, and the Caucasus and exercised full control of the Black Sea. They also dominated the southern and eastern Mediterranean, from Iraq, Syria, Egypt, and the African coast to Algeria. Among their urban strongholds were Belgrade, Aleppo, Baghdad, Damascus, Jerusalem, Mecca, Medina, and Cairo. But Constantinople was the magnificent capital.

The Ottomans were Muslim in faith but spoke Ottoman Turkish and allowed Christians a large degree of freedom within their territories, especially the Balkans. The Ottoman period has been considered a dark one by Arab Muslim historians, while Europeans dreamed back to what they conceived as a lost world of decadence, splendor, and secrets.

The word *harem* is derived from *haram*, which in Arabic means "unlawful," as opposed to *halal*. The Turks softened the word to *haremlik* and let it refer to the wives', children's, and servants' part of the house. Parallel with this, the Franks in the Levantine developed a Persian word for "shelter" into *serail* and *seraglio*.

Ottoman chiefs had harems in smaller and bigger cities around the empire, the most notable ones in Baghdad and Cairo. The sultan's harem in Constantinople at the most lodged three hundred wives and mistresses: fifty *sultanas* or *kadins*, plus the more humble *odalisques*, all headed by the *validée*, or queen, the sultan's mother. Ordinary Ottoman Turks had only one wife and one black slave. But slavery dominated the whole Ottoman Empire, and slaves were used for agriculture, domestic work, and military and sexual purposes, including urban bordellos for commoners.

The harems caused little anxiety even among feminist ideologues who have concerned themselves mostly with the Western world, and in any case considered even traditional marriage an institution of prostitution. However, some young neo-feminists of the 1990s tried to paint the harem as a female paradise. The women lived in a female world and hardly ever slept with a husband, and castrated males served them. But the harems were not women's paradises or brothels, although they preserved some significant links to prostitution, demographically and historically. Most of the people who ended up in the harems had been sold by their parents to, or taken prisoner by, slave traders who then took them across borders to faraway lands. The exceptions to the rule were European, mostly northern Italian adventuresses who sought the harems purely to live out their dreams.

Apart from the sultan, only one man held power in the harem in Constantinople: the grand vizier. All other males were eunuchs, headed by the chief black *kislar aga* and the white *kapi aga*. The latter traditionally was the confidant of the sultan, head of the schools, and master of ceremonies in the palace. Together with a few other high-ranked eunuchs, they constituted the divan and exercised power.

Common eunuchs guarded doors and passages, courtyards and store-rooms, while more personal offices were given to either the young *icoglans,* pages, or experienced elderly eunuchs.

The early Ottoman period had been marked by a rich supply of white eunuchs: German, Slavic, and Hungarian prisoners from Ottoman conquest. Later, white eunuchs were gathered mostly from the Caucasus, some by war, some through peaceful negotiations. In time, black eunuchs would come to dominate. They normally came from the Upper Nile Valley, were taken down the Nile in tiny boats like sardines, or had crossed the Sahara on foot or on the backs of camels. The slave trade was forbidden in 1864, without much loss for the traders. But as the black eunuchs rose in number and importance, the chief black eunuch took over more functions from his white rival.

Most of the eunuchs had had their testicles plucked out or crushed, to incapacitate the seminal glands. Some black eunuchs and all the white eunuchs lacked both penis and testicles. The castration took place far from the cities, then the surviving eunuchs were sent to the harems to be educated and disciplined. The changes to their bodies were more striking—and the risks, including death, greater—the later the operation was undertaken. Lack of body hair, a high voice, gradual flabbiness of the physique, early wrinkling of the skin, loss of memory, insomnia, and bad eyesight were common and most pronounced when castration took place after puberty. Eunuchs might nurse a grievance about their fate for years, but they took revenge when opportunity knocked, as is known from a number of stories, some fictional, and some obviously referring to actual events.

Despite the brutality of these operations, sexual lust among eunuchs did not disappear. Secret semimarriages between eunuchs and women were well known. "Tales of the First Eunuch, Bukhyath" in the *Arabian Nights* is only one account of the sexual joys of eunuchs with one testicle left; they were said to enjoy more frequent and longer erections than noncastrates, to the pleasure of women.

By the late 1700s, the Ottoman Empire reached a critical state, with Bedouin tribes sliding out of control in the eastern provinces and the West triumphing in wars. Sultan Suleiman II tried to take a leaf out of

Europe's books, with an army reform along European lines and French instructors in his military schools. But the Ottomans were bound to lose, and did so, throughout the nineteenth century, as Greece regained its liberty and England and France expanded in North Africa and conquered Egypt in 1882. Meanwhile, the Austro-Hungarian and Russian emperors regained control in the Balkans and the Caucasus. Late sultans of the 1800s tried to modernize their rule with new technology and contract relationships to their subjects. But more reform was needed, according to the Young Turks, led by Mustafa Kemal Atatürk. They managed to keep the Ottoman heartlands independent by overthrowing the sultan and setting up a modernized state in Turkey. The Ottoman Empire had gone with the wind when the last sultan of Constantinople was sent into exile by the Young Turks. Gone also were most of the Ottoman institutions and culture, including those that had been most romanticized in the West: the harems.

When the grand harem of Constantinople closed down in 1909, 370 wives and attendants and 127 eunuchs became homeless. The deposed sultan was allowed to take a few favorites into exile in Salonica. The others were set free. It was up to them to make new lives for themselves. But how?

Some were rescued. A large number of Circassian mountaineers were informed and came to get their women back. In picturesque garb, they marched into Constantinople just in time and were ushered into a long hall filled with the ex-sultan's concubines, kadins, and odalisques, who were allowed to unveil themselves. Daughters fell into the arms of fathers whom they had not seen for years. Sisters embraced brothers and cousins. In other cases, the women did not recognize any relatives but still reestablished connections to the wider society.

The majority of the Circassian females seemed glad to get away and lost little time in packing their belongings, after an affectionate leave-taking. Most women born in more distant areas seem to have continued their lives as secular prostitutes, which is only logical, as they had been victims of the same recruitment channels as the brothels, and some might have actually become reacquainted with their sisters and cousins there. A few, absolutely refusing any change in lifestyle, managed to slip into the few small harems that continued to exist in Medina and the domains of a few Arab sheikhs or North African chiefs.

The Circassian beauties would have been hard to recognize only weeks later, clad in peasant dress, milking cows, and tending Anatolian farms. How they would have compared their new freedom to their former lives or how many would have begun to long for the harem, we know very little about. The harem passed into history with many of its smaller stories untold. *Sic transit gloria mundi.*

TWENTY-FIVE

THE WHITE SLAVE TRADE

T he dime-store novels from around World War I swarm with virtuous schoolgirls and domestic servants, on the way to school or
shops, kidnapped by foul-natured men of evil intent. Many suffer a hellish fate in a Turkish harem, or in a sleazy brothel in New Orleans,
where they are forced to serve Afro-American clients.

Few remember that Victor Hugo constructed the metaphoric *bondage*
between prostitution and black slavery in 1870, to distinguish between free
and unfree prostitution. He chose to call the latter the white slave trade. But
the rationale for the newspapers' continuing gratuitous—and injurious—
use of the concept was the fact that the sex trade had become more widespread than at any previous period in history. The existence of sex for sale,
and the availability of brothels, extended around the globe, and one found
white girls working as prostitutes in Shanghai, Alexandria, Johannesburg,
and other exotic cities full of dark-skinned men. Only the very fewest women
had been kidnapped, and only a minority could be described as slaves.

Never before had so many women supported themselves through
prostitution as during the years from 1870 to 1930. New York, London,
Paris, and Shanghai had the highest numbers of prostitutes, but the phenomenon was far more apparent in Alexandria, Istanbul, and New Orleans,
"the greatest brothel city of all times." In San Francisco, Calcutta, Havana,
Naples, Marseilles, Cape Town, and Hong Kong, the prostitutes were far
more visible in the cityscape.

Opponents of prostitution frequently use wild estimates and seldom distinguish between prostitution as a profession, prostitution as a
source of casual supplementary income, and general promiscuity. Civil
and medical authorities have the opposite tendency, and often make
prostitution estimates too low, because they base their figures on women
afflicted with venereal disease or involved in crime.

By 1905 it was reported that 21 percent of Mexico City's women—altogether one hundred thousand—were working as prostitutes. If this statement is correct, only Shanghai had a larger prostitute population. However many they were, almost all prostitutes in Mexico were indigenous, or of unmixed aboriginal origin. In Shanghai 90 percent were from the interior of China and from Japan. These estimates never caused headlines in the European press. What was considered most shocking there was the prostitution in Buenos Aires and Rio de Janeiro, where 75 to 80 percent of the prostitutes were first-generation-immigrant, European-born women.

Since the 1870s, steamships and railways had made a vast world a lot smaller. Capital and labor power streamed freely over increasing numbers of borders. The entire world seemed to be migrating. Agricultural settlers and industrial workers moved to North America, Argentina, Australia, and South Africa. One could find European entrepreneurs and Chinese and Indian coolies in mines and on plantations in Africa, Southeast Asia, and the Pacific. The workers were young single men with a minimum of economic surplus and earnings that were too meager to allow them to marry, while lots of husbands left their families in their home province or country. Mass migrations of single men, in almost every instance, drew female prostitutes into their wake.

As the Industrial Revolution became internationalized, professional prostitution transformed from a system of small independent enterprises to a broad economic network: big money and hundreds of thousands of women, a radical shift from the past. In pure numbers, the migration rate of prostitutes and other single women was lower than that of men. But particularly in Southeast Asia and Latin America, so many first-generation female immigrants worked as prostitutes that it has continued to create problems for the historians commissioned to write up respectable national histories. A great many prostitutes ended up as matriarchs of successive generations in their new homelands. But in nationalist histories, the matriarchs' past is hardly ever mentioned.

"We have positive evidence that to almost all parts of North and South America, to India, China, Japan, the Philippine Islands, North and South America, and also to many of the countries of Europe, Yiddish-speaking Jews are maintaining a regular flow of Jewesses trafficked solely for the purpose of prostitution." This statement, put forth as a fact in 1902 by the Jewish Society of London, was made in defense of young girls and women. The speaker went on to explain that the reason for this mass migration was hunger and need and, in part, pogroms against Jews in eastern and central Europe.

Out of Shanghai's two thousand European prostitutes in the year 1900, two-thirds were Jewish and the remainder French. The Jewish girls had arrived on the Trans-Siberian Railway via Moscow and Vladivostok, while the French had come by boat from Marseilles through the Suez Canal and south around India.

The European and American press took good notice of the Jewish women in the business, and the tabloid newspapers often prominently featured the Jewish middlemen. Many newspapers portrayed prostitution as a worldwide Jewish pimping conspiracy, and their favorite stories were about cynical Jews who earned fortunes in the trafficking of human beings.

Sadie Solomon became world famous as a sex-madam millionairess around 1914. She was a well-known figure in the New York underworld, but the press reported that she owned brothels in Johannesburg, Rio de Janeiro, Buenos Aires, and outposts like Panama and Texas, too. Another highflier from the pimping world was Nathan Spieler, who quit baking pretzels in New York to open brothels in Shanghai, Constantinople, Bombay, and Singapore. He was reported seen in Manila as well.

The League of Nations would become the first worldwide organization to work for peace and international cooperation. It was founded by the Allied powers, led by Woodrow Wilson, under the terms of the Treaty of Versailles in 1919, and established its center in Geneva. The Scandinavian countries and a few other states that had remained neutral during the war joined in 1920, followed by the revolutionary Soviet Union, and finally the pacified Germany in 1926. The League of Nations played a particularly important role in the years just before and after 1930—before Japan, Germany, and Italy left and the Soviet Union was expelled.

International trade in prostitutes, and women's conditions within the sex industry, were among the important issues on the agenda. Between 1924 and 1927, a commission of experts visited 28 countries and 112 cities and conducted 6,500 interviews with female prostitutes and others in the sex industry. In 1929 the commission brought out a major report on world prostitution. Even today this document remains the most extensive body of material for illuminating prostitution's social, psychological, and economic aspects from an international perspective.

A 1927 interview with a twenty-two-year-old French woman in Calcutta was one of the exemplary cases in this report. The woman started her career in the sex industry at the age of thirteen and spent three years in a bordello in Paris. A few years later, still a teenager, she traveled to Saigon in French Indochina with the help and support of an elderly woman in the trade, then to Manila in the American Philippines. She spent two years in each city before she became pregnant in Singapore and returned to Paris to give birth to a daughter she placed with a sister. By that point, this woman had seen more of the world than almost any French girl of her age, and expressed no regrets other than that she had used up almost all of her savings. When she returned to the Paris bordello where she had worked ten years earlier, she ran into a colleague from Manila who helped to get her back to Asia, this time to Calcutta. All of her travels were assisted by her older sisters in the trade. As she arrived, she was twenty-six years old and very experienced. According to her own calculations, she would still be able to sell her body for another ten years.

In general, conditions in the Asian sex industry were far more brutal than those in Europe and the U.S., just as the greater poverty and stronger pressure of population in the East had led to worse working conditions in general. In the coastal areas of China and Japan, prostitutes were recruited under conditions that might, more than in the European context, be appropriately compared to slavery.

The conditions for European women in the Asian sex industry were far better. The French woman in the report was no sex slave but an independent businesswoman. She handed over her profits only to colleagues of her own sex, and only when she received help from them. Although she had started her prostitution career at a very early age, she was counted as an adult in the report, where minors comprised only 10 percent of the samples. Accordingly, the commission concluded that those under eighteen played "a smaller role in the trade in women than had been assumed."

Sadly, even today we cannot know whether the commission was right or wrong. In many important ways, the investigation collected facts, which in turn were used wrongly, in support of contemporary myths about prostitution. Due to a lack of precision and reflection, the investigation would make generalizations about world prostitution that led to new public delusions.

Sex slavery created headlines in the West only if it had to do with European women; Western newspapers had not the slightest interest in the plight of Asian women. Unfortunately, a similar lack of interest, together with an ingrained racist bias, was characteristic of the League of Nations' experts.

China and Japan were patriarchal societies where women had particularly low status. In a period of economic transition marked by great poverty, overpopulation, and debt slavery, many peasant families lightened the pressure on the family unit by killing newborn baby girls; they also sold their teenage daughters to itinerant buyers. These girls were transported over great distances to Asia and the Pacific, where they seldom were allowed to move freely outside the red-light districts. Girls from the coast of Canton and Fukkien, in South China, were shipped via Hong Kong to Manila, Saigon, British Malaya, and the Dutch East Indies, as well as Hawaii and San Francisco. Japanese girls were taken from overpopulated conditions in coastal southeastern Japan to Shanghai, Harbin, Vladivostok, Australia, or via Singapore to Rangoon, Calcutta, and Madras. A few were smuggled into their destination harbors. The majority were furnished with legal papers and camouflaged as "daughters" or "nieces" of their *mamasan,* usually their purchaser's wife or sister.

Japanese women were reputed to master the skills of the trade best of all Asian women. But among the girls shipped abroad, scarcely any were schooled at the famous Yoshiwara sex metropolis in Tokyo. Chinese women were known to become depressed and weep a great deal, particularly when they received European clients. A number of them were unable to function sexually with non-Asian men, for physical or psychological reasons. They arrived in the large foreign cities in shabby clothing and without belongings, which contributed to their immediate indebtedness, since they had to extend their work period to pay off the costs incurred in outfitting them for the trade. The frequency of suicide was so high among Chinese prostitutes working abroad that specific personnel were employed to prevent it.

In Japan, China, and India, native women dominated the sex industry, while in Southeast Asia, local girls worked alongside women from East Asia and Europe. But there was almost no emigration among local Southeast Asian prostitutes; nor were they forcibly recruited. They chose the work more freely than even the Western girls, stayed in it a short period, and were said to behave more warmly and naturally. Local prostitutes cried less, smiled more, and were just as pretty. But since they cost less, they were not considered as valuable among Western sex customers.

By 1899, Singapore could be described as a midsize Asian city, with room for 311 brothels and 1,400 registered prostitutes, three-quarters of them Chinese. There were also male brothels in Singapore, populated by three hundred boys. The second largest ethnic group among Singapore's prostitutes was Japanese. Indians and Malays made up 5 percent, and approximately the same proportion was European. The other midsize cities in British Malaya—Johor, Malacca, Ippoh, and Penang—contained seven thousand registered prostitutes, with about the same race and gender mix as in Singapore.

European women were at the top of the price list in all Asian brothels, although there was no scarcity of them. Most of them had their own houses and did not live as separated from the local population and the European enclaves as did the Chinese and Japanese prostitutes. The Chinese girls lived almost imprisoned in large, clean Chinese prostitution suburbs.

Asia was and is the largest part of the world, in terms of both population and landmass. By the 1920s, Asia had the largest sex industry in the world and, without contest, the highest number of prostitutes. Nevertheless, the League of Nations report repeated that prostitution in Asia "gave no grounds for worry." How could the League of Nations conclude something so apparently ludicrous? What this statement actually meant was that *European* prostitutes in Asia had good earnings and that scarcely one of them lived in hunger and want or was exposed to force and violence. Today we would demand such a "Western" emphasis at least be stated explicitly. This was simply not the case in the 1930s.

Alexandria has always played a key role in the sex industry. South African prostitution dates back to the 1600s. In the late 1800s, prostitution had become an important business in Lagos, Leopoldville, Addis Ababa, Nairobi, Mombasa, Dar es Salaam, and Salisbury.

African prostitution was no one-way ticket out of poverty, but research into the end of the nineteenth century has pointed out how important the business was for women who wanted to advance in society. A female prostitute made significantly more than a male wage earner and was unlikely to marry. The result was an accumulation of capital, often sunk into urban real estate.

For decades, prostitution in Tanganyika was the most lucrative business an African woman could enter. Dar es Salaam's best-educated and most highly esteemed women were prostitutes. During World War I, both supply and demand in East Africa's sex industry increased enormously. Some women were domestic servants and babysitters by day and did a "double shift" in the evenings.

Between the world wars, in Nairobi and other African cities, one saw a new form of prostitution develop. In the earlier African form, it was assumed that the men knew where the prostitutes lived, and discreetly knocked on their doors. The "woman on the balcony" entered East Africa, less discreetly dressed and far more made up than her predecessor. She could be encountered outside her house during the day and in the evening. The lodgings were often no more than ten square yards, and the clients were no longer discreetly served food. These new balcony women were easier to locate, since their clients needed only their eyes, and not the local language, to find the right place.

Africa's prostitutes had lost all traces of the substitute-wife relationship with their clients. The price was determined beforehand, and it no longer led to an itemized bill. Violence increased in proportion to the blatant visibility of the trade, and women no longer worried about having the respect of their neighbors. On the other hand, profits increased, and the women had more clients, often one in the morning and one at night.

The black prostitutes of Africa distinguished themselves in every way from the rest of the world. The League of Nations limited its findings to five cities in Africa—Johannesburg, Cape Town, Alexandria, Algiers, and Tunis—and concluded: "In the cities of Africa one found the majority of the prostitutes to be French and Jewish. Local Arab girls made up twenty percent of the staff in Alexandria. There were few Negresses." Today we estimate the number of black African prostitutes to be far above a hundred thousand, and spread over almost the whole of Africa.

When the League of Nations was gathering its data, Africa's black prostitutes were independent businesswomen. They were first- and second-generation urban dwellers in the process of destroying their bonds with the tribal society that had restricted them earlier. They had stopped investing their capital in livestock or land and were putting it in the bank and into urban real estate. African miners and railway workers traveled back and forth over half the continent during the 1920s. A prostitute seldom crossed more than one border, and none of them traveled to Europe, Asia, or Latin America. Africa's black women figure most incorrectly in the League of Nations' view of the world.

Around this time, the tabloid press increased its inquiries into Jewish "transactions in women." A strong focus in parts of the prostitution debate had to do with the so-called Jewish mentality.

Obviously, many Jewish girls ended up in prostitution in every corner of the world; there were also many Jewish men involved in the business. But Jews did not dominate it. They were made scapegoats in the prostitution debate, precisely as they were with so many other social ills during the years around 1930.

In the years between the two world wars, the Jews became a comfortable object of hatred for moralistic Europeans, particularly in Germany, Poland, and France. The role that so-called Jewish backers had been ascribed in world prostitution was played down in the League of Nations report, and it was stated that there were not as many Jewish prostitutes in the world as there were French prostitutes within the borders of France. French physicians were considered the front-runners in prostitution research, and the working language of the League of Nations also was French, so considerable interest was devoted to the conditions of French prostitutes, partly for linguistic reasons. There is much to indicate that the French derived greater profit from prostitution than any other national group. But could it be that this was only a natural reflection of the industry's long tradition in France? In any case, the League of Nations guarded against pointing out any new ethnic or religious group as the main force in the worldwide sex industry.

TWENTY-SIX

KAMIKAZE AND COMFORT

*M*ein Leben fur die Liebe—Jawohl,*" sings the sepulchral-voiced Zarah Leander in *Die grosse Liebe*, a Nazi film from 1941. She is in love with a German pilot who, like her, is willing to give everything for true love, the führer, and the fatherland.

Japan's war propaganda contained more sex and less love. Some consider the red imperial sun of Japan's flag a phallic symbol; at the very least, it is a male god. Japan's war leaders were fixated on sex before attack as a form of psychic armor for the soldiers; celibate warriors were believed doomed to defeat. Kamikaze pilots flew to their deaths with amulets and bracelets made out of pubic hair from the prostitutes they had slept with the night before.

Paradoxically enough, the Americans and Russians would posit a third, historically brand-new warrior ideal: the virtuous and faithful soldier-husband. In both Russian and American war propaganda, family and motherland were key concepts. The Soviets and major parts of the Western world tried to tone down old associations between war and promiscuous sex. The Japanese, however, wove the mystique of sex and war more tightly. Thus World War II was full of conflicts on the questions of sexuality, sex life, and prostitution.

A standing army always contains a significant proportion of a nation's most vigorous young men, at the phase of their lives when their sexual energy is at its peak. Soldiers live in a controlled environment, with few chances of social or emotional diversion. Sex is a favorite topic of conversation.

More than two thousand years of tradition had established as a quasi-scientific "fact" that soldiers need brothels and that the need increases as an army switches over from passive readiness to active warfare. Discipline and the line of command are strengthened, and stress factors expand exponentially. This accentuates the need for diversion among the soldiers, no matter how little free time they have.

Whether an intimate situation lasts for a day or fifteen minutes, it implies that the soldier is once again an individual—a unique human being free from the fear of bullets and bombs, released from lines of command and the military hierarchy. The basic angst of never again being able to experience such intimacy weighs each encounter heavily with a sense of existential fate, regardless of whether the sex is paid for. However, all those who have cried their way through *Waterloo Bridge,* from 1940, in which Robert Taylor plays an English officer and Vivien Leigh the eternally beautiful ballerina Myra—who eventually becomes a prostitute—will have a dim perception of such existential pain.

Arguably, the most classic of World War II movies is *From Here to Eternity.* Private Bob Prewitt, unforgettably played by Montgomery Clift, is serving in the U.S. Air Force in Honolulu, together with Private Angelo Maggio (Frank Sinatra) and Sergeant Milton Warden (Burt Lancaster). The film ends as the Japanese attack Pearl Harbor. It is December 1941, and all the young men have been killed. The two girls, Karen and Lorene—respectively, Donna Reed and Deborah Kerr—board the ship to the mainland to escape the Japanese. With empty eyes, they stare out to sea while they calmly list all the men they have loved and lost.

The film is full of hot love, fighting, and military intrigue against the backdrop of the impending world war. The girls are adventuresome, fun-loving, and lighthearted bar girls, not real prostitutes. Karen and Lorene take men, drinks, love, and nylon stockings as they come, retaining vague dreams about the day their prince would come.

Before World War II, the number of prostitutes fell in the U.S., U.K., Germany, and other Western countries, both in total number and in proportion to the conscripted soldiers. But soldiers had more sex. Political democracy, increasing social equality, and cheap contraceptives led to the sexual liberation of middle-class and working-class girls, which gave organized prostitution effective competition. The soldiers were the first to discover that times had changed. Why pay for sex when it was available free? They were making a patriotic effort for God and country, which gave the girls an even greater incentive. A few years earlier, U.S. military authorities had obtained far-reaching powers to intern and inspect prostitutes, particularly those around the military bases, but they soon realized that they were losing control over the soldiers' sex lives, since an increasing number of soldiers no longer visited whorehouses. A new sexual moralism spread among army doctors and higher officers, with one concrete cause: syphilis. The fear of this disease increased between the wars because the number of infected soldiers rose at such an alarming rate. Five percent of white American soldiers and 30 percent of African-Americans were infected every year.

The health authorities registered fewer soldiers who referred to prostitutes as the cause of their disease. "The whore with red lips and her hair down has been replaced by the nice girl from around the corner," wrote an army doctor in 1941. The military authorities expressed concern, but civilian U.S. society did not feel it was acceptable to register and inspect ordinary girls. Even if such girls could not be interned for VD inspection, however, the military authorities started to warn against them, urging soldiers to stay away from "khaki wackies" and patriotic girls, "women of low moral standards, even if they are eager to support our war effort."

U.S. war propaganda presented promiscuous girls as the war's "third peril." Women who had casual sex should be regarded as enemies because, like Hitler and Emperor Hirohito, they could lead to the fall of the U.S. and its Western allies. The new and somewhat surprising slogan became: "If you can't say no, take a pro," because when all was said and done, the risk of infection was smallest for those who visited prostitutes who were checked by the authorities. The same could not be said for the "nice girls."

How were the health authorities to gain acceptance for such a message? And how rational did the West's young men want to be when it came to sensitive matters like sex and manhood? In practice, at least, the Allied soldiers from the U.S. and the U.K., Canada, Australia, Norway, and New Zealand looked for both real love and free sex. This was reinforced by a movie industry unwilling to produce films at the behest of the army's health authorities. Hollywood's war films are free of syphilis but depict intense, flirtatious, romantic, and mostly impossible love affairs.

Hitler's Germany would regulate prostitution and sexuality to a far greater degree. The Nazi party borrowed legislation and surveillance initiatives from Mussolini's Italy when it came to power in Germany in 1933.

Supervision and control of prostitution and free sex were introduced in all the countries Germany later occupied. It was officially declared that the German army would take over existing brothels and reserve them for their own military forces, though these orders were implemented differently from one country to another.

An army on the attack will naturally meet a less warm welcome in a foreign country than a liberation army. For this reason, the Germans had greater demand for prostitutes than the Americans, who almost without exception operated in Allied countries. In France, the Netherlands, and Belgium, there were many brothels. The German takeover was apparent in the strict new health inspectorate and changing of brothels' names. German signs would clarify to passing military personnel whether they were outside a "hotel" for German officers or one for the rank and file. Separate brothels avoided conflicts, and the officers were secured the best women the local sex markets had to offer.

German authorities evidently turned a blind eye to French customers who made use of any available surplus at the brothels. Innumerable stories from the French resistance tell of prostitutes with contacts on the home front, and of how German soldiers and French freedom fighters—who in principle were deadly enemies—were serviced in adjacent rooms. Edith Piaf loved to recount how during the war she and her sister sometimes hid away in a whorehouse where a third friend worked as a prostitute. Later, her biographer gave more precise details, duly reporting that this friend, Andrée Bigaud, received only clients from the liberation front. If that was the case, it is one more indication that French brothels were also centers for the resistance.

In the less populous north, there were many soldiers and few sex workers. Civilian and military sharing of prostitutes was virtually impossible in Norway's and Denmark's few cities, since they had just a handful of brothels. High-class French prostitutes were brought in to service German officers and high officials, and new brothels were opened with German *einsatzfrauen* to attend to the rank and file. Scandinavian girls were officially banned from the sex industry by the Nazis, but a few continued to work the streets, while city restaurants and dance halls supplied some northern sex for cash.

New military brothels were established in places where there was no local provision, usually on the order of the high command of the

Wehrmacht or *Kriegsmarine*. Local military leaders at the intermediate level were responsible for equipment, supervision, and food, for cleaning and other inspection, and for distribution of condoms, soap, and lubricants. Whole ships loaded with *einsatzfrauen* for the forces in northern Norway dropped anchor close to the German fleet or military camps as often as the course of the war allowed. But all over the urbanized and largely sexually liberated Western Europe, the polite and handsome German officers and soldiers could find a number of girlfriends independent of the brothels, even though they represented an occupation force.

It was especially easy for German army men to find girlfriends in Scandinavia, France, and the Netherlands, and the farther north the Germans reached, the easier it became to find the best recreation locally, and for free. Even if they did not pay in cash, they were very generous with clothes, jewelry, food, and other gifts, which were greatly appreciated at a time when luxury items were at a premium. The German army and navy were characterized by strict discipline. Stern measures were meted out to soldiers suspected of sexual violence, which was rarely seen in northern and western Europe.

Awareness of the health risks attached to sex was almost as great in Germany as in the U.K. and the U.S. During World War I, Germany had learned that venereal disease impaired an army at war; their two million afflicted soldiers had been a colossal lesson. During Hitler's war, physicians were ordered to inspect all sex establishments in collaboration with the *Wehrmacht*'s own medical officers. The health authorities were to observe German regulations for the supervision of unorganized promiscuity; the national police was to keep all infectious women under surveillance, whether or not they earned money for sex. This was practiced more strictly in Norway than in other German-occupied countries, due to local traditions. According to German law, unregistered prostitutes were supposed to be marked with a black star, even sent to concentration camps; Norway's vice squad did not go that far, but they interned large groups of "infectious" girls in special camps, although nine out of ten were in no way prostitutes. In Denmark things were more lax, even though venereal disease was just as rife. Neither was anything similar done in France, Belgium, or the Netherlands.

Sex and prostitution were conducted in an entirely different way in occupied Eastern Europe. The Germans were fighting a harder and crueler war on the eastern front and were more removed from the local inhabitants. In Eastern Europe, the free population was either strictly Catholic, Russian Orthodox, or Communist. Eastern European cities were small and nonindustrialized; village-based society and the Communist Party enforced a certain conformity of attitudes and opinions. This left very little space for free sexual activity. Puritanism and anti-German feelings ruled supreme. Exceptionally few girls made contact with German soldiers. As a result, the Germans had to implement stricter measures to ensure that the soldiers had a sex life.

The vast majority among the home-recruited *einsatzfrauen* were sent eastward. But it soon became clear that they were far from enough—and an increasing number of sexual attacks on civilian women began to be reported from the Ukraine and White Russia. In Poland and the Ukraine, and partly in Serbia, the Germans started to draft local girls into the *einsatzfrauen*. Officially, the girls were given a choice between draconian forced labor and a more comfortable and better-paid life in a brothel.

Japan and the American Philippines were the most modern countries in Asia. Both experienced a similar increase in venereal disease, and a fall in recruitment to the sex industry, as the West did during the 1930s. But as World War II broke out, Asia went the opposite direction, adopting a policy of forced recruitment to brothels.

Is there any connection between a man's capacity as a lover and as a warrior? Can a young man without sexual experience have ability as a warrior? Is there an inexplicable link between a man's sexual organ and a warrior's ability to utilize his military weapon? Superstitions exist in military circles, and they are often sex-related. They may seem spurious today, but in Japan in the 1930s and '40s this was the dominant view.

Among all sexual rites, the ceremonies where youths are initiated into manhood may be the most common and well known. Compulsory visits to brothels belong to the initiation ceremonies for sailors and soldiers all over the world. But no Western male culture practiced such rigidly enforced brothel visits as the Japanese army before and during World War II. If an army unit discovered a sexually inexperienced soldier in its midst, he was forced by his comrades to visit a brothel, where they would watch his initiation through holes in the wall. Woe betide the young man who resisted. A deviant was a threat not only to the military hierarchy but also to the emperor himself.

The involvement of the Japanese state in prostitution dates back over four hundred years, much longer than that of any other nation. From the 1880s, the private entrepreneurs in the sex industry began exporting itinerant women of pleasure, *karayuki-san,* to China, Southeast Asia, Australia, and the U.S. This export of sexual services played an astonishingly central role as the country transformed economically, starting in the early 1900s and continuing into the 1920s.

During the same years, Japan began its advance toward great power. In 1885, Okinawa and the Ryuku Islands were annexed, followed by the island of Formosa. Korea, which the Japanese renamed Chosen, was annexed in 1910. As the Japanese established themselves in Sakhalin and Micronesia, the Western powers hurriedly annexed the remaining islands in the Pacific. Japan regarded Korea differently from all its other annexed territories. Many Japanese dreamed of a fusion between their islands and Korea, the peninsula to the west of the Japanese mainland, and called the Koreans "the emperor's stepchildren." In terms of race, language, and culture, the Koreans had much more in common with the Japanese than the primitive natives to the north and the brown islanders to the south and east. As Japan set out to assimilate its occupied nation of "stepchildren," Shinto religion and Japanese names were introduced in Korea, but with less optimal results than most Japanese had expected.

Meanwhile, Japan had set its sights on a China that was breaking up internally. In 1931 and 1932, Japan annexed Manchuria, renamed it Manchukuo, and installed the former Chinese emperor as its puppet head of state. Japan's army grew as swiftly as its ambitious politics. So did the brothels, until the sex industry began to experience recruitment problems. The incoming stream of young women stagnated due to Japan's economic growth, which removed pressure for families to get rid of superfluous daughters. More and more jobs for women were created outside agriculture. The demand for prostitutes slowly began to exceed the supply. Around 1920 the average age of Japanese prostitutes had increased toward middle age, while an increasing number of women had contracted venereal disease again and again.

In the semifeudal, puritanical, agricultural Korea, there was practically no other prostitution aside from a high-status geisha variety called *kisaeng.* But during these years the Japanese began to implement changes, first by subsidizing a red-light district in Seoul, then by supplementing Japan's brothels with young women from the Korean peninsula. Special agents traveled around the countryside drawing new recruits to the sex industry from the families of poor tenant farmers. Enlistment was done privately, but the agents collaborated with the Japanese health authorities. The newly recruited Korean prostitutes were expected to behave in a Japanese fashion and received both Japanese names and clothing—this in stark contrast to the more indigenous Korean prostitutes. As these new, young, fresh Korean women, decked out as Japanese comfort women, entered the brothels, all clients rejoiced, scarcely noticing the extreme silence and sorrow that accompanied these particular sex workers.

The position of daughters in the half-Confucian, half-shamanistic Korea was even weaker than in their patriarchal neighboring states of China and Japan. Since poor peasant families were well paid to give away daughters, and no young girls dared protest, the process could continue almost unnoticed. However, some of the pressure on Korea's peasant girls was erased when Manchuria was annexed. This meant new supplies of girls to Japan's sex industry—this time well-trained and professional girls of Russian, Jewish, or Chinese origin.

Shanghai Express, with Marlene Dietrich starring as Lily, revealed to moviegoers the frightening possibility of an extreme escalation of conflict between China and Japan. Another revelation from the movie was that Shanghai, China's biggest city, was one of the metropoles of prostitution.

During the battles around Shanghai in 1932, the Japanese military authorities lost partial control of their troops. In spite of the innumerable bordellos, the soldiers embarked on the mass rape of civilians. The military leadership took up the matter immediately and undertook a number of preventive civil measures. From now on, prostitution would be provided under the direct control of the army leadership. As soon as the military brothels were in place, the number of rapes declined drastically, and the authorities took this as evidence of a successful policy.

At first the military-run brothels were stocked with girls from Korean working-class families. Although they were much less experienced than Japanese and Chinese prostitutes, they were guaranteed syphilis-free.

While the soldiers were given no choice, the younger officers closed their ears and continued to patronize the most professional, better-looking, but less healthy sex workers of their own island of origin.

In 1937 an armed confrontation at the Marco Polo Bridge outside Beijing finally led Japan into open war with China. Nanjing, which at that time was the Chinese capital, was conquered in an orgy of killing and rape. War with China had not been the wish of the Japanese army, but now it became a bloody reality. After this, the German military offensive in Europe took on global consequences. The Germans seemed to beat France and the Netherlands without resistance in Europe; similarly, it was an almost bloodless task for Japan to seize French Indo-China, the Dutch East Indies, and British Malaya. The West had lost all prestige in the eyes of the local population and never regained it. Japan secured military control over half a continent, along with huge quantities of raw materials.

An alliance among Japan, Germany, and Italy followed, to mutually secure the new sphere of power and to frighten the U.S. The result was the opposite. The U.S. applied tough economic sanctions and moved its whole fleet westward in the Pacific, toward Japan. The December 1941 attacks on the bases in Pearl Harbor and the Philippines, the largest U.S. stronghold in Asia, shocked the Japanese just as much as the Americans. Germany and Japan suddenly found themselves allies, and at once it seemed as though the whole world was at war.

The Shanghai military brothels set the pattern for the comprehensive bordello system that arose after Japan conquered most of Asia and the Pacific. More and more Korean girls were sent to the military brothels, supplemented with further womanpower from China and the Philippines—where the Pacific theater had wreaked some of its worst violence—and the former European colonies that Japan had virtually been given. Some among the recruits had experience, but the vast majority had no idea what prostitution was like. Very few received a share; almost all of it disappeared into the pockets of middlemen.

Regulations got tougher as the war proceeded. Increased pressure on the soldiers meant increased pressure on the prostitutes. It has been claimed that Japanese and Korean paramilitary buyers forced their way into the peasant homes of Asia, raped and kidnapped young girls, and sent them in chains to the brothels, but this is a caricature from a politicized later debate. Almost all the girls came from families in a state of dissolution and need. Most Asian mothers knew that they were sending their daughters off to the sex industry, and most of them were paid. However, they could not have foreseen the dreadful fates their daughters would actually meet.

Movies like *Bridge on the River Kwai* and reports from Britons, Australians, Filipinos, French, Dutch, Norwegian, and American prisoners in war camps seem to satisfy the West's need for a picture of the war with Japan in Asia and the Pacific. The Japanese army was extremely hierarchical and authoritarian. Both officers and men committed atrocities against interned Europeans and the civilian population, particularly in the countryside. Reports on the rape of civilians continued to remain numerous on the Malay Peninsula and the Pacific islands.

Nevertheless, more than its acts of violence characterized Japan's wartime occupations. The authorities set up by Japan were puppet regimes but contained varying degrees of national leadership. Japan saw itself as the liberator of Asia and the Pacific from the colonial powers. The partial truth in this was revealed through the wars for independence in Vietnam, Malaysia, and Indonesia: Only against the background of the Japanese intervention is it possible to fully understand these wars.

In the midst of warfare, Japan played both occupier and liberator. Between 1942 and 1945, some of the civilian population in the cities of Southeast Asia must have regarded the Japanese as a lesser evil than the former colonial powers. Such assessments paved the way for political collaboration and for emotional ties to Japanese men. True love could defy political edicts in Asia, too. In Indonesia, Malaya, Vietnam, and the Philippines, Japanese officers and bureaucrats entered into short-term marriages with local women, a tradition in the region, which provided greater recreation and relief than any brothel and paved the way for gentler forms of contact with the local community.

A complete sexual history of the 1942–1945 Pacific war would have to include all of the marriages and genuine love affairs. In addition to Japan's military sex service, most of the civilian brothels in the major cities of Southeast Asia remained open during the occupation. Working conditions were better, and the girls were paid for their services.

Even forcibly recruited Korean women of pleasure have told of exceptions, of Japanese customers who were kind and sensitive. There were always soldiers who had regard for the girls in the brothels and made sure that they, too, experienced some kind of comfort in a confusing and distressing time. In her autobiography, Jan Rulf, a European-born forced prostitute of whom we will learn more shortly, explains how, when she was a young teenager, an older sister desperately tried to give her days of freedom before her first rape. She appealed to a nice young Japanese soldier named Yodi, who promised to help as far as he could:

> That evening, a friendly looking, slightly built Japanese man came looking for me. . . . He was so understanding and so ashamed at what the Japanese had done to us. Apologizing with humble gestures, he showed me the ticket he had bought for the whole night. . . . For a week, he came to the house every night to keep me safe. To pass the time, I thought of all the childhood games we could play where language is not a barrier, and so we played tic-tac-toe and other games where drawing was the basis. This short period of Yodi's visits could not last. He told me he was being teased and laughed at by his Japanese friends because he visited the brothel every night and stayed all night. It must have been very hard on him, especially as he never once touched me.

Yet however many shades of gray may be introduced, the portrait of Japan as an occupying power is predominantly painted in black. Never before in history had a "liberator" played its political hand in a worse way than Japan did in the occupied territories; never has any relative newcomer on the international stage received so much bad press so quickly—and deserved it. Japan would use more force and violence than any other warring power in living memory as the Asia and Pacific war proceeded.

It is conceivable that Japan's forcible recruitment of women to its military brothels was one of the worst abuses of power. More than two hundred thousand women were transported over great distances, the majority of them recruited by force. Both they and those who were donated by their families or had reported for duty themselves ended up in a rigidly organized, compulsory sexual system that had little in common with classic prostitution. Only a few were paid, and very few managed to escape from their sexual workplace no matter how intensely they wished to.

During breaks in the war, most of the Japanese military enjoyed recreation in big cities: Singapore, Manila, Hong Kong, Nanjing, Batavia, Surabaya, Saigon, and Shanghai all provided a civilian sex industry of considerable size. When officers and soldiers had a choice, they always elected privately run brothels, no matter how much more expensive they

were. But most of the time these heavenly red zones were too far away.
The majority of the military brothels were located in small towns or tiny
military sex stations in the immediate vicinity of army units—spread from
the Andaman Islands, in the Indian Ocean, to Timor to the Solomon Islands, even on tiny islands like Palau and Yap and the northern Aleutians.
In tiny rooms or in tents, a hundred thousand Asian girls had to service up
to forty visitors a day each with only a one-hour lunch break and two breaks
to wash their nether regions. Wherever the circumstances made it possible,
the service was class-divided. Japanese officers rarely had to stand in
brothel lines. But the private soldiers had to wait hours for their ascribed
ten to fifteen minutes.

Some short stories and novelistic biographies about East and Southeast Asia's forced war prostitutes appeared sporadically, especially during the 1970s, often by a young female relative with feminist ambitions.
The theme seemed archetypal: "My aunt was a military pleasure woman"
or "I was forced into prostitution by the Japanese." Few books contained
documentation, but even when some quasi-documentary films were made
in the 1970s, they were belittled and rejected as modern women's nonsense
and rarely reached a broader audience.

During the 1990s, professional researchers interviewed hundreds of
Korean women, who comprised the majority of the forced war prostitutes
but remained the most silent and shamed of all the nationalities in Japan's
service. In *True Stories of the Korean Comfort Women*, Hwang Kumju recounts:

> One day when I was unable to serve soldiers because my womb had
> swollen and was bleeding, an officer ordered me to suck his penis. He
> claimed I was not able to do what he called my "duty." I shouted at
> him: "I'd rather eat your shit than suck you!" This made him very an-
> gry. He beat me and threw me about, shouting, *"Konoyaro koroside
> yarouka,"* something like "I am going to kill you, you bitch." I blacked
> out, and when I came around I was told that I had been in a coma for
> three days.

The material contains a few cinematic stories about dramatic flights
from sex stations and of successful integration in other Asian nations. The
material also gives accounts of both happy and unhappy marriages with
men of their own or other races, in their own or new homelands. But whatever fate they met, these women shared one intense, unforgettable trauma

of rapes, starvation during the war, and the following years of endless shame. A number of the women recall in full detail mass murder, rapes, disease, abortion, suicides during the war, and the sterility, self-hatred, and stigmatization if they ever came "home" to Korea.

For the vast majority of the Korean women, the homecoming they had dreamed about was a deeply painful experience. The poor, still rural, and primitive Korea had hardly been at war, it seemed, and few of its people had any understanding of what had happened in the world war. Consequently, there was little consolation, while vague rumors about sex with many foreign men resulted in social stigma and deprivation. A number of the women had become sterile and ended up as spinsters, an especially bad fate in an agrarian society like Korea. At night these women would be wakened by their own screams, while during the day they fought to suppress a past no one wanted to know about.

An unusually high number of prostitutes were to die in the final phase of the war. This high death rate puts the forced sex workers almost on par with the soldiers they served. But death has many variations. Some of the girls committed hara-kiri in line with the soldiers as the Japanese army started to withdraw from occupied territories in Asia and the Pacific in late 1944. In other cases, the Japanese shot girls they could not retreat with. In March 1945 the American air attack on Tokyo destroyed the well-known red-light area of Yoshiwara, which is on an island and is very easy to identify from the air. The bombs hit their targets unerringly and must have been dropped with intent. Four hundred prostitutes died in the inferno, and more than a hundred drowned in the Sumida River in an attempt to escape.

The brave Philippine liberation guerrilla army was saluted by their "own girls." But there was collateral damage among prostitutes on the other side as well. It was not easy to discern the difference between Japanese and Koreans, and since the "foreign" prostitutes seemed to be part of the enemy's army, the guerrillas in the Philippines killed a large number of Korean women as they liberated their own country.

Early in 1943, American medical laboratories discovered that penicillin had a remarkable effect in combating venereal disease. The high numbers of syphilis patients from the war years provided a huge quantity of human material for research. The results were beyond all expectation. Within a year, there was a noteworthy percentage of cures, sometimes as high as 97 percent.

The fear of syphilis waned as the world war neared its end, and the U.S. military command began to relax its requirements regarding soldiers' morals—not least in Asia. In Norway and Germany, the American and British authorities insisted on health checks for loose women and prostitutes. But the Americans showed far from the same eagerness that they had previously. In Asia the evaporating fear of syphilis must have been one of the reasons why the Japanese were not held especially to account for their forcible recruitment of prostitutes.

When the British liberated Burma in 1945, they found more than three thousand forcibly recruited prostitutes in their former colony, most of them from Korea but some from India, Burma, or China. Similar patterns emerged all over Asia. In 1945 and 1946 the U.S. and the reinstated European colonial masters carried out statistical surveys of prostitutes and venereal disease in the countries they had reconquered. All the brothels were to be privatized, but a large American peacekeeping force would need to take over the prostitution facilities from the Japanese in a number of countries.

The arriving Americans registered only two thousand prostitutes in Korea, due to the fact that the peninsula had never been a battleground. The girls forced into prostitution still were in the former war zones. Manila, on the other hand, had been bombed by Japanese and Americans from the beginning to the end of the war and had nevertheless kept its brothels open. There had been large Japanese forces in major cities like Davao, Iloilo, and Cebu, and in smaller towns on the islands of Leyte and Mindanao—and military brothels of comparable size. There were more than two thousand remaining foreign prostitutes in the Philippines when the Americans took the country, in spite of the hundreds who had been killed and the thousands who had fled with the Japanese army. The military and private bordellos in Manila housed sex workers of several races who were ready to receive the Americans—girls of Spanish, Jewish, and Russian origin, and Asians from the country, as well as from China and Korea.

In the Philippines and in Dutch East India, the victors took up the causes of some women who felt they had been sexually abused by the Japanese military. In the eyes of the West, it was particularly serious that Dutch women had been forced to work in military brothels. Neither Europeans nor Americans found reason to react on behalf of the Chinese or Korean women the Japanese had exploited. This would have made it impossible to make their own use of the sex industry. The fact was that Allied soldiers, too, might commit rape if they did not get women in some other way, as the military authorities were soon to discover.

When the Allied powers captured the brothels, they checked the girls' health and filed away the documents the Japanese had left behind. Since they did not take the question of war prostitution particularly seriously, it became less likely for other countries to do so. China was occupied with revolution. Korea's women were traumatized. To Japan's high command, compulsory sex was an insignificant, mundane phenomenon.

The commander in chief of the U.S. forces in the Pacific, General Douglas MacArthur, was in many eyes the man who had won the war. He was also given the task of organizing the peace. He soon realized that it would be a good idea to utilize the sexual institutions the Japanese had built up. And so it went in the Philippines, on Okinawa, and in Korea, where large American military contingents were now stationed.

Japanese businessmen expressed a strong wish to reopen their brothels with freshly recruited girls, and were given high-level support by their country's top bureaucrats, who clearly wanted to keep American troops away from better-class Japanese girls. But General MacArthur abruptly and surprisingly declared that he found brothels inhumane. How could they be inhumane in Japan but acceptable in Korea and the Philippines? Of course, MacArthur's views reflected practical American considerations, not principles. In his view, it was inhumane to reopen Japan's brothels to American soldiers—though he did not say so in public, the Americans were fully aware of the high syphilis figures in Japan's brothels. It is harder to accept that a man so concerned with humane conditions could have ordered the bombing of the Yoshiwara brothels just a few months earlier.

But Japanese businessmen know how to mollify foreigners. The eventual result was a compromise: new brothels with newly recruited healthy girls. None of the old prostitutes would be admitted to the reorganized sex industry, the Americans were told. This cannot have been completely true, for syphilis burgeoned. When an American battalion reached 680 infected soldiers per year per thousand, they set a world syphilis record. But since medicine had made progress, this was less terrifying than before. After some time, love affairs between Americans and Japanese girls were also allowed to flourish, and a new wave of prostitution films came to give the world a new, romantic, and syphilis-free version of Asia. In the 1950s the world met *Sayonara* and *The World of Suzie Wong*, and thus began a new phase in the film history of prostitution, in spite of the largely unchanged social realities among Asian prostitutes.

The fate of what the Norwegian press termed the Germans' whores—Norwegian girls who had had German soldiers as boyfriends during the war—was hotly discussed in 1945 and then promptly forgotten. Almost forty years would pass before their harsh fate in Norwegian internment camps became known. In the 1980s, a new wave of historians with a keener sensitivity to women's fates changed Norwegian notions of what was important and unimportant in history.

A similar pattern developed for those forced into prostitution by the Japanese over large parts of Asia. Forty-five years had to pass before society was able to comprehend what they had been through. Without shared initiatives and the exchange of information and experiences between female activists and the liberal press in the Philippines, Korea, and Japan, it is doubtful whether their fate would have gotten beyond rumor.

South Korea and Japan are now both industrial nations and enjoy the highest average standard of living in Asia, but thinking has not been modernized at the same tempo. Women's rights are weak in male-dominated East Asia. Southeast Asian countries have traditionally given higher status to women, and in the Philippines, the Catholic Church and American influence contributed to the spread of a Western ethos long before World War II. During this time, well-educated women followed the women's movement in the West more vigilantly than any other place in Asia. Finally, even Japan and South Korea joined in the movement, and in the 1980s, criticism arose against men's sex tourism in Southeast Asia, while Filipina feminists complained about young girls working for the sex industry in Japan.

In 1989 the body of Maricris Siosin was brought home to Manila from Tokyo, full of stab wounds to the head and the sexual organs. The Japanese autopsy neglected all evidence of sexual abuse, torture, and murder and stated that the cause of death was hepatitis. Manila boiled with rage, and the case created interest in tracing the history of the sex trade and earlier incidences of sexual abuse on a transnational scale.

A candid autobiography by an elderly Japanese officer, *My War Crimes: On the Forced Mobilization in Korea,* had the power to shift public opinion. This was a major problem in Japan's military and political history that required attention from all leading figures in Asian politics. All of a sudden Japan, Korea, and the Philippines allowed for public debate on forced prostitution during the Pacific war. Two elderly, unmarried Korean women—with the staunch assistance of a Protestant women's group—dared to go public and demand apology and financial compensation from Japan. A Korean women's council got thousands of Korean women to sign its petition to Japan. The Japanese authorities vacillated among humiliated silence, lies, and obfuscation.

One year later, Manila made world news when a sweet grandmother confessed the abuse she had suffered at the hands of the Japanese. First Japan angrily denied all accusations and then followed with diplomatic posturing and threats.

Public debate in the Philippines being characterized by high drama, the dialogue on the comfort women was in danger of becoming overplayed. An endless stream of elderly Filipinas emerged, each apparently trying to outdo the others, perhaps believing that the worst story would bring the most reparations money. As the long line of witnesses came forward, some spurious evidence was disclosed, and a few false witnesses tainted the reliability of the others who spoke the truth. What was this? A tragedy turning into a soap opera? It was also a complex detective story. Shortly afterward, the Philippines' investigating body seemed unable to find evidence of any sex industry at all in Manila during World War II: Tons of documents had mysteriously disappeared. Japanese, Americans, and the Filipino brothel owners who had collaborated with the Japanese would have had equally good reasons to destroy evidence.

No degree of maneuvering in Manila could ease the pressure on Japan. International media, the UN, and international diplomatic and public interest organizations were watching. As the cream of international experts mobilized, documentation surfaced verifying similar sex industries established in Indonesia and Burma.

For four decades, Japanese official history had presented a self-serving picture of its World War II activities with most of the unpleasant facts removed, but now the authorities had gone too far. Japanese officialdom was rocked when a group of well-respected elderly Japanese officers spoke out, attacking the government and two generations of leaders for having falsified history. This was immediately effective. As the officers submitted private copies of revealing military documents to justify their criticism, the authorities' case collapsed.

Finally, in December 1992, a public hearing was arranged in Tokyo. A large group of comfort women from all over Asia had been assembled to testify. One woman had everything the world media wanted—a sad smile and a clear voice, a supportive husband with a military background, perfect English, and white skin. Dutch-born Jan Ruff was forced to become a sex slave at sixteen and was still a skinny teenager when, in 1945, her sex prison in central Java was liberated by Australian soldiers. Her first free gaze proved to be of the man who was to be her true love. Her testimony was cool, sober, and eloquent and was followed up by an equally convincing autobiography, *50 Years of Silence,* which expresses the solidarity she and the other comfort women would share through their later lives. The book recounts how, as the girls gathered at the veranda one morning before working hours began, Jan Ruff took out the white handkerchief that had been pushed into her hands when she was taken from the Dutch prisoners' camp to the Japanese quarters: "I got out a pencil and asked each girl to write her name there. Afterwards I embroidered over the writing, each name a different color. I kept this white handkerchief with seven names on it hidden for fifty years, afraid my family would ask me, 'What do the names on this hankie mean?' It has been one of my dearest possessions but also my most hidden, the secret evidence of the brutal crimes that had been done to us."

The Korean women who had made up the majority of the forced prostitutes were unable to play a leading role in the media debate. Everyone who tried seemed too full of tears, rage, shame, and hate for the interpreters to make sense of their words. The Filipinas and Jan Ruff brought the message home. Together the women had managed to establish all the elementary facts; together they had testified to a fate so grim and dreadful that it remains almost incomprehensible.

TWENTY-SEVEN

CALL GIRLS

C
an't you see that these are pretty girls?" an elderly judge reprimanded New York assistant district attorney Dennis Wade
in March 1984, when he charged three beautiful young middle-
class girls—two students and one secretary—with prostitution. "What are
you actually expecting to happen during the time you usually spend in a
hotel with a client?" the judge asked one of them. "To meet a gentleman
who treats me with respect," came the reply. The judge found it problematic to interrogate such beautiful and well-dressed women—who did not
use narcotics and drank nothing stronger than champagne—about sexual
liaisons with leaders of society in expensive hotels.

Prostitution is unlawful in New York, as in most other U.S. states,
but the other sex workers who ended up in court had always been street
prostitutes who appeared in the only gear they knew: clinging fabric and
plunging necklines, with heavy makeup and colored hair.

Policemen in New York felt completely within their rights when they
took the odd trick for free upon hauling hookers into the station; indeed,
there were some girls the police enjoyed arresting so much that they
brought them in twice a week. However, with the payment of a fee, it was
possible—particularly for the white girls—to avoid being brought in.
Fewer than half of New York's prostitutes were black, but they were
brought in seven times more often than white girls.

In the early 1980s, the New York police arrested about 2,700 women
annually for prostitution. More than five thousand were fined and released
on the spot. Such a warning was a simple matter, but every arrest, with
subsequent court appearances, cost the police and court system $3,000. The
small sums that the police collected in addition to, or instead of, arrest were
never used to defray public disbursements.

It was no everyday affair in New York to find discreetly made-up
girls, freshly coiffured and wearing tailored outfits, charged with prostitution. They were Westchester County and Scarsdale types. Within the
police force, there was extreme pride in the catch, but the judge felt they
had wasted valuable time and far too much money on the pursuit of these
lovelies. Besides, it had come out that one policeman had forced a girl to
have sex with him while another had asked "his" blonde for oral sex and
arrested her as soon as she consented. The police had done things in their
normal way, certain that the whores would never mention such things in
the courtroom, but these women had the courage to do so.

The New York Police Department had contacted the girls by calling up an escort service called Cachet, which advertised in *The International
Herald-Tribune*. There was no discussion of money, but the police could
demonstrate that it was possible to order prostitutes by telephone. However, it had taken four policemen one month to discover this—a lot of work
for meager results. The judge reprimanded the policemen, dismissed the
indictment, and sent the girls home, but they received no compensation
for their stay in prison or for the sexually harassing behavior of the police.

Nonetheless, the New York police continued to work the case, largely
on their own initiative. The driving force was Elmo Smith, a former un-
dercover agent with experience in the CIA. He had a lively imagination
and a burning desire to be famous one day. In the following year, he behaved like a parody of an action hero, ordering illegal telephone wiretap-
ping, breaking into the girls' apartments, smashing in their doors, and
threatening them with loaded pistols. His aim was to demolish the ring, at
any cost. Elmo Smith and his team managed to spend about $1 million on
this bit of fun.

In March 1985 a thirty-three-year-old woman who called herself
Sheila Devin reported to the district attorney's office in the hope of avoiding more unpleasantness. Without a search warrant, the police had raided
both her home and office, breaking down doors, confiscating her office in-
ventory and toilet articles, and scaring the life out of five or six switchboard operators. She was not home, but the police also destroyed some of
her undergarments and "tested" the capacity of her bed, destroying it. Ms.
Devin arrived at the DA's office with her lawyer, Risa Dickstein. Half of
New York's press had been alerted, but all were looking for the madam
without realizing that one of these two businesslike, well-groomed women

was actually the accused. Both journalists and photographers assumed the two to be lawyers. But soon Sheila Devin would be a media sensation in New York and the national press. Ten years earlier, Xaviera Hollander had published her autobiography, *The Happy Hooker*, which sold in sky-high numbers and went on to be filmed several times, each time with increasing infusions of fiction. Several books were written in the wake of this success, including a 1986 best seller about the New York call-girl ring Cachet, entitled *Mayflower Madam: The Queen of Credit Card Sex*.

No matter what people think about prostitution as a phenomenon, many want to read about it. That there is money to be earned from whores and the sex industry has always been a known fact, just as much by publishers and film companies as by brothel keepers.

"Will you go to bed with me for ten thousand dollars?" goes the query a philandering businessman is said to have posed to an attractive lady of the fashion world in a story that is variously said to have taken place in New York, Paris, Milan, or London in the mid-1960s.

"Your proposition will not be excluded from consideration," she replied with an engaging smile.

"Will you do it for ten dollars, then?"

The woman's smile became a thin line. "What do you take me for?"

"But my dear, you have already indicated that you are for sale. I'm just trying to negotiate the price."

Luxury prostitution is located in a gray zone of the public imagination, accepted one second, then overlooked, then condemned. In the spring of 1985, in a slow news season, the great springtime page-filler in the New York newspapers was the case of the million-dollar girls. The police had managed to break up the call-girl ring they had worked on for a year and a half. The tabloid press reported every last detail of the case. *The New York Times* gave it lead coverage; the scandal made the cover of *Newsweek* and national television.

The name of the ring—Cachet—was chosen simply because it was difficult for the uneducated to pronounce correctly, which helped sort out unwanted clients. A financial newspaper, *Barron's*, was the only one to give an unequivocal account of the company purely as a business. The paper praised Cachet's sound professional management and good business practices and suggested that the only punishment its chief really deserved would be to teach administration at a business school. The director of this enterprise had first appeared under the name Sheila Devin, but the press quickly revealed her real name: Sydney Biddle Barrows. She had attended good schools and was descended from venerable families in Philadelphia and New England on both sides, and several of her ancestors had been associates of George Washington. Ms. Biddle Barrows participated in meetings of the exclusive Mayflower Club and played tennis at West-hampton with all of New York's young up-and-comers. It turned out, however, that she was not a buyer in the fashion world, as most of her peripheral acquaintances had thought—she ran an escort service. The press began to refer to her as the Mayflower Madam.

Cachet was founded in 1979. The Cachet girls were thoroughly in-terviewed, physically inspected, and given an intensive course in sex eti-quette. The starting point was that they were almost all well educated. Those who were students generally studied law and economics. Quite a few had aspirations to the theater and dance; a number of them worked in law offices or brokerage houses. Not all were dazzlingly beautiful, but all of them possessed style and intelligence. They looked like typical uptown girls and were slim, self-assured, well dressed, and normally between eigh-teen and twenty-eight.

Over a period of five years, sociologist Lewis Diana studied a much larger number of call girls than the two hundred employed by Cachet. He confirmed that most call girls are middle-class young women who are also students or full-time employees elsewhere. Few stay in the job longer than five years. The typical call girl takes up prostitution as a secondary source of income for a certain number of hours a week. Only a few end up mak-ing the work their primary occupation.

"She was small and agile, with honey-blonde hair, a calm, profound type of woman, but at the same time, unusually well-dressed. Her outfit matched her hair perfectly. Her only adornment was a pair of modern eardrops in copper. She projected the aura of a ballet dancer or an art student, in any case, a girl from a good background. Her language was educated, her voice well modulated. Not a single foul word passed her lips during twelve months of therapy."

"Sandra," the most important of New York psychiatrist Harold Greenwald's patients, was thus described in the book that would become the first exhaustive portrayal of the call-girl phenomenon. His first impression of Sandra did not prove entirely correct. She grew up in humble circumstances in New Jersey, partly in an orphanage, and partly with foster parents; her foster father had sexually abused her. Sandra had not received a college education. After high school, she went to work in a store, and then she began to work part-time as a prostitute. Sandra was in therapy with Greenwald for five years, and in the course of her treatment, she admitted that she had dreamed of growing up a boy, and that she'd had fantasies about her mother marrying a pimp.

Sandra and her psychiatrist exchanged letters for several years after the therapy ended. He never forgot her. But how extensive could the conclusions of a psychiatrist be based on five years' treatment of one patient? Later, Greenwald would have a total of six call-girl patients; they all came to him on their own and paid out of their own pockets. Greenwald's research assistants interviewed more than twenty other girls. The data were thin, particularly when one takes into account the broad conclusions Greenwald drew.

Greenwald got a whole world to accept the following as a psychiatric truth: "The prostitute lacks the ability for . . . stable relations implied in a marriage. This indicates either a damaged system of values, or a destroyed sense of reality." He explained to the curious that a call girl was a beautiful woman with mink coats and Cadillacs, a child of divorce with suicidal and lesbian tendencies, most frequently frigid and with problems when faced by real love; she had a tendency to shoplift for her own pleasure, but never stole from a client. Perhaps a few call girls of the 1950s fit Greenwald's stereotype, but not many.

Call girls were discernibly a postwar phenomenon. They were a product of the 1950s emphasis on prostitution legislation, a postwar economic boom, an increase in travel, and improved telephone technology. The growing number reduced the number of street prostitutes and brothel girls in Western countries.

Europe learned of the concept through the media in 1963, when the British Conservative Party's minister of defense, John Profumo, saw his affair with call girl Christine Keeler revealed to a shocked world. The British secret service was particularly alarmed: During her affair with

Profumo, Christine Keeler had visited an attaché at the Soviet embassy. Like any Russian of that time, he was practically by definition a KGB agent. Profumo resigned in the summer of 1963 and wrote to Prime Minister Harold Macmillan that he had lied when he solemnly swore that there had not been anything indecent about his affair with Keeler.

Indecent? This was far too weak a word. The newspapers recounted stories of orgies with call girls among the gods of British high society, in fashionable London apartments. At one party in Bayswater, Christine Keeler, Mandy Rice-Davies, and a young man by the name of Stephen Ward had been present. The latter had introduced the girls to all the top leaders of the Conservative Party. A prominent politician was said to have served roast peacock at the dinner table, naked except for a bow tie and a mask. He had a card attached to his stomach that read, "Whip me!" On another occasion, eight High Court justices took part in an orgy with a handful of call girls.

Prime Minister Harold Macmillan was sick with a respiratory illness and had difficulty breathing when he read this story in the newspapers, but he managed to burst out to one of the party faithful, "One I could have accepted, two I could have tried to forget. But eight! Think of it! It is un-believable!" Unfortunately for him, it was not something that the newspaper-reading British public chose to doubt. A rumor that is titillating enough makes the truth irrelevant. Over the course of that autumn, an official report was published about the Profumo affair, and Stephen Ward was charged with procurement. However, he committed suicide before the judgment came down. The press concluded that the British establishment had used him to distance themselves from the scandal. Macmillan extricated himself the following year, when the Conservative government lost power. Harold Wilson and the British Labour Party formed the next government. Ironically enough, Profumo and Christine Keeler had contributed to the radicalizing of British politics.

Although call girls were the period's new form of prostitution, ordinary brothels also enjoyed a new Renaissance across Europe in the sex-friendly 1960s, now packaged for the consumer as Eros Centers. In New York, there were still high-priced brothels camouflaged as members-only clubs. The remaining U.S. whorehouses were shady, depressing establishments. Since prostitution was illegal in most American states, brothel keepers had to bribe the local police to an astonishing degree. In her memoir, Xaviera Hollander recalled paying the police $10,000 a month.

Prostitution researchers Eileen McLeod and Lewis Diana have estimated that street prostitution made up one-fourth of all prostitution in the U.S. and Western Europe in the 1980s, a conclusion consistent with the estimates undertaken by the International Committee for Prostitutes' Rights (ICPR). Today only one prostitute out of ten in the West works in a brothel. A somewhat greater proportion work "independently," based in restaurants and bars where they have to give a percentage of what they take in to the hosts, bartenders, and others who might be construed as assisting them.

Since call girls normally work for only a few years and are rarely organized or registered by police or VD clinics, all statistics are estimates. Whether they are made by epidemiologists, state authorities, or the organized prostitutes' movements, they all seem to make the rough conclusion that at least since the 1980s, half of Western prostitutes are call girls for whom the telephone is the most important external working tool. Most such prostitutes obtain technical assistance from call-girl companies, although many work from their own telephones.

After 1970 telephone sex also became common among male prostitutes. Men and boys have organized through agencies, some specializing in athletes and musclemen and others in leather, rubber, and fetish; still others have invested in the image of youth that had become classic in male prostitution. More men than women work independently. A great number advertise through the extensive gay press. Male hustlers are less dependent on the security and control of an agency than their female counterparts. The other advantage of working alone is, of course, that one keeps all the earnings.

The escort service run by Sydney Biddle Barrows was known for its high quality. A Cachet girl never appeared in trousers; she used New York's most fabulous undergarments, garter belts, and sheer stockings without seams or patterns. The Cachet girls showed off their long legs by means of short skirts and high heels, but this was their only concession toward a sexy look. In all other ways, they were discreetly attired. They might paint their toenails, but their fingernails were left natural. They would generally wear hat and gloves and arrived with a briefcase or a theater program in hand, depending on the time of day. There was nothing about the gait of these girls or their accent that separated them from businesswomen when, completely self-possessed, they strolled through the lobbies of New York's most renowned hotels. Manhattan was usually their only field of operation, though it was totally unacceptable to employ women with a New York accent. By definition, all girls should appear educated and highly articulate.

Cachet employees worked under names suitable to their type. Nicole, Monique, and Tiffany were too widespread among the street prostitutes to be tolerated at Cachet. But a client understood that if he ordered Alexandra, he would meet a tall, blonde, and striking creature; were he to choose a Natalia, he would meet someone softer, warmer, with deep brown eyes and long dark hair. Kristin and Sonja also had to be very tall, blond, and European, with a sexy, slightly foreign accent. Only four female names were held by more than one girl, in keeping with the wishes of the service: Heather, Melissa, Kelly, and Jennifer. This was due to the suggestive power of clichéd American soap operas.

A fictitious work identity was part of the call girl's allure. All of Cachet's clients loved stewardesses. Models are appealing in magazines but were patently more threatening to Cachet's clients, because this line of work was not common in the economy of the day. All Cachet's girls had to read *The New York Times* or *Newsweek*. They received weekly material from a clipping service that kept them up to date on current topics of conversation. It would have reflected badly on the firm if a Cachet girl did not know what the World Bank was or confused Morocco with Malaysia.

In the eyes of a typical Cachet client, art history, fashion, and music studies were less alluring than economics or law. A woman studying law or business who revealed too much expert knowledge could destroy a fledgling erotic experience just as easily as could the "dumb blonde" who might give a sneering "Huh?" when the client, with deep emotion, began to recall Verdi, Violetta, and *La Traviata*. Cachet guaranteed an unforgettable memory of two to three hours, at the cost of $200 to $400.

Cachet's business hours ran from four o'clock in the afternoon until one in the morning. Rush hours were between six and eight in the evening, and twelve-fifteen to closing time. Many sought sex before an important dinner, in order to lower their stress level; others wanted late sex by way of celebration or to stave off loneliness. Saturday was and is the deadest day of the week for call girls. Married men spend time with their families; business travelers have other social diversions.

The girls normally were asked to be available by telephone three evenings a week, and when an appointment was arranged, they had to appear freshly coiffed, made-up, and dressed such that they could throw themselves into a taxi at ten minutes' notice. No one staying at a cheap hotel was accepted as a client, unless it was the exceptional circumstance of an out-of-town businessman who usually lived high on an expense account, and now, in New York on a private visit, wanted to save money. The natural habitat of Cachet girls did not extend beyond the Upper East Side, Upper West Side, Midtown, SoHo, Tribeca, and the more gentrified parts of Greenwich Village.

"We are in the business of selling fantasy and success," Sydney Barrows stressed to her handpicked girls. She herself was graced with knowledge of human beings and good taste, but she had also inherited her parents' stuffiness. What she marketed was precisely the subdued snobbery that one might expect from the East Coast elite.

Sydney Barrows repeatedly hammered into the heads of her girls the importance of being a good listener. Beepers were not allowed. They were a rude interruption of intercourse and created suspicion that the girl would be meeting someone else later. Nobody relished this thought. One of Cachet's best-kept secrets was that girls often had several clients in one evening. If the first appointment unfolded in such a way that the girl did not have time to get to her next, the switchboard had to improvise: "Barbara's board meeting is taking longer than expected. Can we send you someone else instead?" "Melody is still shooting a scene in a film she is in. I am so very sorry." Both the client and the girl were free to say no if they did not feel comfortable with the arrangement made by the escort service. But in most instances things went well—not least, thanks to the switchboard.

Whoever answered the client's call had to understand the client's wishes, dreams, and needs with the aim of satisfying them as well as possible with one of the girls available that evening. The woman at the switchboard had to possess a unique combination of intuition, a sympathetic tone of voice, and social intelligence. Cachet was known for a tall, blond, and shapely upper-middle-class look; it was usually easy to match the right girl to the right client. But neither in life nor at Cachet were there enough of the ideal tall blondes. With time, a couple of Asian girls proved themselves socially acceptable, and there was also a constant supply of Western European girls. African-American and Puerto Rican girls were excluded without any consideration of language, style, or elegance. On the other hand, a somewhat shorter, dark, or redheaded American or European girl could be just as elegant as a blonde, and just as intelligent and sensual.

Some men desired women who were taller and whose breasts were exceedingly well endowed. Such clients might have totally warped notions about the extent of breast size it was possible for Cachet to put on offer, so it was up to the switchboard to discreetly make Mr. Andrews aware that even Dolly Parton did not have the breast size he wanted.

Many short men fell for taller women than themselves; height might intimidate others. For some men, intelligent conversation was more important than tits and hips. A lot of men were simply terrified by dazzlingly beautiful women—even though they wanted attractive girls, there were upward limits to their desires.

"Ah, it was so great to be working those nights when the telephone was constantly ringing and business was booming! The girls were bursting to go out, the clients in high expectations waiting to meet them. Of course sex was part of it, but I didn't actually feel it. I felt more like a representative of the bliss and joy brigade." Many years later, this was how Cachet's most brilliant telephone receptionist recalled her former job.

Cachet's youngest client was the seventeen-year-old son of a big wheel, a lonely, inexperienced kid who fell fatally in love with the first girl who visited him. A lonesome Arab prince made all the girls' hearts bleed. His highest wish was pillow fights, perhaps in compensation for the childhood he never had. A tough Vietnam veteran whose legs had been amputated was a client for years. Almost all of Cachet's girls fell in love with him, yet all of them pledged to refuse him next time—not for sexual reasons; indeed, this man always scored—because afterward the girls were seized with profound sadness.

If a client had a favorite, he got her if she was working that day. But the service never sent the same girl unless requested, no matter how pleased the client had been with the first meeting. Both parties to a commercial sex relationship deserve a professional distance between sex and private life, was the philosophy of the escort service. Accordingly, the staff did their best to prevent the development of strong feelings between a client and a girl. Variation was advantageous for everyone and less threatening to a married man's private life. If the bureau detected genuine love behind eager requests for the same girl, the standard response was, "Oh dear, Stephanie has moved to Louisiana, and no, she has not given us a forwarding address."

For Liza, who only worked the switchboard, things were different. A longtime client used to call her in New York from other faraway cities when he was on business trips, always just to hear how it was going. Liza never took him up on his offers. Not until a good two years of telephone flirting had gone by did she accept a dinner, with full decorum. In the end, it became apparent that they had more in common than voice appeal, and Cachet lost one of its most faithful clients and its best telephone receptionist.

To be a debutante is difficult, even in the sex business. Cachet's policy was that a steady, experienced customer should be allowed to initiate a new girl into the trade. Most of them took this as an honor and viewed it as deflowering a virgin. Cachet kept records of all clients, by name, address, and vital statistics. The telephone receptionist did a short interview with the client and the girl afterward, to check that things had gone well and to improve the quality next time. *LP* was the code for a client who was abnormally long, or well endowed, something that certain girls wanted to avoid. This abbreviation was considered something approaching obscenity, when it came to light later, as attorneys for the prosecution were preparing their case against the escort service.

Narcissistic men who primarily wanted admiring and tender words from a woman were accepted by the service without objection. Requests for two girls were accepted, provided the girls were willing, but the service refused to set up girls for several men at the same time. Ninety percent of Cachet's clients wanted "ordinary" sex; even oral sex was an exception. If a client signaled a need for sadomasochism, this person was referred to a colleague, Olga—Baronesse von Stein—who at the time was New York's most advanced and professional dominatrix.

The average Cachet client was between twenty-eight and fifty. The Rolodex of clients included a number of very big names. Most were businessmen, diplomats, stockbrokers, doctors, and lawyers—a total of 340 New York lawyers, which put a lot of pressure on the district attorney when it looked as though the matter would go to trial. Many of the steady customers were workaholics. It could be that they dared not invest the time necessary for a permanent relationship and preferred casual but well-organized sex. Many men were tired of the "swinging singles" culture of New York. One had to be flush to spend time with the beautiful and intelligent blondes, but actual swingers were extremely demanding and capricious.

A Cachet girl was guaranteed free of feminism, substance abuse, and infection. But they were not devoid of principles. If a man opened the door in a state of undress, he was told politely to dress before receiving his lady visitor. Men who were not physically clean, particularly Englishmen, were instructed to take a shower, first with discretion and, if they hesitated, then firmly. The girls would remain in bed for a while after orgasm, and they did not shower afterward, since many men found it mortifying, as it implied that something dirty had taken place. The procedure was to touch up one's makeup at the hotel, and shower at home.

Cachet's reputation for perfect hygiene and health took a blow in 1984 when gonorrhea invaded the service. This made it essential to contact all steady customers, close down for three weeks, and use obligatory condom sex in the weeks that followed, something that earlier had been a violation of company policy. At the time, Sydney Barrows tried to build a coalition with several other escort services. Since many clients used several services, this ought to have been beneficial to all, but even a purely business cooperation was not possible. The competition was too strong.

Cachet had two high seasons. In summer, married men dominated the client list; in October, it was the UN general assembly. A core of steady clients were first-rate lovers, something one girl or another took pleasure in from time to time. But a job was a job, and most preferred a short, satisfactory liaison with a little less passion, preferably with normally endowed, straightforward, polite married men. The majority liked Japanese clients, who were often sexually placid and very pleasant. Middle Eastern clients were reported to be more difficult. First they haggled over the price, in violation of the service's policy; the fact that they tended to tip well played a less important role. Worse, they did not all treat the girls with respect. Fortunately, some of the girls developed a knack for dealing with this type of client, to the relief of the others.

African-American clients were never accepted, regardless of social background, and only under exceptional circumstances were African diplomats taken as clients. Strangely enough, there were several gay men who regularly used the girls as escorts; such services were free of sex and involved no more than behaving like a fiancée on important occasions. The girls loved these jobs, so long as they were able to stay clear of tactless questions about the client's female relatives.

In the early 1980s, there were many companies like Cachet in Manhattan, but no others with such a high profile. Other services might charge higher prices and offer more tits and ass. Some of New York's larger firms had call girls on salary as PR consultants. The downside was that one couldn't reject a client found to be unsympathetic. Other services exerted a lot more surveillance over their girls. Some no-frills services had male telephone receptionists, but it did not create the same magic to arrange all the details beforehand, man to man. Both the girls and the clients seemed to feel less comfortable when they finally met. It was somehow more romantic when the search for happiness was conducted with the help of a charming young female voice.

Only one of the Cachet girls traveled the world, and that was on her own recognizance. To the joy of the service, she continued to coordinate all her sex business exclusively through them.

The world's most expensive male prostitutes travel the world more frequently and earn one and a half to two times as much. Gender-related salary differences are a reality—even in the world of luxury prostitution.

Sydney Biddle Barrows reported to the office of the district attorney in March 1985, when the police ransacked her apartment. The district attorney was easier to work with, partly because his people were schooled in jurisprudence, and partly because they tended to feel the political and social pressures more directly than did the "tough guys" in the police force.

After one day in custody, Barrows was released on bail raised by good friends. In the course of twenty-four hours, she learned a considerable amount about the daily conditions of street prostitutes. Meanwhile, the New York press was aboil, having caught the scent of a sex- and scandal-permeated trial. New York's lawyers understood how complicated it would be to get Sydney Biddle Barrows and Cachet hauled into court. Their taxes, rent, and telephone bills were paid; their telephone receptionists were employed legally.

If things came to trial against the proprietor of an escort service, it would be impossible not to expose the clients, and a number of them had immediately let their feelings be known. The prosecution was totally paralyzed for a while, terrified, as the wrath of the implicated juridical community mounted higher and higher.

Things were viewed differently in the police force. The media-savvy constable Elmo Smith became almost a superhero to the media, precisely as he had dreamed and imagined. His smile shone from the front pages of the tabloids almost daily. He and his colleagues fed new details to the press every week. Not until the district attorney became aware that they were about to release the clients' names were the police bound by a gag order.

The media were unanimous in their condemnation of the Mayflower Madam. A couple of papers later gave space for readers' reactions, along with the views of indignant moralists. Barbara Walters broached an in-depth interview with Sydney Biddle Barrows, but the highly influential Biddle clan stopped this.

A boyfriend from Sydney's student days sold the tabloids fifteen-year-old private photographs that showed her half naked on a beach near Amsterdam. The prestigious social register of the *Mayflower* descendants undertook a falsification of history when it systematically erased all traces of Sydney Biddle Barrows and her mother from its Rolodex list, as though neither of them had ever been born.

In preliminary hearings, Sydney's defense lawyer, Risa Dickstein, argued in a feminist vein: If the men who sought out prostitutes were allowed to go free, how could the court expect to punish this escort service, which operated a discreet, hygienic, and well-organized form of prostitution and paid its taxes?

Sydney Barrows had few objections to trying the case in court; she had nothing to lose. She was worried for the girls; despite any guarantee of anonymity, some would fall into the clutches of the media. However, Sydney felt she had a moral duty to her clients. After much deliberation, she opted for a compromise. The case was dismissed, she was immune from further indictments, but the legal costs were not covered. She had to give up on the question of reimbursement for the destruction of her property by the police; it would be considered an indirect conviction by the police and entailed protracted, unwanted future consequences.

The press sulked when the balloon they had blown up to such gigantic dimensions began to lose its air. They proclaimed that the Mayflower Madam had been freed, that the elite always protect their own. Elmo Smith and the police took the settlement as a personal defeat, and even though they remained publicly critical, they were reprimanded behind closed doors.

Meanwhile, at the office, the bills had mounted up. The capital that Sydney Barrows was left with, before fines and court costs, was less than an American industrial worker's annual income. The solution came out of the blue—a charity ball!

The invitation read as follows: "The friends of Sydney Biddle Barrows have the honor of inviting you to a ball at the Limelight on the 30th of April, 1985. Black tie. Tiaras not essential." Nevertheless, Sydney's relative Anna Biddle from Philadelphia arrived wearing the family tiara. Sydney herself appeared in a rose-colored floor-length strapless taffeta gown, with a triple row of real pearls and diamonds at her throat and elbow-length white gloves.

The press poured in without paying. Sydney's friends clamored to be there, but many of her girlfriends were afraid of being taken for members of the ring, and certain men of this circle feared being taken for clients. Male and female cousins from the Biddle and Barrows clans arrived with pink balloons that read: "We don't condone everything, but the family stands together." Publishing, movies, and media were well represented among the guests, together with all the other trendy, nonconformist, elegant, or just plain curious New Yorkers. Everything proceeded in high style. The dancing continued into the wee hours.

Next morning the tabloid *Newsday* reported, "Sydney Biddle Barrows showed her body to the upper crust—for a price, as usual. The snobs paid through the nose to see her." From her point of view, things looked rather different. In an old-fashioned way, she had long thought that her wedding day would be the high point of her life. But this particular evening would stand as her most paradoxical and significant day.

TWENTY-EIGHT

ACADEMIC SEX TOURISM

A long day of paddling down a northern Thai river in torrential flood lends itself to flirtation. After her final doctoral research, Cleo Odzer, a slim, bouncy blonde in her late thirties, treated herself to a cool jungle holiday. She spoke Thai very well, since her fieldwork had been conducted in Bangkok. The nimble guide seemed to like her very much, and he winked as the sun set—an invitation to join him in further excitement.

With considerable frankness, Cleo Odzer later stated that "Thailand was also a paradise for Western women," and made it part of the conclusion of her dissertation on prostitution in Bangkok, published in 1994 under the title *Patpong Sisters: An American Woman's View of the Bangkok Sex World.*

Odzer was by no means the first female Western academic who had been fascinated by sex under the southern sun. The paradigm was long-standing, not least thanks to Margaret Mead, who from the 1920s to the 1940s conducted eminent studies of Samoa, Bali, and New Guinea. But her pioneer generation of female researchers placed the same stringent demands on their research as the men did on theirs—perhaps even greater. Consequently Margaret Mead's work deserves attentive reading even today.

During the 1990s, partly due to influence from postmodernism, a new subjective attitude became prevalent among younger female anthropologists. There was a combination of skepticism about scientific truths in the social world and a sense of women's solidarity without theoretical foundation. One should perhaps not be astonished to uncover a whole wave of studies on prostitution that might be summarized with the following formula: Western woman combines holidays and fieldwork by placing herself inside the sex industry of an exotic Third World country. Back home she delivers a vivid narrative about her new friends and experiences—engaged, spontaneous, and consciously subjective. In a number of cases, the research turns into a book, with amateur photographs as evidence. We might see the girls dolling themselves up for a night shift while the researcher assists with makeup, or the researcher and the girls in best-buddy embraces.

Norwegian Annick Prieur's life among the Mexico City transsexuals at "Mema's house" received such excited reviews at home that it was translated immediately. Internationally, the response was equally positive. Cleo Odzer's book also became an international success, if more a media sensation than an academic one. But it might be worth a comparison with two similar books, based on prostitution research during the same years in the same part of the world, both also written by women: Allison Murray's studies of Jakarta girls, published under the title *No Money, No Honey,* and Sandra Pollock Sturdevant and Brenda Stoltzfus's book about prostitution near the U.S. military bases in the Philippines, called *Let the Good Times Roll.*

All of these books limit themselves to description and analysis of only a segment within their chosen nation's prostitutes. But how valuable does this make their conclusions? A reader needs no academic training to feel somewhat uneasy with a researcher who so openly identifies with the object of the research. Murray explicitly acknowledges this problem. The self-evident paradox is that no male researcher could earn academic acclaim in any serious institution for this sort of participant observation. One must conclude that all three autobiographical books in no way follow up the legacy of Margaret Mead, which was engaged and female, but far more dispassionate.

In ancient and early colonial times, Southeast Asia was noted for its polygamy and short-term marriage between itinerant men and local women. Prostitution was unknown. In recent centuries, the sex trade has developed, aimed first at merchants from the West and China, and later toward Chinese coolies and soldiers in service to the colonial powers.

The Americans arrived in the Philippines as a late colonial power but remained there as a military force after liberation in 1945. The Vietnam War would create a constant congestion of American GIs taking rest and recreation in Saigon and Bangkok, and these factors have been used as a major explanation of why the Philippines, Vietnam, and Thailand have more developed sex economies than other nations in the region.

Thailand's sex industry grew into an economic force during the Vietnam War. Today it leads in the export of prostitutes to the rest of the world and in the sale of sexual services to its own population and itinerant male visitors. There are variations within the sex industry of Southeast Asia of today; local religion and culture, as well as foreign influence, contribute to this.

As Southeast Asian prostitution grew during the 1900s, it started to influence the sexual behavior of local men in the large cities and smaller provincial centers, with the greatest effect on policemen, soldiers, and the well off. In the Muslim areas to the south of the region, prostitution is less prevalent, particularly among young men; young divorced women dominate the trade. Due to the tradition of marrying young and practicing polygamy, it is easy for women to drift out of family life and into the sex trade. In the larger cities, it is common to find periodic prostitution lasting from three to four weeks during certain periods of the year. It is easy to keep this hidden and does not cause strong stigmatization if it becomes known in the woman's hometown. In Muslim Southeast Asia, the clients are usually local men, foreigners who are permanent residents, and seamen from the country. Tourism is too infrequent to produce a client base.

In tourist hot spots like Phuket, Pattaya, and Puerto Galera, prostitution is organized exactly as in Manila and Bangkok, while in the less visited Cambodia and Vietnam, the small segment of prostitutes who market themselves to foreign customers mix clothing and symbols of the East Asian and Western sex trades. Buddhist Thailand and Catholic Philippines are also known for their well-organized man and boy prostitution, which seems to be equally geared to local citizens and foreigners.

"Would you like a girl or a boy, young or old?" is the question posed to thousands of tourists every day by the professional touts of Patpong. Cleo Odzer heard it the very first evening she ventured out into Bangkok's sexual underworld. She replied immediately that she did not like tall and muscular boys but preferred them small and sensual.

Patpong is not the largest among the prostitution districts in Bangkok but is the best known and has the most Western mix. In addition, it is a tourist destination independent of prostitution. The neighborhood is close to the river, between main streets Silom and Suriwong, and is visited by thousands in the early hours of every evening. They stroll through the street markets, shop a little, and cast shy glances into the sex bars behind, and then they go back to their hotels. Later in the evening, some might sneak back to the bars, where girls, transsexuals, slim teenage boys, or young bodybuilders go-go dance in skintight fabrics. Some girls open twist-off beer bottles with their sexual organs and simulate, or perhaps actually produce, an orgasm. In some boy bars, the proof of orgasm is proudly displayed to the customers. Such is the everyday life of Patpong between ten in the evening and three in the morning.

Occasional tourists lured into the seediest bars end up with a tab they did not expect and may be unable to pay. Most customers know the rules of the game and are careful about ordering drinks whose price they do not know. A "free purchase" of a prostitute for the night or the morning costs little more than the price of one drink, about $9 paid at the bar, but one later pays three or four times as much in the form of a tip. Most clients do so with pleasure. Both girls and boys in Patpong are attractive, polite, and accustomed to dealing with visitors.

Cleo Odzer knew some Thai before she arrived, but she still must have been blessed with a lot of good luck on her first evening of research. On that day she met Pong, the girl who would become her best friend and informant, and she also met her future lover, Jet. Before leaving New York, Odzer told her professor at the New School for Social Research that her aim was to show the best sides of prostitution. Despite her blond hair, she blended in as one of the girls—two years before a torrent of Russian prostitutes made light hair a common sight in Bangkok's red-light districts.

Patpong's gossip mill heated up as the new American girl started a relationship with Jet, who made his living by drumming up customers for a gay bar in the neighborhood. Jet referred to himself as a hardworking pimp, which might sound slightly odd. He certainly was not Cleo Odzer's pimp, since she never prostituted herself. Nor could Jet be considered her gigolo, because he had his own independent income.

Female and male prostitution in Patpong and resorts like Phuket and Pattaya are oriented toward visitors from East and West, and priced accordingly. But high-class prostitutes in Thailand earn hundreds of times more, since they cater to Thailand's military leaders and Japan's richest businessmen.

The majority of the prostitutes, on the other hand, earn one-tenth as much as the girls in Patpong. The twenty thousand prostitutes in Patpong have to be seen in comparison with the three hundred thousand in metropolitan Bangkok and the close to a million Thai prostitutes who live all over the world. The incidence of HIV is highest in northern Thailand, where heroin is readily available and where the friends and clients of the girl prostitutes are for the most part addicted to drugs. The majority of prostitutes in Thailand live in very sad conditions, have few Western clothes, must service several customers a day, and are far from well nourished, lively, and sexy. Academic researchers or journalists from the West are unlikely to fall in love with the emaciated and toothless local sex workers, or identify as a "close friend" a girl from among the HIV-positive of north and east Thailand. As soon as prostitution loses the aura of fairy tale and appears as social misery, the lust weakens. Anybody interested in obtaining the whole truth ought not to ignore this problem—a very real dilemma for the field.

During the 1990s, Yunnan in south China, Laos, the Shan states, and the rest of Burma sent a flood of migrants to Thailand's borders. Hundreds of thousands dreamed about work and money in this rich, industrialized neighbor state. The most lively young girls, especially those with light skin, would be approached about trying their hand at prostitution. Some, naturally, succumbed. In the border areas, some girls might have had ideas about what this entailed, but hardly anyone would have been prepared for how long and narrow the path to a good income really was.

Scarcely a single migrant is wanted in Thailand; it is essential to have an agent if one is to receive pay for work. To cross the most important border in the north, at Mae Sai, and go south to the largest city in the north, Chiang Mai, costs over $50, a large sum for those who do not own so much as a nail in the wall. The agent can also obtain suitable clothing, makeup, shoes, and networking contacts in a brothel. In a very short time, a young person can get involved in a system of dependency that might take years to emerge from. Boys can move on, but few girls dare to or are even capable of doing so. The expenses of transportation mount. At the same time, it becomes more costly and difficult to send money home.

Another stream of young girls flows from Vietnam via Cambodia to Thailand. The Vietnamese still practice the old Asiatic custom of selling a daughter to an agent on a short-term contract, in return for the reduction of one's own debt. Kidnapping, violence, and rape, the worst imaginable introduction to prostitution, are statistically rare, but such reports consistently come from fishing towns in southern Burma. One and all, the girls end up in Thailand, but none of them are to be found in Patpong.

The girls Cleo Odzer befriended were not from Burma, China, or Vietnam; all were from central Thailand. None of them had been raped, kidnapped, or sold into prostitution; they had all chosen their way of life. They were cheerful and self-reflective, and earned enough to visit their home provinces quite frequently. Cleo Odzer got to go along on several family visits. Because she followed only the same paths as her girlfriends, she never came up against the coercion and control that mark the Thai sex industry. Odzer reported truthfully, but described only one segment of Thai prostitution.

Odzer's book gives an apt description of temporary marriages between Asian women and Western men, an institution that continued to feature in Bangkok. Some Western romantics may certainly feel that the bar girl Hoi was fortunate when she met Alex, a shy, passably good-looking, and warm-hearted twenty-two-year-old "Belgian Pygmalion." After their first meeting, Alex decided to move in with Hoi, bought furniture and books, paid for her English lessons, and found her a respectable waitress job. The money his parents had thought would purchase him a car during his studies in Bangkok was used to finance his "family life" with his heart's desire. It is possible that Hoi was never as enthusiastic about the arrangement as Alex. Hoi's family, in Ubon, put a stop to the relationship as soon as they discovered it. There was no money in it, and what would become of all the needy relatives back in Ubon?

In 1987, Allison Murray moved from Australia to Indonesia to do field-work. She was younger and had less life experience than Cleo Odzer, but she seems to have been more professionally ambitious: Her study bears the stamp of sociological and geographical theories and perspectives. The book she later wrote contains a sprinkling of autobiographical details, but her point of departure was not subjective in the same sense as Odzer's.

Indonesia is the largest country in Southeast Asia, and the fourth largest in the world in terms of population. In ethnic, religious, and linguistic terms, Indonesia is so composite that it is more natural to speak of an island empire than a nation, although it has a widely understood national language and a majority Muslim population.

Allison Murray decided to analyze a middle-class nightlife district in the metropolitan capital, Jakarta. Block M is located between a bus terminal and an expensive shopping center frequented by rich Indonesians and foreigners. During the 1980s, a series of American-style bars with pool tables, dartboards, and tranquil music attracted long-term expat foreigners who felt lonely in Jakarta and wanted to talk and drink with people in the same situation, and perhaps pick up some female company for the night.

When the Block M bars closed, between one and two, the remaining customers made their way over to the only place in the area that the police allowed to stay open, the disco in the basement of the Paradise Hotel. It had no cover charge for girls or foreigners, but there was a solid security system. The several hundred prostitutes who frequented Block M were known as the Bintang girls, named after the national beer and the first bar in the neighborhood.

A number of Western-oriented Indonesians also visited Block M, but the girls found their best customers among the expats from Australia and Europe. Clients from Arab countries were considered domineering and brutal. The Bintang girls had little interest in or understanding of typical tourists. One evening Murray's friend asked her to find out how much money an attractive Australian backpacker had in his jeans. When Murray whispered, "Twenty bucks," the girl sneered with contempt.

The Bintang girls took care of their customers' needs either in small rooms near the bars, rented by the hour, or at home. Allison Murray surely got to witness this. In a backyard area sandwiched between modern apartment buildings, in a lot extending only a few hundred square feet, Allison Murray lived with fifty hens and five Indonesian girls in their twenties, three of them prostitutes from the countryside. Murray shared a small hut with one of the prostitutes but heard everything that happened in the other dwellings; whatever she failed to hear, she learned the following morning. Two elderly widows were also part of this little extended family, the owners of both houses and hens. There were no children. One man lived in the backyard colony, a quiet old fellow who owned a tiny tofu factory.

Allison Murray's girlfriends used the mornings for shopping, trimming or coloring their hair, and otherwise making themselves attractive for the evening. They all spoke a certain amount of English and liked to dress according to Western fashion. They had enough clothing to vary their appearance considerably. Jeans with sexy holes could be combined with a beautiful blouse or skintight sleeveless top, depending on the mood.

Despite their apparently modern lifestyle, all of Murray's friends believed in black magic and used talismans and amulets, whether they had been born in Muslim, Christian, or animist villages. Partly because prostitution is officially illegal in Indonesia, the Bintang girls did not dance naked or half naked on any podium. If a Bintang girl got a client, he was not required to pay a fee to the bar or disco owner, but any elderly "auntie" who helped a girl to get a date received 10 percent. Occasionally, and on behalf of the collective, the girls—some of the youngest and newest—had to contribute to the goodwill of security guards, local police, and politicians, generally by means of gratis custom.

Most Bintang girls had had short-term marriages with itinerant foreigners at various times in their lives. Many received support from previous lovers who had returned to their homelands or were on board ships or oil-drilling platforms. Many of the girls visited the Bintang bars only when they were hard up. Almost all preferred long-term relationships with foreigners. Many dreamed of moving abroad with a lover and hoped that a temporary marriage might lead to eternal happiness.

The Bintang girls were independent businesswomen with no employer relationships to the bar owners. They earned up to $50 from each client, and required at most a couple of clients a week when not in a long-term relationship. Most could afford visits home to relatives about once a month. A girl could support up to eighteen family members. They were honored and esteemed at home, although the nature of their work in the city was camouflaged, especially in the Muslim villages.

In the hierarchy of Indonesian prostitution, the Bintang girls were in the middle, between a few well-to-do luxury prostitutes and the poor sisters of the street. Allison Murray wanted to place the Bintang girls correctly in the hierarchy, making comparisons and seeking out other sources. Kramat Tunggak, centrally located in the port district, was the center for cut-rate prostitution. Indonesian officials maintained that the place was a rehabilitation center for ex-prostitutes, but in reality, it was the most undisguised and cheapest sex quarter. In contrast to Block M, the girls in Kramat Tunggak were under direct control of pimps and bar owners, but since drug abuse and violent behavior were widespread among their customers, this gave them a certain degree of protection.

In 1990 there were more than two thousand women prostitutes and six or seven hundred guards, pimps, and bar owners in Kramat Tunggak, ten times as many as in the Bintang area. It has been estimated that the whole of Jakarta has twenty thousand prostitutes, which is a very low number in comparison with big cities like Bangkok, Manila, and Saigon.

The Kramat Tunggak prostitutes were young and uneducated; almost all of them were divorced. But scarcely a single client paid more than $4 or $5 a trick in Kramat Tunggak, less than a tenth of what was earned in Bintang. But only at this low price could poorly paid Indonesian sailors and construction workers be tempted to assuage their burning needs.

Sandra Sturdevant and Brenda Stoltzfus met at a conference about prostitution at U.S. military bases in Asia and the Pacific. Both were then working for Christian organizations, one as an interpreter and the other as a specialist on Asian history. They had also lived and worked among the Filipina prostitutes at Olongapo, a port city in the northern Philippines strategically located just half a mile south of Subic Bay, the largest U.S. military base in Asia in the post-Vietnam period. The two women rapidly concluded that they had done all the necessary fieldwork; the book that came of it seemed almost to develop by itself.

After the United States had won the Pacific war against Japan in 1945, it continued to be the region's military power, despite Japan's ascendancy as the strongest economic one. Although the U.S. almost lost the Korean War and suffered defeat in Vietnam, it continued to dominate Asia and the Pacific militarily. Hawaii, Guam, and parts of the Samoan Islands were American territory, while they had additional bases in Okinawa and Korea. But until 1991–1992, the U.S. military headquarters in Asia were in the Philippines, with Olongapo and Subic as main centers.

About forty thousand men, young and mostly unmarried, were stationed permanently at Subic Bay, near Olongapo. Twenty or thirty miles inland, in the shadow of the volcanic Mount Pinatubo, lay the Clark air field. A few thousand American military personnel were based there.

Sandra Sturdevant and Brenda Stoltzfus had both lived in Olongapo in the late 1980s, when there were seventeen thousand girls working as prostitutes there. The number could double in a matter of hours if rumors of a visit by the fleet reached Manila and the smaller town of Luzon. A fleet visit meant fun on the beaches, all-out partying at bars and discos, and a lot of money in circulation.

Sturdevant and Stoltzfus had lived long enough in Olongapo to know both the city and its women very well. Their book gives an impression of participant observation; their account presents a description of the Olongapo environment as seen through the eyes of a women's group. Sturdevant and Stoltzfus tried to give voice to that stratum of Filipinas who became their best informants: the middle-aged and elderly who lived with the young prostitutes, washed their clothes, prepared food, and looked after the children. In its best parts, this book makes its points from a sincere, grandmotherly perspective.

The single individual who came to life most strongly was Manang, a good-hearted older woman whose life is a slice of Philippines history. Manang was born in the 1930s on the strongly Catholic island of Leyte, which was to become the Normandy of the Pacific war. It was here that General MacArthur and his army waded ashore in October 1944, the historical moment that signaled the beginning of the end for Japan's war. At this important moment Manang was only eleven years old, and she certainly did not hail the Americans as liberators; she was terrified that the foreigners would behave in as dreadful a manner toward her as the Japanese had toward her aunts and cousins two or three years earlier.

Manang and her family stayed hidden in the mountains. They could have saved themselves the effort, for hardly any of the young Filipinas were hurt by the newcomers. On the contrary, if they sang for them or danced with them, they were showered with gifts and money. Manang eventually married a native boy who was an industrious and loving husband. God blessed the couple with twelve children, and their life was one of both exhaustion and hunger. Widowed at fifty, Manang praised God daily that eight of her children were still alive.

It was with her youngest daughter, Lita, that she had the most to do, perhaps because the girl needed her the most. Lita went her own way and experienced poignantly the depredations of factory work and domestic work. Urged by girlfriends, she sought her luck in Manila, then Olongapo. Manang followed her to keep an eye on both her daughter and a niece who had followed Lita's example. It was not long before she had a grand-nephew to care for; sometime afterward she also had a grand-son, Michael.

The agricultural and coastal parts of the central and northern Philippines have been Catholic since the 1600s; the people are hospitable, but in accordance with the pope, birth control, abortion, and prostitution are illegal. This official policy of virtue is full of double standards. Formally, the Olongapo girls were registered as artists and bar hostesses. Clad in bikinis and high heels, they performed elaborate bodily movements, but not what would be considered the dances of high culture.

Despite all the laws, prostitution in Olongapo was big business and very well organized. Bar owners cooperated with one another and with the local police and health officials. Communications with the American military authorities also went remarkably smoothly. All female "artists" were registered by the city authorities, issued identification papers, and submitted to regular health checkups.

The American bases and their need for sexual services caused this provincial city to develop a sex industry much better organized, specialized, and professional than anything to be found in Manila—the capital, with its population of twelve million—or in any of the Philippines' small seaside holiday towns. Olongapo had its own cool, funky bars for African-Americans, stylish jazz clubs where the officers could go out discreetly, country-and-western bars, salsa clubs, and glitzy discos.

In Olongapo, disgruntled customers would get their money back; the bar owner simply deducted the sum from the girl's monthly wage. Any girl who went around in the streets at night without an escort was fined by the local police if she did not show a valid card from the bar where she was registered. That card alone indicated whether she had been legally redeemed from bar work for the evening.

Beer and alcohol were as cheap in Olongapo as anywhere else in the Philippines. A navy man could easily afford to treat a young Filipina to several drinks, something a tourist in Bangkok would have reason to avoid. Payment was never a problem, even though the bar girls took a profit on the drinks and pressed the boys to drink as much as possible. On the other hand, the sum that a young private had to pay later for the girl's services was higher than in Thailand, about $12. It was common to tip when the night or the evening was over.

The Philippine islands are overpopulated, industry is underdeveloped, and the one-sided export of agricultural products attests to dependency upon the U.S. The ruling elite lives on former glory, while the well-educated and Westernized middle class is impoverished. The village and urban underclass live a life one would believe possible only in the movies. Earthquakes, typhoons, and volcanic eruptions occur more frequently than in any other country and constantly throw islands and villages into acute crisis. Many follow a survival strategy that involves one or more family members traveling to the cities or abroad to earn money for those at home, who hardly have enough to eat, while their debts reach staggering heights. When prostitution becomes the solution, it is the girl, the boy, or the relatives who make the decision. Kidnapping, rape, and forced recruitment into prostitution occur extremely rarely in the Philippines.

No Olongapo girl interviewed by Sturdevant and Stoltzfus was sold or forced into prostitution. They all got their start by their own choice or according to advice from girlfriends, relatives, or their mothers. Grandmother Manang reiterated as often as the occasion arose that she was not such a mother; she never condoned her daughter's decision. First and foremost, Manang was a mother and grandmother who deeply loved her daughter and her grandson.

Lita and the other girls from Olongapo's heyday earned on average five or six times more than girls of the same age in the textile industry, and eight times more than domestic servants in Manila. The Olongapo girls earned enough to support themselves and ten relatives in their home province, and they had considerably more pleasure, food, free time, and sleep. Most of them were very lively, indeed—as one venerable saying declares—true daughters of joy. They also had occasion to drink beer and wine, something only upper-class Filipinas could otherwise allow themselves on a daily basis.

The sacrifice was a staggering degree of discipline. The Olongapo girls had to pay fines if they wore slippers instead of high heels; there were fines for being drunk, for being aggressive, for falling asleep on a job unequaled for boredom on evenings when clients were few. The largest fine was levied against a girl who sneaked away to meet a U.S. Marine for whom she had a particular sympathy—either because she hoped for a higher gratuity or because she wanted to save him the expense. It was also possible that she wanted to demonstrate to him and all the other girls, and to God and the whole world as well, that now things were serious. Those who dared to do this played for high stakes. The fines were set high to quell any tendency toward romance. Professional Filipina whores and American military men all were trained to obey orders and control their bodies.

The Olongapo sex industry was marked by a businesslike desire to ensure that both parties behaved rationally and economically but with warmth and sensuality. On this issue there prevailed a general agreement between the top American military officials at Subic Bay and the local sex-industry magnates. What was one to do when it was really the love of a lifetime? To the very end, the man remained in doubt, while the woman gambled with everything.

Filipinas are raised in a more entertainment-oriented culture and have much greater facility with English than other Asians; many are also the product of Catholic church choirs and sing beautifully. It is only a few steps from the religious hymns of the provincial cathedral to American love songs. And perhaps it is the girl singing the song by heart who moves the young U.S. military man the most. Beautiful singing, lots of beer, an intimate bar, and sexy half-naked girls' bodies turn many men to jelly, and some combination of these factors has made Filipinas the most successful of Asian prostitutes at finding Western mates to "rescue" them, frequently to the consternation of the American military authorities.

When a Filipina in one of the small prostitution communities became a mother—whether she was married or in a strong romantic attachment— life could get chaotic. A girl who did not have a mother or an aunt to help with the child, or was not among the fortunate few whose soldier accepted his responsibility, would be forced out of the prostitution community back to her home province. She had few possibilities of finding work and would stand at the end of the line when the head of the family dealt out the money that came home from other relatives. No matter how sweet the young mother, a child of mixed heritage was evidence of a doubtful past and would frighten away a local suitor.

At Olongapo's peak hundreds of girls went home annually to their home provinces with children, destroyed reputations, and gloomy futures, but at the same time, hundreds of Filipinas who were mothers of small children traveled to the U.S. to marry the father of their child and establish residency. Even a young man and a young woman who meet in a hookers' bar in Olongapo can, despite all the rules, experience true love, have children, and spend the future together.

Perhaps it was Lita's bubbly little son, Michael, who contributed most to a seemingly happy ending. They all now live in a small town in Ohio as American citizens. Was this love? Was it chance? Grandmother Manang never did find out. But it was not in her nature to struggle too deeply over it. The only things that gave her life meaning were prayer and trust in God.

Bangkok's Mahidol University has calculated that Thailand's sex industry is worth $20 billion annually. WHO and UNAIDS—the two UN organizations that most explicitly deal with sex and prostitution—have estimated the total number of sex workers in Southeast Asia to be ten million, out of a total regional population of five hundred million.

In the course of the last fifty years, the prostitution market in the East has changed more than has the West's. In Asia, the typical local prostitution customer—as in Europe two generations ago—is a young man between eighteen and thirty who has a burning desire for recreation and release and usually little money to spare. He is an Asian native, a student or a soldier, a sailor or a worker. He is young and unmarried or perhaps lives a little too far away from his lover. The average customers of the Asian prostitution market are younger and earn less on average than do the modern urban inhabitants of their homelands. The sexual supply and demand are driven by supply, for when sexual services are cheaper, many purchase them. In some places, sex is the cheapest form of entertainment.

Rough calculations indicate that about 80 percent of the sex workers in Southeast Asia serve these local clients. The rest of the market is composed of men from Japan, Korea, and Taiwan, students, businessmen, and tourists from the Arab world. Men from the U.S. and Europe hardly make up over 5 percent of the client base of Southeast Asia's sex industry. But when does the West get to read anything about the Asian clients on the sex market? The Western press writes as though it is the West that keeps the whole Asian sex trade alive.

Madama Butterfly seems to have become an archetype, as older myths about Asian women were reformulated in the 1990s with prostitution musicals like *Miss Saigon* and *Patpong*. Thus the tension behind the man from the West using the woman from the East has an almost eternal appeal. But every time we encounter this theme in a musical or a film, the message is double. In one moment the affair is romantic, while in the next, it is sharply focused and remorseless. The result gratifies two different sets of Western needs: dream and romance, remorse and self-contempt.

International aid organizations and Western media are hung up on the same simplified ideas, and both place too much focus on prostitution with Western clients. When the League of Nations undertook its large-scale inquiry into prostitution in the 1920s, its focus was white European prostitutes in Asia and Africa. One might be tempted to draw the comparison to contemporary Western antiprostitution activists, who, unlike Odzer, Murray, and Sturdevant and Stoltzfus, show hardly any concern for the lives and health of Asian prostitutes. They focus solely on the Western male clients, because their main concern is with Western morality.

Many books are available on contemporary prostitution in Asia, but none can be considered a standard or truly scientific work. The publications are too many and too bad, engaged but poor on facts or the bigger picture. Media inquiries into prostitution suffer strongly from this malady as well. The UN bodies and voluntary organizations working with prostitution are consequently hampered by the lack of objective information. Nowhere else in the world is prostitution as prevalent as in Southeast Asia. In almost every village, one encounters mouths fed with food paid for by relatives in the sex industry. If prostitution in any part of the present-day world ought to be given priority, and be studied in depth, it ought to be Southeast Asia.

TWENTY-NINE

FEMINISM AND THE SEX WORKERS' MOVEMENT

Margo St. James was truly a child of the post–World War II period, a late-blooming beatnik and groupie from North Beach, San Francisco. As a law student in the 1960s, she supplemented her income with part-time work as a cocktail waitress at catered parties. At home, her circle of friends smoked marijuana, danced, and tested the new ideals of the time about full sexual freedom.

However, the San Francisco police considered the house she rented a "hippie den" and put it under surveillance. One day someone rang Margo's doorbell. When she answered, a complete stranger asked her if she would accept money for sleeping with him. Utterly flabbergasted, she refused. He then showed his police badge and arrested her for allegedly propositioning him, and she was hauled into court and convicted of prostitution. The judge placed great weight on Margo's ready ability to define the word *trick*. Only a whore could know the meaning of the word, he maintained in his written ruling. After the conviction, Margo was freed and fined, but it came with a heavy burden. All of her secondary sources of income dried up; the rumors always preceded her.

After having seen the law in practice, Margo St. James lost all taste for it as a profession. What became much more tempting was to engage herself in the political work of securing social and legal rights for prostitutes. It was all too easy to identify with them, since she had experienced how badly protected by law even emancipated women were.

In 1970, Margo St. James spearheaded the organizing of the Whores' Masquerade Ball in San Francisco, which generated the capital necessary to start history's first modern trade union for prostitutes. Lawyers, journalists, and social workers, both male and female, supported this initiative, which ultimately resulted in an organization named COYOTE, or Call Off

Your Old Tired Ethics. The howling coyote was symbolic, too: Ranchers blamed this animal for every type of mischief and hunted it down, even though, apart from being a menace to dogs, cats, and chickens, the coyote is a relatively harmless animal.

Margo St. James and many of her contemporaries embraced the word *feminist* and admired pioneers like Emma Goldman, Margaret Mead, Karen Horney, and Simone de Beauvoir—female theoreticians and researchers concerned with sex and gender, sensuality and society. They posed deep and critical questions about history and society, and all of them struggled for freedom up to and including sexual liberation. The emancipation of women had to include a woman's right to both choose and reject men.

Emma "Red" Goldman had worked as a prostitute in New York to provide for her husband and son, and urged others to do the same if they needed to. Margaret Mead had informed her contemporaries about sexual development in non-Western societies, while Simone de Beauvoir observed in 1949: "One must not ask how women prostitute themselves, but rather why more do not do so."

Women's liberation of the 1950s and 1960s in many ways followed this tradition. A woman was considered liberated if she used a diaphragm or birth-control pills: She gave a signal to herself and the wider world that she was setting herself free from her biological role. A liberated woman decided for herself when she would become a mother; accordingly, her sexual relationships could be free of obligation. Any woman with many partners knew the risk of being stamped as a whore, particularly by conservative religious men. The leftist segment of women's libbers spontaneously identified with prostitutes, partly due to the tradition from European Communist feminist elders. It was the Christian-minded male moralists, with their old-fashioned idea of womanhood, who were, they reasoned, the real enemy.

In the 1960s, women's liberation was considered a women's issue and of not much concern for men, although many feminists hoped that men would also try to liberate themselves from the traditional gender roles. It was a good beginning when gay men spoke out on behalf of prostitutes. They also identified with prostitutes, because they, too, lived in a sexual subculture and often had many partners and cruised on the streets. As homosexuals began to work for the decriminalization of gay sex and the right to organize, many feminists considered this a parallel struggle for sexual liberation. "Prostitutes sell their morals, not their bodies. Married women do the reverse," wrote Nicolaus Cybinsky in a slightly patronizing manner. "The prostitute does it with many for money. The housewife does it with one for pocket money" was the slogan of the German cabaret singer Lore Lorentz, who hoped to draw married women into a movement for greater sexual liberation.

Few women's activists in this pioneer phase voiced strong objections to prostitutes. Many showed themselves to be a little naive, however, in believing that as soon as economic conditions improved for all women, and liberation had been achieved, then prostitution and much else they did not appreciate would disappear spontaneously.

Earlier in history, young men from the upper and middle classes in Europe and the U.S. traditionally obtained sexual fulfillment in two different sex markets, and satisfied their sexual and emotional needs with women from different classes.

Students and young functionaries would visit, promenade with, and woo women of their own class before marrying one of them. But until matrimony, they secretly took part in a parallel sex market where they met working-class women, serving girls, and prostitutes.

The average middle-class male had his sexual debut with a waitress, maid, or prostitute. Middle-class women traditionally had no sexual debut—they were virgins until their wedding night. After World War I, better education brought more middle-class women into the workforce, as teachers, nurses, and secretaries. During their school years and early working years, many of them lived in lodgings or boardinghouses. Of course, middle-class men could be more sexually forthcoming with women who lived on their own, if they promised marriage. Some women began to try out different partners in their search for Mr. Right, although fear of venereal disease and pregnancy restrained their ardor; they knew very well it was the fate of working-class women and prostitutes. Especially after World War II, as all fear of syphilis fell away, methods of birth control and increased access to abortion made sexual life freer and more open. Both working-class and middle-class men would, to an increasing degree, find sexual gratification in the same stratum where they looked for their life partners. Differences between the class-specific sex markets were being wiped away, just as other class differences were diminishing in significance.

In the conservatives' view, all women of the West were becoming harlots. As a jest, women activists called one another whores in order to beat back moral prejudice and remind one another of their goal for sexual liberation. During and after World War I, doctors had seen the majority of registered syphilis and gonorrhea sufferers shift from prostitutes to the general population. And just as middle-class women became whores in a playful sense, their sexual habits became competition for professional prostitutes. From decade to decade, prostitution diminished in extent and importance: The numbers of prostitutes went down despite a population increase, and relatively fewer men were partaking of them.

Prostitution lost its former basic functions as pastime and training ground for bachelors. Even more important was that the sex industry lost its most important customer group: Students, soldiers, sailors, and young immigrants could get sex with no strings and no marriage proposal more and more often. The commercial sex market had to adjust to the "deviants" and those who lost out in the general sex market. Prostitution decreased but did not disappear. Instead, it began to specialize and differentiate, to turn toward minority tastes within heterosexual society. Some men had strange or kinky tastes: role-playing, fetishism, and complex sexual games became more important to the sex industry.

On the increasingly unfettered general market, sex was free, although not without costs. This sex market rapidly developed new strategies, rules, and norms. Women were reluctant to go to bed too soon, though they had the desire and the birth control. Simply put, it would ruin their reputation in the eyes of their paramour or their girlfriends. Even though the men did not have to pay for sexual intercourse, wooing and foreplay could be costly and time-consuming. Some of them did enjoy the thrill of the chase and delighted in each new conquest. Others felt that pursuing new lovers was not a very rational use of time, so they continued to buy sex because they found it the most efficient solution.

Unpaid sex is competitive, and it creates winners and losers. Some men never tried to get a woman in bed without a marriage proposal; others got no results for all their efforts. Many lost out for purely psychological reasons. Women's increasing freedom corresponded to an increase in their self-reliance, and later to more sexual pleasure for women.

Others found the more woman-dominant, out-in-the-open sexual culture so demanding and dangerous that their own strength deserted them. Alternatives were found with their own sex and on the commercial sex market. Prostitution's therapeutic function grew to become one of its chief characteristics.

A New York working girl professionally known as Marie spoke of her therapeutic function as follows: "Sex is business, and I do the same thing anyone does who runs a store. I smile and make the customer feel at home, and never get mad the way some ladies do these days. To tell the truth, it is not really me and my body that count. I have to think of the poor sucker who's paying to meet me." Few prostitutes felt threatened by women's liberation. Many female sex workers actually thought their efforts to improve their working conditions were part of what other women called the movement.

Two brutal murders of prostitutes in Lyon, France, in the mid-1970s led prostitute activists to start a high-profile campaign for increased police protection for them. The Lyon police had long supplemented their income through fines levied on local prostitutes. Now, as they began to organize, the police stepped up their fining. Those who did not have the money were jailed. In the end, it was a bitter battle for the whores and their new organization. On June 3, 1975, 150 women sought asylum at the Church of St. Nizier and hung banners out the church windows on behalf of their children. The banners read: "We do not want to see our mothers in prison."

The prostitutes achieved no breakthrough with the French police, but they won total victory in the media. Sympathizers flocked to the church with food and clothing. All of France stood up in solidarity with the Lyon sex workers, and churches in Montpellier, Toulouse, Cannes, and finally even St. Bernard Chapel, in Montparnasse, granted prostitutes' groups sanctuary. The French police sprang into action. In the gray light of dawn, while the sympathizers were asleep outside, the Lyon police tricked one of the priests into opening the door of the church. Forty policemen stormed in and dragged several girls out by the hair. Other churches were emptied in equally ungallant ways. The police may have won the battle, but they lost the war. The long-term effect was an enormous growth in trade-union activities among France's sex workers.

*   *   *

Peter Sutcliffe, known as the Yorkshire Ripper, was on the rampage in England during the same years. In general, the 1970s were characterized by violence conducted by both police and civilians against prostitutes. Sutcliffe told the newspapers, "Whores are filthy bitches contaminating the streets," and he felt that knifing them to death was a positive contribution to society. The public prosecutor's comments about these ghastly murders revealed how deep-seated antiprostitute prejudices were in British society: "What is saddest of all is indeed that some of the murder victims were not in fact prostitutes."

Violence and intimidation can spread fear but also engender solidarity. In the 1970s and 1980s, strong prostitute trade unions were formed in various states of the U.S., in France, England, Australia, the Netherlands, and Germany. Many, particularly the U.S. organizations, followed the paradigm of COYOTE and adopted similarly dramatic names: PONY, PUMA, HYDRA, PASSION, and OCELOT. In Social Democratic Scandinavia, with its state-supported health, education, and welfare, the public sector was so actively involved in social work among prostitutes that self-organizing occurred later there than in other European countries.

The older, the experienced, and the proud set the tone. The best-paid call girls, the very young, and the worst paid were the least inclined to get organized. Seventy percent of the organized prostitutes in England during the mid-1980s were single mothers, a much higher percentage than their overall representation in the sex trade. Obviously, a trade union was a crucial need for prostitute mothers.

The idea about prostitutes' unions was established internationally by the early 1980s, but it did not spread without pain. The first Irish prostitute leader was killed by arson; in Ecuador the brothels instituted a lockout of unionized girls. Brazil, the Philippines, and Thailand soon got significant organizations under way, although they developed more slowly and drew a smaller proportion of the sex industry than in the highly industrialized countries.

The sex workers' main demands were nearly universal: decriminalization, freedom of speech, the right to marry without criminalizing one's partner, the right to travel without a special stamp in one's passport, and the assurance that violent customers will be prosecuted. In most countries where sex workers are organized, they have set up centers for legal assistance and health care. Prostitutes' struggle to keep their children when the social-welfare authorities consider them unfit mothers has also been a top priority.

The feminism of the 1960s regularly raised questions such as: What is women's oppression? What is women's liberation? But more and more energy was expended on strategic and tactical plans to defend, consolidate, and extend power among "correct" women and "correct" positions, just as in more traditional politics. While the slogans from the 1970s about extinction and total battle or the enemy evinced radicalism, the theoretical discussion degenerated. The questions raised by the feminism of the 1970s increasingly became: Who is supporting us? And who is opposing us?

Kate Millett's 1975 *Prostitution Papers* established the boilerplate for feminist analysis of prostitution in the late 1970s, and she steered the debate with an iron hand. But what passed for debate included no problematizing of prostitution as a societal phenomenon; it was limited to a purely strategic discussion. It had become an indisputable assumption that prostitution, like pornography, was an evil to be combated relentlessly. Just as some student groups of the period appointed themselves spokespersons for the workers' movement, Kate Millett expressed herself with full conviction about the interests of all women, even if her supporters were mainly educated middle-class women. The program became fixed, the problems were considered analyzed, and the consensus solutions established as doctrine. The epoch of feminist dogma, myth, and catchwords had arrived.

Women who chose the housewife role over wage work were considered either reactionary or lacking consciousness. Prostitutes were viewed as damaged or bestial, inferior creatures unable to speak or act on behalf of their gender. According to Millett, they were "unconscious as women" and were "driven by instinct, not by thought."

"This is my body and I can do what I want with it" was a standard expression from female activists in the abortion debate of the 1970s. A few prostitutes borrowed this analogy to defend their right to sell their bodies. A French activist who preferred to go public under her professional name, Diana, put it like this: "The whole world is talking about what to 'do about' prostitutes. Christ! Why don't they ask what should be 'done about' journalists or the police? Ever since I first started to rent out my body, I have known it was my business and nobody else's. My body belongs to me. Period." Filipina activist Nelia Sancho, a nationally admired former Miss Philippines who founded the women's organization Gabriela in the early 1980s, and pioneered bridging gaps between prostitute and nonprostitute women, never failed to mention prostitution whenever women's issues were on the agenda. She gave the following version of the analogy between abortion and prostitution by adult women: "Who said that abortion is a good choice, or pleasant? It must be every woman's right to choose prostitution just as much as abortion if she judges this necessary." Few European or American feminist leaders agreed with this. The prostitutes' movement and trade unions were seldom commented upon or supported by the women's movement. The few ex-prostitutes who became feminists chose to keep their pasts hidden. The British antirape activist Sheila Jeffrey bluntly phrased the antagonism between feminists and prostitutes: "Prostitution is the guerrilla training camp and rehabilitation center for sexual terrorists." As the 1970s gave way to the 1980s, the conflict deepened. Historians have described this phase as authoritarian, some even totalitarian.

In 1981, Kathleen Barry, an elegant New York feminist of the Kate Millett school, brought out her book *Female Sex Slavery,* and with this received a degree of world renown. Margo St. James had become nationally known because of her union activities. Kathleen Barry contacted her as she was preparing a conference on prostitution in Rotterdam in 1981, and St. James happily agreed to participate. As she and other representatives for the union-organized prostitutes began their preparations, however, a war was on. The prostitutes proposed that the main goal should be to "focus on the feminist struggle against male violence, and the feminist struggle for self-determination." The hot-button issue turned out to be self-determination.

St. James and her colleagues expected to speak, but, reduced to the role of "resource persons," they were allowed only to answer concrete questions about their experiences. Every prostitute had to leave the podium the second she had been interviewed. The press was informed about this silencing of opinion, but when confronted after the conference, Kathleen Barry answered confidently, "We would do an injustice to our gender if we did not make weak and immature women responsible for their wrong choices." She went on to criticize the groups where she expected to find her closest allies, UNESCO and the World Council of Churches, for "weakness in the struggle against prostitution." But above all, she criticized anyone who dared to view such a way of life as acceptable. The press likes bold speech, and Kathleen Barry's got her proclaimed "Wonder Woman" of the year by one U.S. newspaper.

Margo St. James struck back with a slogan no good journalist could resist citing: "A blow job is better than no job." Did the feminists presume to pressure women out of prostitution because they felt uncomfortable with the idea of paid sex?

Organized prostitution's international umbrella organization, the International Committee for Prostitutes' Rights, held its first congress in Amsterdam in 1985. The next was in Brussels in 1987, together with the European Green Alternative Coalition, an umbrella group for smaller ecological and political organizations in Germany and central Europe. Here, too, Margo St. James was a key figure. "You don't repeat history! Finally something new is happening," the prostitution historian Judith Walkowitz said powerfully at the opening.

The prostitutes had more opponents than allies. The International Abolition Federation, founded by Josephine Butler, was an archenemy. In 1987 the abolitionists held their twenty-ninth conference in Stuttgart under the slogan "Prostitution: A World Problem, a Threat to Humanity." Well-intentioned women from Christian and cultural organizations attended. UNESCO and the World Council of Churches sponsored the conference. By principle, the forum refused to distinguish between the children and the adults of the sex industry; nor did it accept any significant difference between people who voluntarily took up prostitution and those who were forced into it. By its very nature, prostitution in all forms was coercive and enslaving, as bad for adults as for the young. Accordingly, it had to be combated in all its forms and by all means.

Prostitutes were refused entry, but some managed to get in, camouflaged as abolitionists. "They treated us like dogs, but we fought like tigers," one of them said afterward. A thirty-year-old German prostitute managed to make her way up to the podium and shout, "You're just hysterical! I am fed up with all these lies. How can you call prostitution a threat against humanity? It is ridiculous to mix coercion, slavery, and child prostitution with what I live from. I am a free and adult human being!" However, even at this conference, the whores received some public support. The European Green Alternative Coalition sent a resolution declaring the gathering an abomination, saying, "We consider your conference to be a declaration of war against prostitutes and a clear attempt to push forward repressive legislation."

The antagonism between prostitutes and the women who want to save them remains sharpest on the question of the sex workers' nonprostitute partners. Many activists claim that they support the prostitutes but combat their workplaces; they give the women full backing as victims, but take an entirely different tack on their male spouses, who are defamed as whoremongers and criminalized as pimps.

Quite a few prostitutes have grown up with fathers and uncles who are unemployed. But if a prostitute marries a man without work, or if her boyfriend becomes unemployed, she is punished and he criminalized. In the eyes of most Western societies, it is his unemployment that makes him a pimp. Pimping paragraphs forbid any woman who earns money by means of sex to support a man. "A man who wholly or partly allows himself to be supported by a woman who has fornication as her occupation can be punished by a prison sentence of up to two years," according to Norway's current penal code. Most European countries have similar laws, some even worse.

Few modern Westerners have problems accepting that a woman who works in the business sector can have a devoted stay-at-home husband; it is even considered a positive result of the struggle for gender equality. But if a prostitute has a man at home, this is regarded not as equality but as exploitation. A U.S. prostitute commented, "Some of us are in fact proud that we earn enough to support our boyfriends and avoid sending them off to work in a factory where they would only turn sour and get worn out." One has to wonder why prostitutes should be the only exception from the view that any woman (or man) should be allowed to weigh good against bad in their lives.

The question of domestic violence might be the pinpoint of the issue. Hollywood films may have contributed to the popular impression that all prostitute women regularly get beaten up by their lovers. Word travels fast in the world of prostitution about clients with violent behavior. If a woman is beaten by her husband, or suffers another form of domestic violence, it is considered a private matter, just as in the rest of the society. Both medical sources and police reports and numbers given by the prostitutes' organizations point to a higher frequency of domestic violence in prostitute women's lives. But for most prostitutes, violence is the exception, not the rule.

"People think because a girl's been beaten up by her boyfriend, it's because she's not earning enough money. There are other reasons. My boyfriend's threatened to kill me if I go off with another man, so if I get a beating, it's not because he wants money off me, it's because I'm going out with another man," quotes Eileen MacLeod from a court case against the prostitute Carol, on charges of public nuisance. Her neighbors sent the police, not to protect her against domestic violence—for she herself was a criminal and not worthy of such protection—but to get the immoral woman out of the neighborhood. "Every man does it, really," Carol cried, referring to the many violent episodes that occurred in nonprostitute neighboring women's homes without any interruption from the police.

This remark was answered with silence.

Human mating patterns differ a great deal between cultures and different periods of history. In Asia, in the Arab world, in sub-Saharan Africa, the promiscuous male who never marries is a more common phenomenon than in the white West. In Asia, second and third wives are widely accepted despite lacking legal status. Marriage also has lower frequency among African-Americans, a social phenomenon often criticized by white conservatives and some black activists, and which some claim is rooted in slavery.

Whenever married life holds a dominant position in society and ideology, the unmarried males are considered losers in the sex market, unable to get wives or companions. But a growing number of losers allows for more variety among the winners—such as the heterosexual promiscuous male who, by choice, never marries. This pattern is repeated, or reaches its zenith, in the prostitute subculture. The promiscuous stereotype looks far different from the ordinary boyfriend, and is in prostitution named a stable pimp.

The laws make no distinction between faithful and polygamous partners of prostitute women, but female sex workers make it themselves. The
degree of promiscuity or actual polygamy among prostitutes' nonpaying
male sex partners has received little attention in legal, medical, and sociological work on the sex industry. A rough estimate may conclude that stable
pimps account for between 5 and 20 percent of the men whom prostitute
women chose in their free time, and it would be likely to peak among
freelancers or streetwalkers who work outside of organized sex establishments, a category that includes most black American prostitutes.

In the better strata of white society, socially successful, impeccably
dressed, handsome men appear in innumerable women's sexual lives and
fantasies, because the women choose them, in spite of or because of their
reputation. Don Giovanni (Casanova) is perhaps the most familiar Western archetype. The classic stable pimp shows these similarities but also a
more obvious one: size. He is not only more potent physically and sexually than other males, but bigger and stronger.

Men's sex appeal and physical capacities are openly discussed among
prostitutes, and may be more appreciated, too. Some of them do not want
to spend their leisure nights or hours with someone as boring as their clients and prefer to share the local male sex idol with others girls in the trade,
just as some women in the days of the Ottoman harems ended up in those
institutions by choice. For those girls who have not succeeded in finding
the protection of a brothel or other establishment, he affords some protection on the streets.

Big and strong men tend to show their muscles frequently, and even
more in a subculture partly beyond the law. We might expect more violent behavior from pimp boyfriends than from less sexually aggressive and
dominant males, toward weaker males especially. Most of the men who
fight at bars and clubs seem to limit their violence to their own sex; men
expressing their violence toward women rarely fight with men. The laws
of civil society might not protect prostitutes to the same degree as other
women, but to escape these violent men is easy whenever a woman stops
working as a freelance or streetwalker and for a bigger sex establishment,
where her health is of too high a value to be endangered.

The stable pimp is no myth, but the glamour attached to him might
be more representative of the fantasies of the outside heterosexual male
world, which seems intensely preoccupied with the idea that some few men

triumph over all others on the sexual market, without the costs of cash or marriage. Two recent U.S. documentaries about the black pimp subculture, *Pimps Up Hoes Down* and *American Pimp,* have become cult successes. The stable-pimp image, like that of a rapper, athlete, or gang member, is among the few glamorous, powerful images available of African-American men, whether targeted to young black men or to the larger white society.

The rapper 50 Cent recently performed his song "P.I.M.P." on MTV's music awards, accompanied by Snoop Dogg and a group of dancers in clothing and accessories typical to the image of the pimp and streetwalker. A cartoon called "Lil' Pimp," voiced by rappers Ludacris and Lil' Kim, is now in production. The predominance of the stable-pimp image in the media may be based on estimates of the future viewers' puerile sexual jealousy; sociological studies or representative numbers never set the standard in Hollywood.

"To say that a woman sells her body is bullshit. What she does is to give a customer access to her body for a short time, at a fixed price, just as a shrink allows a patient access to his brain for a higher price," a British call girl told the media in 1980. A number of interview-based investigations from the 1980s give the impression that most prostitutes are satisfied with their work. U.S. sociologist Lewis Diana's investigations from 1985 concluded that 60 percent of prostitutes—street hookers as well as call girls—were content with their work. African prostitutes give the same answer. More coercion and dire poverty in the Asian sex industries yield more negative responses. Sociologist Bernard Cohen interviewed an estimated half of New York City's Puerto Rican prostitutes in 1979 and summarized the responses by stating that they had "as women an unusually positive attitude toward their work." The most satisfied stay in the business longer, and the older, experienced, and work-proud dominate the unions. In the 1980s many organizations started to accept transsexuals and male prostitutes.

French prostitute spokeswoman Marie Arrington has maintained that the sex industry's traditional division between two separate markets, the homosexual and the heterosexual, is extinct: "Boys sell themselves until they are no longer sweet enough or do not have tight enough asses for the clients. Then some start dressing up in women's clothing to remain on the market. No way are all men who pay for lads homosexuals; they certainly do not look for someone of their own kind. I often have noticed the same men buying both young boys and young girls."

Transsexual prostitutes find clients among working-class men who would never consider themselves homosexual. In Mediterranean and Latin American countries, sex with males of one's own age or standing identify a man as not only homosexual but outright as a eunuch or a woman, according to the dominating macho codes, while sex with extremely feminine men, teenagers, or transsexuals belongs to a less threatening gray zone. Only a small segment of clients of transsexual or transvestite prostitutes are turned on specifically by sexual hybrids. The phenomenon has another explanation: Strictly speaking, a man who buys a transsexual or a feminine boy can honestly swear that he has not had sex with another woman and consequently has never "cheated" on his wife.

Middle- and upper-class Latin men have a bit more freedom to dabble in homosexuality and the purchase of sex from masculine-appearing prostitutes. But to see a Latin man with a male prostitute much older than twenty is rare, as Latin clients to a much larger degree want absolute control of the sexual act they pay for, according to the ICPR. In Australia, Europe, and the U.S., thirty years of vital gay subcultures have caused greater variations within the male role and beauty standard inside and outside the subculture. Along with the traditional devotion to pretty young men, a noticeable demand has sprung up for muscular, extremely masculine male prostitutes, who seem to remain in demand up to the age of about forty-five, a development in male prostitution almost completely without historical precedent.

According to the standard definition of prostitution, the price has to be bargained before the sexual act. Women's liberation in the West has led to many adult women supporting younger lovers over longer periods; by definition, this makes the young man a gigolo, not a prostitute. Men receiving regular gifts or a permanent salary from female lovers have historically never identified themselves as prostitutes, and many would consider the term a threat to their male egos. Other than in the Roman Empire, hardly any male prostitutes in history—other than those who serve men—have ever been called prostitutes. This, too, has changed in recent decades. "Male whores with female clients is the most recent market in the sex industry. It is growing, but slowly," concluded Canada's foremost prostitute activist, Valerie Scott, in 1990. An avant-garde of Western women may channel their sexuality into isolated, rational, and business-like one-night stands or casual and clearly defined sex-only relationships, a development that may contribute to lessening social condemnation of sex for money. The women who take advantage of such arrangements hold leading positions in business, politics, and administration, and may be said to have fully adopted a traditionally male role in other important aspects of their lives.

Lesbian demand for paid sexual services does exist; it is not only a pure pornographic fantasy, the prostitutes' organizations have more than once informally confirmed. Statistics are hard to come by, however, since such arrangements are highly sensitive issues in the lesbian community (if their participants even self-identify as lesbian) and consequently are bound to occur with extreme discretion. In spite of written references in memoirs by ex-prostitutes, and informal confirmation from the ICPR, no independent researcher has taken up the challenge of gathering or analyzing even tentative statistics yet.

Male demand dominates prostitutes' lives and in a thousand different ways marks their profession; only those men who identify as prostitutes are found in the prostitutes' organizations and unions, and almost all of them tend to have a purely male clientele. Just as in all previous periods of history, the majority of male prostitutes serve their own sex. The best-paid male prostitutes make far better money than their best-paid female colleagues; while this may occasionally create small frictions within the profession, it has not significantly hindered common organizing.

Interviews with young male prostitutes do reveal an astonishing fact—that one out of three male prostitutes earning income from sex with men prefers women in his free time. The interpretation of this fact may cause highly political debates among gays. In any case, it gives more weight to the argument that prostitution and acting are close cousins.

The best-paid call girls and boys in the world travel first class across the globe to their wealthiest clients, well aware of the optimal pleasure—sexually, and in conspicuous consumption—the clients get as they are flown in. Prostitutes with more modest ambitions find it satisfactory to be based in the richest country in which he or she has connections, and to move from one country to another is quite common. Prostitute migration, well known from the end of the nineteenth century and the years between the two world wars, reached a new high at the end of the twentieth century.

"At home in Bogotá I was promised work in a club with a swimming pool. But here I only have a little room. Oh, how I envy the Dutch women for their mastery of the language," Colombian Conchita confirmed to an activist in 1994. Conchita arrived in the Netherlands on false papers and expected to be threatened. No way would she return to Colombia. Of course, she did want out of the sex industry, even without legal papers. Conchita was stuck in a vicious circle, like most illegal immigrants.

Low-end prostitution has always had greater turnover and a higher rate of foreign labor supply than well-paid call girls, from whom appearance and skill are required, linguistically, physically, and sexually. Low-end prostitution started to suffer from serious recruitment problems during the late 1970s, in both Europe and the U.S., where few now entered the trade without the idea of reaching its high end. The segment of heroin addicts in Europe, and crack addicts somewhat later in the U.S., mostly worked on their own and were not trusted by the management of brothels and massage parlors. But client demand remained stable, and many cared little about striking looks and intelligent conversation; they wanted a female body at a cheap price. As the demand for cheap prostitutes grew and recruitment failed, the vacancies had to be filled with imported foreign labor.

Prostitutes migrate according to the same pattern as other labor; the increasing hurdles put up to stop the poorer segments of society from crossing borders cannot stop the migrants with the strongest drive. In all economic sectors where cheap immigrant labor is utilized, much of it is illegal. Labor migration in itself must be examined separately from illegal migration. Illegal migration, with forged documents and the like, must be looked at in light of jurisprudence and criminology, legal migration for the purposes of work, according to the standard patterns it follows.

All migration occurs in stages, with its first stream away from the village and toward the towns, from there toward the cities, the coast, and abroad. The main route stretches from semi-industrialized countries to the largest and richest nations (and often to a wealthier country with old colonial ties to the home country). From Brazil, Uruguay, Argentina, and the Caribbean, people travel to the U.S., Germany, and France. Many of the most recent U.S. immigrants, from Cuba, Puerto Rico, Mexico, and the

South Pacific end up in prostitution. West African women seek work in the sex industries in France and Belgium. A stream of Asian sex workers flows into Europe from Mumbai, Calcutta, and Bangkok. Some men, and still more women, abandon Hong Kong and the Philippines for Europe, Australia, Japan, and the U.S. with the plan to sell their bodies only during their first year in this new world. The emigration of sex workers causes vacancies in the sex business of the semideveloped countries they leave behind, so bars and clubs fill with new migrants from outlying districts or poor neighboring countries of the same region. Cheap brothels in Thailand recruit from Laos, Vietnam, and Cambodia, from Myanmar and Hunan in southern China. A family from the countryside of north Thailand or Vietnam with an obedient daughter in the sex industry can buy a television set before their neighbors—a message to the rest of the village about what is the best solution when the crops fail.

Annually, hundreds of thousands of new prostitutes stream into India's large cities from Nepal and Assam and India's other interior and coastal regions. Hong Kong's sex industry traditionally was based on girls from Communist China. Manila girls with the urge for quick money go abroad, while the girls in the metropolis's own trade come from outlying islands in the Visayas. Brothels in Brazil and Argentina recruit from that continent's poorest regions; poor Arab boys prostitute themselves in Tokyo. Poland and the Ukraine send hopeful sex workers of both sexes westward.

Whenever prostitutes of another skin color are discovered in a neighborhood, it may reinforce the locals' moral condemnation of prostitution. Many feel that foreign and racially different prostitutes are tangible symbols of a world that is becoming a moral cesspool. Political activists who already condemn prostitution find it additionally immoral for a sex worker to cross a national frontier. Both key legislators and engaged women activists zealously declare that particularly strong initiatives must be taken to prevent the migration of prostitutes. It is, therefore, a worldwide custom for migration authorities to physically mark prostitutes' passports to prevent them from traveling abroad. ICPR and other groups regard such measures against prostitutes as classic violations of basic human rights. They naturally defend the sex workers' right to travel the way others can, and combat all specific restrictions linked to either lifestyle or occupation.

*   *   *

In 1995, Kathleen Barry once again received intense attention from world media for her book *The Prostitution of Sexuality*. She stressed the politically charged nature of her perspective by systematically describing adult, self-chosen prostitution as willing sex slavery. At her book party, she deplored the fact that there were still prostitutes naive enough to believe that their immorality could be acceptable. Prostitution by nature, she argued, convinced men that all women were sexually available, for free or by purchase. The logical next step was violence in marriage and rape on the streets. The threat of prostitution placed all women in bondage and slavery.

Ardent opponents of prostitution have taken to constantly introducing new, negatively charged terms in their speeches and slogans against prostitution—a strategy that is highly mediagenic and creates the impression of ever worsening conditions. This strategy can even increase their political influence and, not least, harvest more funding for their organizations. Accordingly, Indian temple prostitution recently has started to be called ritual rape, and voluntary prostitution named *sex slavery*. With such emotionally and politically charged terminology, illegal immigration of sex workers may be called people smuggling, and all blame may be placed on the backers involved in this trafficking.

Human trafficking does exist; women and men are transported across borders like sacks of mail—gagged, handcuffed, or, especially for males, drugged unconscious. This phenomenon is known along Thailand's southwest frontier. Burmese girls are doped close to the border and often do not regain consciousness until they wake up in Bangkok and, out of fear, end up obeying the brothel keeper. Such smuggling accounts for less than 1 percent of the region's sex migration, according to the UN International Organization of Migration (IOM).

It is absurd to speak of human trafficking as Philippine nationals fly to Japan to serve clients who pay ten times more than those at home. Along an equally classic labor-migration pattern, Moscow prostitutes move to Thailand, Germany, or Norway. They normally have to borrow the money for the ticket at the highest rate of interest, but that does not make the travel less voluntary. And while it is true that immigrants in prostitution, as in other fields, tend to earn less than native-born workers, the inaccurate notion of such coercion being ubiquitous must be credited to the hyperbole of activists, rather than the facts of social anthropology.

A 1999 IOM report on the illegal migration of prostitutes between Vietnam, Cambodia, and Thailand concluded that almost all these women and girls traveled alone or with family members. There were a few poorly organized "coyotes." The sex smugglers, or male local helpers, made only a small percentage of the money invested by the illegal migrants; the rest ended up with the police and immigration authorities.

The sale of daughters is an age-old practice in East Asia and Vietnam; limited-term contracts are the rule. When Vietnamese mothers sell their daughters to brothel owners from neighboring countries, they do as their maternal ancestors have done for centuries in calculating the suffering of their daughters against the survival of the remaining family members. The Western moralist argument against the evil of prostitution fails to account for the starving relatives the prostitute migrants intend to feed.

Prostitution in the third world must be analyzed as a housekeeping strategy, not an individual choice. A Western volunteer or paid aid worker who analyzes the roots of the institution and the social and economic misery in the local communities will almost always refrain from stigmatizing the solution, as long as there are no alternative economic opportunities.

Prostitution takes on an infinitely more negative aspect when the daughter offered on behalf of her family, or kidnapped into the industry, is underage. In addition, the likelihood of a return home after a stint in the sex industry is radically lower for girls under the age of seventeen. Prostitute unions and mature prostitute women readily support this view; ultimately, it can be accepted in traditional communities, too. Child prostitution in the third world is a scourge that can be limited, maybe even eliminated.

But when a realistic approach loses ground and the field gets taken over by agitators who lump child prostitution together with all prostitution-related work and oppose it all, all local support gets lost. These are the main reasons behind the tensions among the different UN organizations and NGOs in the field, between agencies who work with prostitutes and the agencies working against them.

Sexual child labor must be combated as an issue distinct from prostitution, or along with other forms of child labor. To force underage children to work is also unconscionable; the working hours may be just as long, and, depending on the work, the rate of illness and the risk of an early death even higher. Mining and industry base themselves to a much greater degree on the doping, violent coercion, and smuggling of children than does the sex industry. Such forced migration occurs almost daily and must be counted among the worst injustices imaginable, but very few smuggled children end up in prostitution. Nevertheless, quite a few nongovernmental volunteer organizations and even some exceptional UN reports systematically use the term *smuggling* or *trafficking* of women and children as a reference to prostitution in general, thereby establishing a close association between children in the sex industry and prostitution, an elision that is both inaccurate and offensive. A single reference to child prostitution gets these activists twice the press coverage and much more financial support for their particular organizations, and diverts attention from children involved in other forms of labor. Because child sexuality is so troubling, both the media and the authorities lose interest in forced child labor in mining and other industries. Sex always sells best—including to politicians and bureaucrats.

Beautiful twenty-seven-year-old Lisa from Manila became an unparalleled sensation in the Dutch media when she grasped the microphone during a 1987 parliamentary hearing on the smuggling of humans and thundered: "Stop this abomination!" Lisa herself immigrated illegally in 1981, on the promise of work in a respectable beauty parlor. Bad luck landed her in a seedy bordello. But salvation was not far away; a young farmer instantly fell in love with the sweet girl, helped her escape, and married her. Love, luck, and good helpers soon got Lisa the good life she had traveled to the Netherlands to obtain.

Legal migration from third-world countries became increasingly complicated during the 1980s; for certain nationalities, like those of the Philippines, a visa was required to most countries. Only a few hopefuls obtained visas, since every tourist journey was suspected to be an illegal immigration. But all the various obstructions might be gotten around with false passports and fake documents for a tourist visa; and a girl working as a prostitute had the same opportunity to remain abroad after her visa expired as did a sailor, construction worker, or maid. The sex industry, with its inherent fraud and criminality, rarely favors legal solutions to such stumbling blocks.

Like any other illegal migrant, Lisa was dependent on others as she made her way from Manila to Amsterdam. She was twenty-one years old, with a high school degree and a truly admirable mastery of English. Could she possibly be ignorant of what every other Filipino maid or oil worker from Hong Kong to Kuwait knows so well—that Filipinos always need visas and are met with suspicion from immigration authorities all around the world? As Lisa later chose to see it, all her contacts in Manila had been bad men full of lies and false promises, while she herself was naive, good-hearted, and ignorant about the world. Lisa's story, like a Hollywood movie, seemed a battle between good and evil, with good luck intervening every time she needed it. She lucked out again when, after her marriage ended, she met a group of activists out to combat prostitution and illegal migration.

Disputes about immigration politics are extremely polarized. Some oppose or want to restrict immigration to protect their own standard of living; those who are most concerned about living conditions in poor and war-torn countries desire an open immigration policy with little or no consideration about the consequences for life in their own country. What of Lisa the media darling? Would she like to make immigration easier for women in her own situation? Would she like to spare them the problems she went through? Oh no! Third-world girls with expectations of a new life in the first world could not count on Lisa. Her looks and charm may have contributed to her fame, but it was her attitude toward foreigners that made her a star. Her main argument was for better border controls. Secondly, she demanded strong penalties against everybody who gave assistance to illegal migrants. In 1990 she and her supporters took legal action against the brothel owner she had worked for in Amsterdam, and won. Next they filed suit against her former helpers in Manila, on the charge of people smuggling. She lost this case. Meanwhile, television programs and magazine articles about Lisa sprouted like toadstools after rain. Though her Filipino helpers escaped punishment for helping her migrate, they were vilified in the press. Her Dutch helpers, the activists, got a better return on their investment.

While the sex market in the West has changed character from decade to decade, the changes in Asia have been fewer. Asia's sex industries are, like the West's, patronized mostly by local clients, but the Asian market also has a significant tourist clientele, especially in countries where tourism is flourishing. Vacation, recreation, leisure, and sex are closely connected, but in most tourist destinations, local noncommercial sex is rarely available to the average Western male. A young male surfer from Australia who vacations in Southeast Asia has to choose among Scandinavian, Australian, or German girls, or paid sex. The Filipino, Thai, or Balinese beach boy he rents his surfboards from during the day is not in a much better position. He might have better access to native girls, but without serious promises, he has to pay. Free sex is to be obtained only from a Western girl. In the eyes of the locals, such females are not only sluts but stupid, too.

Tourists of both genders get more for their money in Southeast Asia: Some buy clothing, jewelry, and watches; some women get free love, if drinks and gifts to the beach boy are excluded, but the horny male has to pay cash. Men who could not countenance paid sex at home do so abroad because it is cheap. The low price has to be explained by the local economy, worker surplus, and easy recruitment among women in the outlying areas or in the neighboring country or province. But the sex industry acts like the tailoring business; new market niches are created for tourists where prices rise above the local market.

Three out of four men between the ages of twenty and fifty who have visited Asia or Africa have paid for sex; the statistics show no significant variation between those who temporarily work in the region and the regular tourists. Among the nontourists, military and maritime personnel have the highest numbers; in the latter category, there seem to be no differences between levels of income or professions. The figures show a correspondence between many sex partners at home and abroad; to put it in terms from the market economy, the winners in the sexual home market dominate the losers with sex in foreign lands. But men who have little to no sexual experience at home have remedied this with several partners in the third world. This creates a sort of social argument for a worldwide sex market. The young and the unmarried males dominate; in historical perspective, this is just as it has always been.

In the sex industries in some poor Southeast Asian and African countries—like Cambodia by the mid-1990s—observers stated a phenomenon they named boredom inflation. As, periodically, the supply of girls became very high, the price for one sex encounter became cheaper than a bottle of beer or a movie ticket. Young men went to the brothels almost more out of boredom than physical need. There was nothing else to do in the evening at that price. The prostitutes' demand for the prices to rise is easy to understand. All sex workers want to improve their quality of life, save money, or support their relatives. If they do not manage to do so, both they and the business have a problem. Union-organized prostitutes lobby to raise the price for sex encounters in poor countries, and for related issues: alternative workplaces for young girls who would otherwise turn to prostitution, and alternative leisure, sports, social, or cultural activities for the local young men. Neither cheap nor bored customers are good for business.

A stable income and fewer customers per day enable better sleep, meals, personal hygiene, better health in general. Foreign demand always causes prices to rise. But the Western clientele accounts for only 10 to 20 percent of the surplus, according to figures from Southeast Asian countries, and East Asian foreign clients occupy a similar share of the market. There are few statistics available showing the profiles of the local clients. One tendency is clear: Young men dominate the provincial low-price brothels; adult and married men tend to patronize the midprice institutions in the cities or near the high-priced red-light district.

Most research on the Southeast Asian sex industry has focused on the Western (minority) client segment. This might be seen as lacking interest for the sex workers and their region, but it has an open theoretical base in slogans about third-world prostitution being derived from first-world demand. It is true that prostitution, centuries ago, was a cultural implant from Europe and East Asia to sub-Saharan Africa and Southeast Asia. But for at least a century, local customers have been the dominant social base of the sex industry, measured in number of clients or in purely economic terms. The Vietnam War and Western military bases have contributed to growth and further adjustments to Western tastes, which have again facilitated the access to paid sex for men who visit those countries for recreation, and added a surplus to the gross national product in poor countries.

Short flight times and cheap tickets have contributed significantly to the establishment of a world sex market. The past two decades have been marked by a previously unknown phenomenon in the travel business: package tours to Southeast Asian red-light districts, including guides to the girls. The Western participants are well over thirty and tend to lack experience since they live mostly in rural districts where no commercial sex is available. Ultimately, sex is an activity and not a disease. If a sex tourist should be ascribed a particular predilection or psychological disposition, then you could call most Western males abnormal, or, rather, all men in history.

A population imbalance between the sexes has been common through-out history. It is much greater in rural areas than in the cities. In isolated European or American backwaters, in the mountains and along the coast, a surplus of unmarried men is left alone: The women have left for the cities and refuse to move back. Australia's census still shows an absolute male majority because of its open immigration policies, since young males always make up the majority of immigrants, often on a journey for a bride.

Cheap fares and quick travel have facilitated not only cross-cultural sex but cross-cultural marriages. Lonesome young or middle-aged men with little success or bitter experiences regularly experience much better luck if they open their search to a third-world country. Southeast Asian women are especially well known for their tender care and soft-spoken housekeeping, and will consider a less good-looking low-income West-ern weakling and appreciate his modest income. Many Eastern European women also seem to find their dreams come true in a marriage to a man from the West. Marriage bureaus might offer necessary help and can, in this respect, be included among the phenomena labeled as sex tourism. But Western newspapers are also full of personal advertisements for marriage, not to mention online personals, and many a man exchanges letters with his possible future bride for a long time, without any interference from a bureau, and finally travels abroad to test his real feelings. The result might be a happy marriage, but the husband often has to face racist assumptions and accusations of "yellow fever," while his wife might suffer from end-less implicit or explicit hints about her past.

It is an old and widespread prejudice that all foreign girls are ex-prostitutes, and that a man who finds his wife in a foreign country cannot experience real love. Cross-cultural marriages overwhelmingly dominate the total number of marriages in which the couple first met in a sex estab-lishment. In these cases, the husband is likely a soldier or a sailor who knew no other places to meet girls in his early mating days. But to make general statements about all cross-cultural marriages represents a misunderstand-ing of male feelings and other national cultures, where sex before a mar-riage proposal may be inconceivable for the majority of the female population. These misconceptions continue to flourish on a general fear of everything foreign and the widespread though somewhat rational tendency for skepticism toward anybody with a mysterious history. It is worse that the vast majority of literature on sex tourism repeats and strengthens these prejudices with a mixture of ignorance and regular falsification of available data. Most of the literature classified as sex tourism is a mess of dogma, assumptions, and hypothesis, based on loosely cited anecdotes from random interviews and travel literature.

Demographers, migration researchers, and epidemiologists have far more reliable knowledge about these complicated matters, but they seldom make their arguments in a mediagenic political or public forum, and as scientists, they take care to speak precisely. As a result, the false information lives on, occasionally finding its way into reports and political documents in the international arena.

One mind-boggling demographic fact made its way out of the close circle of the world's population experts several years ago. China's one-child policy and the abortion of girl fetuses have produced an enormous surplus of male children. Demographically, there are fifty million more Chinese men reaching sexual maturity than there are women of the same age; we can predict that China will soon exhibit a demand for sexual services and mail-order brides such as history has never seen.

What right have the dogmatic adherents of true love in the homeland to refuse so many men sex outside their own national borders? Some may find satisfaction in homosexuality, others will come to terms with celibacy, but neither of these alternatives will provide satisfactory solutions for all. International migration and sexual politics seem destined to be intertwined for some time to come.

Since World War II, the international pharmaceutical industry and the worldwide spread of illegal drugs have become two increasingly important forces in the modern world. Even legal drugs have created arguably as many new problems as they've solved. But hardly any study has undertaken the ambitious goal of analyzing legal and illegal drugs together.

Sex workers function as both pariah and avant-garde. Exposed to many diseases (physical and psychological) and much psychological pain, they are ahead of the rest of society with regard to illegal drugs and the medical establishment. After years of heavy medication in the war against syphilis, sex workers became front-runners in the use of preventive and prophylactic medicine. Illegal abortions have flourished among prostitutes, and they started experiments with sex changes and plastic surgery long before these phenomena gained their limited present acceptance. A minority subculture of male bodybuilder prostitutes in the U.S., Australia, and parts of Southeast Asia uses anabolic steroids.

Some data about the use and abuse of legal and illegal drugs and other intoxicants, including alcohol, are available from medical and police reports. But these sources cover mainly the lower-priced segment among sex workers, who are less likely to hide their profession or to have access to private medical care. Interview-based research and information from the prostitutes' organizations may add valuable information, but these data, too, have been accused of bias, this time in underestimating the use of intoxicants. Prostitutes assume names to meet clients, they fake their orgasms, and they constantly play cat and mouse with the police. They work under extreme control inside sex establishments but live beyond the social norms of their neighborhoods and may not be considered the most reliable informants about their alcohol and drug habits. Hardly any of the interview-based reports have done a medical test to double-check personal information.

Even accounting for this statistical unreliability, one blunt generalization seems to be accepted inside and outside the sex industry, in medical circles, and among researchers: The sex industry worldwide is a subpopulation with higher degrees of the use and abuse of drugs and intoxicants than the general population, but it still varies according to age and region.

A famous 1985 study by Lewis Diana included statistics on intoxication habits among unionized U.S. female sex workers, stating 4 percent heroin abuse and 2 percent cocaine abuse without overlap between these socially distinct subgroups. For the vast majority, a daily intake of combinations of alcohol, amphetamines, marijuana, sleeping pills, and antidepressants was normal. This was before crack made its way to a new subgroup of female abusers, mostly black. The picture of Western and Eastern Europe seems compatible, though the lack of cocaine and crack steers users to higher use of amphetamines and heroin; in Africa the use of recreational drugs among sex workers has been given low priority on a research agenda fully occupied with sexual disease. The Asian and Southeast Asian sex industries don't resemble Europe, partly because the almost nonexistent intoxication habits among the Asian female population, as well as the strict discipline of the sex industry, continue to dominate over the urge to use drugs, so the rare drug user tends to intake relatively moderate amounts. Heroin is nonexistent in the Philippines, where crystal meth is more common, slightly more similar to a U.S. pattern than a European one. In mainland Asia, the low price of heroin is compensated with fear of its dangers, not least due to observance of male lovers and relatives and the exchange of information among women in the trade.

ICPR and other prostitute organizations make no effort to hide the fact that alcohol and recreational drugs add new risks to the already unhealthy work environment. The intake of light drugs seems to have found a use before work, to motivate for the job, to better the performance, and to minimize the burden of fantasy play. After a night's work, the prostitute is confronted with her colleagues' or boyfriend's demand for fun, and her own need to make sure her real-life happiness overshadows the fake happiness of work. At Western parties, alcohol may be mandatory, and drugs easy to obtain and accept, so the best of intentions from earlier in the day can be lost.

In spite of the collective worries about the long-term effects of drug and liquor abuse, all organized prostitutes criticize a recent stereotype as unrepresentative of the profession: the heroin junkie dying in the streets, almost too familiar from movies and documentary novels. Heroin-abusing young prostitutes account for a substantial part of those who come in contact with the police and health authorities around the world. Both sexes demonstrate the same pattern: The heroin abuse precedes the sale of sex, which does not start until dependency forces them into the streets. After a few years' practice, their time is up; during their working years, the network to others in the profession is very limited, and hardly any heroin junkies join prostitutes' organizations. They usually underprice themselves and are accused of destroying the market and the general working conditions of nonaddicted prostitutes. Only in exceptional cases does heroin addiction develop among prostitutes with experience in the trade. This demonstrates that solidarity and mutual responsibility inside the sex industry has its clear preventive side effects, far beyond questions about income.

In the decades following World War II, modern medicine neutralized syphilis and gonorrhea and much of the fear of venereal diseases. But the two diseases, as well as chlamydia, remained widespread, particularly among poorly paid prostitutes in parts of the world where health services were primitive. In the early 1970s, only 20 percent of U.S. and European men with venereal disease contracted it from prostitutes, while the number in Asia and Africa was 80 percent. Western prostitutes were at that time extremely health-conscious; their public-health systems had more success among sex workers than in the rest of the population. Among U.S. prostitutes, traditional venereal diseases had a frequency of infection of 5 percent in the mid-1980s, while the rate among female university students was 25 percent.

By the early 1980s, when AIDS entered the public eye, the world had a new and greater worry, and the almost forgotten sex industry started to regain its traditional attention. The prostitutes were, despite popular belief, not a major cause of AIDS infection in the early years of the epidemic. Interestingly enough, the prostitutes of the West practiced safe sex many years before AIDS reached the gay male culture, safe-sex campaigns were instituted, and condoms started to be distributed by aid agencies. In 1980, three years before the AIDS virus was identified, Margo St. James stated: "Condoms establish private life . . . it is a method for prostitutes to distinguish between work and play!" AIDS is a life-threatening disease but significantly more difficult to transmit than other venereal diseases. It required a very promiscuous lifestyle to develop its epidemic character, and such was found in the gay ghettos of the U.S., Europe, and Australia. While female prostitutes might have between five hundred and fifteen hundred partners annually, as a world average according to estimates from WHO, UNAIDS, and ICPR, the average client had very few partners a year, rarely more than ten—with some exceptions—and so exposed his prostitute partner to fewer tertiary contacts.

But the real infection risk becomes much higher when the internal-exchange effect between the milieus is taken into consideration. The gay ghettos were very tightly connected with several hundred thousand mutual visitors or migrants; the industrial-sex enclaves were quiet and isolated, with few migrants and even very few clients visiting multiple sex zones in one year.

As the total history of the AIDS epidemic has been reconstructed, it has been stated beyond reasonable doubt that the virus, before it reached the sex industry, penetrated a third and more susceptible subculture: heroin addicts, from whom the virus was passed through the sharing of needles.

During the early years of the epidemic, hardly any sex workers were infected, not even in Africa. Contemporary and retrospective medical research and reports from WHO and UNAIDS confirm this. One reason was the widespread misinterpretation of patient information; many of the infected preferred to say—and some believed—that they had been infected in a whorehouse. In any case, they avoided sharing other unpleasant facts with the physicians and their relatives: homosexual experiences or inject-able drugs.

Ultimately AIDS infested the sex industry, mostly as heroin-abusing male partners of prostitutes infected the women. The prostitutes started to pass on the virus to non-condom-using male clients. Just as the research-ers of the West began to become familiar with this transmission pattern, it repeated itself in East and southeastern Africa toward the end of the 1980s, when it started to spread more rapidly than in any previous geographical area. By the late 1980s, 3 to 4 percent of Europe's prostitutes had become HIV positive, while the U.S. percentage was 5 or 6 percent. The com-parative numbers from Africa were almost beyond belief, up to 80 percent in certain areas.

Antiprostitution activists widely propagated the notion that sex tour-ism caused AIDS in Southeast Asia; this should be taken as the ultimate proof of the total neglect for scientific fact in this type of literature. AIDS was established in Asia much later than the observers of the epidemic had feared and predicted. For a couple of years, it seemed restricted to the river systems in southern China, where heroin was transported from the moun-tains and east toward the coast. But AIDS finally reached Bangkok and slowly made its entrance to the sex industry, again with male heroin ad-dicts and needle sharers as the middlemen.

Attempts to stop or diminish the spread of the virus have been wide-spread internationally, with propaganda for the use of condoms a disputed spearhead of many campaigns. Condoms are a necessary defense against AIDS and other infections, but many countries have limited access to them. Some have insisted that they encourage immorality, while others empha-size that condoms hinder natural insemination.

Opposition to the use of condoms is unfortunately common among clients of prostitutes, much to the exasperation of the professionals. This clash in attitudes between female sex workers and male clients is at its sharpest in sub-Saharan Africa, where safe-sex campaigns have made a deep impression on the professional women but fall on deaf ears as far as their clients are concerned. All evaluations, all studies in the field, communicate the same despair as did this experienced Hausa prostitute: "Men with both wives and children . . . come here and say, 'I'll give you so and so much more if you do it without'. . . . Ugh, it's like eating candy with the wrapper on!" Not only among African males, but also across race in the West the avoidance of condoms is far too common.

The capital-accumulating African woman prostitute had been an archetype of the postwar period. For decades, black African prostitutes had been prominent in their societies, to the surprise of Western observers. During decolonization and national consolidation, many former prostitutes could be found working as political activists, and as experts on housing and health matters. During the 1970s, prostitution ceased to be as prestigious or remunerative, but it remained an attractive option. Information about AIDS-related health costs and high mortality had an astonishingly low influence on the recruitment to prostitution in Africa; many females still view it as the only route to a self-determined life. Fati, a Hausa, married and divorced three times and now a prostitute, put it like this in 1988: "As a wife I got beaten. When I sell sex, I get paid. . . . Go back to the village to find a new husband? I have to plow. I have to haul water. I have to cook. I have to do the whole job. Ha ha ha! No. No. No! Things are much better for me here in the city." Africa's AIDS has aggravated an existing crisis in society, with its poverty, underdevelopment, and lack of access to health care, and, in the sex industry, with its poor working conditions.

Western HIV-positive gay men have defended the right to continue having sex. Similar demands from female prostitutes have neither been understood nor won acceptance. In most countries around the world, authorities have been quick to come up with initiatives aimed at producing an HIV-free sex industry. Generally, consideration for the client has been placed ahead of concern for the worker, a bit of an ethical inconsistency but not surprising.

In several U.S. states sex workers are exposed to forced tests for HIV whenever they are arrested, and several third-world countries practice mandatory testing for all prostitutes. In countries that practice registration, HIV-positive women lose their license; in most countries, they are forcibly removed from the prostitution district. Semilegal initiatives have closed down establishments where there is a high incidence of HIV. In smaller countries, pictures of HIV-positive prostitutes are broadcast on TV as a sort of customer service. Many of these initiatives may be viewed as violations of basic human rights, and they run directly counter to the AIDS-preventive policy advocated by WHO, UNAIDS, and most NGOs; they force infected prostitutes underground and severely undercut health education, the use of condoms, and the control of the epidemic. Prostitutes' rights organizations and a couple of international organizations, like WHO and ILO, have tried to advance such arguments but without much success.

AIDS remains a world problem. The number of newly infected AIDS patients has remained high in Africa. In the West, they are consistently low. In countries like India, Thailand, and Cambodia, AIDS has reached considerable proportions, but in spite of the late arrival, health institutions have major problems with handling the diseased. The contrast between possible treatment and eventual medical support remains most marked in the world's poorest countries. Many good medicines are available on the international market, but they are priced too high for an underpaid prostitute. AIDS-sick women and unsuccessful safe-sex campaigns mark today's Africa to a grotesque degree; the continent remains the worst proof of the Western world's limited attention and commitment. AIDS has lost most of its former scare effect on Western governments' aid budgets, as well as most of its media power, so it will go into history with a dying African prostitute as its most vivid metaphor.

As the world passed from one millennium to the next, the Butlerian tradition of propaganda for war and the total abolishment of prostitution as a social evil still has innumerable adherents, even on the left. The dominant trend worldwide is, however, the willingness among politically and socially concerned women to assist prostitutes without any subtext of saving them.

In Western Europe, the organized prostitutes have worked hard to establish an open dialogue with women outside the trade. Belgium and the Netherlands have many cooperative organizations for women: For example, the Red Thread, which organizes professional sex workers, is complemented by the Pink Thread, which organizes their nonprofessional friends. A Belgian middle-class housewife and member of the Pink Thread summarized her recent experiences like this: "The fact is, I had never really thought very much about prostitution before. It was as though prostitutes lived on another planet. They were the sort of ladies one read about in the newspaper when they were murdered and so on. . . . Now I have had both strippers and porno actresses living under my own roof! They say they like what they do. So should I let loose on them and tell them to quit? My God, I'm certainly not their mother!"

The contrast between moralistic feminism and a realistic approach to the field of prostitution is still easy to detect in the most distant corners of the world. The abolitionists, in strategic alliance with Christian organizations, have left their mark on the UN cultural and children's organizations, UNESCO and UNICEF, and a number of nongovernmental organizations. On the other hand, ILO, WHO, UNAIDS, the World Bank, and others have put politics and absolutist worldviews aside in favor of care for life and health. Their acceptance and cooperation with prostitutes' groups have extended over a decade, due to the prostitutes' abilities as lobbyists.

Prostitutes have crossed many borders and achieved considerable results within the sex industry and in international society. Australia's top prostitution agencies are listed on the stock exchange. The prostitutes' clients in Amsterdam have formed their own organization and regularly negotiate on fees, much as large cities regulate taxi fares. Denmark and the Netherlands provide the handicapped and people in a number of government-run institutions with regular visits from professional sex therapists, with taxi fare included.

This concern for the mental and physical health and happiness of the handicapped in no way reflects a similar rise in concern for prostitutes; not even AIDS, with its grave problems for prostitutes, seems to have contributed to that. The general view of prostitute women has changed very little. They continue to be seen as a second-class species, with the double stigma of their gender and profession. They have a long way to go before being granted the rights otherwise considered inherent in humankind.

The attitude of the police has also remained firm. Gloria Lockett, former California prostitute and present activist, tells stories about the Los Angeles police. One dark night in late 1990, the police stopped her car. After searching it, they found a large parcel of condoms. What was this? The policemen took the condoms out of the package one by one and punched holes in them with a pocketknife. Then they broke into laughter. One of them said, "Try and use 'em now!"

An almost identical episode took place a few weeks later. Gloria had gone into a drugstore and bought twelve dozen condoms. The boys in blue must have had her under surveillance. In any case, they accosted her outside the drugstore. They grabbed her purse and shook it upside down. Then they punctured every single condom, one by one, pushing the knife down into the latex membrane, slowly and with great enjoyment. Gloria got her purse back, along with the pile of useless rubber. As they handed over her belongings, the hard-boiled cops flirted with her: "G'night, honey! Happy hunting!"

QUOTES AND REFERENCES

Introduction

Camille Paglia: *Vamps and Tramps: New Essays*. New York, 1994./ Johann Jacob Bachofen: *Evolutionist Tradition*. Das Mutterrecht, Stuttgart, 1861./ Friedrich Engels: *The Origin of the Family, State and Society*. London, 1884./ Henry Maine: *Ancient Law*. London, 1861./Lewis Morgan: *Ancient Society*. New York, 1871./Robert Briffault: *The Mothers: A Study of the Origins of Sentiments and Institutions*. New York, 1927./Clellan Ford: *Patterns of Sexual Behavior*. New York, 1951./Gilbert Herdt and Robert Stoller: *Intimate Communications: Erotics and the Study of Culture*. New York, 1990./Kirk and Sylvia van Kirk: *Many Tender Ties: Women in Fur Trade Societies in Western Canada 1679–1870*. Winnipeg, 1980./Bronislaw Malinowskij: *The Sexual Life of Savages*. New York, 1929./ Margaret Mead: *Male and Female: A Study of Sexes in a Changing World*. New York and London, 1949.

1. The Whore of Babylon

Averil Cameron, Amelie Kuhrt, Barbra Lesko, Paul Hardmann, and Gerda Lerner, op. cit. /Egyptian section based on Sarah Pomeroy, Lise Manniche, Barbara Lesko. /Special thanks to critical reading by Bente Groth. / Herodotus: *Persian Wars,* trans. by A. D. Goodley. London, 1904./Sir James Frazer, James George: *The Golden Bough: A Study in Magic and Religion I–XIII*. London and New York, 1911–15. /Margaret Ehrenberg: *Women in Prehistory*. London, 1989. / Marija Marij Gimbutas: *The Language of the Goddess*. London, 1989; *The Civilization of the Goddess*. London, 1991./ L. Meskell: "Goddesses, Gimbutas and New Age Archeology," in *Antiquity* 69, 1995./Timothy Taylor: *The Prehistory of Sex: Four Million Years of Human Sexual Culture*. London, 1996./Giovanni Pettinato: *Samuramat/ Semiramis*. 1989.

2. Patriarchs and Priestesses
Averil Cameron, Amelie Kuhrt, Carol Meyers, Barbara Lesko, op. cit. / Old Testament references: Tamar and Judah: Genesis 38. / Rahab: Joshua 2, 1 ff. / Samson: Judges 11, 2, 161, 16:4–40./Proverbs 6:20, 24, 25, 32, 7: 6:10– 12./ Solomon: 1 Kings 3: 16–28./Jezebel: 1 Kings 21./Isaiah 23:16. I have mainly used the King James English Bible, but in a few instances the Living Bible. Tyndale House Publishers, 1971. I would also like to acknowledge Professor of Theology Tun'd Seim Karlsen for critical comments at the launching of the Norwegian edition in 1997.

3. Fallen Angels
Barbara Lesko, Geoffrey Parrinder, Karen Armstrong, Bullough and Brundage, op. cit. / Walter Burkert: *Ancient Mystery Cults.* Harvard, 1987.

4. Greek Liberalism
Hans Licht, John Winkler, Carola Reinsberg, Keneth Dover, Aline Rouselle, op. cit. / Vase paintings: on Eva Keuls, op. cit. /Different notions of homosexuality: John Winkler, op. cit./Lucian: *Dialogues of Courtesans,* ed. and trans. by M. D. MacLeod. London, 1961. / Aristophanes: *The Acharnians,* ed. and trans. by Benjamin Rickley. London, 1950. / Alciphron: *Letters of Courtesans,* ed. and trans. by Allen Rogers. London, 1962. / Aeschines: *Against Timarchos*, ed. and trans. by Charles Darwin Adams. London, 1957. / Demosthenes: *Contra Naerem: Orations Vol . VI,* trans. by A. T. Murray. London, 1957. / Letter by the *hetæra* Bakkis cited after Lujo Basserman, 1965. / Philemon's comedy fragment from Eva Keuls, 1985.

5. Hindu Ambiguity
Main text based on Abbe Dubois, J. J. Meyer, Norman J. Penzer, S. C. Banjerij, and Ch. Chakraborty, op. cit. / Vatsayana: *Kama Sutra,* trans. by Richard Burton and F. F. Arbuthnot. London and New York, 1963, 1980. / *Ramayana and the Mahabharatha,* trans. by Romesc C. Dutt. London and New York, 1950. / Buddha and followers after *A Life of the Buddha,* ed. and trans by Michael Edwards. London, 1959; and Radhgovinda Basak: *Lectures on Buddha and Buddhism.* Calcutta, 1961. I would also like to acknowledge Audun Beyer for his valuable assistance with Sanskrit.

6. Rome's Daughters

Cicero: *Pro Caelio,* trans. by Michael Grant. London, 1941. / Horace: *The Complete Works,* intro. by John Marshall. London, 1931. / Ovid: *Amores,* trans. by Grant Showerman. London, 1962. / Properts: *Elegies,* ed. and trans. by H. F. Butler. London, 1962. / Martial: *The Satires, Book 1,* Satire 11, p. 155, and Plautus: *Mostellaria,* trans. by Paul Nixon. London, 1963./Atti/ Galli: *Der entmannte eros: Eine Kultyurgeschichte der Eunuchen und Kastraten.* Düsseldorf/Zurich, 1997. / Konstantin and Christianity: Bullough and Brundage, op. cit. / Theodora/Justinian: John Norwitch and Elisabeth Clarke, op. cit. / Theodora/Justinian and homosexuality: John Boswell: *Same-Sex Unions in Premodern Europe.* New York, 1994. / Procopius: *Anecdota,* trans. by H. B. Dewing and Gløanville Downey. London, 1954. As with the Bible, many translations of Roman verse may be found.

7. Repentant Sinners

New Testament references (see chapter 2 notes for a word on translation): MM at Crux: Matt 27:55–57, 61–67; Mark 15:40–47; Luke 23:27–56; John 19:25–27. / MM at Grave: Matt 28:1–8; Mark 16:1–13; Luke 24:1–12; John 20:1–18. / MM in Bethany: Luke 10:38–42; John 12:1–8. / Female sinner: John 8:1–11. In Simon's house: Luke 7:36–50. / Sophia in John's Revelations: 22:17. / Reconstruction of MM legends based on Anstett-Jansen, op. cit./ Eccl. history: Peter Brown, Bullough and Brundage, op. cit. / Special thanks to Turid Seim Karlsen. / Prostitute saints after: Stephen Wilson, Elisabeth Clark, op. cit. / *Butler's Lives of the Saints,* ed. and suppl. by Herbert Thurston and Donald Attwater./Tertullian: *Apology,* trans. by Emilia Joseph Daly. New York, 1950. / Augustine: *Confessions,* trans. by Albert C. Outler. London, 1955.

8. Tang China's Pleasure Women

M. Beurdeley, Ruang Fang Fuy, and R. H. van Gulich, op. cit. / Yü's poems quoted from van Gulich.

9. Muhammad's Women

The Qu'ran on prostitution: Surah Nur 24:33. / Abnormal sex: 24:19./ Decency: 24:20–31./ Zina: Surah Nur 24:31, Sura Isra: 17:32. / Poetry after Ahmad al-Tifahi: *The Delight of Hearts,* trans. by Edward Lacey. San Francisco, 1988.

10. Guilds and Cloisters, Rogues and Rapists
Philippe Aries, Bronislaw Geremek, Baker, Leah Otis, and Jacques Rossiaud, op. cit. / François Villon: *The Complete Works,* trans. notes by Anthony Bonner, intro. by William Carlos Williams. New York, 1964.

11. Celestial Whores
Iconography of MM figure based on Marga Anstet-Jansen, op. cit. / Canon law and ecclesiestical history based on Bullough and Brundage, Jacques Rossiaud, Jeffrey Richards, op. cit. / Eustache Mercade is quoted from Rossiaud. / Oscar Wilde: *De Profundis.* 27th ed. London, 1913.

12. War of the Roses
Main arguments based on Jacques Rossiaud, op. cit. / *Christine de Pizan: The Book of the City of Ladies,* trans. by E. J. Richard. New York, 1982. / E. McLeod: *The Order of the Rose. The Life and Ideas of Christine de Pizan.* London, 1976. / Joan Kelly: "Early Feminist Theory and the Querelle des Femmes," in *The Essays of Joan Kelly.* Oxford, 1977. / M. P. Cosman and C. C. Willard, eds.: *A Medieval Woman's Mirror of Honour: The Treasury of the City of Ladies.* New York, 1989. / E. D. Bornstein: *Ideals for Women in the Works of Christine de Pizan.* Ann Arbor, 1981. / Andreas Capellanus: *The Art of Courtly Love,* trans. by J. J. Parry. New York, 1941. / Jean Froissart: quoted from Lorenz von Nummer, 1962.

13. Pox, Punishment, and Penitence
Claude Quetel, Bronislaw Geremek, Leah Otis, and Jacques Rossiaud, op. cit. / Ernst Bäumler: *Amors Vergifteter Pfeil: Kulturgeschichte einer verschwiegenen krankhet.* München, 1976.

14. Splendor and Misery of the Courtesans
Archillo Olivieri, Georgina Masson, Lujo Basserman, Guido Ruggiero, and Nickie Roberts./Earl of Rochester quoted by Hillary Evans, op. cit. / *Aretino's Dialogues,* trans. by Raymond Rosenthal. London, 1972.

15. Love in the South Seas
Special credit to the many books of Antony Reid and James Francis Warren on the region. Historical parts in Terence H. Hull et al., op. cit., and

Peter J. Rimmer and Lisa Allen, eds.: *The Underside of Malaysian History: Pullers, Prostitutes, Plantation Workers.* Singapore, 1990. / European travelers: Louis-Antoine de Bougainville: *A Voyage around the World.* New York, 1989. / The lack of prostitution in Southeast Asia and the Pacific caused Denis Diderot to make a series of comments in the 1770s. *Descriptions of Old Siam,* compiled and introduced by Michael Smithies. Oxford, 1995. / Hugh Clifford: *Further India: Being the Story of Exploration from the Earliest Times in Burma, Malaya, Siam and Indo-China.* Bangkok, 1990. / C. R. Boxer: *The Dutch Freeborn Empire 1600–1800.* London, 1967. / Henry Muhout: *Travels in the Cenral Parts of Indochina During the Years 1858, 1859, and 1860.* Bangkok, 1986. / J. M. Gullick: *Adventures and Encounters: Europeans in Southeast Asia.* Kuala Lumpur, 1995. / Henn Mouhot and Francis Garnier: *The French in Indo-China with a Narrative of Garniers Explorations in Cochin China, Annam and Tonquin.* Preface by Dorn Meyers.. Bangkok, 1994. / Chinese travelers: Ying-yai Sheng-lan: *The Overall Survey of the Ocean's Shores (1433).* Bangkok, 1970. / Free love: Richard Hough: *Captain Bligh and Mr. Christian.* Newton Abbot, Devon, 1972. / Chinese influence: C. P. Fitzgerald: *The Southern Expansion of the Chinese People.* Bangkok, 1972. / Sterling Seagrave: *Lords of the Rims.* London, 1995. / Slavery: Anthony Reid: *Slavery, Bondage and Dependency in Southeast Asia.* Sta. Lucia, Queensland, 1983. / B. Lasker: *Human Bondage in Southeast Asia.* North Carolina, 1950. / James Francis Warren: *The Sulu Zone 1768–1898: Dynamics of External Trade, Slavery and Ethnicity.* Singapore, 1981. / Virginia Thomson: *French Indo-China.* New York, 1937.

16. Fanny Hill
Special credit to George Rousseau and Roy Porter.

17. Hara-kiri
Main credit to Cecilia Segawa Seigle, op. cit. / Details from Ernest de Becker, Stephen and Ethel Longstreet, op. cit. / Samurai: Inazo Nitore: *Bushido. The Soul of Japan.* Tokyo, 1969. / Charles Dunn: *Everyday in Traditional Japan.* Tokyo, 1969. / Homosexuality: Tsuneo Watanabe: *The Love of the Samurai: A Thousand Years of Japanese Sexuality.* London, 1989. / *Shikamatsu,* trans. by Donald Keene. New York, 1961. / Poetry after Shuichi Kato: *A History of Japanese Literature,* trans. and ed. by Don Sanderson. Richmond, Surrey, 1997.

18. The Penetration of Africa
Special credit to Ronald Hyam and Louise White. Charles E. Ambler: *Kenyan Communities in the Age of Imperialism.* London, 1988. / Ann Becky: *A History of the British Medical Administration of East Africa 1900–1950.* Cambridge, Mass., 1970. / Anthony Clayton: *Khaki and Blue: Military and Police in British Colonial Africa.* Ohio, 1989. / Maria Rosa Cutrufelli: *Women of Africa: Roots of Oppression.* London, 1983. / John Davis (ed.): *Choice and Change.* London, 1974./Christine Oppong (ed.): *Female and Male in West Africa.* London, 1983./Charles van Onseln: *Studies in the Social and Economic History of Witwatersrand 1886–1914.* New Babylon, London, 1982. / Henry Junod: *The Life of a South African Tribe.* London, 1927. / G. H. Mungeam: *British Rule in Kenya 1895–1912.* Oxford, 1966. / See also: "I'm the Meat, I'm the Knife: Sexual Service, Migration and Repression in Some African Societies," in Gail Phetersen (ed.), op. cit.

19. Nana and Her Times
Hollis Clayson's approach to the prostitute as depicted by French impressionists: credit to Jill Harsin and Theodore Zeldin, op. cit.

20. Moral Crusaders
Based on Alain Corbin, Judith Walkowitz, Mary Gibson, op. cit. / Quotes from Corbin, Walkowitz, and Mary Gibson. Credit also to two female co-students during the late 1970s. I had never been engaged in any discussion about prostitution until I met Kari Melbye (now professor of history) and Aina Schiøtz (who edited my dissertation for publication in 1981): Melbye's article about prostitution politics and Schiøtz's about prostitutes' living conditions in Anne-Marie Gotaas (ed.): *Det kriminelle kjønn,* Oslo, 1980, are still worth reading, and deserve to be translated. I deleted this book from the bibliography to this edition because they are only available in the Norwegian language.

21. Sex in the Wild West
Based on Anne M. Butler, Marion Goldman, and Glenda Riley, op. cit.

22. Imperial Virtue
Special credit to Kenneth Ballhatchet and Ronald Hyam, op. cit.

23. Tango!
Special credit to Donna Guy, op. cit, quoted after her. / Homosexuality: Carlos Luis Jauregui: *La homosexual en la Argentina.* Buenos Aires, 1987. / Tango: Julio Mafud: *Sociologia del Tango.* Buenos Aires, 1966. / Simon Collier: *The Life, Times and Music of Carlos Gardel.* Pittsburgh, 1986.

24. Ottoman Footnote
Credit to Norman Penzer: The Harem. / Andrew Wheatcroft: *The Ottomans.* London, 1993. / Eunuchs: *Der entmannte Eros: Eine Kultyurgeschichte der Eunuchen und Kastraten,* Düsseldorf/Zurich, 1997.

25. The White Slave Trade
Based on James Francis Warren, Louise White, Donna Guy, and Charles Terrot. / Samuel Cohen: *Report of the Secretary on his Visit to South America,* 1919.

26. Kamikaze and Comfort
Based on my own book about the Norwegian police during WWII from 1987 and the earlier, but extremely relevant, book by Grethe Hartmann, op. cit. My life in Manila, 1989–1994, where I followed the newspapers' opening up of the Korean and Filipina comfort women's stories, has played a key role in this chapter and the rest of the book. Credit also to Huie, Hicks, Rohrwasser, Hartmann, Seidler, and Allan M. Brandt.

27. Call Girls
Based on Sydney Biddle Barrows, Martha Stein, Harold Greenwald, Robert Preston, and Lewis Diana, op. cit.

28. Academic Sex Tourism
Based on Allison Murray, Cleo Odzer, Sturdevant and Stoltzfus, Peter Jackson.

29. Feminism and the Sex Workers' Movement
Based on Nickie Roberts, op. cit., "Migration and Prostitution," in Gail Peterson (ed.), Laurie Bell, and Sietske Altink. Kate Millett: *Sexual Politics,* London, 1970, and *The Prostitution Papers,* New York, 1975. AIDS and prostitution: Dennis Altmann, Martin Plant, op. cit.

BIBLIOGRAPHICAL
POSTSCRIPT

Prostitution is by no means the world's oldest profession. It does not derive automatically from human nature, and it cannot be traced in all cultures.

Prostitution requires training, and it is normally transferred from one society to another by imitation or cultural diffusion. Nevertheless, the phenomenon has attracted the attention of the wise and learned in all ancient cultures, and Vatsyayana's *Kama Sutra* from the fourth century B.C. and Ovid's *Ars Amatoria* from the first century A.D. are partly to be regarded as Hindu and Roman textbooks on the art of prostitution. When Greek scholars collected biographical information about famous *hetæræ*, they founded a tradition of anecdotal prostitute studies that was revitalized during the Renaissance.

Eighteenth-century French and British novels, satires, and moral pamphlets initiated a public debate on prostitution that would last well into the next century and finally brought the field from anecdote to science. In the 1830s, J. B. Parent-Duchatelet published exhaustive empirical studies of prostitution in Paris, while Paul Lacroix wrote a historical bibliography and a comprehensive comparative study. This inspired studies of the sex industry in London and several other Western capitals.

William W. Sanger, one of the physicians regarded as the professional experts on prostitution, wrote the first book considered a historical classic. During World War I, the U.S. Bureau of Social Hygiene and John D. Rockefeller initiated exhaustive studies on prostitution. The League of Nations' comprehensive survey from 1927–1929 is clearly Western-ethnocentric, but it is nevertheless broad and systematic in its approach. Fernando Henriques synthesized this modern, ambitious era of prostitution study after World War II with *Prostitution and Society I–III*.

The United Nations and the World Health Organization, founded in 1946 and 1948, respectively, did not continue this broad approach but left such work to special commissions or dedicated organizations. The result would be dwindling research, politicization of any prostitution-related question, and conflict between dedicated NGOs and among UN organizations.

The postwar period and the last decades have seen a formidable number of specialized studies by university scholars, historians, and social scientists. In the 1960s and 1970s, the husband-and-wife team of Vern and Bonnie Bullough compiled a comprehensive annotated bibliography with Barrett Elcano and Margaret Deacon. The last three decades' interest in women's and sex-related studies have partly included prostitution, which has been frequently treated in comparative-literature studies, history, anthropology, and criminology. Medicine and psychology have continued to show interest. The numerous novels on prostitution and an increasing number of prostitutes' autobiographies have further enlarged the literature. A six-hundred-page American filmography concluded that between 1913 and 1990, as many as 338 Hollywood films used prostitution as a primary or secondary theme.

There are a number of bibliographical databases on prostitution, but the *Journal of the History of Sexuality* is the best in English. Much literature is being published by and for the professional sex workers, such as a theoretical international magazine, *Horizontal,* edited in Vienna, while ICPR, the International Committee for Prostitutes' Rights, in Geneva, runs the Centre de Documentation International sur la Prostitution.

The bibliography is selective. Its prime goal is to show the differences in breadth and quality of the literature on prostitution within various historical eras and cultures. Articles are included only when they play a crucial position in a debate or when there is no comprehensive literature on an era or field.

Camille Paglia is quoted from *Vamps and Tramps* and hardly mentions prostitution elsewhere. Her general approach has nevertheless inspired my thinking and reinforced my self-confidence. Ronald Hyam's *Empire and Sexuality* has been an arsenal of arguments and a source of merriment. Nickie Roberts's polemical but incisive *Whores in History* has been another close companion. Roberts is a learned prostitute and activist and writes brilliantly about our recent past.

Vern and Bonnie Bullough's *Women and Prostitution: A Social History*, from 1987, is invaluable in its precise detail and comprehensive references, but the authors' professional expertise is in public health and social science. As a result, chapters like "The Romans" or "Europe in the Middle Ages" seem to be historical but lack chronology and periodization.

The historical literature on Mesopotamia, Israel, and Egypt has proved just as explosive as the political situation in today's Middle East, as a freshly published conference report edited by Barbra S. Lesko demonstrates alarmingly. The complex philology of Mesopotamian and Hebrew terminology is emphasized in my text but might have required a separate thesis. I finally learned to trust Gerda Lerner, Peter Ackroyd, and Bente Groth as I balanced my way through these minefields.

My descriptions of ancient India and China are based in classics like Abbe Dubois, J. J. Meyer, and R. H. van Gulich. The chapters on antiquity were reinforced by an interest and training in classical studies from my youth. A 1996 collection of apocryphal and gnostic writings in Norwegian breathed new life into my fascination for Mary Magdalene, and after some playful interdisciplinary heuristics, I discovered the writings of Marga Anstett-Janssen, which were to become my guide. When I had to reacquaint myself with medieval social and ecclesiastical history twenty years after my student days, Jacques Rossiaud proved a superior helper, while both Philippe Aries and Bronislae Geremek were stimulating and thought-provoking.

Some chapters do summarize material that no author has synthesized and seen in perspective. Anthony Reid's ambitious overview of Southeast Asian social and economic history was so solid in detail that it finally became a pleasure to piece together a coherent view of sexuality and prostitution in the region from older times. Other chapters have almost written themselves; the chapter on Yoshiwara could well have been a eulogistic book review of Cecilia Segawa Seigle, who writes as elegantly as her subject demands.

Among the many historians who have treated nineteenth-century prostitution in an exemplary manner with regard to thorough reading of their sources and brave synthesis in theory, I would emphasize Alain Corbin and Judith Walkowitz. Hollis Clayson's approach to the prostitute paintings of French impressionists was instructive for my chapter on Nana, but also inspired a more independent analysis of Byzantine, medieval, and Renaissance iconography.

My description of prostitution in the interwar period and analysis of the surveys done by the League of Nations are based on James Francis Warren, Louise White, Donna Guy, and Charles Terrot.

My depiction of World War II rests on my own research about the police in German-occupied Norway through the mid-1980s, which resulted in two books in Norwegian and a number of articles. I took a strong interest in the German whores and drew on works on Denmark, France, and the Netherlands. I was living in Manila as the truths about the Korean and Philippine comfort women came out from 1990 on, and I followed the process closely. Herein I have tried to offer a world perspective with the help of books by George Hicks, Franz Seidler, and the inexhaustibly abundant history of venereal disease that Allan M. Brandt has given the world.

Quotations from the modern debate on feminists and whores should be attributed to Nickie Roberts, Gail Peterson, Laurie Bell, or Sietske Altink. I wish I had met many more of the prostitute leaders than the formidable Priscilla Alexander, whom I met in Manila in 1992, but I do hope I have infused my text with some of their sophisticated bitchiness.

The literature on prostitution is terribly uneven. After World War II, historical research improved. The books on the nineteenth century, especially, have set a standard that contrasts sharply with the biased and academically unacceptable books that were published in the same period. "Involved" individuals and strong pressure groups, religious groups, women's rights and gay activists, and organizations for prostitutes or prostitutes' customers have contributed to a politicized literature where unfounded assertions and unalloyed misinformation may carry more weight than serious argument. It would be wrong to exclude all ideological and tainted literature from my bibliography, or to refrain from comments on these realities.

The bottom of the barrel seems to be the twelve white papers from Inquisition 2000, extending from *Criminal Lust: The Sexual Exploitation of Women and Children in Asia* to *Brazil: The Ultimate Immoral Community*. The series is crammed with distorted quotations and libelous statements about individuals and organizations. The practice of naked bathing and the use of condoms are condemned; the Qu'ran and the Bible are presented as moral guides for our world, while the Khmer Rouge is credited for having abolished prostitution in Cambodia. As a taxpayer, I am angry about abused money; as a Scandinavian, I am ashamed of NORAD and SIDA, the foreign aid agencies that sponsor Inquisition 2000 through the Christian feminist lobby ECPAT. Evidently, these are not the only blindly generous aid organizations that rarely bother to check where money is spent as long as a good cause is assumed.

I have expended a great deal of energy on literary research, book collection, and cross-checks on peripheral references. Harald Seip Stubbe double-checked my references against bibliographical databases before the Norwegian edition appeared in 1997. I have also added a number of new entries. With the high quality of earlier prostitution bibliographical work taken into account, I still feel especially proud of this annotated bibliography of my own.

REFERENCES

I. Bibliographies

Elcano, Barrett, Margaret Deacon, Vern and Bonnie Bullough. *A Bibliography of Pros-titution*. New York, 1977.

Krich, Aron. *The Prostitute in Literature*. New York, 1960.

Parish, James. *Prostitution in Hollywood Films*. London, 1992.

II. Classics on Prostitution

Acton, William. *Prostitution, Considered in Its Moral, Social and Sanitary Aspects*. London, 1857.

Bloch, Iwan. *Die Prostitution: Handbuch der gesamten Sexualwissenschaften I–II*. Berlin, 1912–1925.

Dufour, Paul (P. Lacroix-Dufour). *History of Prostitution Among All the Peoples of the World, from the Most Remote Antiquity to the Present Day, I–III*. (Chicago, 1925.) New York, 1932. First published in Paris, 1851–56.

Ettlinger, Karl. *Die Reglementierung der Prostitution*. Leipzig, 1903.

Flexner, Abraham. *Prostitution in Europe*. New York, 1912.

Guyot, Yves. *La prostitution*. Paris, 1882.

Reitman, Ben L. *The Second Oldest Profession*. New York, 1931.

Robinson, William J. *The Oldest Profession in the World*. New York, 1929.

Ryan, M. *Prostitution in London with a Comparative View of That in Paris and New York*. London, 1839.

Sanger, William W. *The History of Prostitution: Its Extent, Causes and Effects Throughout the World*. New York, 1858.

Scott, George Rydley. *The History of Prostitution*. New York, 1936.

Woolston, Howard B. *Prostitution in the United States*. New York, 1921.

III. Modern Comprehensive Studies

Ariés, Philippe, and André Béjin (eds.). *Western Sexuality: Practice and Precept in Past and Present Times.* Oxford, 1985.

Bassermann, Lujo (Hermann Schreiber). *The Oldest Profession: A History of Prostitution.* New York, 1993.

Bullough, Vern. *The History of Prostitution.* New York, 1964.

———. *Sin, Sickness and Sanity.* New York, 1977.

Bullough, Vern and Bonnie. *Women and Prostitution: A Social History.* New York, 1987.

Chauvin, C. *Les chrétiens et la prostitution.* Paris, 1983.

Evans, Hillary. *Harlots, Whores and Hookers: A History of Prostitution.* New York, 1979.

Henriques, Fernando. *Prostitution and Society, I–III.* London, 1962–68.

———. *Prostitution in Europe and the New World.* London, 1963.

Murphy, Emmet. *Great Bordellos of the World.* London, 1983.

Roberts, Nickie. *Whores in History: Prostitution in Western Society.* London, 1992.

Sicot, Marcel. *La prostitution dans le monde.* Paris, 1964.

Symanski, Richard. *The Immoral Landscape: Prostitution in Western Societies.* New York, 1981.

Veyne, Paul (ed.). *A History of Private Life, I–V.* Cambridge, Mass., 1987–1989.

Wells, Jess. *A Herstory of Prostitution in Western Europe.* Berkeley, 1982.

Winick, Charles, and Paul M. Kinsie. *The Lively Commerce: Prostitution in the United States.* Chicago, 1971.

IV. Historical Studies

MESOPOTAMIA, ISRAEL, AND EGYPT

Cameron, Averil, and Amélie Kuhrt (eds.). *Images of Women in Antiquity.* London, 1983.

Epstein, Louis M. *Sex, Laws and Customs in Judaism.* New York, 1948.

Kaufmann, Yehezekel. *The Religion of Israel: From Its Beginnings to the Babylonian Exile.* Chicago, 1961.

Leick, Gwendolyn. *Sex and Eroticism in Mesopotamian Literature.* London, 1994.

Lerner, Gerda. *The Creation of Patriarchy.* New York, 1986.

———. "The Creation of Prostitution in Ancient Mesopotamia," in *Signs: Journal of Women, Culture and Society,* 11:1986.

Lesko, Barbara S. (ed.). *Women's Earliest Records: From Ancient Egypt and Western Asia.* Atlanta, 1989.

Manniche, Lise. *Sexual Life in Ancient Egypt.* London, 1987.

Meyers, Carol. *Discovering Eve: Ancient Israelite Women in Context.* Oxford, 1988.

Pagels, Elaine. *Adam, Eve and the Serpent.* London and New York, 1980.

Parrinder, Geoffrey. *Sex in the World's Religions.* New York, 1980.

Patai, Raphael. *Sex and Family in the Bible and Middle East.* New York, 1959.

————. *The Hebrew Goddess.* New York, 1967.

Pomeroy, Sarah B. *Women in Hellenistic Egypt: From Alexander to Cleopatra.* New York, 1984.

Tyldesley, Joyce. *Daughters of Isis: Women of Ancient Egypt.* London, 1994.

GREECE, HELLENISM, AND ROME

Balsdon, J. V. P. D. *Life and Leisure in Ancient Rome.* London, 1969.

Cantarella, Eva. *Bisexuality in the Ancient World.* Yale, 1992.

Dover, Kenneth James. *Greek Homosexuality.* London, 1978.

Hardman, Paul D. *Homoaffectionalism: Male Bonding from Gilgamesh to the Present.* San Francisco, 1993.

Hauschild, Hans. *Die Gestalt der Hetære in der Griechischen Komoedie.* Leipzig, 1933.

Keuls, Eva C. *The Reign of the Phallus: Sexual Politics in Ancient Athens.* New York, 1985.

Kiefer, Otto. *Sexual Life in Ancient Rome.* London, 1934.

Licht, Hans (P. Brandt). *Sexual Life in Ancient Greece.* London, 1931.

Norwitch, John Julius. *A Short History of Byzantium.* London, 1997.

Pomeroy, Sarah B. *Goddesses, Whores, Wives and Slaves: Women in Classical Antiquity.* New York, 1975.

Reinsberg, Carola. *Ehe, Hetárentum und Knabenliebe im Antiken Griechenland.* Munich, 1989.

Rouselle, Aline. *Porneia: On Desire and the Body in Antiquity.* Oxford, 1988.

Siems, Andreas Karsten (ed.). *Sexualitet und Erotik in der Antike.* Darmstadt, 1988.

Winkler, John J. *The Constraints of Desire: The Anthropology of Sex and Gender in Ancient Greece.* New York, 1990.

EARLY CHRISTIANITY AND BYZANTIUM

Anstett-Janssen, Marga. *Maria Magdalena in der Abendländischen Kunst.* Freiburg, 1961.

Blank, Josef et al. *Die Frau im Urchristentum.* Freiburg, 1983.

Brown, Peter. *The Body and Society: Men, Women and Sexual Renunciation in Early Christianity.* New York, 1988.

Burkert, Walter. *Ancient Mystery Cults.* Harvard, 1987.

Cameron, Averil. *Procopius and the Sixth Century.* London, 1985.

Cameron, Averil, and Amelie Kuhrt (eds.). *Images of Women in Antiquity.* London and Detroit, 1983.

Clark, Elisabeth A. *Women in the Early Church.* Wilmington, Del., 1983.

Clark, Gillian. *Women in Late Antiquity: Pagan and Christian Lifestyles.* Oxford, 1993.

Leontsini, Stavrula. *Die Prostitution im Frühen Bysanz.* Vienna, 1989.

Ward, Benedicta. *Harlots of the Desert.* Oxford, 1987.

Wilson, Stephen (ed.). *Saints and their Cults.* Cambridge, Mass., 1983.

ANCIENT INDIA

Auboyer, J. *Daily Life in Ancient India.* London, 1965.

Banerji, Sures Chandra, and Chanda Chakraborty. *Folklore in Ancient and Medieval India.* Calcutta, 1991.

Banerji, Sures. *Crime and Sex in Ancient India.* Calcutta, 1980.

Chand, Khazan. *Indian Sexology*. New Delhi, 1972.

Dubois, Abbe Jean Antoine *Hindu Manners, Customs and Ceremonies*. Oxford, 1897.

Marglin, Frederique Appfel. *Wives of the God-King: The Rituals of the Dewadasis of Puri*. New Dehli and Oxford, 1985.

Meyer, Johann Jakob. *Sexual Life in Ancient India: A Study in the Comparative History of Indian Culture, I–II*. London, 1930.

Orr, Leslie C. "Women of Medieval South-India in Hindu Temple Ritual: Text and Practice," in *Women in World Religions II*. New York, 1994.

Parrinder, Geoffrey. *Sex in the World's Religions*. New York, 1980.

Penzer, Norman Mosley. *Poison Damsels and Other Essays*. London, 1952.

Yamauchi, Edwin M. "Cultic Prostitution: A Case of Cultural Diffusion," in Harry Hoofer (ed.). *Orient and Occident*. Neukirchen, 1973.

ANCIENT CHINA

Beurdeley, M. et al. *The Clouds and the Rain: The Art of Love in China*. Fribourg, 1969.

van Gulick, Robert Hans. *Sexual Life in Ancient China: A Preliminary Survey of Chinese Sex and Society from ca. 1500 B.C. until 1644*. Leiden, 1974.

Juan, Fang Fu. *Sex in China: Studies in Sexology in Chinese Culture*. New York, 1991.

Mitaimura, Taitsuke. *Chinese Eunuchs: The Structure of Intimate Politics*. Vermont and Tokyo, 1970.

Schlegel, Gustaaf. *Histoire de la prostitution en Chine*. Rouen, 1880.

CELTS, SLAVS, AND VIKINGS

Cherici, Peter. *Celtic Sexuality, Power, Paradigms and Passions*. London, 1995.

Holtan, Inger. *Ekteskap, frillelevnad og hor i norsk høgmellomalder*. Oslo, 1996.

Levin, Eve. *Sex and Society in the World of the Orthodox Slavs, 900–1700*. Ithaca, N.Y., 1989.

Power, Patrick. *Sex and Marriage in Ancient Ireland*. Dublin, 1976.

Preston, James. *Mother Worship*. San Francisco, 1982.

Sigurdsson, Jon Vidar. "*Börn go gamalmenni á tjodveldisöld*," in Gunnar Karlsson (ed.). *Yfir Islandsála*. Reykjavík, 1991.

MEDIEVAL EUROPE

Baker, Derek (ed.). *Medieval Women*. Oxford, 1978.

Brundage, James A. *Law, Sex and Christian Society in Medieval Europe*. Chicago, 1987.

Bullough, Vern L., and James A. Brundage. *Sexual Practice in the Medieval Church*. Buffalo, N.Y., 1982.

Carter, John Marshall. *Rape in Medieval England*. Landham, Md., 1985.

Cleugh, James. *Love Locked Out: An Examination of the Irrepressible Sexuality of the Middle Ages*. New York, 1964.

Geremek, Bronislaw. *The Margins of Society in Late Medieval Paris*. Cambridge, 1987.

Otis, Leah Lydia. *Prostitution in Medieval Society*. Chicago, 1985.

Payer, P. J. *Sex and the Penitentials: The Development of a Sexual Code, 550–1150*. Toronto, 1984.

Richard, Jeffrey. *Sex, Dissidence and Damnation: Minority Groups in the Middle Ages.* London, 1991.

Rossiaud, Jacques. *Medieval Prostitution.* Oxford, 1988.

Weir, A., and J. Jerman. *Images of Lust: Sexual Carvings on Medieval Churches.* London, 1986.

RENAISSANCE AND EARLY MODERN EUROPE

Benabou, Erica-Maria. *La prostitution et la police des moers au 18e siècle.* Paris, 1987.

Burford, E. J. *Gawds and Lodgings: A History of the London Bankside Brothels, ca. 1000–1675.* London, 1976.

Burford, E. J. (G. R. Quaife). *Wits, Wenches and Wantons: London's Low-Life: Covent Garden in the 18th Century.* London, 1986.

Davenport-Hines, Richard. *Sex, Death and Punishment: Attitudes to Sex and Sexuality in Britain Since the Renaissance.* London, 1990.

Hagstrum, J. H. *Sex and Sensibility: Ideal and Erotic Love from Milton to Mozart.* Chicago, 1980.

Laslett, Peter et al. *Bastardy and Its Comparative History.* Cambridge, Mass., 1980.

Maccubbin, Robert Purks (ed.). *"Tis Nature's Fault": Unauthorized Sexuality During the Enlightenment.* Williamsburg, Va., 1985.

Masson, Georgina. *Courtesans of the Italian Renaissance.* London, 1975.

Quetel, Claude. *History of Syphilis.* Baltimore, 1990.

Rousseau, George Sebastian, and Roy Porter (eds.). *Sexual Underworlds of the Enlightenment.* Manchester, 1987.

Rowse, A., and Simon Forman. *Sex and Society in Shakespeare's Age.* London, 1974.

Stone, Lawrence. *Family, Sex and Marriage in England 1500–1800.* London, 1977.

MALE PROSTITUTION IN EARLY MODERN TIMES

Burford, E. J. *The Orrible Synne: A Look at London Lechery from Roman to Cromwellian Times.* London, 1973.

Hinsch, Bret. *Passions of the Cut Sleeve: The Male Homosexual Tradition in China.* Berkeley, 1990.

Norton, Rictor. *Mother Clap's Molly House: The Gay Subcultures in England, 1700–1830.* London, 1992.

Ruggiero, Guido. *The Boundaries of Eros: Sex, Crime and Sexuality in Rennaissance Venice.* New York, 1985.

Saslow, James M. *Ganymede in the Renaissance: Homosexuality in Art and Society.* New Haven, 1986.

Shepherd, Simon. *Marlowe and the Politics of Elizabethan Theatre.* Brighton and New York, 1986.

VICTORIAN BRITAIN

Bristow, Edward J. *Vice and Vigilance: Purity Movements in Britain Since 1700.* Dublin, 1977.

Finnegan, Frances. *Poverty and Prostitution: A Study of Victorian Prostitutes in York.* Cambridge, 1979.

Gorham, Deborah. "The Maiden Tribute to Modern Babylon Reexamined: Child Prostitution and the Idea of Childhood in Late Victorian England," in *Victorian Studies XXI*. 1977.

Mangan, J., and James Walvin (eds.). *Manliness and Morality. Middle-Class Masculinity in Britain and America, 1800–1940*. Manchester, 1987.

Marcus, Steven. *The Other Victorians: A Study of Sexuality and Pornography in Mid-Nineteenth Century England*. New York, 1966.

Mason, Michael. *The Making of Victorian Sexuality*. Oxford, 1992.

———. *The Making of Victorian Sexual Attitudes*. Oxford, 1994.

McHugh, Paul. *Prostitution and Victorian Social Reform*. London and New York, 1980.

Pearsall, Ronald. *The Worm in the Bud: The World of Victorian Sexuality*. London, 1969.

Pearson, Michael. *The Age of Consent: Victorian Prostitution and Its Enemies*. Newton Abbot, 1972.

Pivar, David. *Purity Crusade: Sexual Morality and Social Control, 1868–1900*. Westport, Conn., 1973.

Trudgill, Eric. *Madonnas and Magdalens: The Origins and Development of Victorian Sexual Attitudes*. New York, 1976.

Vicinus, Martha (ed.). *Suffer and Be Still: Women in the Victorian Age*. Bloomington, Ind., 1973.

Walkowitz, Judith R. *Prostitution and Victorian Society: Women, Class and the State*. Cambridge, Mass., 1980.

Weeks, Jeffrey. *Sex, Politics and Society: The Regulation of Sexuality Since 1800*. London, 1981.

WESTERN EUROPE 1800–1920

Bernheimer, Charles. *Figures of Ill Repute: Representing Prostitution in Nineteenth-Century France*. Cambridge, 1989.

Clayson, Hollis. *Painted Love: Prostitution in French Art of the Impressionist Era*. New Haven and London, 1991.

Corbin, Alain. *Women for Hire: Prostitution and Sexuality in France After 1850*. Boston, 1990.

Evans, Richard. "Prostitution, State and Society in Imperial Germany," in the journal *Past and Present*. 1976.

Gibson, Mary. *Prostitution and the State in Italy, 1860–1915*. New Brunswick, N.J., 1986.

Gotaas, Anne Marie. *Det kriminelle kjønn*. Oslo, 1980.

Harsin, Jill. *Policing Prostitution in 19th-Century Paris*. Princeton, 1985.

Hartmann, Grethe. *Boliger og bordeller: oversigt over postitusjonens forskjellige former og tilholdssteder i København til forskjellige tider*. Copenhagen, 1949.

Johansson, Gunilla. *Life Chances: Prostitutes in the Swedish Reglementation System, 1850–1950*. Wellesley, 1987.

Mosse, G. L. *Nationalism and Sexuality: Respectability and Abnormal Sexuality in Modern Europe*. New York, 1985.

Nield, Keith (ed.). *Prostitution in the Victorian Age: Debates on the Issue from Nineteenth-Century Critical Journals*. Westmead, Farnborough, 1973.

Richardson, Joanna. *The Courtesans: The Demimonde in 19th-Century France.* Cleveland, 1967.

Zeldin, Theodore. *France 1848–1945, I: Ambition, Love and Politics.* Oxford, 1973.

NORTH AMERICA 1800–1920

Barnhart, Jacqueline Baker. *The Fair but Frail: Prostitution in San Francisco, 1849–1900.* Reno, 1986.

Butler, Anne M. *Daughters of Joy, Sisters of Misery: Prostitutes in the American West, 1865–1890.* Illinois, 1985.

D'Emilio, John, and Estelle B. Freedman. *Intimate Matters: A History of Sexuality in America.* New York, 1988.

Ehrenberg, Lewis A. *Steppin' Out: New York Night Life and the Transformation of American Culture, 1890–1930.* Westport, Conn., 1981.

Freedman, Estelle B. *Their Sister's Keepers: Women's Prison Reform in America, 1830–1930.* Michigan, 1981.

Frost, H. Gordon. *The Gentlemen's Club: The Story of Prostitution in El Paso.* El Paso, Tex., 1983.

Gentry, Curt. *The Madams of San Francisco.* New York, 1964.

Gilfoyle, Timothy. *City of Eros: New York City: Prostitution and the Commercialization of Sex, 1790–1920.* New York, 1992.

Goldman, Marion S. *Gold Diggers and Silver Miners: Prostitution and Social Life on the Comstock Lode.* Ann Arbor, Mich., 1981.

Gray, James H. *Red Lights on the Prairies.* New York, 1971.

Monkkonen, Eric H. *Police in Urban America, 1860–1920.* New York, 1981.

Riley, Glenda. *Women and Indians on the Frontier, 1825–1915.* Albuquerque, N.M., 1984.

Rosen, Ruth. *The Lost Sisterhood: Prostitution in America, 1900–1918.* Baltimore, Md., 1982.

Strange, Carolyn. *Toronto's Girl Problem: The Perils and Pleasures of the City, 1880–1930.* Toronto, 1995.

Tong, Benson. *Unsubmissive Women: Chinese Prostitutes in Nineteenth-Century San Francisco.* Oklahoma, 1994.

MALE PROSTITUTION IN THE NINETEENTH CENTURY

Chauncey, George. *Gay New York: Gender, Urban Culture and the Making of the Gay Male World, 1890–1940.* New York, 1994.

Hyam, Ronald. *Empire and Sexuality: The British Experience.* Manchester, 1991.

Oswald, Hans. *Männliche Prostitution im Kaiser lichen Berlin.* Leipzig, 1906.

CHINA AND JAPAN 1700–1940

Benedict, Ruth. *The Chrysanthemum and the Sword: Patterns of Japanese Culture.* Boston, 1946.

De Becker, Joseph Ernest. *The Nightless City, or the History of Yoshiwara Yuwaku.* London, 1905.

Gronewold, Sue. *Beautiful Merchandise: Prostitution in China, 1869–1936.* New York, 1982.

Hershatter, Gail. "The Hierarchy of Shanghai Prostitution, 1870–1949," in *Modern China* 15, 1989.

Jaschok, Maria. *Concubines and Bondservants: The Social History of a Chinese Custom.* London, 1988.

Longstreet, Stephen, and Ethel Longstreet. *Yoshiwara: City of the Senses.* New York, 1970.

Miners, Norman. *Hong Kong Under Imperial Rule.* Hong Kong, 1987.

Ono, Kazuko. *Chinese Women in a Century of Revolution, 1850–1950.* Stanford, 1989.

Scott, Adolphe Clarence. *The Flower and Willow World: The Story of the Geisha Girl.* London, 1959.

Segawa Seigle, Cecilia. *Yoshiwara: The Glittering World of the Japanese Courtesan.* Honolulu, 1993.

Watson, Rubie S., and Patricia Buckley Ebrey (eds.). *Marriage and Inequality in Chinese Society.* Berkeley, 1991.

COLONIAL SOUTHEAST ASIA

Allen, Lisa M. (ed.). *The Underside of Malaysian History: Pullers, Prostitutes, Plantation Workers.* Singapore, 1990.

Hull, Terence H., Endang Sulystianingsih, and Gavin W. Jones. *Prostitution in Indonesia: Its History and Evolution.* Jakarta, 1996.

Ingleson, John. "Prostitution in Colonial Java," in D. P. Chandler and M. C. Rickles (eds). *Nineteenth- and Twentieth-Century Indonesia: Essays in Honour of Professor J. D. Legge.* Melbourne, 1986.

Jones, Gavin W. *Marriage and Divorce in Islamic South East Asia.* Oxford, 1994.

Motoe, Terami-Wada. "Karayuki-san of Manila, 1890–1920," in *Philippine Studies* 36, 1988.

Ngo, Nonh Long. *Vietnamese Women in Society and Revolution: The French Colonial Period.* Cambridge, Mass., 1974.

Pivar, David. "The Military Prostitution of Colonized People: India and the Philippines, 1885–1917," *Journal of Sex Research* 17, 1981.

Warren, James Francis. *Ah Ku and Karamu-San: Prostitution in Singapore, 1870–1940.* Oxford, 1993.

BRITISH INDIA

Ballhatchet, Kenneth. *Race, Sex and Class Under the Raj: Imperial Attitudes and Policies and Their Critics, 1793–1905.* London, 1980.

Berger, M. "Imperialism and Sexual Exploitation: A Review Article, and R. Hyam: A Reply," in *Journal of Imperial and Commonwealth History* XVII, 1988.
———. *Prostitution in India.* Delhi, 1986.

Hyam, Ronald. *Empire and Sexuality: The British Experience.* Manchester, 1991.

Joardar, Biswanath, *Prostitution in Nineteenth- and Early-Twentieth-Century Calcutta.* Delhi, 1985.

Levine, Philippa. "Venereal Disease, Prostitution and the Politics of Empire: The Case of India," *Journal of Sexual History* 4, 1994.

Mayo, Katherine. *Mother India.* New Delhi, 1927.

Raj, M. Sundara. *Prostitution in Madras: A Study in Historical Perspective.* New Delhi, 1993.

Shankar, Jogan. *The Devadasi Cult: A Sociological Analysis.* New Delhi, 1991.

Trustram, M. *Women of the Regiment: Marriage and the Victorian Army.* Cambridge, 1984.

AUSTRALIA AND THE PACIFIC

Cumes, J.W.C. *Their Chastity Was Not Too Rigid: Leisure Times in Early Australia.* Melbourne, 1979.

Davidson, R. "As Good a Bloody Woman as Any Other Woman: Prostitution in Western Australia," in P. Crawford (ed.). *Exploring Women's Past.* London, 1984.

Hori, Joan. "Japanese Prostitutes in Hawaii During the Immigration Period," in *Hawaiian Journal of History* 15, 1981.

Inglis, Amirak. *The White Woman's Protection Ordinance: Sexual Anxiety and Politics in Papua.* New York and Sussex, 1975.

Knapman, C. *White Women in Fiji 1835–1930: The Ruin of Empire.* Sydney, 1986.

Sissons, D.C.S. "Karayuki-san. Japanese Prostitutes in Australia, 1887–1916," in *Historical Studies* XVII, 1977.

Sturma, Michael. *Vice in a Vicious Society: Crime and Convicts in Mid-Nineteenth-Century New South Wales.* Queensland, 1983.

COLONIAL AFRICA

Dirasse, Laketch. *Commodization of Female Sexuality: Prostitution and Socioeconomic Relations in Addis Abeba, Ethiopia.* Boston, 1992.

Gann, Lewis H., and Peter Duignan. *The Rulers of British Africa, 1870–1914.* Stanford and London, 1978.

Hyam, Ronald. *Empire and Sexuality: The British Experience.* Manchester, 1991.

Mair, Lucy. *African Marriage and Social Change.* London, 1969.

Songue, Paulette. *Prostitution en Afrique: L'Exemple de Yaounde.* Paris, 1986.

Strobel, Margaret. *Muslim Women in Mombasa, 1890–1975.* New Haven and London, 1979.

White, Louise. *The Comforts of Home: Prostitution in Colonial Nairobi.* Massachusetts, 1990.

THE MUSLIM WORLD

Ahmed, Leila. *Women and Gender in Islam: Historical Roots of a Modern Debate.* Yale, 1992.

Al-Sayid-Marsot and Afaf Lutfi (ed.). *Society and the Sexes in Medieval Islam.* Malibu, 1979.

Beck, Lois, and Nickie Keddie. *Women in the Muslim World.* Cambridge, 1978.

Deeken, Annette, and Monika Bösel. *An den süssen Wassern Asiens: Frauenreisen in den Orient.* Frankfurt, 1997.

El Sadaawi, Nawal. *The Hidden Face of Eve: Women in the Arab World.* London, 1980.

Haeri, Shahla. *Law of Desire: Temporary Marriage in Shi'i Iran.* Syracuse, N.Y., 1989.

Houel, Christian. *Maroc: Mariage, adultaire prostitution.* Paris, 1912.

Khalaf, Samir. *Prostitution in a Changing Society.* Beirut, 1965.

Penzer, Norman Mosley. *The Harem: An Account of the Institution as it Existed in the Palace of the Turkish with a History of the Grand Seraglio from its Foundation to Premodern Times.* London, 1965.

Pierce, Leslie Penn. *The Imperial Harem: Women and Sovereignty in the Ottoman Empire.* New York, 1993.

LATIN AMERICA

Cohen, Samuel. *Report of the Secretary of His Visit to South America.* Oxford, 1913.

Guy, Donna J. *Sex and Danger in Buenos Aires: Prostitution, Family and Nation in Argentina.* London, 1991.

Londres, Albert. *The Road to Buenos Ayres.* New York, 1928.

Pareja, Ernesto M. *La prostitución en Buenos Aires.* Buenos Aires, 1936.

PROSTITUTION AND MIGRATION 1890–1940

Bristow, Edward. J. *Prostitution and Prejudice: The Jewish Fight Against White Slavery 1870–1939.* Oxford, 1982.

Champly, Henry. *The Road to Shanghai: White Slave Traffic in Asia.* London, 1934.

De Leew, Handrik. *Cities of Sin.* London, 1934.

Grittner, Frederick K. *White Slavery: Myth, Ideology and American Law.* New York, 1990.

Hall, Gladys Mary. *Prostitution in the Modern World.* New York, 1936.

Harris, H. Wilson. *Human Merchandise: A Study of the International Traffic in Women.* London, 1928.

Hirschfeld, Magnus. *The Sexual History of World War I.* New York, 1941.

Hyam, Ronald. *Empire and Sexuality: The British Experience.* Manchester, 1991.

League of Nations. *Reports of the Special Body of Experts on Traffic of Women and Children I–II.* Geneva, 1923–1937.

O'Callaghan, Sean. *The Yellow Slave Trade: The Traffic in Women and Children in the East.* London, 1968.

Roe, Clifford. *The Great War on White Slavery.* New York, 1911.

Terrot, Charles. *The Maiden Tribute Revisited: A Study of the White Slave Traffic of the Nineteenth Century.* London, 1959.

WORLD WAR II

Brandt, Allan M. *No Magic Bullet: A Social History of Venereal Disease in the United States since 1880.* New York, 1985.

Calica, Dan P., and Nelia Sancho (eds.). *War Crimes on Asian Women: Military Sexual Slavery by Japan During World War II.* Manila, 1993.

Costello, John. *Love, Sex and War: Changing Values, 1939–1945.* London, 1985.

Hartmann, Grethe. *The Girls They Left Behind.* Copenhagen, 1946.

Hicks, George. *The Comfort Women: Sex Slaves of the Japanese Imperial Forces.* Bangkok, 1995.

Howard, Keith (ed.). *True Stories of the Korean Comfort Women.* London/New York, 1995.

Huie, Shirley Fenton. *The Forgotten Ones: Women and Children Under Nippon.* Sydney, 1992.

Parran, Thomas, and Raymond Vonderlehr. *Plain Words About Venereal Diseases.* New York, 1941.

Ringdal, Nils Johan. *Mellom barken og Veden: Politiet under okkupasjonen.* Oslo, 1987.

Rohrwasser, Michael. *Saubere Mädel, Starke Genossen.* Frankfurt, 1975.

Seidler, Franz W. *Prostitution, Homosexuality, Self-Mutilation: Problems of German Hygiene Control, 1939–1945.* London, 1981.

Stouffer, Samuel et al. *The American Soldier: Adjustment During Army Life.* Princeton, 1949.

White, Louise. "Prostitution, Identity and Class Consciousness during World War II," in *Signs* 11, 1986.

SOVIET RUSSIA AND CENTRAL EUROPE

Altink, Sietske. *Stolen Lives: Trading Women into Sex and Slavery.* London, 1995.

Brokhin, Yuri. *Hustling on Gorky Street.* New York, 1975 .

Bronner, V. *La luttre contre la prostitution en USSR.* Moscow, 1936.

Carter, Herbert Dyson. *Sin and Society.* New York, 1946.

Halle, Fannina. *Women in the Soviet East.* London, 1938.

Hellie, Richard. *Slavery in Russia, 1450–1725.* Chicago, 1982.

Mandel, William M. *Soviet Women.* New York, 1975.

Stern, Michael. *Sex in the USSR.* New York, 1980.

VIETNAM WAR

Beredsford, Melanie. *Vietnam: Politics, Economy and Society.* New York, 1988.

Emerson, Gloria. *Winners and Losers: Battles, Retreats, Gains, Losses and Ruins from the Vietnam War.* New York, 1976.

Jeffords, Susan. *The Remasculinisation of America: Gender and the Vietnam War.* London, 1989.

V. Contemporary Prostitution

THE PROSTITUTES' MOVEMENT, MANUALS

Bell, Laurie. *Good Girls/Bad Girls: Feminists and Sex Workers Face-to-Face.* Seattle, 1988.

Delacoste, Frederique, and Priscilla Alexander. *Sex Work: Writings by Women in the Sex Industry.* San Francisco, 1987.

English Collective of Prostitutes. *A–Z for Working Girls: A Guide to the Rules of the Game.* London, nd.

HYDRA (ed.). *Beruf: Hure.* Berlin, 1988.

Jaget, Claude (ed.). *Prostitutes: Our Life.* Bristol, 1980.

Jeness, Valerie. *Making It Work: The Prostitutes' Rights Movement in Perspective.* New York, 1993.

Kempado, Kemala, and J. Dozema. *Global Sex Workers.* New York, 1998.

McLeod, Eileen. *Women Working: Prostitution Now.* London and Canberra, 1982.

Perkins, Roberta, and Gary Bennett (eds.). *Being a Prostitute.* Sydney, 1985.

Pheterson, Gail. *The Whore Stigma.* The Hague, 1986.

———. (ed.). *A Vindication of the Rights of Whores.* Seattle, 1989.

Preston, John A. *Hustling: A Gentleman's Guide to the Fine Art of Homosexual Prostitution.* New York, 1994.

Roberts, Nickie. *The Front Line: Women in the Sex Industry Speak.* London, 1986.

Thistlewaite, Susan. *Casting Stones: Prostitution and Liberalization in Asia and the U.S.* Minneapolis, 1996.

EAST ASIA

Bornoff, Nicholas. *Pink Samurai: The Pursuit and Politics of Sex in Japan.* London, 1991.

Downer, Lesley. *Geisha: The Secret History of a Vanishing World.* London, 2000.

Dutton, Michael. *Streetlife China.* Cambridge, 1998.

Hane, Mikiso. *Peasants, Rebels and Outcasts: The Underside of Modern Japan.* New York, 1982.

Jaschok, Maria, and Suzanne Miers. *Women and Chinese Patriarchy.* Hong Kong, 1994.

Louis, Lisa. *Butterflies of the Night: Mamasans, Geisha, Strippers and the Japanese Men They Serve.* New York/Tokyo, 1992.

Ma, Karen. *The Modern Madame Butterfly: Fantasy and Reality in Japanese Cross-Cultural Relationships.* Tokyo, 1996.

SOUTHEAST ASIA

Bishop, Ryan, and Lillian S. Robinson. *Night Market: Sexual Cultures and the Thai Economic Miracle.* New York and London, 1998.

Blowfield, Michael. *The Commercial Sex Industry in Surabaya.* Jakarta, 1992.

Brazil, David. *No Money, No Honey: A Candid Look at Sex Sites in Singapore.* Singapore, 1998.

Brown, Louise. *Sex Slaves: The Trafficking of Women in Asia.* London, 2000.

Chandler, Glen (ed.). *Development and Displacement: Women in Southeast Asia.* Melbourne, 1988.

Chant, Sylvia, and Cathy McIwaine (eds.). *Women of a Lesser Cost: Female Labour and Philippine Development.* London, 1995.

Dawson, Alan. *Patpong: Bangkok's Big Little Secret.* Bangkok, 1988.

Dunn, Caroline. *The Politics of Prostitution in Thailand and the Philippines: Politics and Practice.* London, 1994.

Hull, Terence H., Endang Sulistyaningsih, and Gavin W. Jones. *Prostitution in Indonesia: Its History and Evolution.* Jakarta, 1999.

Jackson, Peter S., and Nerida M. Cook. *Genders and Sexualities in Modern Thailand.* Bangkok, 1999.

Jones, Gavin. *Marriage and Divorce in Islamic Southeast Asia.* Kuala Lumpur/Oxford, 1994.

Khin, Thitsa. *Nuns, Mediums and Prostitutes in Chiengmai.* Singapore, 1983.

Lim, Lean Lin. *The Sex Sector: The Economic Basis of Prostitution in Southeast Asia.* Geneva, 1998.

Mahatdahanobol, Vorasakdi. *Chinese Women in the Thai Sex Trade.* Bangkok, 1999.

Murray, Allison J. *No Money, No Honey: A Study of Street Traders and Prostitutes in Jakarta.* Singapore, 1991.

Odzer, Cleo. *Patpong Sisters: An American Woman's View of the Bangkok Sex World.* New York, 1994.

Pongpaichit, Pasuk. *From Peasant Girls to Bangkok Masseuses.* Geneva, 1982.

Santos, Aida Fulleros, and Lynn F. Lee. *The Debt Crisis: A Treadmill of Poverty for Filipino Women.* Manila, 1989.

Sturdevant, Sandra Pollock, and Brenda Stoltzfus. *Let the Good Times Roll: Prostitution and the U.S. Military in Asia.* New York, 1992.

Truong, Thanh-Dam. *Sex, Money and Morality: Prostitution and Tourism in Southeast Asia.* London, 1990.

INDIA

D'Cunha, Jean. *The Legalization of Prostitution: A Sociological Inquiry into the Laws in India and the West.* Bangalore, 1991.

Frederick, John, and Thomas Kelly (ed.). *Fallen Angels: The Sex Workers of South Asia.* New Delhi, 2000.

Joardar, Biswanath. *Prostitution in India.* Delhi, 1986.

Kamala, Rao, and S. D. Punekar. *A Study of Prostitutes in Bombay.* Bombay, 1967.

Majupuria, Indra. *Nepalese Women.* Bangkok, 1996.

Mark, Mary Ellen. *Falkland Road: Prostitutes of Bombay.* London, 1981.

Mukherji, Santos Kumar. *Prostitution in India.* New Delhi, 1986.

Nanda, Serena. *Neither Man nor Woman: The Hijras of India.* Belmont, 1990.

Raghuramaiah, Lakshmi. *Night Birds: Indian Prostitutes from Devadasis to Call Girls.* New Delhi, 1991.

MIGRATION AND SEX TOURISM

Altink, Sietzke. *Stolen Lives: Trading Women into Sex and Slavery.* London, 1995.

Barry, Kathleen. *Female Sexual Slavery.* Englewood Cliffs, N.J., 1979.

———. *The Prostitution of Sexuality: The Global Exploitation of Women.* New York, 1995.

Cohen, Eric. *Thai Tourism: Hill Tribes, Islands and Open-Ended Prostitution.* Bangkok, 1996.

Enloe, Cynthia. *Bananas, Beaches and Bases: Making Feminist Sense of International Politics.* Berkeley, 1989.

Haour Knipe, Mary. *Migration, Etnicity and AIDS.* London, 1998.

Jeffrey, Leslie Ann. *Sex and Borders: Gender, National Identity and Prostitution Policy in Thailand.* Bangkok, 2002.

Latza, Berit. *Sextourismus in Südostasien.* Frankfurt, 1987.

Lipka, Susanne. *Das käufliche Glück in Südostasien: Heiratshandel und Sextourismus.* Münster, 1985.

O'Callaghan, Sean. *The Slave Trade Today.* New York, 1961.

Rosario, Virginia. *Lifting the Smoke Screen: Dynamics of Mail-Order Bride Migration from the Philippines.* The Hague, 1994.

Ryan, Chris. *Recreational Tourism.* London, 1991.

Ryan, Chris, and Michael Hall. *Sex Tourism: Marginal People and Liminalities.* London and New York, 2001.

Seabrook, Jeremy. *Travels in the Skin Trade: Tourism and the Sex Industry.* Chicago, 1996.

Thorbek, Susanne, and Bandana Pattanaik. *Transnational Prostitution: Changing Global Patterns.* London and New York, 2002.

Truong, Thanh-Dam. *Sex, Money and Morality. Prostitution and Tourism in Southeast Asia.* London, 1990.

PSYCHOLOGY, LOVERS, AND CUSTOMERS

Banay, Ralph. *We Call Them Criminals.* New York, 1957.

Becker, Howard S. *Outsiders.* New York, 1963.

Benjamin, Harry, and Albert Ellis. *Prostitution and Morality.* New York, 1964.

Boyle, Sharon. *Working Girls and Their Men.* London, 1994.

Choisy, Maryse. *Psychoanalysis of the Prostitute.* New York, 1961.

Cohen, Bernard. *Deviant Street Networks: Prostitution in New York.* Lexington, Ky., 1980.

Diana, Lewis. *The Prostitute and Her Client.* Springfield, Ill., 1985.

Glover, Edward. *The Psychopathology of Prostitution.* London, 1945.

Greenwald, Harold. *The Call Girl: A Social and Psychoanalytical Study.* New York, 1958.

Heyl, Barbara Sherman. *The Madam as Entrepreneur: Career Management in House Prostitution.* New Brunswick, N.J., 1979.

Høigård, Cecilie, and Liv Finstad. *Backstreets: Prostitution, Money and Love.* Cambridge, Mass., 1992.

James, Jennifer, Jean Withers, Marilyn Haft, and Sara Theis. *The Politics of Prostitution.* Seattle, 1975.

Kinsie, Paul M., and Charles Winick. *The Lively Commerce: Prostitution in the United States.* Chicago, 1971.

Mancini, Jean Gabriel. *Prostitutes and Their Parasites: An Historical Survey.* London, 1963.

Miller, Eleanor. *Street Woman.* Philadelphia, 1986.

Prus, Robert, and Iriss Stylianoss. *Hookers, Rounders and Desk Clerks: The Social Organization of a Hotel Community.* New York, 1980.

Sion, Abraham. *Prostitution and the Law.* London, 1977.

Stein, Martha. *Lovers, Friends, Slaves: 9 Male Sexual Types. Psychic-Sexual Transactions with Call Girls.* New York, 1974.

Walkowitz, Judith. *City of Dreadful Delight.* Chicago, 1992.

CHILD AND TEENAGE PROSTITUTION

Aquino, Emilio R. *Tourism and Child Prostitution in Pagsanjan.* Manila, 1987.

Botte, Marie-France. *Le Prix d'un Enfant.* Paris, 1993.

Bracey, Dorothy. *Baby-Pros.* New York, 1979.

Campagna, Daniel J., and Donald Poffenberger. *The Sexual Trafficking of Children.* South Hadley, Mass., 1988.

Carlebach, Julius. *Juvenile Prostitutes in Nairobi.* Kampala, 1962.

Drew, Dennis, and Jonathan Drake. *Boys for Sale: A Sociological Study of Boy Prostitution.* New York, 1969.

Ennew, John. *The Sexual Exploitation of Children*. Cambridge, 1986.

Jersild, Jens. *Boy Prostitution*. Copenhagen, 1956.

Lloyd, Robin. *Playland: A Study of Boy Prostitution*. London, 1977. Originally published under the title *For Money or Love: A Study of Boy Prostitution*. New York, 1976.

Michaelson, Karen (ed.). *And the Poor Get Children*. New York, 1991.

O'Grady, Ron. *Gebrochene Rosen: Kinderprostituton und Tourismus in Asien*. Bad Honnef, 1992.

Schmidt, Heinz G. *Kindermarkt: Reportagen vom schmutzigsten Gerschäft der Welt*. Basel, 1988.

Sereny, Gitta. *The Invisible Children: Child Prostitution in America, Germany and Great Britain*. New York, 1985.

Srisang, Koson et al. *Caught in Modern Slavery: Tourism and Child Prostitution in Asia*. Bangkok, 1991.

Weisberg, Kelly D. *Children of the Night: A Study of Adolescent Prostitution*. Lexington, 1985.

Zelizer, Viviana. *Pricing the Priceless Child: The Changing Social Value of Children*. New York, 1985.

ADULT MALE PROSTITUTION, EUROPE AND THE U.S.

Gauthier-Hamon, C., and R. Teboul. *Entre Pere et Fils: La prostitution homosexuelle des garçons*. Paris, 1988.

Luckenbill, David. "Deviant Career Mobility: The Case of Male Prostitution," in *Social Problems* 3, 1986.

McNamara, Robert P. *The Times Square Hustler: Male Prostitution in New York City*. New York, 1994.

Pleak, Richard R. "Sexual Behavior and AIDS: Knowledge of Young Male Prostitutes in Manhattan," *Journal of Sex Research* 27, 1990.

Polsky, Ned. *Hustlers, Beats and Others*. Chicago, 1967.

Steward, Samuel M. *Understanding the Male Hustler*. New York, 1991.

West, Donald, and Buz de Villiers. *Male Prostitution*. New York, 1993.

ADULT MALE PROSTITUTION, ASIA AND LATIN AMERICA

Garcia, Ranulfo L. *Male Prostitutes Servicing Male Homosexuals in the Metropolitan Manila Area*. Manila, 1976.

Jackson, Peter S. *Dear Uncle Go: Male Homosexuality in Thailand*. Bangkok, 1995.

Jackson, Peter S., and Gerard Sullivan. *Lady Boys, Tom Boys, Rent Boys: Male and Female Homosexualities in Contemporary Thailand*. Bangkok, 1999.

Parker, Richard. *Bodies, Pleasures and Passion: Sexual Culture in Contemporary Brazil*. Boston, 1991.

Schmitt, Arno, and Jehoeda Sofer. *Sexuality and Eroticism Among Males in Moslem Societies*. Binghamton, N.Y., 1992.

Whitam, Frederick L. Bayot. "Callboy in the Philippines," in Murray (ed.). *Cultural Diversities in Homosexualities*. New York, 1987.

PROSTITUTION AND AIDS

Aggleton, Peter (ed.). *Men Who Sell Sex: International Perspectives on Prostitution and HIV/AIDS.* London and Hong Kong, 1999.

Altman, Dennis. *Global Sex.* London, 2001.

Brandt, Allan M. *No Magic Bullet: A Social History of Venereal Disease in the United States Since 1880.* New York, 1985.

Cleland, John, and Benoit Ferry. *Sexual Behavior and AIDS in the Developing World.* London, 1995.

Mann, Jonathan et al. *AIDS in the World: A Global Report.* Cambridge, 1992.

Peterson, Gail (ed.). *A Vindication of the Rights of Whores.* Seattle, 1989.

Plant, Martin (ed.). *AIDS, Drugs and Prostitution.* London, 1990.

TRANSVESTITES AND TRANSSEXUALS

Feinblom, Deborah Heller. *Transvestites and Transsexuals.* New York, 1976.

Levine, Laura. *Men in Women's Clothing: Anti-Theatricality and Effeminization.* Melbourne, 1994.

Prieur, Annick. *Mema's House, Mexico City.* Chicago, 1998.

Raymond, Janice G. *The Transsexual Empire: The Making of the She-Male.* Boston, 1979.

Walters, William A. W., and Michael W. Ross (eds.). *Transsexualism and Sex Reassignment.* Oxford, 1986.

VI. Biographies and Autobiographies

FAMOUS COURTESANS 1500–1800

Du Castelot, André. *Madame du Barry.* Paris, 1989.

Rosenthal, Margaret F. *The Honest Courtesan: Veronica Franco, Citizen and Writer in Sixteenth-Century Venice.* Chicago, 1992.

Sanders, Joan. *La Petite: The Life of Louise de la Valliere.* Boston, 1959.

Wilson, John Harold. *Nell Gwynn: Royal Mistress.* New York, 1952.

SEX CUSTOMERS 1800–1940

Anonymous. *The Romance of Lust I–IV.* London, 1873–1876.

Buruma, Ian. *The Missionary and the Libertine: Love and War in East and West.* New York, 1998.

Butler, Iris. *The Eldest Brother: The Marquess Wellesley.* London, 1973.

Casanova de Seingalt, Giovanni Jacopo. *Memoirs 1–12.* Leipzig, 1828–1832.

Chitty, Susan. *The Beast and the Monk: A Life of Charles Kingsley.* London, 1974.

Devereux, Charles. *Venus in India, or Love Adventures in Hindustan.* Paris, 1959.

Ellmann, Richard. *Oscar Wilde.* London, 1987.

Hanger, George. *The Life, Adventures and Opinions of Colonel George Hanger.* London, 1801.

Logan, William. *An Exposure from Personal Observation on Female Prostitution in London, Leeds and Roxdale and Especially in the City of Glasgow.* Glasgow, 1843.

Perham, M. Lugard. *The Years of Adventure 1858–1898.* London, 1956.

Purcell, Victor. *The Memoirs of a Malayan Official.* London, 1965.

Rosen, Ruth, and Sue Davidson. *The Maimie Papers.* New York, 1977.

Royle, Trevor. *Death Before Dishonour: The True Story of Fighting Mac.* London, 1982.

Rukavina, K. S. *Jungle Pathfinder: The Biography of "Chirupula" Stephenson.* London, 1951.

Saikaku, Ihara. *The Life of an Amorous Man.* Tokyo, 1963.

Searight, K. *Paidikion.* "An Autobiography, or The Book of Hyakintos and Narcissos" (unpublished). 1917.

Sellon, Edward. *The Ups and Downs of Life: My Life . . . a Veritable History.* London, 1869.

Singleton-Gates, Peter, and Maurice Girodias (eds.). *The Black Diaries: Account of Roger Casement's Life and Times.* Paris, 1959.

Trevor-Roper, Hugh Redwald. *A Hidden Life: The Enigma of Sir Edmund Backhouse.* London, 1976.

"Walter" (pseud.). *My Secret Life I–II.* New York, 1966.

PROSTITUTES OF THE NINETEENTH AND EARLY TWENTIETH CENTURY

Adler, Polly. *A House Is Not a Home.* New York, 1953.

Aikman, Duncan. *Calamity Jane and the Lady Wildcats.* New York, 1927.

Cousins, Sheila (pseud.). *To Beg I Am Ashamed.* New York, 1938.

Cromwell, Helen Worley, and Robert Dougherty. *Dirty Helen.* Los Angeles, 1966.

Dean, Nancy, and Jack Powell. *Twenty Years Behind Red Curtains.* Chicago, 1959.

Kimball, Nell. *Nell Kimball: Her Life as an American Madam.* (Introduction by Stephen Longstreet.) New York, 1970.

Lim, Janet. *Sold for Silver: An Autobiography.* Oxford and Singapore, 1958.

McDonald, Douglas. *The Legend of Julia Bulette and the Red Light Ladies of Nevada.* Las Vegas, 1980.

Pruitt, Ida. *Old Madam Yin: A Memoir of Peking Life, 1926–1938.* Stanford, 1979.

Reitman, Ben L. *Sister of the Road: The Autobiography of Box Car Bertha.* New York, 1937.

Smith, Marjorie (alias "O.W."). *No Bed of Roses: The Diary of a Lost Soul.* New York, 1930.

Watts, Martha. *The Men in My Life.* New York, 1960 .

Wolsey, Serge. *Call House Madam: The Story of the Career of Beverly Davis.* New York, 1942.

ANTIPROSTITUTION CRUSADERS

Bell, Enid Moberly. *Josephine Butler: Flame of Fire.* London, 1963.

Besant, Anne. *An Autobiography.* London, 1893.

Butler, Josephine. *An Autobiographical Memoir.* Bristol, 1928.

Forster, Margaret. *Significant Sisters: The Grassroots of Active Feminism 1839–1939.* New York, 1985.

Hammond, J. L., and Barbara Hammond. *James Stansfeld: A Victorian Champion of Sex Equality.* London, 1932.

Taylor, Anne. *Annie Besant*. Oxford, 1992.

Williamson, Joseph. *Josephine Butler: The Forgotten Saint*. London, 1977.

CONTEMPORARY FEMALE SEX WORKERS

Barrows, Sydney Biddle, and William Novak. *Mayflower Madam: The Queen of Credit Card Sex*. London and Sydney, 1986.

Dalby, Liza. *Geisha*. Berkeley, 1983.

Golden, Arthur. *Memoirs of a Geisha*. New York, 1997.

Hollander, Xaviera, and Robin Moore. *The Happy Hooker*. New York, 1972.

Levine, June, and Lyn Madden. *Lyn: A Story of Prostitution*. Dublin, 1987.

Louis, Lisa. *Butterflies of the Night: Mama-sans, Geisha, Strippers and the Japanese Men They Serve*. New York, 1992.

Mitsuku, Iolana. *Honolulu Madam*. Los Angeles, 1969.

O'Herne, Jan Ruff. *Fifty Years of Silence: Comfort Women in Indonesia*. Sydney, 1994.

Payne, Cynthia. *Personal Services*. London, 1983.

CONTEMPORARY MALE SEX WORKERS

Ambé, Reidar. *Tagebuch eines Callboys*. Berlin, 1994.

Boggs, Thomas. *Tokyo Vanilla*. London, 1998.

Carroll, Jim. *The Basketball Diaries*. New York, 1978

DeLillo, Don. *Underworld*. London, 1998.

Gibson, Barbara. *Male Order: Life Stories from Boys Who Sell Sex*. London, 1995.

CONTEMPORARY SEX CUSTOMERS

Benderson, Bruce. *User*. New York, 1994.

Bole, Daniel. *Bei Anruf Sex: Liebe mit Callboys*. Hamburg, 1999.

Walker, Dave, and Richard S. Ehrlich. *Hello My Big Honey: Love Letters to Bangkok Bar Girls and Other Revealing Interviews*. Bangkok, 1992.

VII: Prostitution Movies

A Girl in Every Port, 1928 (Louise Brooks).

Madame X, 1929 (Ruth Chatterton).

The Blue Angel, 1930 (Marlene Dietrich).

Anna Christie, 1930 (Greta Garbo).

Shanghai Express, 1932 (Marlene Dietrich).

I'm No Angel, 1933 (Mae West).

Lady for a Day, 1933 (Glenda Farrell).

Nana, 1934 (Anna Sten).

Madame Dubarry, 1934 (Dolores del Rio).

Camille, 1936 (Greta Garbo).

Stagecoach, 1939 (Claire Trevor).

Gone with the Wind, 1939 (Hatty McDaniel).

Waterloo Bridge, 1940 (Vivien Leigh).

China Girl, 1942 (Gene Tierney).

The Outlaw, 1943 (Jane Russell).

Cover Girl, 1944 (Rita Hayworth).

Flamingo Road, 1949 (Joan Crawford).

From Here to Eternity, 1953 (Deborah Kerr/Donna Reed).

Miss Sadie Thompson, 1953 (Rita Hayworth).

La Strada, 1954 (Giulietta Masina).

Teahouse of the August Moon, 1956 (Machiko Kyô).

The Revolt of Mamie Stower, 1956 (Jane Russell).

Sayonara, 1957 (Miiko Taka).

Gigi, 1958 (Leslie Caron).

Never on Sunday, 1960 (Melina Mercouri).

The World of Suzie Wong, 1960 (Nancy Kwan).

Irma la Douce, 1963 (Shirley MacLaine).

Belle de Jour, 1967 (Catherine Deneuve).

Flesh, 1968 (Joe Dallesandro).

Justine, 1969 (Anouk Aimée).

Midnight Cowboy, 1969 (Jon Voight).

The Boys in the Band, 1970 (Robert la Tourneaux).

Cheyenne Social Club, 1970 (Shirley Jones/Elaine Devry/Jackie Russell).

Klute, 1971 (Jane Fonda).

Taxi Driver, 1976 (Jodie Foster).

Just a Gigolo, 1979 (David Bowie/Marlene Dietrich).

American Gigolo, 1980 (Richard Gere).

The Best Little Whorehouse in Texas, 1982 (Dolly Parton).

Cannery Row, 1982 (Debra Winger).

Beverly Hills Madam, 1986 (Faye Dunaway).

Pretty Woman, 1990 (Julia Roberts).